CHRIST ON A DONKEY

Early Social Performance

This series publishes monographs, themed collections of essays, and editions relating to performance in the Middle Ages and Early Modern Period that includes, but is not confined to, drama, visual art, music, and dance. It addresses those areas of social performance which slip down the conventional disciplinary cracks, such as processions, tournaments, proclamations, and other courtly, civic, and rural ritual practices. It also considers treatments of, for instance, clothing, poetry, architecture, sport, story-telling, and any other human social activity which can be construed as performative.

Editorial Contact

Pam King

Series Editors

Andrew Kirkman, *University of Birmingham*
Elizabet L'Estrange, *University of Birmingham*

CHRIST ON A DONKEY

PALM SUNDAY, TRIUMPHAL ENTRIES, AND BLASPHEMOUS PAGEANTS

MAX HARRIS

To Ann, again

"Her children rise up and call her happy;
her husband too, and he praises her:
'Many women have done excellently,
but you surpass them all.' "

(Proverbs 31:28–29)

British Library Cataloguing in Publication Data
A catalogue record for this book is available from the British Library.

© **2019, Arc Humanities Press, Leeds**

The author asserts their moral right to be identified as the author of this work.

ISBN (print): 9781641892872
eISBN (PDF): 9781641892896

arc- humanities.org
Printed and bound by CPI Group (UK) Ltd, Croydon, CR0 4YY

CONTENTS

PART ONE:
POMP

I.   TRIUMPHAL ENTRIES:
FROM CHARLEMAGNE TO OLIVER CROMWELL

II.   PALM SUNDAY PROCESSIONS:
FROM EGERIA TO PETER THE GREAT

PART TWO:
PARODIES

JAMES NAYLER AND JESUS OF NAZARETH

PART THREE:
DONKEYS

I.   A SCARCITY OF DONKEYS: FROM UDINE TO EL ALTO

II.   WOODEN CHRISTS ON WOODEN DONKEYS:
FROM AUGSBURG TO CHIQUITOS

LIST OF ILLUSTRATIONS

ACKNOWLEDGEMENTS

WHILE WRITING THIS book, I spent two years as a fellow at the University of Wisconsin-Madison's Institute for Research in the Humanities. I am grateful to Susan Friedman, director of the institute, to Ann Harris, assistant to the director, and to the other members of staff for their support and encouragement. My time was enriched by conversations with other fellows, past and present, especially those whose area of scholarly expertise or gift for clear thinking enabled them to shed light on my work in progress. I think, in particular, of Karen Britland, Sidnie Crawford, Devaleena Das, Andrey Ivanov, David Loewenstein, Steven Nadler, Jennifer Pruitt, Paul Taylor, and Lee Palmer Wandel. Several fellows also helped me with translation from foreign languages: Tina Chronopoulos, John-Henry Clay, Anne Duncan, and Brett Whalen each helped me find my way through a tricky Latin passage or two; Andreas Schwab helped me with obscure German; Tomislav Longinovic, Sara Trevisan, and Lisa Woodson translated Russian. Colleagues and friends elsewhere helped in this regard as well: Petr Uličný and Eliška Poláčková translated Czech; Elsa Strietman deciphered a misleading Dutch paragraph; Glenn Ehrstine and Michaela Vatcheva made a couple of difficult German texts seem much easier; Rachel Brenner, Jan and Ewa Miernowski, and Michaela Vatcheva translated Polish; Inna Bohn translated Russian. Final versions, as well as any errors in my own translations from these and other languages, remain my responsibility.

Other friends and colleagues who graciously responded to individual queries, supplied personal materials, corrected drafts, drew my attention to essential reading, or shed sudden light with off-the-cuff comments, include Diana Anderson, Philip Butterworth, Cara Strauss Contreras, Thomas Dale, Kathryn Dickason, Glenn Ehrstine, Christian Ender, Alison Fraze, Markus Freitag, Corinna Gramatke, Jonathan Grieser, Margaret Hebblethwaite, Kevin Kain, Pamela King, Samuel Kinser, Gordon Kipling, Jude Leimer, Leonora Neville, Katie Normington, David M. Perry, Peter van der Krogt, Martin Walsh, Kenneth Way, Susan Verdi Webster, Clare Woods, and Stephen K. Wright. Directors, curators, and custodians of museums, churches, and convents who generously took time to answer my many questions about their palmesels include Sophie Begel (Musée Théodore Deck et des Pays du Florival, Guebwiller), Monika Boosen and her staff (Museum im Prediger, Schwäbisch Gmünd), Umberto Calafà (Chiesa di Santa Maria in Organo, Verona), Helga Cirello (Hohenzollerisches Landesmuseum, Hechingen), Stefan Demetz (Museo Civico, Bolzano), Rosa Pittà-Settelmeyer (Rosgartenmuseum, Konstanz), Robert Stauder (Musée Historique de Kaysersberg), Olaf Ude (Kloster Wettenhausen), and the custodian of the Stadtpfarrkirche Maria Himmelfahrt, Landsberg am Lech. The members of the Medieval and Renaissance Drama Society and the Société Internationale pour l'Étude du Théâtre Médiéval also deserve thanks for providing me for many years with a congenial, stimulating, and often very entertaining environment in which to discuss my own research and to learn from that of others.

I am also grateful to the many University of Wisconsin-Madison librarians who helped me during the writing of this book. Stephanie Harris and her staff at the InterLibrary Loan office have again been unfailingly efficient in obtaining books for me from libraries far and near. Lyn Korenic, Linda Duychak, and Soren Schoff at the Kohler Art Library and Tom Tews at the Geography Library responded to my inquiries with kindness and expertise.

Finally, I am immeasurably grateful to my wife Ann, to whom I owe so much and from whom I have received such patient love. It is only fitting that she should be named last, in the place of greatest processional honour, acclaimed above all preceding luminaries.

ABBREVIATIONS

AB	Anchor Bible
ACW	Ancient Christian Writers
ANF	The Ante-Nicene Fathers: Translations of the Writings of the Fathers down to AD 325
CCCM	Corpus Christianorum Continuatio Mediaevalis
CCM	Corpus Consuetudinum Monasticarum
CCMET	*The Cambridge Companion to Medieval English Theatre*
CCSL	Corpus Christianorum Series Latina
CSCO	Corpus Scriptorum Christianorum Orientalium
EMD	*European Medieval Drama*
FC	Fathers of the Church
HBS	Henry Bradshaw Society
JBL	*Journal of Biblical Literature*
Knapen	Knapen and Valvekens, eds., *Palmezelprocessie*
LCL	Loeb Classical Library
Lib. Cens.	*Liber Censuum*
Lib. pont.	*Liber pontificalis*
LPPTS	Library of the Palestine Pilgrims' Text Society
MGH,DRIG	Monumenta Germaniae Historica, Diplomatum regum et imperatorum Germaniae
MGH,E	Monumenta Germaniae Historica, Epistolae
MGH,FIGA,USSE	Monumenta Germaniae Historica, Fontes iuris Germanici antiqui in usum scholarum separatim editi
MGH,L	Monumenta Germaniae Historica, Legum
MGH,PLMA	Monumenta Germaniae Historica, Poetarum Latinorum medii aevi
MGH,SRG,NS	Monumenta Germaniae Historica, Scriptorum rerum Germanicarum, Nova Series
MGH,SS	Monumenta Germaniae Historica, Scriptores
MGH,SS,USSE	Monumenta Germaniae Historica, Scriptores rerum Germanicarum in usum scholarum separatim editi
MP	*Mercurius Politicus*
NPNF,FS	A Select Library of Nicene and Post-Nicene Fathers of the Christian Church, First Series
NPNF,SS	A Select Library of Nicene and Post-Nicene Fathers of the Christian Church, Second Series
OAE	Orientalia Christiana Analecta
ODB	*Oxford Dictionary of Byzantium*

OLD	*Oxford Latin Dictionary*
PG	*Patrologiae cursus completus [...] series Graeca*
PL	*Patrologiae cursus completus [...] series Latina*
PO	Patrologia Orientalis
SC	Sources chrétiennes
SRG	Scriptores rerum Germanicarum
SRL	Scriptores rerum Livonicarum
TDNT	*Theological Dictionary of the New Testament*
TTH	Translated Texts for Historians
TTH,LS	Translated Texts for Historians, Latin Series
Wenger	Wenger, ed., *Palmesel*

NOTE ON FORM

I HAVE MODERNIZED fifteenth-, sixteenth-, and seventeenth-century English spelling and grammar. Since translations from foreign languages, however ancient the original, are rendered into modern English, it seems only fair to grant the reader the same degree of accessibility to early modern English.

For similar reasons, I use the terms "Byzantine Empire" and "Holy Roman Empire" to refer to the eastern and western Roman empires after the times of Constantine and Charlemagne respectively. In their day, each power preferred the exclusive designation "the Empire," but the non-specialist modern reader may prefer a clear distinction.

I have adopted two distinct ways of citing online sources. When directing readers to a specific web page, I have provided full bibliographical data. When multiple websites offer pertinent text, images, or video, I have provided select keywords.

Finally, scholarly convention requires me to note that "Mark" signifies "the author of the gospel traditionally ascribed to Mark." Similar caution applies to "Matthew," "Luke," and "John." Unless otherwise identified, biblical quotations are from the New Revised Standard Version.

INTRODUCTION: FROM POMP TO DONKEYS

ON PALM SUNDAY, 1558, a prosperous English merchant by the name of Anthony Jenkinson was in Moscow, representing both his queen, Elizabeth I, and an international trading enterprise known as the Muscovy Company. While there, he saw Moscow's annual "donkey walk," like many other Palm Sunday processions an elaborate outdoor liturgical rite recalling Christ's entry into Jerusalem on a donkey five days before his crucifixion. Despite the name of the event, no donkey took part. The metropolitan archbishop of Moscow and all Russia was led in procession seated on "a horse, covered with white linen down to the ground, his ears being made long with the same cloth, like to an ass's ears." The archbishop, in full pontifical regalia, played the part of Christ, while a white horse, wearing white linen ass's ears, played the part of the donkey. Holding the end of the horse's rein was no less a dignitary than Tsar Ivan IV (1547–1584), also known to history as Ivan the Terrible.[1]

Three centuries later, in 1865, a Russian realist painter, Vyacheslav Schwartz, completed a large oil painting called *Palm Sunday in Moscow under Tsar Alexei Mikhailovich: The Procession of the Patriarch on a Donkey*.[2] The painting, which now hangs in the State Russian Museum in St. Petersburg, depicts in meticulous detail a later instance of the same processional tradition (Fig. 1). A grey-bearded boyar guides the reins of the patriarch's horse, while Tsar Alexis I (1645–1676), holding the tasseled end of the rein in his right hand and a palm in his left hand, walks ahead. The metropolitan archbishop of Moscow and all Russia, whose predecessor had been elevated to the status of patriarch in 1589, sits atop the white horse. Crowned and richly vested, he holds a golden, three-beamed orthodox cross in his right hand and a gilded gospel book in his left. The animal's costume remains the same: a full-length white linen cloth, topped with long, white, pointed donkey's ears.

Moscow's horse with donkey's ears is one of the more colourful cases of historical dissonance between an enacted representation of Christ's entry and the biblical story it was believed to represent. The horse's false ears testified to the shared conviction of those taking part that Christ rode a donkey. The white horse bore annual witness to the fact that no archbishop of Moscow deigned to ride a real donkey in the city's Palm Sunday procession. Nor did a tsar ever lead one.

A more modest Palm Sunday celebration takes place each year in the village of San José de Chiquitos in lowland Bolivia. There, a life-size wooden image of Christ on a donkey, mounted on a low, wheeled platform, is the star of the show. In the late afternoon, a crowd of people accompany the image through the village to the church, where "Jesus of Nazareth" and "his little donkey" are received "with a shower of yellow flowers, the fluttering of palms, the chiming of bells, songs proclaiming him the son of David …

---

1 Morgan and Coote, *Early*, 2:364.

2 Vereshchagina, *Viacheslav*, 75–79.

Figure 1 Vyacheslav Schwartz, *Palm Sunday in Moscow under Tsar Alexei Mikhailovich: The Procession of the Patriarch on a Donkey*. Oil on canvas, 1865. State Russian Museum, St. Petersburg. Wikimedia Commons. (The Yorck Project (2002), 10.000 Meisterwerke der Malerei (DVD-ROM), distributed by DIRECTMEDIA Publishing.)

and the sound of bass drums and violins" (Fig. 2).[3] The tradition of wheeled processional images of Christ on a donkey probably travelled to South America with German-speaking Jesuit missionaries in the late seventeenth and early eighteenth centuries.

Christ on a Donkey explores Palm Sunday processions and other public representations of Christ's entry into Jerusalem as both spectacular instances of processional theatre and highly charged interpretations of the biblical narrative to which they claim allegiance. Biblical scholars generally understand Christ's donkey as a sign that he came neither as a warrior nor as one drawn to the trappings of power, but in peace and humility. A wheeled wooden image of Christ on a donkey is arguably consistent with this interpretation. A Palm Sunday procession that gives pride of place to a high-ranking member of the clergy on a white horse is not.

Even more at odds with the biblical model are those triumphal royal entries that borrow the language and iconography of Palm Sunday, allowing a king to play the role of Christ while celebrating military victory. Charlemagne, king of the Franks, entered Rome for the first time on Easter Saturday, April 2, 774. Fresh from military victories against the Lombards, Charlemagne was met outside the city by young boys carrying palm and olive branches and singing acclamations. As Charlemagne and the pope entered the Basilica of Saint Peter, clergy and monks sang the Palm Sunday antiphon, "Blessed is he who comes in the name of the Lord." The ceremony's allusions to Christ's entry into Jerusalem not only set a precedent for subsequent appropriations of the language and iconography of Palm Sunday by rulers of church and state, but also for elite Palm Sunday processions themselves to appropriate the language and iconography of royal entries.

---

3 Cambara Flores, "Semana."

Figure 2 Palm Sunday, San José de Chiquitos, Bolivia (2011).
Photograph by Limber Lionel Cambara Flores.

The narrative arc of my book moves from this dissonant mingling of elite genres toward the simpler and more congruent use of wheeled images of Christ on a donkey. Although I have respected chronological order within each chapter and, to a lesser extent, within each cluster of chapters, I have arranged the parts themselves according to their place in this thematic arc.

In the first half of Part 1, I evaluate the phenomenon of triumphal pomp in selective royal (and not quite royal) entries from the time of Charlemagne to that of Oliver Cromwell and in papal entries, some of them explicitly celebrating military triumph, from the twelfth to the sixteenth centuries. In the second half of Part 1, I assess the same phenomenon in Palm Sunday processions. The first surviving record of a Palm Sunday procession comes from late fourth-century Jerusalem. Neither this nor any other record of such a procession during the next four and a half centuries betrays any sign of triumphal pomp. Palm Sunday processions only began to resemble royal entries some eighty years after Charlemagne rode into Rome.

Part 2 serves as the hinge on which my story turns from pomp to donkeys. It does so by focusing on two arguably unique moments in the entangled history of Palm Sunday and triumphal entries. The first took place in Bristol on October 24, 1656. James Nayler, a leader of the first generation of Quakers in England, approached the city on horseback, accompanied by a small group of men and women reportedly singing "holy, holy, holy." It was raining heavily, and the Quakers trudged knee-deep through mud in the part of the road where only horses and carts usually travelled. Charged with "horrid blasphemy," Nayler was tried in London by the Puritan-dominated parliament. Found guilty, he narrowly escaped the death penalty and was condemned instead to a series of painful humiliations: he was pilloried, his tongue was bored through with a red-hot iron (Fig. 10), and his forehead was branded with the letter B for blasphemer. He was then returned to Bristol, where he was made to enter the city seated backwards on a horse, after which he was whipped through the streets and finally imprisoned. With few exceptions, historians have assumed that Nayler's entry into Bristol was a deliberate "reenactment of Christ's entrance into Jerusalem on Palm Sunday."[4] The records, I believe, suggest a different reading: Nayler's entry is better understood not as a shabby imitation of the first Palm Sunday, but as a muddy parody of triumphal royal entries.

The second arguably unique moment is Jesus of Nazareth's own entry into Jerusalem. Biblical scholars have come to understand Jesus's entry as a parody of the imperial and other military entries of his own time. Stanley Hauerwas describes Jesus's entry into Jerusalem as "an unmistakable political act," one that "parodies the entry of kings and their armies."[5] Marcus Borg and John Dominic Crossan see it as "a deliberate lampoon" of such entries,[6] including that of Pontius Pilate, who probably rode into Jerusalem "seated upon a horse or riding a chariot," and accompanied by "something on the order of one thousand" cavalry and foot soldiers.[7] Jesus's entry was not the "triumphal entry" imagined by a long tradition of later Christian rhetoric and processional performance; it was "nontriumphal,"[8] "atriumphal,"[9] or even "anti-triumphal."[10] James Nayler's rain-soaked parody of royal entries may have been more faithful to the biblical story of Jesus of Nazareth's entry into Jerusalem than were any number of royal triumphs or elite Palm Sunday processions.

If not pomp, then what? One might suppose that live donkeys would have played a major part in Palm Sunday processions over the centuries, but to the best of my knowledge the earliest surviving record of anyone riding a live donkey in a Palm Sunday procession is found only in 1424. In that year, a brief entry in the chapter accounts of Udine cathedral records payment of "twelve soldi [pence]" on Palm Sunday "to the boy who went on the ass in place of Christ."[11] The question naturally arises of why, if all Christendom believed that Jesus rode a donkey, so few live donkeys and so many white horses were ridden in Palm Sunday processions. The first half of Part 3 finds the answer at least in part in medieval bestiaries and in a forged papal document known as the *Donation of Constantine*. These chapters also note the absence of triumphalism from Palm Sunday processions under Muslim rule in Jerusalem, where a donkey was first ridden in liturgical procession in the late fifteenth century.

---

4 Loewenstein, *Treacherous*, 227.

5 Hauerwas, *Matthew*, 181–82.

6 Borg and Crossan, *Last*, 32.

7 Kinman, *Jesus*, 160–72.

8 Duff, "March," 55.

9 Kinman, *Jesus*, 90–122; Blomberg, "Matthew," 65.

10 Crossan, *Jesus*, 128; Borg and Crossan, *Last*, 32.

11 Vale, "Liturgia," 29, citing the "libri dei Dapiferi del Capitolo di Aquileia (Udine, Archivio Capitolare)."

Life-size wooden images of Christ on a donkey arrived on the Palm Sunday processional scene nearly five hundred years before live donkeys. Gerhard of Augsburg's *Life of Saint Ulrich*, written within two decades of the death of Ulrich, prince-bishop of Augsburg, in 973, reports that Ulrich walked in procession each Palm Sunday in the company of "an image of the Lord seated on an ass."[12] This is believed to be the earliest surviving record of a class of processional images known to English-speaking scholars by the German name of *Palmesel* (palm donkey). The timing is noteworthy. Introduced less than two hundred years after Charlemagne rode into Rome and around a hundred years after elite Palm Sunday processions began to resemble royal entries, palmesels offered a strikingly different mode of representing Christ's entry into Jerusalem. Not only were they the first processional images to acknowledge that Christ rode a donkey, but they also avoided the urge to visual splendour evident in other processional images of the period. Moreover, they were mounted on wheels and pulled at street level rather than held aloft or carried in ornate portable shrines on the shoulders of their bearers. In the second half of Part 3, I trace the history of palmesels, which were for many centuries a popular feature of the processional theatre of Palm Sunday in Germany and its immediate neighbours. In many towns, children were given rides on the donkey behind Jesus. In Biberach, Palm Sunday with the palmesel was known as "the day of the humble king."[13]

Palmesels were also victims of religious violence. Hussite radicals threw a palmesel from the battlements of Prague's cathedral in 1421. A century later, during outbreaks of Zwinglian iconoclasm in and around Zurich, palmesels were denounced as "idols" and burned, hacked into pieces, used as firewood, or drowned in lakes. During the late eighteenth-century Catholic Enlightenment, in southern Germany, Austria, and Poland, palmesels were condemned as "superstitious" and destroyed or forcibly retired by order of regional archbishops. Most of those that survive have found homes in museums; some are on display in their original churches. A growing number, including a few new models, are taking part in Palm Sunday processions as far apart as Tokarnia (Poland), Thaur (Austria), Ammerschwihr (Alsace), and lowland Bolivia. The final chapter of Part 3 includes an account of my own participation in two such Palm Sunday processions in the Austrian Tirol.

The narrative arc of *Christ on a Donkey* thus moves, not without its bumps and detours, from elite dissonance to a greater (but never complete) popular accord between professed beliefs and processional practice. A curious theme emerges: those embodied representations of Christ's entry into Jerusalem that were, at one time or another, labelled blasphemous, idolatrous, or superstitious by those in power were arguably most faithful to the biblical narrative of Palm Sunday, while those staged with the purpose of exalting those in power and celebrating military triumph were arguably blasphemous pageants.

---

12 Gerhard, *Vita*, 124–25.
13 Schilling, "Religiösen," 120.

PART ONE:

POMP

I. Triumphal Entries:
From Charlemagne to Oliver Cromwell

Chapter 1

CHARLEMAGNE'S BIRTHDAY POMP

CHARLEMAGNE APPROACHED ROME for the first time on April 2, 774. Not only was it Easter Saturday, just six days after Palm Sunday, but it may also have been Charlemagne's twenty-sixth birthday.[1] Fresh from victories in the war against the Lombards, Charlemagne rode towards Rome at the head of an entourage of bishops, abbots, officials (*iudices*), dukes, and counts. Although the bulk of his army remained outside the besieged Lombard city of Pavia, Charlemagne and his court travelled "with very many armed forces." Learning of Charlemagne's approach, Pope Adrian I sent "all his officials" to welcome the king some thirty miles north of Rome.[2] Within a mile or so of the city, Charlemagne was met by "the entire ceremonial military guard" (*universas scolas militae*), by young boys carrying palm and olive branches and singing acclamations (*laudes*), and by the "venerable crosses, that is to say standards (*signa*)." It is not clear whether the "standards" were military banners bearing the sign of the cross or liturgical crosses ordinarily used in Roman outdoor processions.[3] In either case, they enhanced the message of triumph. The cross had been understood as a promise of military victory since Constantine's decisive victory just north of Rome at the Battle of Milvian Bridge in 312 CE. Constantine was said to have seen in the sky a bright cross and the Greek words "En toutō níka" (In this sign you will conquer).[4]

Seeing the processional crosses, Charlemagne dismounted from his horse and continued on foot to the Basilica of Saint Peter, where he was greeted by the pope, clergy, and people of Rome. In a show of humility, Charlemagne kissed each step leading up to the church doors where the pope awaited him. As Charlemagne and Adrian entered the basilica, clergy and monks sang the Palm Sunday antiphon "Blessed is he who comes in the name of the Lord," recalling the cry of the crowd as Jesus entered Jerusalem.[5] Inside, all prostrated themselves in prayer, giving glory to God who had granted so great a victory. Afterwards, pope and king together crossed the bridge over the River Tiber to enter the city itself.[6] The allusions to Christ's entry into Jerusalem had been explicit: children waving palm branches, public acclamations, and the singing of the "Benedictus qui venit." The fact that Charlemagne's entry took place less than a week after Palm Sunday underlined their significance. As Edward Muir remarks, "The liturgical images" of the

---

1 Story, "Carolingians," 271. Becher, "Neue," 60, concludes that Charlemagne "was born on April 2, 748." For April 2 ("IIII Non. Apr"), see Ganshof, "Over," 45; for 748, see "Annales Sancti," 11, where, if the calendar year began at Easter, "747 ipso anno fuit natus Karolus rex" should now be read as 748.

2 *Lib. pont.* 1:496, trans. Davis, *Lives*, 138, identifies the meeting point.

3 Twyman, *Papal*, 75.

4 Eusebius, *Life* 1.28–32, trans. Cameron and Hall, 80–82 (commentary, 204–13); Lactantius, "Deaths," 44.5, trans. McDonald, 191–92.

5 Matt. 21:9; Mark 11:9; Luke 19:38; John 12:12; see also Ps. 118:26.

6 *Lib. pont.* 1:496–97; translation adapted from Davis, *Lives*, 138–39.

Figure 3 Agostino Cornacchini, Monumental equestrian statue of Charlemagne, 1725.
Basilica of Saint Peter, Vatican City. Myrabella / Wikimedia Commons.
Creative Commons licence and GFDL.

entry "transformed a king [Charlemagne] into the likeness of Christ, and a terrestrial city
[Rome] into another Jerusalem."[7] The military images served a contrary purpose, captured well by Agostino Cornacchini's 1725 statue of Charlemagne on horseback (Fig. 3).
Paired at the entrance to the Vatican Palace with Bernini's 1670 equestrian statue of
the emperor Constantine, Cornacchini's work transforms Charlemagne instead into the
likeness of the first Christian emperor. Charlemagne's entry to Rome invoked both biblical and imperial precedents.

Charlemagne may have been greeted on other occasions in a manner intended to
recall Christ's entry into Jerusalem. In March 798, Charlemagne was in Saxony, to the

---

7 Muir, *Civic*, 116.

northeast of his capital city of Aachen, trying yet again to complete his brutal pacification of the pagan Saxons. Alcuin of York, the preeminent scholar of Charlemagne's court, closed a letter to the king by saying that he hoped, on Charlemagne's return, to "greet the triumph of your glory with palm branches and singing children." Alcuin further compared Aachen to Jerusalem and the Palatine Chapel then under construction to Solomon's temple.[8] Michael McCormick observes: "The elaborate metaphor intimates the king would be met by some sort of welcoming ceremony,"[9] in which Charlemagne would play the part of Christ entering both the city and the temple of Jerusalem. Alcuin's proposal, made in March, may have been prompted by the proximity of Palm Sunday.

Charlemagne returned to Rome in November, 800, a month before his coronation as emperor by Pope Leo III. The pope himself met Charlemagne on November 23, twelve miles from the city. Returning to Rome overnight, Leo the next day "sent the banners (*vexilla*) of the city of Rome" to honour Charlemagne, and ordered crowds of townspeople and pilgrims to line the streets and acclaim the king on his arrival. Pope, bishops, and clergy waited to greet Charlemagne at the Basilica of Saint Peter. The chronicler makes no mention of palms being waved or the "Benedictus qui venit" being sung on this occasion. Perhaps he took such details for granted; perhaps the fact that Christmas rather than Easter was approaching explains their absence; or perhaps these markers of Palm Sunday were not suited to a very different political occasion. Charlemagne was in Rome this time not as a military victor but as the royal judge due to preside over the trial of Leo III on charges of adultery and perjury. Although the favourable outcome of the trial was assured in advance, it was only on December 23 that the pope was permitted to clear himself by swearing a solemn oath of innocence. Two days later, on Christmas Day, he crowned Charlemagne ruler of a revived western Roman Empire.[10] Receiving the news in Aachen, Alcuin wrote a poem wishing Charlemagne a triumphant return. The final lines envisaged "Francia" greeting the victorious emperor "with palms and applause" (*palmatis et manibus*).[11] If Charlemagne's arrival in Rome had failed to invoke Christ's entry, his imperial return to Aachen may have rectified matters.

Or perhaps not. It would be unwise to assume that all references, however vague, to royal entries of the period indicated a single format. Ernst Kantorowicz's celebrated claim that Charlemagne's entry into Rome in 774 exercised an enduring influence, "remain[ing] authoritative for all imperial receptions in Rome during the Middle Ages,"[12] and further that all royal entries during "fifteen or more Christian centuries" recalled Christ's entry into Jerusalem, whether "historical" or "eschatological,"[13] supposes too

---

8 Alcuin, *Epistolae* 145 (235).

9 McCormick, *Eternal*, 372–73.

10 Pertz and Kurze, *Annales Regni*, 110–12; trans. Scholz and Rogers, *Carolingian*, 80.

11 Alcuin, *Carmina* 45 (259). "Francia" is now used in English to distinguish the medieval kingdom of the Franks from modern France.

12 Kantorowicz, "King's," 211n23.

13 Kantorowicz, "King's," 210–12, 221; Kantorowicz, *Laudes*, 71–72.

great a uniformity.[14] Gordon Kipling's carefully argued and more chronologically focused conclusion that late medieval civic triumphs between 1377 and 1615 drew variously on one or more of Christ's multiple advents and on other classical and historical referents is more judicious.[15] How much earlier this breadth of reference may have been in play lies beyond the scope of Kipling's study, but if Kantorowicz was wrong about the uniformity of civic triumphs after 1377, he may also have been wrong about those that more closely followed Charlemagne's entry into Rome in 774. For my purpose, which is not to write a history of royal entries, but to determine the degree to which early medieval entries appropriated the language and iconography of Palm Sunday, it will be enough to examine the admittedly scant surviving evidence of royal and imperial entries and of royal and imperial participation in Palm Sunday processions between 774 and 1118. I choose the latter date because in that year the crusader king of Jerusalem, Baldwin I, played a post-humous (and thus somewhat macabre) starring role in the city's Palm Sunday procession.

I begin with the question of innovation. Was Charlemagne the first Christian ruler to enhance his own celebration of royal power and military triumph by evoking Christ's entry into Jerusalem? And, if so, was this why Palm Sunday processions first began to borrow the language and iconography of triumphal entries in the second half of the ninth century? Clarifying the timing of these innovations is an important step in my overall argument. If Charlemagne was the first to confuse the public celebration of human power with the processional recollection of Christ's entry, then such a confusion is not inherent in enacted representations of the biblical story, but was introduced at the particular his-torical moment when aspirations to imperial rule were revived in western Europe.

There are two rival, but demonstrably false, claims to precedence. The first, advanced by Kantorowicz, is that Charlemagne's entry was modelled after "the entry into Rome of the Exarch of Ravenna."[16] Kantorowicz based this assertion on a passing observation in the *Liber pontificalis* that in 774 Pope Adrian I "despatched venerable crosses, that is to say standards (*signa*), to meet [Charlemagne], just like greeting an exarch or patri-cian (*sicut mos est exarchum aut patricium suscipiendum*)."[17] The exarch of Ravenna had been the Byzantine emperor's representative in Italy, often compared in status to a Roman patrician; both had become largely honorific titles. The last exarch of Ravenna died when the Lombards captured the city in 751, ending Byzantine rule in northern Italy.[18] I know of only one account of an exarch's reception in Rome. When the exarch

---

14 For Kantorowicz's susceptibility to what Thomas Mathews has called "the Emperor Mystique," see Mathews, *Clash*, 12–22. For the influence of Kantorowicz's "nostalgia for lost empire" (*Clash*, 19) and assimilated German Jewish heritage on his study of royal entries, see Harris, "Charlemagne," 85–86. For a sympathetic and judicious biography of Kantorowicz, including his transition from far-right German nationalism to a post-war liberal defence of individual freedom of conscience, see Lerner, *Ernst*.

15 Kipling, *Enter*, 23–27, includes the incarnation, historical entry into Jerusalem, ascension, "spiri-tual advent into individual souls," and still-future second coming among the multiple advents of Christ.

16 Kantorowicz, "King's," 211.

17 *Lib. pont.* 1:497; Davis, *Lives*, 139.

18 Brown, *Gentlemen*, 48–53.

John Platyn entered Rome in 687, invited by one of three rival candidates for the vacant papacy, he did so "in such secrecy ... that the crosses (*signa*) and standards and soldiery of the Roman army did not go to meet him as was customary at the appropriate place, but only near the city itself."[19] Even in more settled times, then, the arrival of an exarch in Rome did not borrow the language and iconography of Palm Sunday. Like Platyn, albeit at a more prestigious distance from the city, other visiting exarchs were greeted with crosses, standards, and a military guard. A straightforward reading of the papal chronicler's comparison of Charlemagne's entry to the lapsed tradition of welcoming "an exarch or patrician" finds the similarity not in every detail of Charlemagne's triumphal entry—and certainly not in an evocation of Christ's Palm Sunday entry—but in the customary use of crosses and military standards.

It may be worth noting, too, that there was as yet no annual Palm Sunday procession in Rome. The first record of such a procession in papal Rome comes from the mid-twelfth century.[20] This may be one more reason why Charlemagne chose to celebrate his birthday by entering the city on Easter Saturday rather than six days earlier on Palm Sunday itself. The later date allowed him not only to model his own royal entry into Rome on Christ's "triumphal" entry into Jerusalem but also to play a prominent role in the established Easter ceremonies that followed.[21] Nor was there an annual Palm Sunday procession in Byzantine Ravenna or in Constantinople itself before the late ninth century.[22] By contrast, Palm Sunday processions are recorded in Francia by at least 800 and may well have arrived a little earlier.[23] If Charlemagne's entry owed anything to Palm Sunday processions rather than to the biblical narrative alone, the influence came from Francia rather than from Rome or Ravenna.

The second, older claimant to the novelty of combining military triumph and the iconography of Palm Sunday comes from Jerusalem itself sometime around the year 630/631. Christian Jerusalem had fallen to the forces of the Sasanian Persian Empire in 614. As part of their spoil, the Persians had removed the city's treasured relic of Christ's true cross to their capital, Ctesiphon, south of present-day Baghdad. Between 622 and 628, the Byzantine emperor Heraclius (610–641) conducted an eventually successful campaign to defeat the Persians and recover the cross.[24] Some time afterwards, possibly in March 1630,[25] he entered Jerusalem in triumphant possession of the reliquary chest containing the cross. Contemporary testimony to his entry is sparse; none comes from an eyewitness.

---

19 *Lib. pont.* 1:372; translation adapted from Davis, *Book*, 86.

20 See chap. 6.

21 *Lib. pont.* 1:497–98; Davis, *Lives*, 140.

22 See chap. 7.

23 See chap. 5.

24 Kaegi, *Heraclius*, 112–91.

25 The date "is notoriously difficult to establish" (Schick, *Christian*, 50). See Garitte, *Prise*, 1:82–83 (Georgian), 2:54–55 (Latin translation), trans. Conybeare, "Antiochus," 516, and for scholarly commentary, e.g., Frolow, "Vraie"; Pertusi, in George of Pisidia, *Poemi*, 230–37; Grumel, "Reposition," 142–44; and Kaegi, *Heraclius*, 206.

A seventh-century Armenian chronicle imagined in retrospect the fervent emotions of all who took part in Heraclius's triumphal entry: "They entered Jerusalem" to "the sound of weeping and wailing; their tears flowed from the awesome fervour of the emotion of their hearts and from the rending of the entrails of the king, the princes, all the troops, and the inhabitants of the city."[26] Writing beforehand in Constantinople, the court poet George of Pisidia called on a personified Golgotha to "prepare new palm branches for the welcome of [Heraclius] the new bearer of victory."[27] In the Roman empire, of which Constantinople was the hereditary capital, palms had been used to acclaim successful warriors long before Christ rode into Jerusalem on a donkey. Palm Sunday processions would not reach Constantinople for another three hundred years or so. For George of Pisidia, palms waved in welcome were markers of military victory.

Much later Latin Christian sources, however, were confident that Heraclius's entry had been "meant to evoke Christ's entry on Palm Sunday."[28] They also added legendary material. The version of the story in Jacob of Voragine's *Golden Legend* (ca. 1260) is the best known: "Heraclius ... rode down the Mount of Olives, mounted on his royal palfrey and arrayed in imperial regalia, intending to enter the city by the gate through which Christ had passed on his way to crucifixion. But suddenly the stones of the gateway fell down and locked together, forming an unbroken wall. To the amazement of everyone, an angel of the Lord, carrying a cross in his hands, appeared above the wall and said, 'When the King of heaven passed through this gate to suffer death, there was no royal pomp. He rode a lowly ass, to leave an example of humility to his worshipers.'" Moved to tears, the emperor removed his boots, stripped to his shirt, and carried the relic of the true cross on foot to the gate, which miraculously reopened to admit him.[29]

An earlier version, found in a sermon formerly attributed to Hrabanus Maurus (ca. 780–856), but now thought to be by a contemporary of Hrabanus,[30] told the story in almost identical terms, noting in addition that "all the people [were] rejoicing with palm branches, candles, and torches," and that Christ himself "did not display himself in [imperial] purple or shining crown, or require the conveyance of a powerful horse."[31] The sermon in question was composed some fifty years or so after Charlemagne's entry into Rome in 774. Its rhetorical link between Heraclius's entry and Christ's own entry into Jerusalem was probably forged with more interest in moral application than in historical accuracy. It is even possible that the ninth-century sermon, stressing the dissonance between the pomp of Heraclius's entry and the simplicity of Christ's, was written not to document a past angelic rebuke of Heraclius but indirectly to challenge a more

---

26 Thomson and Howard-Johnston, *Armenian*, 90.

27 George of Pisidia, "Improvisations ... on the Restoration of the Holy Cross," 7–8, (*Poemi*, 225); translation from MacCormack, *Art*, 86. For the argument that George's poem anticipated, rather than commemorated, Heraclius's entry into Jerusalem, see Grumel, "Reposition," 146–49.

28 Drijvers, "Heraclius," 186.

29 Jacob of Voragine, *Golden*, 2:169–70.

30 Étaix, "Receuil," 125–26.

31 Hrabanus, *Homilia* 70 (*PL* 110:131–34).

recent Carolingian confusion of Palm Sunday and military triumph. There is, in any case, no reason to believe that the sermon contains a reliable account of Heraclius's historical entry into Jerusalem.

If neither Heraclius nor the exarch of Ravenna anticipated Charlemagne's appropriation of the language and iconography of Palm Sunday for the celebration of military triumph, then we can affirm with some confidence that Charlemagne's reception in Rome in 774 was the first (or at least the first recorded) civic entry to do so. The extent of Charlemagne's innovation can be brought into even sharper relief by comparing his Easter Saturday triumph to the earlier entry into Rome in 663 of Constans II (641–668), "the first and last Byzantine emperor" to visit Rome in person.[32] Although Constans, like Charlemagne, arrived after a military victory over the Lombards, no evidence suggests that he concerned himself with the language or iconography of Palm Sunday. On Wednesday, July 6, 663, Constans and his army were met "at the sixth milestone from the city" by Pope Vitalian "with his priests and the Roman people."[33] Andrew Ekonomou understands this ceremonial encounter as the first step in a lavish, traditional, imperial spectacle: "The emperor's arrival in the ancient capital of the empire was thus transformed into an 'imperial epiphany' assuming all the attributes of an *adventus* in the ancient style."[34] From there all proceeded to Saint Peter's Basilica, where Constans prayed and presented a gift. The following Sunday, Constans returned to Saint Peter's "with his army, all with wax tapers, and on its altar he presented a gold-wrought pallium, and mass was celebrated."[35] The records afford no allusion to Christ's entry into Jerusalem. If Ekonomou is correct, it was a standard imperial entry, with its roots in classical Roman practice rather than in Christian narrative.

Charlemagne's victorious entry, a century later, was the first to add the language and iconography of Palm Sunday to the inherited signs and symbols of classical Roman triumphs. He may have believed that he was claiming a historically pagan ceremonial for Christ, just as his many military campaigns aimed at claiming pagan peoples and territories for Christ. The political norms of his day expected a Christian ruler to spread his faith by force. Adding the language and iconography of Palm Sunday to a civic entry celebrating military triumph was innovative, but it may not have struck his contemporaries as dissonant. The consequences, however, were far-reaching. Charlemagne set in motion a process by which not only could triumphal entries become acceptably Christian but elite Palm Sunday processions could became increasingly triumphal.

---

32 Ekonomou, *Byzantine*, 171.

33 Paul the Deacon, *Historia* 5.11 (190–91), trans. Foulke, 223–24.

34 Ekonomou, *Byzantine*, 172.

35 *Lib. pont.* 1:343, trans. Davis, *Book*, 73.

Chapter 2

KINGS DEAD OR ALIVE

Any inquiry into how far Charlemagne's innovation shaped his successors' roles in triumphal entries and Palm Sunday processions over the next 350 years is hampered both by the sketchy nature of the contemporary records and the tendency of historians to read those records through the lens of Kantorowic's exaggerated claims. In Chapter 2, I offer tentative conclusions rather than definitive answers.

In 801, after a prolonged siege, the citizens of Barcelona surrendered to the forces of Louis the Pious, Charlemagne's youngest son and the duke of Aquitaine. The city had been under Muslim rule for some eighty years. According to his anonymous contemporary biographer, now known only by his nickname (the Astronomer), Louis delayed his entry "until he could decide how to consecrate this desired and welcome victory to God's name with suitable thanksgiving. On the next day his priests and clergy preceded him and his army through the gate of the city. With solemn splendour and hymnic praise, they processed to the church [i.e., the Visigothic cathedral] of the holy and most victorious Cross, where they gave thanks to God for the victory divinely bestowed upon them."[1] Ermold the Black, a contemporary court poet, dates the opening of the city gates to Holy Saturday and the entry itself to Easter Sunday, which fell that year on April 4. He adds that Louis "purified" the places of worship appropriated by Muslims for use as mosques before "he gave reverent thanks to God."[2] Louis's entry into Barcelona shared significant features with his father's entry into Rome in 774. Common to both are the juxtaposition of clergy and soldiers; the singing of "hymnic praise," which in both cases may have been acclamations (*laudes*) directed towards the king; the celebration of a decisive military conquest and annexation of new territory; the acknowledgment of the power of the "victorious cross"; and, if Ermold is correct, the timing of the entry just a few days after Palm Sunday. The contemporary accounts, however, yield no decisive reference to palms or to any other elements of the Palm Sunday story or liturgy.[3]

The few other records of Carolingian triumphal entries that survive are even sketchier. In the summer of 818, Louis led "a great army" to quell a rebellion in Brittany. He was by then, as his father had been, both king of the Franks and emperor. He was met in the autumn on his return to Aachen—or perhaps in his palace at Herstal (now in

---

1 Astronomus, *Vita* 13 (318–21), translation adapted from Noble, *Charlemagne*, 238, and Cabaniss, *Son*, 43–44.

2 Ermold, *Poème*, 45–47; trans. Noble, *Charlemagne*, 140.

3 Louis's entry into Barcelona may have been more akin to his father's triumphal entry into Pavia in June 774, when the chronicles also speak of "hymns and *laudes*" but not of palms or Palm Sunday (McCormick, *Eternal*, 374–75; Schnorr von Carolsfeld, "Chronicon," 31; Pertz and Kurze, *Annales Fuldenses*, 9).

Belgium), some thirty miles west of Aachen—"with a victorious triumph."[4] The chronicle gives no details of the triumph. In 823 and 824, Louis twice sent his son Lothair to Italy. On the first occasion, Lothair was received in Rome by Pope Paschal I "with stately pomp" (*clarissima ambitione*) and crowned co-emperor with his father,[5] and on the second by Paschal's successor, Eugene II, "most willingly and most honourably (*libentissime atque clarissime*)."[6] If Charlemagne's entry into Rome in 774 were indeed the prototype "for all imperial receptions in Rome during the Middle Ages,"[7] then Lothair's entries in 823 and 824 would have resembled that of his grandfather. But this is to rely on Kantorowicz rather than on documentary evidence. Lothair's entries were linked to diplomatic mission, not military triumph, and possibly followed a different pattern.

On January 15, 859, Charles the Bald, king of West Francia and another son of Louis, defeated his brother, Louis the German, king of East Francia, at Jouy (now Aizy-Jouy), between Soissons and Laon.[8] John Scot Eriugena, theologian and royal poet, wrote a poem in celebration of the victory, two lines of which may suggest a triumphal entry: "Now we celebrate the return of Charles with a grateful song (*carmine grato*): / After many lamentations our joys shine forth."[9] But Paul Edward Dutton translates "carmine grato" as "with this thankful poem," and suggests a private reading of the poem in the presence of the king, rather than a public triumph.[10] Again, the records leave us uncertain.

Seventy-four years after the death in 888 of Charles the Fat, a grandson of Louis the Pious, control of the western Roman Empire passed to the kings of Germany. In 962, after a nearly forty-year hiatus during which there had been no papally anointed emperor, Otto I, king of Germany, was crowned emperor by Pope John XII in Rome. John Bernhardt believes that Otto's arrival in Magdeburg for Easter week in 948, a full twelve years before his imperial coronation, had "liturgically re-enacted the triumphal entry of Christ as king into Jerusalem."[11] Although the contemporary records establish only that Otto was in Magdeburg from at least March 27 (the day after Palm Sunday) to April 1 (Holy Saturday),[12] Bernhardt plausibly assumes that Otto celebrated both Palm Sunday and Easter Sunday in the royal monastery. Even so, there is no documentary evidence that Otto's entry into Magdeburg shortly before Palm Sunday recalled Christ's entry. Bernhardt's sole authority for his claim is Kantorowicz's general principle.

---

4 Ketteman, "Chronicon," 141; *Chronicon Moissiacense*, MGH,SS, 1:280–313 (313); see also Astronomus, *Vita* 31 (388–91); trans. Noble, *Charlemagne*, 258.

5 Astronomus, *Vita* 36 (414–15); trans. Cabaniss, *Son*, 75.

6 Astronomus, *Vita* 38 (422–25); trans. Noble, *Charlemagne*, 267.

7 Kantorowicz, "King's," 21n23.

8 Poupardin, "Carolingian," 37; Nelson, *Charles*, 190.

9 Eriugena, "Hellinas Troasque suos," MGH,PLMA 3:527–29 (528). For a triumphal reading of these lines, see McCormick, *Eternal*, 373; Nelson, *Charles*, 190.

10 Dutton, "Royal," 63.

11 Bernhardt, *Itinerant*, 168.

12 "Otto I: Diplome," 96–99 (179–81).

More well-founded is the scenario suggested by Thietmar of Merseburg's account of Otto's subsequent Holy Week visit, in 973, to Magdeburg, where Otto "celebrated Palm Sunday with great solemnity. Indeed, it was his custom on all feast days to be led to the church for vespers, matins, and the mass by a procession composed of bishops and other orders of clerics carrying crosses, relics of saints, and censers."[13] By then, Otto was emperor and the abbey church was the seat of an archbishop. If Otto's royal procession formed part of the cathedral's own Palm Sunday procession, it would have been accompanied not only by crosses, relics, and censers, but also by palms or other foliage, and by the singing of Palm Sunday hymns, antiphons, and responses. Royal and Palm Sunday processions would have been indistinguishable. Perhaps this had also been the case in 948.

Something similar may have happened on Palm Sunday, 958. On that day "in the city of Mainz," Otto signed a deed granting property to Saint Alban's Abbey in return for the care of the soul of his son Liudolf.[14] The abbey was on high ground outside the city walls. Franz Staab has proposed that the charter was signed after prime, that Liudolf's corpse was carried to the abbey as part of the customary first stage (*Vorprozession*) of the Palm Sunday procession, that he was buried inside the abbey, and that the deed of gift was laid on the altar of the abbey church. The Palm Sunday liturgy then continued with the blessing of the palms, after which the procession re-formed and made its way downhill from the Albansberg into the city, ending at the cathedral, where terce and mass were celebrated.[15] If Staab is right, Otto's royal participation in the Palm Sunday procession would have allowed for "a triumphal *adventus* through the Mainz city walls," recalling Christ's descent from the Mount of Olives, through the Golden Gate, and into Jerusalem.[16] Mapping Jerusalem onto the local terrain was, as we shall see, a common feature of medieval Palm Sunday processions.

Royal participation in a Palm Sunday procession was, of course, not the same as incorporation of the signs and symbols of Christ's entry into a royal military triumph. In the former, the king was still—at least in principle—playing a supporting role to the Christ who was represented in procession by crosses and gospel books. In the latter, the evocation of Christ's entry magnified the king's starring role in his own show. Such had been the case when Charlemagne entered Rome in 774. Nearly two hundred years later, on January 31, 962, Otto also entered Rome in the wake of a military victory of sorts. As Liudprand of Cremona tells it, "the most pious king" Otto had been "moved by the tears" of papal, episcopal, and secular ambassadors from Rome, Milan, and elsewhere in northern Italy to act against the "savage tyranny" of Berengar II, king of Italy. "Considering not his

---

13 Thietmar, *Chronik* 2.30 (76–77); trans. Warner, 114.

14 "Otto I: Diplome" 192 (273–74).

15 Staab, *Erzstift*, 99, 108, 170–73.

16 Parkes, *Making*, 77–78, 123. Later sources show that in Mainz "on Palm Sunday all the collegiate churches gathered in the cathedral and made their way together to Saint Alban's, where the blessing of the palms took place" (Gottron, "Stationsfeiern," 21). After the abbey was destroyed in 1552, the Collegiate Church of Saint Stephen, also on high ground but within the city walls, was substituted for Saint Alban's (Würdtwein, *Commentatio*, 4.141).

own interests, but those of Jesus Christ, [Otto] gathered his forces" and marched on Italy. Berengar fled. Otto took Pavia by default, declared Berengar deposed, and continued to Rome, where "he was received with wondrous pomp and new ceremonial."[17] Thietmar confirms that Otto "celebrated a glorious entry into the city,"[18] while the *Liber pontificalis* notes with somewhat less flair that "the Roman emperor Otto was honourably received" by Pope John XII.[19] In the absence of further details, we can only guess as to whether Otto invoked Christ's entry. Two days after his triumphal entry, Otto was crowned emperor by the pope in Saint Peter's Basilica.

One of the more bizarre episodes in Palm Sunday's entangled relationship with royal entries began with the death of Otto III, grandson of Otto I, on January 24, 1002. Otto III was twenty-one and childless when he died, outside Rome, of high fever and "internal sores which gradually burst."[20] He had been preparing to enter the city to avenge an earlier revolt against German imperial rule.[21] Sensitive to the precarious political situation, the emperor's retinue kept his death a secret until the full complement of imperial troops had arrived. Otto's body was then escorted north not only by soldiers but also by his friend and counsellor Archbishop Heribert of Cologne, who had been with him in Italy. For the first part of the journey, according to later reports, the king's corpse was dressed in imperial purple and secured to his horse in an upright position, so that it looked as if he were still alive and riding at the head of his army.[22]

After crossing the Alps in winter, the entourage was joined by Duke Henry IV of Bavaria, one of the rival claimants for the now vacant imperial throne. Henry "gave the beloved emperor's intestines, carefully preserved in two small vessels, an honourable burial" in Augsburg's Church of Saint Afra.[23] The removal and separate burial of internal organs was a normal practice when corpses had to be transported a long distance.[24] Duke Henry reluctantly left the cortège in Neuburg an der Donau, the last town under his rule on the way to Cologne.

On Palm Sunday, the king's corpse was solemnly received into the city of Cologne by Archbishop Heribert. The timing of its arrival was deliberate, for as Henry Mayr-Harting remarks, it not only allowed Otto's corpse to be acclaimed "as if it were Christ entering Jerusalem," but it also gave "the archbishop a wonderful opportunity to apotheosize the emperor by making his body an image of Christ for the Holy Week ceremonies, and an opportunity to elevate his own city" as an image of the holy city Jerusalem.[25]

---

17 Liudprand, "Historia" 3 (170); trans. Squatriti, 221; see also Mann, *Lives*, 4:247–48.

18 Thietmar, *Chronik* 2.13 (52–53); trans. Warner, 101.

19 *Lib. pont.* 2:246, 248n6; see also Böhmer, *Regesta*, 2.1:149.

20 Thietmar, *Chronik* 4.49 (188–89); trans. Warner, 187.

21 Althoff, *Otto*, 118–29.

22 Glaber, *Historiarum* 1.15 (30–31); Wolfhelm, *Brunwilarensis* 10 (131); Böhmer, *Regesta*, 2.3:829. Althoff, *Otto*, 129, considers the later reports "embroidered."

23 Thietmar, *Chronik* 4.51 (190–91); trans. Warner, 188.

24 Warner, "Thietmar," 71n102.

25 Mayr-Harting, *Ottonian*, 1:119; see also Bornscheuer, *Miseriae*, 210.

The archbishop integrated the royal body into the ongoing liturgy of Holy Week, having the corpse carried on Monday "to the Church of Saint Severinus, on Tuesday to Saint Pantaleon ... on Wednesday to Saint Gereon," and on Maundy Thursday to the Cathedral Church of Saint Peter.[26] On Saturday the remains of Otto III were taken a further forty-four miles to Aachen, where on Sunday they were buried in the imperial basilica established by Charlemagne.

Religious ritual betrayed a political agenda. Beginning with the triumphal entry on Palm Sunday, the events of Holy Week in Cologne and Aachen had been designed to "counteract" Duke Henry's preemptive burial of Otto's intestines in Augsburg.[27] Archbishop Heribert favoured a rival claimant for the imperial crown, Duke Herman of Swabia, who, we are told, secured promises of support from "the majority of nobles who attended the funeral procession."[28] Herman's efforts proved insufficient. In July, Duke Henry succeeded to the throne of Germany as Henry II, and twelve years later was formally crowned emperor by the pope. Thietmar of Merseburg, the chronicler and bishop to whom we owe details of Otto's death and long funeral journey north, was Henry's appointee.

The Palm Sunday entry of Otto's corpse to Cologne was not unique. A century later, another dead king rode into the midst of a Palm Sunday procession, this time in Jerusalem. In 1099, the forces of the First Crusade under Frankish leadership had conquered Jerusalem, reportedly slaughtering tens of thousands of Muslims and Jews, and establishing a crusader kingdom that was to last until 1187. In March 1118, the second crusader king of Jerusalem, Baldwin I, died during a military incursion into Egypt. The cause of his death is disputed. Albert of Aachen reports that the king died on March 26 from heat exhaustion (and possibly burns) incurred while setting fire to the conquered Egyptian town of Farama (now al-Farama, some twelve miles east of the Suez Canal). After his internal organs were removed and buried, his body was embalmed, sewn into a hide, wrapped in carpets, and tied on horseback. Concealment of the corpse kept enemy forces from learning of the king's death. After reaching Ashkelon, the army gained in confidence and advanced the remaining forty-five miles inland to Jerusalem "with banners flying and [in] battle formation."[29] Fulcher of Chartres, who was in Jerusalem at the time, tells a different story: the king fell ill after eating fish, and died on the way home on April 2 in Laris (now al-Arish, about fifty miles east of al-Farama).[30]

Both are agreed, however, that Baldwin's eviscerated corpse reached Jerusalem on Palm Sunday, which fell that year on April 7. Despite Fulcher's insistence that the timing of the royal corpse's arrival was "by the will of God and by a most unexpected

---

26 The Romanesque churches of Saint Severin, Saint Pantaleon, and Saint Gereon all survive, although considerably modified since the time of Otto III. The "old cathedral" of Saint Peter was destroyed by fire in 1248.

27 Bornscheuer, *Miseriae*, 210.

28 Thietmar, *Chronik* 4.53–54 (192–93); trans. Warner, 189–90.

29 Albert, *Historia*, 868–71.

30 Fulcher, *Historia* 2.64 (609–12); trans. Ryan, 221–22.

circumstance,"[31] one suspects that Baldwin's followers took full advantage of the opportunity. Albert writes:

> On that same day the lord patriarch Arnulf [of Choques] had come down from the Mount of Olives with his clergy after the consecration of palms, and his brothers came out from the Temple of the Lord[32] and from all the churches to meet him for the festival, with hymns and songs of praise in celebration of the holy day on which the Lord Jesus, riding on a donkey, deigned to enter the holy city of Jerusalem. So, with all the Christian congregations gathered together for the festival in praise of God, suddenly the dead king was borne into the middle of the people as they sang. At the sight of him their voices were hushed and their praises were brought low, and a very great weeping was heard from the clergy and people alike. Nevertheless the Palm Sunday service was completed, and everyone came in with the dead king through the gate which is called Golden, through which Lord Jesus had entered when coming to his Passion.[33]

The dead Baldwin thus went one better than Otto, entering Jerusalem itself, and doing so though the same gate that Christ was believed to have used. If, as Colin Morris claims, the reenactment of Christ's entry into Jerusalem was "code for the triumph of the First Crusade,"[34] then the timing of the dead crusader king's entry was particularly apt. The procession may have claimed to celebrate Christ's entry on a donkey, but the entry of a dead crusader king on horseback served the more immediate political end of upholding the legitimacy of the crusader kingdom.

These two Palm Sunday entries of dead kings not only illustrate the perverse degree to which Palm Sunday processions and royal entries could become entangled, but they also offer indirect confirmation that the practice of live kings making royal entries of Palm Sunday processions was common enough. The posthumous entries of Otto III to Cologne and Baldwin I to Jerusalem are credible only if they were particularly eccentric adaptations of a widely accepted practice of mingling the language and iconography of Palm Sunday processions and royal entries in the wider Ottonian empire and the Frankish homeland. Even so, it is important to retain the distinction between Palm Sunday processions, of which these posthumous entries are peculiar examples, and royal entries at other times of the year. We can, I think, safely conclude that royal participation in Palm Sunday processions was not unusual and that, where it happened, the processsion became in addition something of a royal entry. We can be less certain that royal entries routinely appropriated the language and iconography of Palm Sunday for their own celebrations of power and military triumph. The records are, at best, unclear.

---

31 Fulcher, *Historia* 2.64 (612); trans. Ryan, 222.

32 Under the crusader state, the Muslim Dome of the Rock was converted into an Augustinian church known as the Templum Domini.

33 Albert, *Historia*, 870–71.

34 Morris, *Sepulchre*, 221.

Chapter 3

WARRIOR POPES

We turn now from emperors and kings to popes, dipping into the story of papal entries shortly after the point at which we left the story of royal entries.[1] My purpose here, as elsewhere in Part 1.1, is not to give a complete account of either royal or papal triumphal entries, but to highlight specific examples of dissonance between civic pomp and the evocation of Christ's entry. In this chapter, I consider just four papal entries. Two come from the first half of the twelfth century, around the time of the first Palm Sunday processions in papal Rome. Another, in which the elected pope insisted on riding a donkey to his coronation but was persuaded to change to a white horse for the triumphal procession that followed, took place in 1294. The fourth, much later, instance comes from 1507, when even the pope's master of ceremonies was troubled by a spectacular instance of tension between military triumph and Palm Sunday's liturgical anticipation of Christ's passion. Cultural circumstances, of course, changed over the intervening four centuries, but the dissonance between biblical story and its ceremonial representation by rulers of church and state proved remarkably persistent.

Pope Calixtus II entered Rome on June 3, 1120, just two years after King Baldwin I's corpse had ridden into Jerusalem. Calixtus had been elected pope at Cluny on February 2, 1119, and crowned seven days later at his archiepiscopal see of Vienne.[2] After more than a year spent consolidating his power north of the Alps but failing to make peace with the current king of Germany and Holy Roman emperor, Henry V, Calixtus set out for Rome.[3] Everywhere along the way, according to Boso, the pope's twelfth-century biographer, "innumerable multitudes of people" gathered. Crowds "venerated (*venerabantur*) him … as the vicar of Christ" and "prostrated themselves before him with great devotion."[4]

Uodalscalcus, a monk from the abbey of Saint Afra and Saint Ulrich in Augsburg, left an eyewitness account of Calixtus's entry into Rome. He describes how the Roman militia came out to meet the pope while he was still three days away from the city. "So magnificent was the procession that Caesar himself, had he been present, would have marvelled at the sight and even Tullius Cicero would have been impressed." As the pope neared the city, "young men and children bearing branches of all kinds hurried toward him shouting acclamations." Closing around him, the children were forced back, but Calixtus intervened: "Let the little children come to me, and do not stop them; for it is to such as these that the kingdom of heaven belongs."[5] After his coronation in Saint Peter's Basilica, the pope was led through the streets of Rome, which "were everywhere adorned with gold and precious jewels," and was greeted with "harmonious

---

1 For earlier papal entries, see Twyman, *Papal*, 41–92; Blaauw, "Contrasts."

2 *Lib. pont.* 2:376; Twyman, *Papal*, 92; Stroll, "Calixtus," 18–25.

3 Stroll, "Calixtus," 25–42.

4 *Lib. pont.* 2:377.

5 Compare Matt. 19:14.

praises sung in Latin and Greek" and with acclamations in Hebrew by members of the city's Jewish community.[6] Calixtus finally reached the Lateran Basilica, where he was enthroned.[7] Uodalscalcus thus invokes not only the magnificence of Roman imperial triumphs and the Palm Sunday acclamation of Christ by children bearing palms, but also the trilingual inscription identifying the crucified Christ as "King of the Jews … in Hebrew, in Latin, and in Greek,"[8] and the risen Christ's triumphant ascension to a heavenly throne from which he rules over "a great multitude … from every nation, from all tribes and peoples and languages, standing before the throne and before the Lamb … with palm branches in their hands."[9] Papal dogma taught that the heavenly rule of Christ sanctioned the vicarious and, in principle, universal power of the papacy on earth.

Boso's account of Calixtus's inaugural entry into Rome also incorporates details of a second triumphal entry that took place a year later, on April 22, 1121. At the time of his first entry, Calixtus had not been the only claimant to the papacy. In 1118, the emperor Henry V had installed Maurice Burdinus, Archbishop of Braga, as Pope Gregory VIII. Burdinus fled Rome before Calixtus's arrival, but in the spring of 1121 was captured by an army loyal to Calixtus.[10] Calixtus led the captive antipope into Rome, staging Burdinus's humiliation by having him sit backwards on "a camel instead of a white horse," holding the animal's tail, and wearing a "shaggy wether's pelt (*pilosa pelle vervecum*) instead of a red mantle."[11] Calixtus, befitting his status as the legitimate pope, rode a white horse and wore a red papal mantle.

Two decades later, Eugene III became the first Cistercian monk to be elected pope. He entered Rome in December 1145, after testy negotiations over the degree of temporal

---

6 Uodalscalcus mentions "the confused cheering of the Jews." Champagne and Boustan, "Walking," 489, gloss this as "the Jews' acclamation in Hebrew … Such trilingual acclamations in Greek, Latin, and Hebrew had long been performed for secular rulers"; see also Twyman, *Papal*, 201–6. For the participation of Jews in other royal and papal entries, see Coulet, "Intégration." For the mutually supportive relationship of Calixtus and the Roman Jews, see Stow, *Jews*, 1:xxi–xxii.

7 Uodalscalcus, "De Eginone et Herimano," ed. Philippe Jaffé, in MGH,SS 12:429–47 (446); translation adapted from Twyman, *Papal*, 93–94. See also the letter written by Calixtus himself, dated June 3, 1120, in *PL* 163:1180–81; and Falco of Benevento, *Chronicon*, in *PL* 173:1146–262 (1179).

8 John 19:19–20.

9 Rev. 7:9. Contemporary teaching held that Christ's entry into the earthly Jerusalem had prefigured both his ascension, forty days later, from the Mount of Olives to the heavenly Jerusalem (Durand, *Rationale*, 1.3.14, 6.67.7–9 [1:40, 2:323–24]) and his final triumphant entry into the heavenly city with all the saved after the Last Judgment (Bernard of Clairvaux, "In Ramis Palmarum, Sermo Primus," 2–3, in *Opera*, 5:43–44; Bernard, *Sermons*, 2:113–15).

10 *Lib. pont.* 2:323; Twyman, *Papal*, 96.

11 *Lib. pont.* 2:377; Falco of Benevento, *Chronicon*, *PL* 173:1183; Twyman, *Papal*, 97. For the practice of condemning an offender to ride backwards on an animal, see Mellinkoff, "Riding." *Vervex*, meaning a wether or a castrated male sheep, was commonly used as "a term of abuse for a stupid or sluggish person" (*OLD*, s.v. ueruex).

power he might properly exercise in the city. Eugene's immediate predecessor, Lucius II, is reported to have marched against the senators and people of Rome "with a huge army" and to have died after being struck by a large stone thrown in the ensuing battle.[12] Eugene preferred negotiation and the implicit threat of armed intervention by Roger II of Sicily. According to Boso, Eugene was led into the city by "a great crowd of people carrying branches." Also taking part in the procession were standard-bearers, papal archivists and officials, Jews bearing scrolls of the Torah on their shoulders,[13] and "all the Roman clergy singing as one, 'Blessed is he who comes in the name of the Lord.' "[14] Eugene was no doubt dressed in fine silk vestments and rode a richly caparisoned white horse.[15]

Bernard of Clairvaux, the primary reformer of the Cistercian order, warned Eugene, his friend and former disciple, against the pomp enjoyed and enjoined by the Roman curia:

> You see the entire zeal of the church burn solely to protect its dignity. Everything is given to honour, little or nothing to sanctity. If, when circumstances require, you should try to act a little more humbly and to present yourself as more approachable, they say, "Heaven forbid! It is not fitting; it does not suit the times; it is unbecoming to your majesty; remember the position you hold." ... [Saint] Peter is known never to have gone in procession adorned with either jewels or silks, covered with gold, carried on a white horse, attended by a soldier, or surrounded by clamoring servants ... In this finery, you are the successor not of Peter, but of Constantine.[16]

Constantine, the first Christian emperor, had been a triumphant warrior.

Despite his mentor's counsel, Eugene submitted to the ceremonial demands of office. I know of only one pope who resisted such demands to the point of riding a donkey in public procession. Peter of Morrone was an eighty-four-year-old hermit who had no aspirations to be pope, initially resisted election to the office, and only reluctantly agreed to serve.[17] The news that he had been chosen as pope, after an electoral process that had remained unresolved for nearly two years, reached Peter in his grotto on Mount Morrone, north of Sulmona (Abruzzo), in late July 1294. It was brought by two groups: a royal embassy led by Charles II, king of Naples, and his son Charles Martel, the titular

---

12 Godfrey of Viterbo, *Pantheon*, 461; Twyman, *Papal*, 100.

13 For the role of the Torah in papal entries, see Twyman, *Papal*, 197–200.

14 *Lib. pont.* 2:387; Twyman, *Papal*, 100–1.

15 Blaauw, "Contrasts," 362–66.

16 Bernard of Clairvaux, *De consideratione* 4.2–3 (*Opera*, 3:452–53); trans. Anderson and Kennan, 115–17. For the date of the work, which was sent to Eugene in five installments between 1149 and 1153, see Jacqueline, "Appendices," in Bernard, *Five*, 184. For a similar rebuke, comparing the "horses and chariots" of the higher clergy with the "poverty" of Christ, in a sermon delivered by Arnulf of Lisieux at the Council of Tours (1163), see *PL* 201:160.

17 For modern biographies of Celestine V, see Mann, *Lives*, 17:247–341; Golinelli, *Papa*; Sweeney, *Pope*.

king of Hungary; and a delegation from the college of cardinals, led by Bérard of Got, archbishop of Lyon.[18] Peter chose the name Celestine V.

Charles II suggested that Celestine be spared the journey to Rome and crowned instead in L'Aquila, some forty miles away. L'Aquila was the second city in the kingdom of Naples; Rome was outside Charles's jurisdiction. The Roman cardinals grudgingly complied.[19] According to Giacomo Stefaneschi, who witnessed the new pope's entry into L'Aquila on a "donkey (*asellus*)" with Charles II on his right and Charles Martel on his left holding the animal's bridle, Celestine's choice of mount reminded "the astonished multitide" of Christ's entry into Jerusalem.[20] This may well have been Celestine's intent. The earliest prose hagiography of Celestine, written "between 1303 and 1306,"[21] observes that Celestine "ordered a donkey to be brought" so that he might follow "the example of his Lord." The cardinals, "astonished" by Celestine's "great humility," tried to dissuade him "lest the church of God be seen to suffer an indignity."[22] Stefaneschi granted that Celestine set a good example to the more ostentatious clergy, but wondered if he might have done better humbly to ride a horse.[23]

The coronation overcame Celestine's resistance. On August 29, in L'Aquila's Basilica of Santa Maria di Collemaggio, Celestine was weighed down with the papal tiara, red imperial mantle, and other regalia of the office. An eyewitness estimated the crowd at "more than two hundred thousand."[24] After the ceremony, Celestine rode into the city on the obligatory white horse.[25] The new pope never made it to Rome, establishing his residence in Naples instead. There, on December 13, he resigned, the last pope to do so before Benedict XVI in 2013. Imprisoned by his successor, Boniface VIII—who was not in the least embarrassed to ride a "snow-white" (*niveus*) horse[26]—Celestine died two years later. Pope Clement V (1305–1314), whose brother Bérard of Got had led the delegation of cardinals to Mount Morrone in 1296, declared Celestine a saint in 1313.

Celestine's sanctity was acknowledged in his canonization, but only after he had failed to be taken seriously as pope. For a very different approach to papal rule, we can fast-forward to Julius II, whose entry into Rome on Palm Sunday, March 28, 1507, was

---

18 Sweeney, *Pope*, 63–66; Mann, *Lives*, 17:280–84.

19 Mann, *Lives*, 17:284–89.

20 Stefaneschi, *Opus*, 58. For a biography of Stefaneschi, see Dykmans, *Cérémonial*, 2:25–131.

21 Ortroy, "S. Pierre," 378.

22 "Vie et miracles de S. Pierre Célestin par deux des ses disciples," in Ortroy, "S. Pierre," 393–458 (418).

23 Stefaneschi, *Opus*, 59, note to line 65; Stefaneschi's Latin verse is convoluted at this point, forcing me to rely, as others have done (e.g., Mann, *Lives*, 17:286), on Seppelt's suggested editorial paraphrase.

24 Tolomeo, *Historia* 24.29 (634); Golinelli, *Papa*, 120–21, regards this as "a symbolic number, which signified a great multitude." For Tolomeo's "firsthand knowledge" of Celestine's papacy, see Blythe, *Life*, 86–88.

25 Stefaneschi, *Opus*, 65; Mann, *Lives*, 17:290; Sweeney, *Pope*, 145–49.

26 Stefaneschi, *Opus*, 101; Mann, *Lives*, 18:57.

perhaps the most spectacular (or outrageous) integration of military triumph, Palm Sunday iconography, and sheer *chutzpah* in the history of the papacy.

The military victory celebrated by Julius's entry into Rome had been won four months earlier. At the head of his own mercenary army, the sixty-three-year-old pontiff had advanced on Bologna, supported by a French expeditionary force that had already placed the city under siege. The threat of imminent attack forced the "tyrant" Giovanni Bentivoglio to flee Bologna without a fight, and restored the city to the temporal dominion of the Papal States. In the first of multiple entries that were to culminate with his arrival in Rome, Julius rode into Bologna on November 11, 1506, passing through a dozen triumphal arches on his way from the city gate to the cathedral.[27] The arches displayed flattering mottoes hailing Julius as the liberator of Bologna from tyranny and the bestower of peace on the city. At the first arch, prepared by the city's Jewish community, a hundred or more Jewish elders stood "with palms, and olives, and oak branches in their hands." Hanging from their shoulders were gold-lettered inscriptions, calling for loud and unabashed acclamation of the pope.[28]

A more sceptical response to Julius's Bologna triumph was penned by the Christian humanist Erasmus, who had taken up residence in the city earlier in the year, but had fled to Florence "for fear of the siege." Returning to Bologna once the threat of attack had passed, he was present for Julius's entry.[29] On November 17, he wrote to a colleague in Flanders: "At this moment studies are remarkably dormant in Italy, whereas wars are hotly pursued. Pope Julius is waging war, conquering, leading triumphal processions; in fact, playing Julius [Caesar] to the life."[30] Later, after the pope's death in 1513, Erasmus wrote *Julius Exclusus*, a satirical dialogue between Saint Peter and Pope Julius. When Peter refuses the fictionalized pope entry to heaven, Julius boasts of his worldly achievements, including the capture of Bologna and the "regal triumph" as he entered the city.[31] Finally, he threatens to recruit, from the "several thousand more soldiers" who will soon be "slaughtered in the wars," a vast army with which to besiege heaven and "throw [Peter] out by force."[32] "It was Julius II," it has been said, "who turned Erasmus into a pacifist."[33]

Julius himself remained in Bologna until February 22, 1507, when he set off on a triumphal return journey to Rome that would last over a month. On March 15, in Viterbo, the pope told his master of ceremonies, Paride de' Grassi, that he would time his formal reentry into Rome to coincide with Palm Sunday, and that he had written accordingly to Cardinal Allessandrino, the papal legate in Rome. The pope stipulated that he would

---

27 Frati, *Due*, 84–96. For an account of Julius's Bologna campaign, see Shaw, *Julius*, 148–61, 204–14.

28 Frati, *Due*, 87–88.

29 Erasmus, *Opus*, 1:431–33; Erasmus, *Collected*, 2:122–25. For Erasmus's presence at Julius's entry to Bologna, see Halkin, *Erasmus*, 66; Stinger, *Renaissance*, 236.

30 Erasmus, *Opera*, 1.1:573; Erasmus, *Opus*, 1:435; Erasmus, *Collected*, 2:128.

31 Erasmus, "Iulius," 234, 242–44; Erasmus, "Julius," 172, 176. *Julius Exclusus* was published anonymously; for the arguments in favour of Erasmus's authorship, see Erasmus, "Julius," 156–60.

32 Erasmus, "Iulius," 296; Erasmus, "Julius," 197.

33 Phillips, *Adages*, 105.

bless palms and hear mass at the Church of Santa Maria del Popolo on the morning of Palm Sunday, and proceed "with due ceremony" (*solemniter*) through the centre of the city to his palace in the Vatican after eight in the evening.

Grassi tactfully asked whether he should prepare something "more than was customary" for a papal entry. He clearly felt—but was not yet ready to say so directly—that the pope's process through Rome on Palm Sunday should not only be a secular triumph, but should also contain liturgical elements recalling Christ's entry into Jerusalem. Grassi wondered, too, what he should do if the people of Rome "were not prepared to receive the pope with due ceremony." Relations between the pope and Rome's secular officials and citizens were rarely straightforward.

Visibly displeased, Julius demanded to know what could be more important than the pontiff returning from a long absence. Grassi begged the pope to consider whether it was suitable, while Christ was liturgically in the midst of "his passion," for the pope, as the vicar of Christ, to engage "in triumphal procession, and pomp, and glory." The pope became agitated, insisting that if the Roman people and clergy came out to meet him, crying "Blessed is he who comes in the name of the Lord," his entry would be entirely appropriate for the occasion. When Grassi tried to point out that the lengthy reading of the passion story at mass on Palm Sunday "saddened" the church, and so rendered even such a modified celebration of papal triumph unsuitable, the pope ordered him to be silent. He allowed that Grassi need not order the Romans to stage such an entry, but insisted that he not stand in their way should they wish to do so. In subsequent discussion, Grassi and Allessandrino conceded that they must obey the pope's command for a ceremonial entry, but agreed nonetheless to plan a procession that would be "ecclesiastical and spiritual rather than worldly and triumphal."[34]

In the event, on the evening of Saturday, March 27, Julius arrived in considerable pomp aboard a galley on the river Tiber.[35] Trumpeters aboard ship heralded his approach. Disembarking at the Ponte Milvio, the scene of the emperor Constantine's decisive military victory in 312, Julius was met by his legate and other cardinals who had remained in Rome, by a group of Roman senators and conservators, all of whom kissed the pope's feet, and by a large crowd. Ceremonially mounting his horse (*equum ascendens pompose*), the pope proceeded to the Augustinian monastery of Santa Maria del Popolo, where he spent the night.[36] On the morning of Palm Sunday, the pope attended divine office in the church. Twenty-six cardinals joined him, wearing red copes suited to a papal entry rather than the violet appropriate to the liturgical season.[37] An abundance of palms and even more olive branches were blessed and distributed. After a brief procession, mass was celebrated, and the pope returned to the monastery for lunch.[38]

---

34 Frati, *Due*, 168–69; see also Shaw, *Julius*, 213.

35 Beltrando Costabili, "Lettera da Roma, 28 marzo 1507, al duca di Ferrara," in Cruciano, *Teatro*, 322–23, places Julius's arrival "circa a le XXII hore" (at around 10 p.m.).

36 Frati, *Due*, 169–71.

37 Red replaced violet as the liturgical colour of Palm Sunday in 1969 in the wake of Vatican II.

38 Frati, *Due*, 171–72.

In terms of sheer spectacle, the evening's triumphal entry was the major event of the day. The processional route from Santa Maria del Popolo to the papal palace in the Vatican "was very richly prepared in all parts," with cloths covering the streets, and tapestries and decorations of every kind hanging from the walls. About eight triumphal arches, "no less magnificent and costly," had been built, not at public expense but by private "friends and members of the Roman Curia."[39] Grassi and Allesandrino, doing their best to balance these signs of triumphal pomp with an appropriate liturgical counterpoint, had arranged for every collegiate and parish church along the way to set up an outdoor altar," adorned "as festively as possible with songs, and sounds, and smells [i.e., incense], and the most magnificent preparations possible." Rather than processing ahead of the pope, "all the urban clergy, of whatever church without exception, no matter how privileged," remained by the outdoor altars of their own churches, "dressed in ecclesiastical vestments, with a palm in hand." As the pope passed, the stationary clergy acclaimed his advent in song. Moreover, "if some of the churches were a little distant from one another, then altars were erected at equal intervals, and there some religious or secular clergy were added," to ensure that there be no significant interruption in the liturgical praise of the Christ whom the pope represented.[40]

By thus turning the triumphal arches "into small islands in a sea of chanting clerics standing before altars,"[41] Grassi and Allesandrino ensured that Christ's entry into Jerusalem was celebrated along with Julius's military triumph. Even so, despite their insistence on Passion Week being a "season of Christian sadness," they staged Christ's entry as a joyous triumph pointing beyond "the mystery of his passion" to his subsequent ascension to his heavenly throne and his final eschatological victory over all his enemies. Julius, of course, did not ride a donkey. Grassi specifies that the papal mount was a mule (*sua mula insidens*): a white mule was then of the same exalted status as a white horse.[42] Although the Curia were reportedly overjoyed to see the pope again after so long an absence, the Roman people were less enthusiastic: while Grassi hesitates to use the word "sadness," he admits that the Romans did not show "wholehearted joy." He puts this down to a consciousness of "their own fault" at having failed to send any messages to the absent pope congratulating him "on his victory over the expelled tyrant," but grants that there may be "some other cause" of popular discontent.[43]

---

39 Sanudo, *Diarii*, 7:63–65, records some of the laudatory verses placed on the triumphal arches.

40 Frati, *Due*, 172–73. For other contemporary accounts of Julius's entry, see Costabili, "Lettera," and Sigismundo Gonzaga, "Lettera da Roma, 29 marzo 1507, al marchese di Mantova," both in Cruciano, *Teatro*, 322–23; Tedallini, "Diario," 313.

41 Kinser, "Entry," 27.

42 Frati, *Due*, 174. Costabili, "Lettera," in Cruciano, *Teatro*, 323, wrote that Julius was "muntata a cavallo," which can simply mean "mounted," without specifying the animal in question. Cruciani, *Teatro*, 324, translates Grassi's "sua mula insidens" as "a cavallo della su mula." The feminine noun *mula* may signify "mule" without reference to actual gender. Julius's contemporary Cardinal Thomas Wolsey, "richly robed in red velvet, rode on a magnificent white mule caparisoned in gold" (Bough, *Donkey*, 60).

43 Frati, *Due*, 173–75.

In what followed, secular celebration of military victory finally overwhelmed liturgical commemoration of Christ's entry. Near the Castel Sant'Angelo, the pope was greeted by "a noble spectacle that was both delightful to see and of mysterious teaching." A triumphal chariot (*currus triumphalis*) pulled by a team of four white horses, "in accordance with the practice of Roman triumphs,"[44] supported a round platform on which ten winged boys representing angels, each with a palm in his hand, sang and moved "in a slow ring dance."[45] When the chariot stopped, "a small boy rose up on the high summit, waving a palm in his hand, as if presenting it to the pontiff." The boy sang a heroic poem glorifying Julius, who "on the feast day of palms" had brought his own victory palm to Rome, and was himself "most worthy of all palms" for having expelled tyranny. Above the head of the boy was a large orb in the form of an astronomical sphere, signifying "universal dominion,"[46] and above the sphere "a great golden oak, which was set up between two palm trees, and stretched out its branches and its golden acorns to the heavens."[47] The coat of arms of the Della Rovere family, to which the pope belonged, was a golden oak and acorns.

Pyrotechnics followed with unintended effect. "So many explosions and bombs from the Castel Sant'Angelo were heard at that moment that one would have thought that the sky cracked; and on account of this, and the following applause from the immense crowd, the team of four white horses was greatly terrified." The horses bolted, careening in different directions, out of control. Whether the winged boys enjoyed their wild ride or were as terrified as the horses is not recorded. The chariot was finally abandoned half-way to the Vatican. The rest of the cavalcade arrived at Saint Peter's Basilica at around midnight, three hours after it had set out.[48]

After some comparatively simple ceremonies reincorporating the pope into the liturgical life of the basilica, Julius was carried to the Vatican palace on his *gestatorium* (portable throne). A final triumphal arch awaited him in front of the palace. "Equal in size and form and elegance to the Arch of Constantine"—except, of course, that it was made of "painted wood and cloth," not "carved marble"—the arch displayed "all the acts and gestures of the pontiff in all his travels," and announced its theme in writing: "To Julius II, who has returned as the best and greatest pontiff, because through virtue, wisdom, and blessedness, he has liberated the papal states from the servitude of tyranny and has established peace and freedom everywhere."[49] The Arch of Constantine, the largest triumphal arch in Rome, had been erected by the Roman Senate to commemorate the first Christian emperor's victory at the Battle of Milvian Bridge.

To mark his triumphal return to Rome, Julius had also issued a commemorative medal. One side features Julius's bust in profile and the inscription IVLIVS CAESAR PONT[IFEX]

---

44 Stinger, *Renaissance*, 236.
45 Kinser, "Entry," 30.
46 Stinger, *Renaissance*, 236.
47 Frati, *Due*, 175.
48 Frati, *Due*, 174–75.
49 Frati, *Due*, 175–76.

II, while the other side features the Della Rovere golden oak, the papal tiara and crossed keys, and the inscription BENEDI[CTUS] QV[I] VENIT I[N] NO[MINE] D[OMINI]. Charles Stinger concludes: "Julius II entered Rome ... both as a second Julius Caesar, heir to the majesty of Rome's imperial glory, and in the likeness of Christ, whose Vicar the pope was, and who in that capacity governed the universal Roman Church. The things of God and Caesar, far from belonging to separate spheres, were fused in Julius's triumph."[50] It was a far cry from Christ's entry on a donkey, modelling peace to a Jerusalem chafing under Roman imperial rule.

---

50 Stinger, *Renaissance*, 238.

Chapter 4

MUD, PLAGUE, AND THE LORD PROTECTOR

We return now to kings and other secular rulers, rejoining the story of royal entries in 1559, half a century after Julius II's triumphal papal entry into Rome. In the meantime, royal entries had extended their range of referents beyond Christ's entry into Jerusalem to other advents that were less susceptible to "unfortunate suggestions" of imminent betrayal and execution and more permissive of untrammelled splendour and exaltation.[1] Christ's ascension to a heavenly throne and his second coming in undisputed glory were more in keeping with the mimetic aspirations of royalty. Moreover, with the spreading vogue for classical referents occasioned by the Italian Renaissance and the acceptance of ancient philosophical texts by humanist scholars, organizers of royal entries developed a marked preference for classical and allegorical models. These might be given a Christian interpretation but were only occasionally grounded in the New Testament narrative. Julius II's triumphal entry recalled Christ's entry only because Julius chose to schedule the event on Palm Sunday and Grassi insisted on a liturgical balance to the classical allegory and triumphal pomp. For my purpose, which is to explore the dissonances between enacted representations of Christ's entry and the shared story to which they claimed allegiance, I can safely bypass most of these later royal entries. Other scholars, with different interests, have already studied them well and in considerable detail.[2]

One set of civic entries, however, still warrants my attention, not so much because of its occasional evocations of Christ's entry, but because it provides a necessary context for my later discussion of James Nayler's entry into Bristol in October 1656. Before I argue, in Chapter 9, that Nayler engaged in a dishevelled parody of royal entries, I will do well to describe in this chapter the English (and Scottish) entry traditions with which Nayler may have been familiar, either personally or by report. After brief summaries of royal entries and progresses during the reigns of Elizabeth I, James I, and Charles I, I look in more detail at the triumphal entries of Oliver Cromwell, in whose army Nayler had fought and with whom, after Cromwell became Lord Protector in 1653, Nayler grew increasingly disillusioned.

Moving directly from Julius II in papal Rome to Elizabeth I and her successors in Protestant England means, of course, that I pass both chronologically and geographically through the heart of the Reformation. For good reason, however, I have postponed discussion of the Reformation itself. The Protestant Reformation had much less (if any) effect on royal entries than it did on Palm Sunday processions. This was especially true in German-speaking lands, where the reformers' hostility towards religious images extended in many cases to the active destruction of life-size Palm Sunday processional sculptures of Christ on a donkey known as palmesels. Although my story

---

1 Gordon Kipling, personal communication, June 10, 2014.

2 For example, Jacquot and Konigson, *Fêtes*; Kipling, *Enter*; Mulryne, Watanabe-Kelly, and Shewring, *Europa*.

occasionally brushes against the Reformation in the meantime, I have reserved closer examination of its impact on processional representations of Christ's entry until we reach the persecution of the palmesel in Chapters 15 and 16. In the meantime, I remain with royal entries.

Throughout her long reign, Elizabeth I indulged not only in lavish entries but also in extended summer progresses from one city or private estate to another. Lawrence Stone paints a vivid picture:

> Almost every year there set forth a huge caravan led by the queen, accompa-
> nied by her ladies, by some members of the Privy Council, and by noblemen and
> courtiers, waited on by an army of royal servants and supported by a baggage
> train of between 400 and 600 carts forcibly impressed from a reluctant peas-
> antry ... Those anxious to preserve or increase their favour at court could not
> afford to show themselves niggardly in the country on the occasion of a royal
> visit ... Elizabeth ... expected to be richly feasted and elaborately amused, and to
> be sent on [her] way with expensive parting gifts ... Erratic and destructive as a
> hurricane, summer after summer Elizabeth wandered about the English coun-
> tryside bringing ruin in her train, while apprehensive nobleman abandoned
> their homes and fled at the mere rumour of her approach.[3]

For all the expense incurred, even the grandest of royal entries were rarely as splendid as the official records pretend. Elizabeth I's 1559 coronation entry into the city of London is a case in point. Most accounts, whether by eyewitnesses or historians, focus on the five triumphal arches on which allegorical "pageants" were presented, celebrating the new queen's royal ancestry and her commitment to biblical truth, national concord, and the triumph of virtue over vice.[4] But even a laudatory pamphlet published ten days after the event admitted that the design of the arches meant that the queen, seated in an elaborate horse-drawn litter, had a hard time seeing and hearing the children who presented the pageants.[5]

The weather wasn't great either. Although the accounts printed for public consumption avoid the topic, an Italian eyewitness, Aloisio Schivenoglia (also known as Il Schifanoya), reported in a private letter that "it snowed a little" on the morning of the entry. It was not the first precipitation of the winter. "Owing to the deep mud caused by the foul weather and by the multitude of people and of horses, everyone had made preparation by placing sand and gravel in front of their houses." Schivenoglia reckoned that the queen's chariot or "litter," taking the place of greatest honour "last of all" in the procession, followed in

---

3 Stone, *Crisis*, 451–54.

4 Contemporary accounts include "The Quene's Majestie's Passage," in Kinney, *Elizabethan*, 7–39 (also Nichols, *Progresses*, 1:114–39); "Il Schifanoya to the Castellan of Mantua," in *Calendar*, 7:11–19; Machyn, *Diary*, 186; Grafton, *Abridgement*, 194v–195v. For modernized texts of these documents, see Warkentin, *Queen's*. Nichols, *Progresses*, 1:114, and Strong, *Tudor*, 2:33, provide helpful bibli-ographies of scholarly commentary on the entry, to which should be added Kipling, *Enter*, 125–29, 348–52.

5 Kinney, *Elizabethan*, 19, 21, 24, 32.

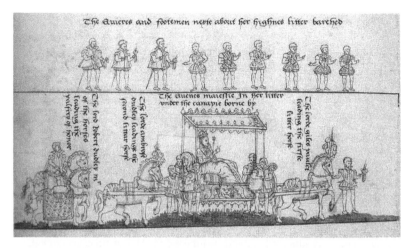

Figure 4 Coronation procession of Elizabeth I of England. Drawing, 1559.
College of Arms, London, MS 6f 41v. © College of Arms. Used with permission.

the hoofprints of "in all 1,000" horses.[6] The mud must by then have been deeply churned and mixed with horse dung, but no trace of fouled conditions underfoot appears in a contemporary drawing of Elizabeth's litter (Fig. 4). Susan Frye observes that private reports such as Schivenoglia's serve "as a reminder of what is missing in the published text—any sense of disorder, the tawdry, and the everyday that might taint the authority represented in the allegories."[7] By contrast, all the published accounts of Nayler's entry into Bristol drew scornful attention to the degrading rain and mud.

James I lacked Elizabeth's tolerance for royal entries. Although he was crowned in July 1603, an outbreak of bubonic plague in London that summer, described in printed records as "the sickness" or "the great mortality,"[8] meant the postponement of his "magnificent coronation entry"[9] until March 1604.[10] Fifty years later, Arthur Wilson recalled James's distaste for the day's events: "The city and suburbs being one great pageant, wherein he must give his ears leave to suck in their gilded oratory, though never so nauseous to the stomach," James had failed to match Elizabeth's display of "well-pleased affection" for "her people's acclamations." Instead, the new king "endured this day's brunt with patience, being assured he would never have such another." Although spared another coronation entry—he had been crowned king of Scotland in 1567,[11] shortly

---

6 *Calendar*, 7:12. Machyn, *Diary*, 186, confirms that the streets were "strewed with gravel."

7 Frye, *Elizabeth*, 159n29.

8 Nichols, *Progresses*, 1:329.

9 Smuts, "Public," 82.

10 Stewart, *Cradle*, 172; for records of the entry, see Nichols, *Progresses*, 1:325–423, and for a judicious summary, Bergeron, *English*, 72–88.

11 Stewart, *Cradle*, 31.

after his first birthday—James could not avoid all public ceremonial: "Afterwards in his public appearances ... the accesses of his people made him so impatient, that he often dispersed them with frowns, that we may not say with curses."[12]

Charles I also preferred to avoid public ceremonial. The City of London began preparing for Charles's coronation entry as early as April 1625, a month after James's death. A recurrence of the plague caused delays, but "five most superb [triumphal] arches" were eventually built and put in place "at the expense of many thousands of ducats." In May 1626, three months after the coronation itself had taken place in Westminster Abbey, Charles abruptly canceled the delayed outdoor entry and ordered the arches torn down, prompting "the murmurs of the people and the disgust of those who [had] spent the money."[13] Like his father, Charles favoured the more contained spectacle of courtly masques. Both kings were probably afraid of catching the plague or some other fatal disease from too close a proximity to the common crowd.

Charles did, however, permit a state entry when he arrived in Edinburgh for his belated coronation as king of Scotland in June 1633. The printed account describes four triumphal arches with pageants mythologizing Scottish history and flattering Charles with relentless classical allegory.[14] Two days later, accompanied by bishops and Scottish lords, Charles rode in an impressive cavalcade from Edinburgh Castle down what is now known as the Royal Mile to Holyrood Abbey Church, where he was crowned.[15] An early twentieth-century Scottish clergyman and historian, defending the cavalcade against the charge that it was "a mere equestrian display," claimed that "it had no less a precedent than our Saviour's entry into Jerusalem, whereby he offered himself as the true king of Zion."[16] Other than, perhaps, the downward slope of the Royal Mile, there is nothing in the contemporary records to suggest such an intent on the part of the organizers.

Finally, in November 1641, on his return from another visit to Scotland, Charles allowed the city of London to give him a state entry of sorts. There were no triumphal arches or dramatic pageants, but there was at least a show of popular acclaim. The Venetian ambassador reported: "Four miles outside London the mayor came out with the aldermen and 600 horsemen of the most substantial citizens, with numerous liveries and richly dressed." All the streets were "decorated" and lined with crowds, such that Charles "was received everywhere with universal acclamations."[17] His popularity was short-lived. The English Civil War broke out in the summer of 1642, and Charles was beheaded in January 1649.

---

12 Wilson, *History*, 12–13. See Smuts, "Public," 84–89, for other factors besides "James's distaste for plebeian crowds" that may have caused the "curtailment in public ceremony" during his reign.

13 *Calendar*, 19:464; see also Bergeron, *English*, 111–13.

14 Drummond, *Entertainment*, 1–30; see also Bergeron, "Charles"; Bergeron, *English*, 111–20; Sharpe, *Personal*, 778–83.

15 Coit, *Life*, 153–62.

16 Cooper, *Four*, 25n2.

17 *Calendar*, 25:254; see also Bergeron, *English*, 122–24.

By contrast with his Stuart predecessors, Oliver Cromwell professed a humble aversion to pomp while presiding over a revival of triumphal entries, even when he was still only commander of the parliamentary army. On July 10, 1649, six months after Charles's execution, Cromwell left London at the head of an army headed for Ireland with the goal of defeating the allied forces of the regrouped Royalists and an independent Irish Catholic Confederation. According to a contemporary report, he "went forth in that state and equipage as the like hath hardly been seen, himself in a coach with six gallant Flanders mares, whitish grey, divers coaches accompanying him, and very many great officers of the army ... with trumpets sounding." Cromwell's army continued "by the way of Windsor and so to Bristol"[18] in what has been called an "already glitteringly stately progress."[19]

Cromwell's Irish campaign left scars that still disfigure the political landscape. His triumphant return to London in June 1650 was met with a "lavish welcome" that continued "the appropriation of monarchical ceremony for the republican state."[20] An unsigned "Letter from Windsor," dated June 1, reports that most of the town's inns were "full of guests ... come from London on purpose to attend him," and that "a great number" would "also meet him by the way, in his passage to London" the next day. In a double show of humility, Cromwell declared that it was "not suitable to his desire, to come up to London in great pomp and glory," but allowed the acclaim to go ahead lest he be "thought guilty of that abominable vice of ingratitude." A postscript adds that Cromwell was accompanied from Windsor to Westminster by "many lords, and most of the members of Parliament and the Council of State, the officers of the army, and many hundred well-affected gentlemen and citizens."[21] A contemporary engraving shows the fêted Cromwell "astride a rearing stallion, wearing full armor." Although "the horse is simply caparisoned and Cromwell is unarmed," the image still idealizes Cromwell, in the words of its inscription, as "the Right Honorable and undaunted Warrior."[22]

In July 1650, Cromwell marched on Scotland, where Charles I's son, later to reign as Charles II, had landed and formed an unlikely alliance with the Scottish Covenanters. After Cromwell's victory, on September 3, at the Battle of Dunbar, the English Parliament commissioned a commemorative medal for all who had taken part in the battle. Cromwell urged that the medal show Parliament on one side and the army, beneath the inscription "The Lord of Hosts," on the other side. The final design of the silver medal showed Cromwell's profile in place of the army.[23] Cromwell was not charged with blasphemy. James Nayler was entitled to a medal. Having enlisted with the rank of corporal in a parliamentary "troop of horse" (cavalry) in 1643, he fought under Cromwell at Dunbar,

---

18 *Moderate Intelligencer* 225 (July 5–12, 1649): 17.

19 Sherwood, *Oliver*, 11.

20 Knoppers, *Constructing*, 50.

21 "A Letter from Windsor," in *Speech*, 4–6.

22 Knoppers, *Constructing*, 50–51.

23 Knoppers, *Constructing*, 56–57. British Museum M.7330, at www.britishmuseum.org/research/collection_online/collection_object_details/collection_image_gallery.aspx?partid=1&assetid=1613052031&objectid=952258.

but was released on the grounds of ill health soon afterwards. Within just over a year, he became a Quaker.[24]

In 1651, Charles and his Scottish allies launched a desperate campaign to invade England and capture London while Cromwell was in Scotland. Cromwell pursued and caught the Scots at Worcester, on September 3, 1651, where he gained a decisive victory over the last of the Royalist forces. Charles fled to the continent. Nine days later, on September 12, Cromwell and his army entered London. According to Samuel Carrington, a contemporary biographer unstinting in his praise, Cromwell "desire[d] no triumphal preparations" and specifically declined the city's proposal "to have bonfires made and … triumphal arches erected."[25] Even so, "at least three hundred coaches" accompanied Cromwell and his "gallant" cavalry into London, along a road lined by "many thousands of citizens both horse and foot … four or five miles together." After he reached Hyde Park Corner, he was saluted by successive regiments of uniformed soldiers, firing volleys of "great and small shot," and by "mighty" shouts of the people." For all Cromwell's professed "meekness and humility,"[26] Laura Knoppers discerns a contrary impulse: "The ceremonial entry and public acclaim marked Cromwell's political ascendancy in a mode that flirted with the more monarchical entries."[27] In a manner reminiscent of pagan imperial triumphs, some 4,000 Scottish prisoners were brought into London under guard the following day.[28]

On Friday, December 16, 1653, Cromwell was installed as Lord Protector of England, Scotland, and Ireland. Dressed in "a black suit and cloak," he rode the half-mile or so from Whitehall to Westminster in the last of many horse-drawn coaches filled with civic dignitaries. Foot soldiers lined "both sides [of] the streets all along, and in the palace at Westminster were many soldiers, both horse and foot."[29] The investiture itself, which took place inside Westminster Hall, drew generously on "the trappings of kingship" while stopping short of a full-blown royal coronation.[30] Even so, the Lord Protector was routinely addressed thereafter as "your Highness."[31]

Printed reports of the day's events were uniformly positive,[32] but surviving private correspondence reveals a measure of dissent. John Thurloe, who was to control Cromwell's department of intelligence (or spies), wrote on the morning after the investiture, "Yesterday [Cromwell] was proclaimed with some pomp, not pleasing to many beholders." In a second letter, Thurloe declined to describe "the solemnities, which

---

24 Neelon, *James*, 49, 65–66.

25 Carrington, *History*, 82.

26 *Another Victory*, 1–3; see also Whitelock, *Memorials*, 3:352.

27 Knoppers, *Constructing*, 58.

28 *Another Victory*, 3–4.

29 *Severall Proceedings of State Affairs* 221 (December 15–22, 1653): 3499.

30 Sherwood, *Oliver*, 9–12.

31 Carrington, *History*, 166; *MP* 192 (February 9–16, 1654); Whitelocke, *Memorials*, 4:71ff.

32 *Great Brittain's Post* 151 (December 14–21, 1653): 1242–23; *MP* 184 (December 16–22, 1653): 3052–54.

were too much after the old fashion, and so grievous to many."[33] Lorenzo Paulucci, the Venetian Secretary in England, sent his ambassador in France a detailed account of the investiture, emphasizing its troubling proximity to a royal rite: Cromwell was seated "on what was once a royal throne," while civil and military officers, "hat in hand, did him homage, in the obsequious and respectful form observed toward the late kings." Three days later, the Lord Mayor and his court of aldermen, preceded by "heralds in rich tabards," proclaimed the new republican government in the streets of London. Paulucci sensed popular apathy. Writing in cipher, he reported "that the people seemed rather amazed and dashed than glad, and no shout of public acclamation was heard."[34]

Even more splendid was Cromwell's entry into the city of London on Ash Wednesday (February 18) 1654, after which he joined the Lord Mayor and aldermen in "a noble banquet."[35] In his typically effusive style, Carrington describes the ceremonial splendour: "His Highness's Life Guard of horse marched in the first place, after which followed the chief officers of the army on horseback, and some of his Council of State; after them rode two pages bareheaded in sumptuous apparel; after them came twelve lackeys in velvet caps and gray liveries, with silk and silver fringe; then followed his Highness seated in a chariot of state drawn by six beautiful horses richly trapped, which by their lofty gait seemed to glory in their drawing so victorious a Hercules, triumphing over so many monsters." Cromwell was initially "clad in a dark-coloured suit and cloak," but when he was met by the Lord Mayor's party at Temple Bar—the principal western gateway to the city—he "alighted from his chariot, and quitting his cloak, put on a rich riding coat embroidered with gold, and got up on horseback on a palfrey richly trapped, and was followed by three other led horses of state."[36] Arriving at the guildhall of the Worshipful Company of Grocers, Cromwell and his entourage were entertained "in a very magnificent manner" with music and feasting.[37] "Thus was enacted a royal ritual dating back to the late fourteenth century."[38]

Some observers took offence, not merely at the monarchical pomp but also at the flouting of older religious sensibilities. To schedule such feasting and show on Ash Wednesday, the first day of Lent, was consistent with the Puritan rejection of religious holidays, but an affront to those of more traditional Anglican convictions. Among the latter group, the Royalist John Evelyn complained to his diary: "In contradiction to all custom and decency, the usurper Cromwell feasted at the L[ord] Mayor's on Ash Wednesday, riding in triumph through the city."[39] The Catholic Venetian diplomat Paulucci noted that "the first day of Lent" was specifically "appointed" by Cromwell as most "suiting him." While acknowledging the splendour of the entry, Paulucci again switched to cipher to

---

33 Thurloe, *Collection*, 1:640.

34 *Calendar*, 29:164–65; see also *MP* 184 (December 16–22, 1653): 3054.

35 *MP* 191 (February 2–9, 1654): 3262.

36 Carrington, *History*, 168.

37 *MP* 191 (February 2–9, 1654): 3262.

38 Sherwood, *Oliver*, 18; see also Knoppers, *Constructing*, 76–79.

39 Evelyn, *Diary*, 3:93.

note popular dissent: "Although the entire population of London came forth to view the pageant, not the faintest sound of applause was heard, nor were any blessings invoked on the head of his Highness." Likewise, during Cromwell's return to his dwelling that evening, there were "very scanty marks of goodwill from the people in general, who ... greeted him with a rancour which increases daily because he has arrogated to himself despotic authority ... under the mask of humility and the public service. He lacks nothing of royalty but the name, as his power is certainly greater than that of the late kings."[40] A written newsletter takes an even more critical tone of "our Ash Wednesday's pageantry which was a triumph made up of dirt and multitude." The near-silent crowd offered only curses and threw "tiles and filthy clouts to accompany the pomp."[41] Cromwell's pomp was more like Nayler's than the official accounts admit.

On September 4, 1654, Cromwell opened the First Protectorate Parliament "with all the ritual and pageantry of a king."[42] There may have been no alternative ceremonial precedent, but over the next couple of years speculation grew rife that Cromwell would in fact be crowned king himself.[43] By June 1655, the Swedish ambassador to London was convinced that Cromwell would "very shortly assume the title of king." In March, 1656, he reported that "the protector is anxious to assume the crown," and that he had himself "thought it not inadvisable to encourage him to do so." Similar claims flowed from the ambassador's pen in July and August.[44] In September, an anonymous tract, *The Unparalleld Monarch*, openly urged Cromwell's matchless qualifications for the crown.[45]

Taking a very different position, radical religious dissenters believed that Cromwell had already usurped the rights of King Jesus. In a letter written in February 1655, Cromwell's spymaster, John Thurloe, quoted John Carew as saying that "when the Little Parliament was dissolved" on December 12, 1653, Cromwell "took the crown off from the head of Christ, and put it upon his own."[46] Carew had himself been a member of the Barebones or "Little" parliament of 1653. He was also, like many of the members of that short-lived parliament, a Fifth Monarchist, convinced that Christ was about to return to establish his millennial kingdom on earth.[47] Another Fifth Monarchist, the preacher John Rogers, reportedly told his congregation in December 1654 that "the saints ... must shortly enjoy and possess the glory of the earth," and that "the Antichrist, the Babylon, the great dragon or the man of sin, Oliver Cromwell in Whitehall, must be pulled down."[48] In February 1655, according to his own supporters, Rogers told Cromwell to his face,

---

40 *Calendar*, 29:185–86.

41 Oxford: Bodleian Library, Clarendon MS 47, fol. 379r–v, quoted in Knoppers, *Constructing*, 79.

42 Sherwood, *Oliver*, 39.

43 Knoppers, *Constructing*, 110–18.

44 Roberts, *Swedish*, 75, 270, 317, 326.

45 *Unparalleld*; Knoppers, *Constructing*, 115–18.

46 Clarke, *Papers*, 2:244. Thurloe's letter to George Monck, 1st Duke of Albemarle, was written in February 1655. See also Knoppers, *Constructing*, 71–72; Rogers, *Fifth*, 60.

47 For the Fifth Monarchists, see Rogers, *Fifth*; Capp, *Fifth*.

48 Thurloe, *Collection*, 3:136.

"The controversy is not now between man and man, one government of the world and another government of the world, or king and people; but it is now between Christ and you (my Lord) Christ's government and yours: and which of these two are the higher powers for us to side with, and be obedient unto, judge ye."[49]

Although, as a Quaker, James Nayler thought of Christ's rule as something present and internal rather than future and external, he shared the Fifth Monarchists' concern that Cromwell was setting himself up in opposition to Christ. The time was ripe for a parody of the revitalized tradition of royal entries in general and of Cromwell's potentially imminent royal coronation entry in particular. On October 24, 1656, Nayler rode through the mud into Bristol, an action that can only be properly understood in its immediate political and religious context. We shall return to Nayler in Part 2. In the meantime, we set royal entries aside to look more closely at Palm Sunday processions.

---

[49] *Faithfull*, 35. The lack of a comma before or after the parenthical "my Lord" leaves its attribution to Cromwell or to Christ ambiguous.

PART ONE:

POMP

II. Palm Sunday Processions:
From Egeria to Peter the Great

Chapter 5

PALMS OF VICTORY

ACCORDING TO THE *Ordo of Beroldus*, a twelfth-century ordinal from Milan, the city's annual Palm Sunday worship began in the Basilica of San Lorenzo with the chanting of "Magnum salutis gaudium" (Great joy of salvation).[1] Several times, the hymn insisted on Christ's "meekness" in riding an "ass's colt." The fifth stanza reads:

O quam stupenda pietas
mira Dei clementia
sessor aselli fieri
dignatur auctor saeculi.

[O tender love how marvellous,
More wondrous meekness yet!
That earth's Creator deigneth thus
On ass's colt to sit.][2]

The entry of the archbishop of Milan to the basilica coincided with the opening line of the seventh stanza, "Rex ecce tuus humilis" (Behold your humble king): the archbishop was understood to represent the Christ of Palm Sunday.

After preaching a sermon and blessing palm and olive branches, the archbishop went back outside, where the branches were distributed among the crowd. Waiting for him was "a white horse covered in a ceremonial saddle cloth."[3] The saddle cloth (*naccum*) was probably made of cloth of gold.[4] The horse's bridle was held by an "elegantly dressed" soldier from the private militia of a noble Milanese family. Once the archbishop had mounted the horse, he was given a "cross made of crystal, decorated with palm and olive leaves," which he held in his left hand while blessing the crowd with his right. Led by the choir from the Basilica of Saint Ambrose, a minor cleric bearing a golden crucifix, and a phalanx of other clergy and monks, and surrounded by a large crowd of laity, the archbishop processed "with triumphal glory" (*cum triumphali gloria*) through the streets of Milan.[5] The procession ended at the Basilica of Saint Ambrose, where the archbishop dismounted and went inside to celebrate mass.[6]

---

1 Magistretti, *Beroldus*, 96–97. The archdiocese of Milan has observed the distinctive Ambrosian Rite since at least the eighth century.

2 For the words of the hymn, as they were sung in Milan on Palm Sunday, see Magistretti, *Manuale*, 3:171–72; for a metrical translation, see Copeland, *Hymns*, 177–80.

3 Magistretti, *Beroldus*, 96.

4 Magistretti, *Beroldus*, 213.

5 McCormick, *Eternal*, 372, notes that phrases "like 'cum magno triumpho' or 'cum gloria triumphi'" were frequently used to qualify contemporary descriptions of Carolingian royal entries.

6 Magistretti, *Beroldus*, 97; Tyrer, *Historical*, 54–55, 64.

Palm Sunday in twelfth-century Milan stopped far short of Julius's II's triumphal Palm Sunday entry into Rome. Nor can it be confused with Charlemagne's triumphal entry into Rome in 774. The Milan ceremony was a Palm Sunday procession, not a military triumph; it was an annual rite, not a special event. Nevertheless, the richly vested archbishop, processing "with triumphal glory" through the streets of Milan on a prestigious white horse led by a soldier, was of a very different order from the humble rider on an ass's colt celebrated in the opening hymn. Visually, the progress of the archbishop resembled a royal entry more than it resembled Christ's entry into Jerusalem. In this chapter, I sketch the history of Palm Sunday processions from their first surviving record in late fourth-century Jerusalem to the first signs of military triumph in Francia during the late Carolingian era. In the rest of Part 1, I follow the spread of triumphal Palm Sunday processions south from imperial Germany to papal Rome (Chapter 6), before turning east to look at Orthodox traditions in Constantinople (Chapter 7) and Moscow (Chapter 8). My intent, here as elsewhere, is not to write an exhaustive history of the processional theatre of Palm Sunday. My more focused goal in this second half of Part 1 is to document the ways in which, after four hundred years of comparative simplicity, some elite examples of the genre came to resemble triumphal entries.

Although the emperor Constantine I's legalization of Christianity in 313 CE had made public Christian celebrations possible, it was the subsequent emergence of Jerusalem as a pilgrimage destination that first nurtured Palm Sunday processions. Since its destruction in 70 CE, Jerusalem had been something of a backwater, known by the Roman colonial name of Aelia Capitolina. This changed radically when the adjacent sites of Jesus's crucifixion and tomb were uncovered, possibly during the visit of Constantine's mother, the dowager empress Helena, in 327. Claims that the remains of Christ's true cross had been unearthed, a discovery later attributed to Helena herself, further enhanced the city's prestige.

Constantine commissioned the building of a large basilica over the sacred sites. The revitalized city, once again identified as Jerusalem, and its magnificent Church of the Holy Sepulchre, completed in 335, soon attracted pilgrims to the places of Christ's passion. During Holy Week, Jerusalem and its basilica "became host to a liturgical round which sought to take pilgrims on a journey alongside Jesus Christ through the events of his last sufferings in Jerusalem, his crucifixion and resurrection."[7] An annual Palm Sunday procession was probably introduced sometime between 350 and 380. The anonymous Bordeaux Pilgrim, who had visited Jerusalem in 333, claimed to have seen at the foot of the Mount of Olives "a palm tree, branches of which the children carried off and strewed in the way when Christ came," but made no mention of a processional commemoration of the biblical event.[8] Cyril of Jerusalem, in catechetical lectures delivered "no later than the early 350s,"[9] also noted "the palm-tree in the valley ... which provided

7 MacCulloch, *Christianity*, 195.

8 Bordeaux Pilgrim, *Itinerarium*, 17, trans. Stewart, 24.

9 Yarnold, *Cyril*, 6.

the palms for the children who greeted Christ there," but likewise made no mention of a Palm Sunday procession.[10] By 381–384, however, when the Spanish pilgrim Egeria visited Jerusalem,[11] an outdoor Palm Sunday procession was an established part of the city's Holy Week worship.

Palm Sunday in late fourth-century Jerusalem opened, like almost every other Sunday in the city's church year, with a series of services in the Church of the Holy Sepulchre, lasting from pre-dawn cockcrow until late morning, and moving between the round Church of the Anastasis (Resurrection), built over the tomb at the western end of the basilica, and the rectangular Great Church or Martyrium (Shrine of Martyrdom) at the eastern end over the rock of Golgotha. After "a quick meal" at home, the worshippers gathered again in the Church of the Eleona (Olive Grove) on the Mount of Olives for hymns, antiphons, prayers, and readings "suitable to the place and the day." At three in the afternoon, they moved to the nearby Church of the Imbomon (Hillock), built on the traditional site of Christ's Ascension.[12]

Finally, around five, the worshippers began to walk downhill in active remembrance of Christ's own Palm Sunday entry. Egeria recalled:

> The passage is read from the Gospel about the children who met the Lord with palm branches, saying, "Blessed is he that comes in the name of the Lord." At this the bishop and all the people rise from their places, and start off on foot down from the summit of the Mount of Olives. All the people go before him with psalms and antiphons, all the time repeating "Blessed is he that comes in the name of the Lord." The babies and the ones too young to walk are carried on their parents' shoulders. Everyone is carrying branches, either palm or olive, and they accompany the bishop in the very way the people did when once they went down with the Lord. They go on foot all down the Mount to the city, and all through the city to the Anastasis, but they have to go pretty gently on account of the older women and men among them who might get tired. So it is already late when they reach the Anastasis; but even though it is late they hold Lucernare

---

10 Cyril, *Catacheses* 10.19, in *PG* 33:331–1059 [cols. 685–86]; trans. Yarnold, *Cyril*, 127. Cabrol, *Églises*, 95, inexplicably rendered Cyril's observation in the present tense ("le palmier dans la vallée, dont les branches servent aux enfants qui acclament joyeusement le Christ"), allowing him to argue that Cyril bore witness to a Palm Sunday procession in his own time. But the Greek original (*ho phoinix ho epi tēs pharaggos ... ta baia paraskhōn paisi tois tote euphēmousi*) uses both an aorist participle (*paraskhōn*) and a temporal adverb (*tote* = at that time) to specify past time.

11 An incomplete eleventh-century copy of Egeria's diary was found by G. F. Gamurrini in 1884 (Gamurrini, *Hilarii*, ix–xiv), who dated her travels to 381–388 (Gamurrini, xxvii–xxxvii). Férotin, "Véritable," identified the author as "the most blessed nun Etheria" of Galicia; the spelling of her name has since been standardized as Egeria. Maraval, in Egeria, *Journal*, 23–27, suggests that she was not a nun, but a devout laywoman with a sustained interest in the monastic life. Devos, "Date," narrowed the date of her stay in the Holy Land to 381–384.

12 Egeria, *Itinerarium* 24–25, 30–31 (69–70, 76–77), trans. Wilkinson, 124–26, 132–33.

[the Service of the Lamps] when they get there, then have a prayer at the Cross, and the people are dismissed.[13]

There are no signs of imperial pomp or military triumph in this procession. The inclusion of old people, who had to move slowly, and of babies and young children riding piggyback on their parents' shoulders, is a mark of its peaceful and unpretentious character. Lay men and women accompanied the bishop on foot, rather than lining the way to watch him pass "with triumphal glory." There was no entourage of richly vested clergy, no white horse draped with cloth of gold, and no "elegantly dressed" soldier walking ahead of the bishop. Hand-carried palm or olive branches and the chanting of "hymns and antiphons," perhaps by a monastic choir with the laity adding the repeated refrain,[14] are the only ornamentation noted. The early Jerusalem Palm Sunday procession was a mobile act of communal worship in which the participants—lay, monastic, and episcopal—understood themselves to be following in Christ's footsteps, walking together the route he was believed to have taken from the Mount of Olives down into the heart of Jerusalem.

The degree of mimesis should not be exaggerated. The route of the procession no doubt permitted a kind of mimetic precision impossible elsewhere: Jerusalem's Palm Sunday procession involved not only "the coincidence of time" of year but also "the coincidence of historical and liturgical space."[15] But to say that "the bishop re-enacted the role of Christ,"[16] while the worshippers played the part of the Jewish crowd, is misleading. The processional mimesis was spatial rather than visual or dramatic. Mistaken notions of reenactment may also account for the discovery by nineteenth-century scholars of an imagined donkey in Egeria's text. In the decades following the first publication of Egeria's diary in 1887, most scholars took her observation that "the bishop is led in the same manner as the Lord once was led" (*sic deducetur episcopus in eo typo, quo tunc Dominus deductus est*)[17] to mean that the bishop was seated, like Christ, on a donkey.[18] E. K. Chambers was the first to dissent: "There is no ass," he wrote, "in the Palm Sunday ceremony" reported by Egeria.[19] Angelo de Santi agreed: "Such is the character of the author, that without any doubt she could have noted this particularity, if there had

---

13 Egeria, *Itinerarium* 31 (77), trans. Wilkinson, 133. For Egeria's description of Lucernare, which ordinarily began "at four o'clock," but much later on Palm Sunday, see Egeria, *Itinerarium* 24 (68–69), trans. Wilkinson, 123–24.

14 See Egeria, *Itinerarium* 25.2, 25.12 (70, 72), trans. Gingras, 93, 96: "the monks, singing hymns"; "monks ... chanting hymns and antiphons."

15 Hardison, *Christian*, 87.

16 Gingras (Egeria, *Diary*), 35; see also Thibaut, *Ordre*, 20, Bludau, *Pilgerreise*, 124.

17 Egeria, *Itinerarium* 31 (77), trans. Gingras, 105.

18 Cabrol, *Églises*, 93–94, remarked: "The bishop, who represents the Lord, is led, like him, on an ass." Bludau, *Pilgerreise*, 124; Baumstark, *Comparative*, 149; and Thibaut, *Ordre*, 15n2, agreed. Leclercq, "Semaine," 1155n1, thought this was "probably" the case. Pétré, in Egeria, *Éthérie*, 223n4, preferred "perhaps."

19 Chambers, *Mediaeval*, 1:334n1.

actually been" a donkey. He saw no reason to exclude the bishop from Egeria's observation that "everyone goes on foot."[20] I agree. Egeria had a good eye for detail. Had there been a donkey, she would have mentioned it.

Several different nations and ecclesiastical traditions lived and worshipped in Jerusalem in the centuries following Egeria's visit. A fifth-century Armenian lectionary sets out an abridged version of the liturgy described by Egeria, specifying the antiphon, psalm, and two Bible readings to be used during morning worship in the Martyrium, the afternoon climb with palm branches to the Mount of Olives, a brief time of "psalmody and prayer" at the summit, and the processional descent to the Anastasis. The chosen texts suggest an emphasis on the heavenly reign of Christ, but not yet in a manner that invites the celebration of Christian military rule on earth.[21] A Georgian lectionary, dated by its modern editor to the "fifth to eighth century," expands the liturgy for Palm Sunday to include all four gospel accounts of Christ's entry, several other biblical readings, and multiple psalms and antiphons. Perhaps for the first time, it adds a blessing of the palms to be distributed to the crowd, and stipulates that the procession should pause at churches at Gethsemane and the Pool of Beth-Zatha before ending with mass and vespers in the Martyrium.[22] In neither case is there any reference to a donkey or, for that matter, to a bishop. Under Byzantine rule, the predominantly monastic Armenian and Georgian communities had no resident bishop in Jerusalem. No extant text testifies to the form of the Palm Sunday liturgy presided over by the Greek patriarch of Jerusalem between the time of Egeria and the fall of Jerusalem to the forces of the Sasanian Persian Empire in 614. Despite Heraclius's triumphant return of the relic of the true cross, the Byzantine recovery of Jerusalem was short-lived. In 638, Jerusalem fell to the Muslim forces of 'Umar ibn Al-Khattāb, after which it was ruled by various Muslim dynasties until the arrival of the First Crusade in 1099. We will return to Muslim Jerusalem in Chapter 11.

From Jerusalem, the observance of Palm Sunday first spread north and east. In 497/8, archbishop Peter of Edessa (now Urfa, Turkey), "added Palm Sunday to the ... yearly festivals" to be observed in churches under his jurisdiction.[23] The patriarch Severus of Antioch (now Antakya, Turkey) (d. 538) noted in a sermon that Palm Sunday had not formerly been widely celebrated, but was "now celebrated among all men."[24] In neither case are we given any indication of the nature of the celebration, but it is probably safe to assume that some form of simple procession was included.

Under Muslim control of the region, Palm Sunday processions were permitted, but required to remain outside city walls. For obvious reasons, they avoided any hint of

---

20 De Santi, "Domenica," 7–8.

21 Renoux, *Codex*, 2:256–59; Conybeare, *Rituale*, 520.

22 Tarchnischvili, *Grand*, 1:100–5 (Georgian), 2:81–85 (Latin translation). Tarchnischvili refers to the Pool of Beth-Zatha (or Bethsaida) as the Probatica, a name taken from the Vulgate translation of John 5:2: "probatica piscina, quæ cognominatur hebraice Bethsaida."

23 Trombley and Watt, *Chronicle*, 31.

24 Severus, *Homiliae* 125 (247–49).

Christian triumphalism. The Rashidun caliph 'Umar ibn Al-Khattāb (634–644) wrote to Abu 'Ubaydah ibn al-Jarrah, his commander-in-chief in Damascus: "Do not prevent [the Christians] from displaying crosses on the day of their feasts, outside the town, without flags and standards, as they have requested, one day a year: but they must not display their crosses inside the town, in the midst of the Muslims and their mosques."[25] The day in question was generally the last day of Lent, either Palm Sunday or the Sunday or Monday of Easter.[26] Processional crosses, stripped of any "flags" or "standards" that might have borne military connotations, were used to represent Christ in the procession. In Mosul, during the time of the Nestorian patriarch Timothy I (780–823), Muslims are said to have joined the Christian Palm Sunday festivities. "On that day, Christians and Muslims gathered together in the green and silent places" outside the city walls, "to join the prayers of the monks and to take part in processions with the cross but also to profit from the good wine which was produced there, to look at and to associate with the women and beautiful young Christian people who came out on this occasion. Even the caliphs ... sometimes took part in these popular rejoicings, alongside the common people."[27] Also in Mosul, a ruling issued in 836 by the Syriac Orthodox patriarch Dionysius of Tel-Mahrē included the observation that on "Palm Sunday ... the whole town gathers for the blessing of the olive branches in the church of the Tagritans," which was the church of those from Tagrit (now Tikrit) who were living in Mosul.[28] Although under Muslim rule, both Mosul and Tikrit had substantial Christian populations.

The celebration of Palm Sunday also spread westward. Some of the earliest traces of the observance of Palm Sunday in western Europe come from Spain. Although news of the feast would have reached Spain with the return of Egeria from Jerusalem, observance of the rite itself may have spread through Christian communities along the north coast of Africa. In his *De ecclesiasticis officis* (ca. 610), Isidore of Seville notes that Palm Sunday "is celebrated," but says very little about the form it takes.[29] Another Spanish document, the eleventh-century *Liber Ordinum*, testifies to liturgical practices in Visigothic Spain from "the fifth to eleventh centuries." Unfortunately, the manuscript page that may have included a description of a Palm Sunday procession is missing. We know from the surrounding pages that Palm Sunday began in one church with an extended rite for the

---

25 Abū Yūsuf, *Livre*, 218; see also 213–14, 219, 227–28; Putman, *Église*, 121. The Rashidun Caliphate (632–661), under which the Muslim empire rapidly expanded, was ruled by the first four caliphs after Muhammed's death. 'Umar ibn Al-Khattāb was the second Rashidun caliph.

26 Abū Yūsuf, *Livre*, 219; Putman, *Église*, 122. At least one version of the Pact of 'Umar, an apocryphal document of uncertain date and authorship commonly attributed to 'Umar ibn Al-Khattāb, included a ban on Palm Sunday processions (Tritton, *Caliphs*, 7), but this was only enforced by the Fatimid caliph Al-Hakim in 1008 (see chap. 11).

27 Putman, *Église*, 122; see also Fiey, *Mossoul*, 126; Brown, *Cult*, 43. Putman names the Abbasid caliph Abū Ja'far Abdullāh al-Ma'mūn ibn Harūn (813–833) as one who took part in Mosul's Palm Sunday festivities.

28 Chabot, *Chronique*, 3:87; the Syriac patriarch Michael I (1166–1199) quotes at length, 3:85–87, from an earlier and now lost history by Dionysius of Tel-Mahrē.

29 Isidore, *De ecclesiasticis* 1.28 (31); trans. Knoebel, 50–51.

blessing of "branches of palm, willow, and olive," and ended in a second church with the reading of a prescribed homily and the celebration of mass. A procession probably took the clergy and congregation from one church to the other.[30]

A short prayer for "the blessing of palms and olives on the altar" is also found in the Bobbio Missal, a compilation of liturgical materials copied "perhaps as early as the later seventh century in south-eastern Gaul, conceivably in or around the city of Vienne,"[31] but containing some earlier materials. The prayer understands the crowd's acclamation of Christ's entry as a celebration of his victory over "the world and the devil." Although the missal contains no further instructions for the communal celebration of Palm Sunday, it indicates that worshippers took blessed palms home with them in the "pious belief" that they helped to drive away "diseases … and all snares of the evil one."[32] Further north, the celebration of Palm Sunday reached Britain by the late seventh century, when Aldhelm (ca. 639–709), abbot of Malmesbury, wrote of taking part himself in the joyful chanting of the "the holy feast of palms."[33]

The list of witnesses to Palm Sunday celebrations in Europe before the Carolingian Renaissance of the late eighth and ninth century is thus very short. While it is unwise to argue too confidently from faint whispers, it is probably safe to suppose that few substantial changes had been made to the rite since the time of Egeria. The Georgian lectionary had introduced the blessing of palms, increased the number of biblical readings, and adopted a pattern of pausing at other churches en route. Processional crosses had been added in Damascus. Most of these practices had probably spread to Europe. But there is no suggestion of any shift from the peaceful commemoration of spiritual victory towards the celebration of military triumph. It was not until the middle of the ninth century, some eighty years after Charlemagne's innovative entry into Rome in 774, that images of military victory began to trespass on Palm Sunday processions. In the meantime, the liturgical celebration of Palm Sunday in Francia appears to have been on the increase. This may have been due to the implicit iconographic link between Christ's "triumphal" entry and the victories of Charlemagne and his successors over pagans and other "enemies of the church," but the connection was not yet made explicit.

---

30 Férotin, *Liber*, 169–74. Férotin, 170, believes this to be "the oldest prescribed liturgy for the blessing and procession of the palms." While the Georgian lectionary mentioned above (see note 22) bears earlier testimony to the blessing of the palms, it does so with only a brief rubric ("Et benedicunt palmam").

31 Hen and Meens, *Bobbio*, 219. The missal was discovered in 1686 in the Italian monastery of Bobbio.

32 *Bobbio*, ed. Lowe, 2:170; see also Tyrer, *Historical*, 50.

33 Aldhelm, *Prosa* 30 (2:381–83); Lapidge and Herren, in Aldhelm, *Prose*, 90, unfortunately translate "in sacrosancta palmarum sollemnitate" as "in the holy celebration of the Psalms." The so-called Pontifical of Ecgberht of York (d. 766) includes several prayers for Palm Sunday and the blessing of palms (Banting, *Two*, 68, 135–36, 142–43), but the attribution to Ecgberht is now regarded as "certainly spurious" (Lapidge, "Ecgbehrt"; see also Banting, *Two*, xv–xvii). Thus the mid-tenth-century manuscript of the pontifical (Paris, BN, lat. 10575) by an unknown author cannot be assumed to bear witness to the earlier celebration of Palm Sunday in Britain.

The earliest description of a Carolingian Palm Sunday celebration is found in Angilbert's *Institutio de diversitate officiorum*, written "shortly after the dedication" of the new abbey of Saint-Riquier in 800.[34] Angilbert describes a short procession of monks and local people between two churches on the abbey's property. In the event of inclement weather, the procession avoided the public road, walking instead beneath the covered walkways that joined the abbey's churches.[35] By 820, Amalarius of Metz was able to remark on the widespread observance of Palm Sunday in the realm: "In memory of [Christ's entry into Jerusalem], we are accustomed throughout our churches to carry branches and to cry 'Hosanna'."[36] Both Angilbert and Amalarius had links to Charlemagne. Angilbert was raised at the royal court, served Charlemagne in various diplomatic and theological roles, enjoyed "a marital relationship" with Charlemagne's daughter Bertha, who bore him two sons, and was appointed lay abbot of Saint-Riquier by Charlemagne.[37] Amalarius was a pupil of Alcuin, Charlemagne's chief theological advisor.

The most enduring Palm Sunday hymn, "Gloria, laus et honor" (Glory, laud, and honour) also comes from this period.[38] The hymn derives from the opening twelve lines of a long poem by Theodulf of Orléans, who had succeeded Alcuin in 804, but fell out of favour under Charlemagne's son and successor, Louis the Pious (814–840). Between 818 and 820 Louis exiled Theodulf to a monastery in Angers. The latter part of Theodulf's poem provides an intriguing glimpse of Angers' Palm Sunday procession.[39] Groups of clergy and lay men and women, chanting, praying, and carrying palm, willow, and olive branches, and in at least one case a cross, made their way from ten different churches and abbeys to the Parish Church of Saint Michael on the Hillock (Saint-Michel-du-Tertre), situated as its name suggests "on a small knoll" at the northeast corner of the city walls.[40] There the gathered company was "joined" by the "sweet love" of Christ,[41] perhaps a processional cross representing, here as elsewhere, the liturgical presence of the Saviour.[42] The events and topography of Christ's entry into Jerusalem were thus

---

34 Rabe, *Faith*, 81. The surviving Abbey Church of Saint-Riquier is five miles northeast of Abbeville (Picardy).

35 Angilbert, *Institutio*, 294; Rabe, *Faith*, 124, 193–94.

36 Amalarius, *Liber*, 58. Palm Sunday was also known among the Franks as Hosanna Sunday (Boretius and Krause, *Capitularia*, 1:28: "dominica in palmis quae Osanna dicitur"; trans. Loyn and Percival, *Reign*, 68).

37 Rabe, *Faith*, 73–74, who also notes (81) that "Charlemagne, Alcuin, and the greatest bishops and dignitaries of the realm attended the dedication" of the abbey. For more on the nature of *Friedelehe*, an ancient Germanic custom of "marriage by mutal consent," see Wemple, *Women*, 12–15, 35.

38 The hymn is still sung in English in a version of J. M. Neale's 1854 translation, "All glory, laud, and honour."

39 For the full text of Theodulf's poem, see Theodulf, *Carmina*, 558–59; Theodulf, *Verse*, 161–63.

40 Rondeau, *Histoire*, 11; Longin, *Paroisses*, 1–2. For a map of Angers, marking most of the churches and abbeys named by Theodulf, including Saint-Michel-du-Tertre, which was destroyed at the time of the Revolution, see Lebrun, *Histoire*, 14.

41 Theodulf, *Carmina*, 559, lines 69–70; Theodulf, *Verse*, 163.

42 For more on the significance of Palm Sunday processional crosses, see chap. 6.

mapped onto the landscape of Angers: the church on the hill represented the Mount of Olives, the worshippers climbing the hill recalled the crowds coming out from Jerusalem, and the cross (if such it was) functioned as an image of Christ arriving from Bethany. From Saint-Michel, the combined procession moved downhill to the Cathedral Church of Saint-Maurice, a distance of about a quarter of a mile, thereby recalling Christ's descent into Jerusalem and its temple. Choirboys sang hosannas. To the best of my knowledge, this is the first record of a Palm Sunday practice that was to became commonplace in medieval Europe: processions travelled across the local terrain in a manner designed to replicate as closely as possible the topography of Christ's entry into Jerusalem. The spatial mimesis of pilgrimage remained more important than the visual mimesis of dramatic reenactment.

It was not long before the governing interests of emperors and popes began to change the character of Palm Sunday processions. McCormick notes that, by at least 853, popes were sending Charlemagne's successors palm branches that were "meant to be carried by the ruler in the palace liturgy's Palm Sunday procession ... The papal letters accompanying the palms emphasize their symbolism of both ethical and military victory."[43] In March 853, "according to custom," Pope Leo IV sent "branches of victory" (victoriae ramos) to the co-emperors Lothair I and his son Louis II "for the Easter feast and as a sign of honour."[44] In February 875, Pope John VIII sent Louis II "palm branches according to custom."[45] On February 13, 877, he sent Charles the Bald "green palms," described as "palms of competitive victory" (palmae bravium [=brabeum]), along with a request for "help against new enemies,"[46] and on March 29, 881, he sent Charles a palm, an apostolic blessing, and a plea for military support against the Saracens. The palm, he wrote, was given as "a sign of victory" so that the emperor "might carry it with joy on the day of such great celebrations."[47] For an emperor to carry so explicit a sign of military victory in a Palm Sunday procession was to welcome the triumphal iconography of imperial entries into the liturgical commemoration of Christ's entry. For the pope to request military aid from the emperor in return for the gift of a processional palm made the rapprochement of the two traditions all the more plausible.

---

43 McCormick, Eternal, 370.

44 Jaffé, Regesta, 1:334.

45 Caspar, Registrum, 302.

46 Caspar, Registrum, 31.

47 Caspar, Registrum, 245. For a similar letter from Pope Stephen V to Emperor Charles III (the Fat), dated March 887, accompanying a gift of "palm branches," see Caspar, Fragmenta, 340.

Chapter 6

EXALTED AND ECCENTRIC IMAGES

WITH THE ASSUMPTION of imperial power by the German Ottonian dynasty, Palm Sunday processions became more elaborate and, in much of continental Europe, more standardized. Sometime between 950 and 964, monks (or perhaps a single monk) at Saint Alban's Abbey in Mainz compiled a pontifical, a book of ceremonies to be presided over by a bishop. Surviving in some thirty-six manuscript copies, the influential Mainz compilation is now known as the Romano-German Pontifical, a name that reflects its dependence on older Roman and Gallican sources, its place of origin, and its subsequent authoritative diffusion throughout Germany and as far south as Rome. The effect of the pontifical on Palm Sunday processions, whether intentional or otherwise, was to codify and disseminate the inclination of the powerful to make elite Palm Sunday processions double as triumphal entries.[1]

In this chapter, I begin with the Mainz pontifical itself, paying particular attention to the belief that processional crosses or other exalted Palm Sunday images embodied the immediate presence of Christ and were therefore worthy of veneration. I then follow the pontifical to Rome, where, as we have already seen in the case of Calixtus II, crowds "venerated" the pope "as the vicar of Christ" and "prostrated themselves before him with great devotion."[2] After Palm Sunday processions were introduced to Rome in the twelfth century, the pope himself became the feast day's object of veneration. I close the chapter with two variations, one strikingly eccentric, on the theme of Palm Sunday processional theatre in fifteenth-century Rome.

Palm Sunday worship, according to the Mainz pontifical, began at a church outside the city gates. This not only allowed the procession to follow more closely the pattern observed by the church in Jerusalem and so to represent more convincingly Christ's historical entry, but it also permitted the procession to approach its own city in the manner of a royal entry. The Carolingian Palm Sunday processions in Saint-Riquier and Angers, remaining within the abbey grounds or city walls, had not exercised this option.

After antiphons, prayers, scripture readings and an optional sermon by the bishop, the officiating priest of the Mainz pontifical exorcised flowers and palm, olive, and other branches, ritually expelling from them "all the armies of devils" and other "hostile powers." The cleansed "palms of victory" were blessed, aspersed, and distributed to the people. The procession then departed for the city church where mass was to be celebrated. Along the way, antiphons were sung. Despite its repeated acknowledgment in scripture, prayers, and antiphons that Christ rode the "colt of an ass," the pontifical offers

---

1 While it may be true that "medieval ceremonial books ... rarely corresponded to actual practice" (Paravicini-Bagliani, *Pope's*, xix), they do at least point us to what was considered normative.

2 *Lib. pont.*, 2:377; see also chap. 3.

no hint of a processional donkey, whether live or wooden.[3] Christ was represented by the customary processional cross.

Still outside the city, at an extended stop en route, "the holy cross" was venerated. Clergy and people reverently waited in groups, while choirboys (*infantes paraphonistae*) sang. The whole choir (*scola*) responded "on behalf of the people" with the antiphon "Occurrunt turbae":

> Occurrunt turbae cum floribus et palmis Redemptori obviam,
> et victori triumphanti digna dant obsequia;
> Filium Dei ore gentes praedicant,
> et in laude Christi voces tonant per nubila: Hosanna.

> [The multitudes go out to meet the Redeemer with flowers and
>   palm-branches,
> and pay the homage due to a triumphant conqueror.
> The nations proclaim the Son of God
> and their voices rend the sky in praise of Christ: Hosanna!][4]

The antiphon, with its triumphal image of conquest over "the nations," is first attested in the Compiègne Antiphonary, possibly prepared for the Carolingian emperor Charles the Bald shortly before his death in 877.[5] While it celebrates the heavenly rule of Christ and the triumph of the gospel, it also brings to the Palm Sunday procession a whiff of the military pretensions of Christian empire. Since the time of Constantine, the cross had been a sign of Christian victory in battle no less than the site of Christ's victory over sin. The two were not easily distinguished in an age of conversion by force of arms.

Choristers approached the cross "with slow steps" and, "with all reverence throwing their capes or caps (*casulas vel cappas*) on the ground," prostrated themselves before the cross while the clergy sang "Pueri Hebreorum vestimenta prosternebant" (The Hebrew children spread their garments). Other children not enrolled in the choir school (*pueri laici*) followed suit, singing the Kyrie and casting palm branches on the ground before they, too, prostrated themselves in adoration. Choir and clergy alternated the refrain and verses of "Gloria, laus et honor," all the while "gazing on the holy gospel book," another customary representation of Christ's processional presence, and "bowing their heads to the holy cross." After another antiphon, "all the people" threw "flowers or branches," and were joined by the bishop in prostrate adoration of the cross while the clergy sang "Scriptus est enim: Percutiam pastorem" (For it is written, "They will strike the shepherd"). Standing again, the bishop delivered a prayer thanking God for his "victorious triumphs and abundance of mercy."[6]

---

3 Vogel and Elze, *Pontifical*, 2:40–47.

4 Hesbert, *Corpus*, 3:380, no. 4107; trans. Borders, *Early*, 3:xxxi.

5 Hesbert, *Corpus*, 3:380, no. 4107, and for the date and character of the antiphonary [C], 1:xvii–xix; see also Huglo, "Observations"; Jacobsson, "Antiphoner," 147–52.

6 Vogel and Elze, *Pontifical*, 2:47–49.

The procession formed again, following "the cross and banners." Although the pontifical, designed to be used in cities of varying terrain, neither required nor ruled out descent from a hill resembling the Mount of Olives, it did assume passage through a city gate representing Jerusalem's Golden Gate. As the cross passed beneath the gate, the head chorister intoned the responsory "Ingrediente domino in sanctam civitatem" (As the Lord entered the holy city). Finally, entering the church where mass was to be said, the choir sang "Benedictus dominus Deus Israel" (Blessed be the Lord God of Israel).[7] Clergy and people held on to their palms at least until the completion of the mass.[8]

The extended veneration of the cross, followed by its entry through the city gates, is the most striking feature of the Mainz pontifical's Palm Sunday liturgy. This order of events allowed the procession not only to recall Christ's past entry into Jerusalem five days before his crucifixion, but also to stage a present triumphal entry of Christ the risen and exalted king. In the pontifical's Palm Sunday procession, Christ was not only making his way to the sacrifice of the mass (in which, it was believed, a past event in Jerusalem became again a present event at the local altar) but also reaffirming his long-standing victorious rule over the city where the procession took place. To say that Christ was "represented" by the cross is to understate the case. It was, to use Caroline Walker Bynum's distinction, "not a matter of mimesis," but rather one of embodying the "power or presence" of Christ. "People behaved as if images *were* what they represented."[9]

Belief that the cross displayed the presence of Christ was not only integral to the rite's simultaneous celebration of past and present entries, but was also believed to be a safeguard against improper worship of images. Contemporary othodoxy insisted that it was not the cross itself that was adored, but the person of Christ made present in the cross. The *Liber de divinis officiis*, formerly ascribed to Alcuin, but now believed to have been composed "shortly before 950,"[10] drew the distinction: "We prostrate ourselves in our bodies before the cross, but in our minds to the Lord. We venerate the cross, by which we are redeemed, but we pray to him who redeemed us."[11] In an alternative version of the Palm Sunday office, copied by the pontifical from pseudo-Alcuin's *Liber*, the focal point of the procession was a "gospel book, by which Christ is signified (*quod intelligitur Christus*)." The same principle applied to the gospel book as to the cross: worship was offered not to the object itself but to the Christ whose presence it signifed. In keeping with Christ's exalted status, the book was carried aloft in "a most noble processional litter (*portatorium*)."[12]

---

7 The words are those of Zechariah, father of John the Baptist, in Luke 1:68–79.

8 Vogel and Elze, *Pontifical*, 2:49–51.

9 Bynum, *Christian*, 59, 125.

10 Ryan, "Pseudo-Alcuin," 160.

11 Pseudo-Alcuin, *Liber de divinis officiis* 18 (*PL* 101:1210).

12 Vogel and Elze, *Pontifical*, 2:51–52; Pseudo-Alcuin, *Liber de divinis officiis* 14 (*PL* 101:1201).

A more specific image of the Palm Sunday Christ was venerated at the Benedictine abbey of Fruttuaria, in what is now the small town of San Benigno Canavese, some twelve miles north of Turin. According to the abbey's *Consuetudines* (Customary), compiled around 1003,[13] Christ was represented on Palm Sunday by an image known as the "Osanna," generally believed to have been a painted panel depicting Christ's entry into Jerusalem.[14] Acolytes carried the Osanna towards the abbey from "another church," recalling Jesus and his disciples approaching Jerusalem. A second, more elaborate, procession, representing the crowd going out from the city to meet Jesus, began at the abbey. Monks and choirboys carried a cross, candelabra, gospel books, and palms. The two groups met at a designated spot, where carpets had been laid on the ground. The Osanna was placed on a cushion between the candelabra and gospel books. All stood reverently before the image "as if God himself were present" (*quasi ipse deus sit presens*). The antiphons "Dignus es domine" (Worthy are you, O Lord) and "Osanna filio David" (Hosanna to the Son of David) were sung to the Christ revealed in the image. Boys and monks prostrated themselves three times before the Osanna. Further antiphons and hymns, including "Gloria, laus et honor," were sung at the gates of the monastic complex and the doors of the abbey church, representing Jerusalem's gates and temple.[15] The customary's rubrics insist on the transcendent significance of these acts of veneration: "If we were permitted to contemplate with our bodily eyes, it would seem that we had ourselves gone to meet the Son of God, which we must without any doubt believe we have done. Although he may not indeed be seen physically, yet the person whose inner eyes he will have opened has the power to see that we have gone forth to meet our Lord Jesus Christ."[16] Christ himself was passing through the abbey gates in triumph.

The abbey of Fruttuaria was not the only community to venerate Christ's Palm Sunday presence with the help of a painting. One of several early Cluniac customaries, copied in Dijon in the mid-1020s, refers briefly to the preparation and removal of an "Osanna" after matins on Palm Sunday and to its veneration later at the far point of the procession.[17] An eleventh-century manuscript from the Vatican Library specifies the use in Italian cloisters of a "painting (*tabula*) on which is the likeness of the Lord our Saviour seated on an ass."[18] *Tabulae* were also used in secular cathedrals. A small double-sided painting was carried in procession in thirteenth-century Magdeburg. One side of the tabula depicted Christ's passion, while the other showed Christ being met with palms. During the procession, the image of Christ was venerated with song, prostration, and the scattering of branches.[19] Cathedral accounts from fourteenth-century Cambrai also

---

13 The abbey was founded by William of Volpiano in 1003; its customary was "in large measure framed by William himself" (Williams, *Monastic*, 112; see also Spätling and Dinter, *Consuetudines*, 1:xiv–xv).

14 Gräf, *Palmenweihe*, 78; Lipsmeyer, "Devotion," 21, 27n10.

15 Spätling and Dinter, *Consuetudines*, 1:146–53; Lipsmeyer, "Devotion," 21–22.

16 Spätling and Dinter, *Consuetudines*, 1:150; translation adapted from Lipsmeyer, "Devotion," 22.

17 Hallinger, *Consuetudines*, 62, 65; for the date of the customary, see Hallinger, *Consuetudinum*, 237.

18 Gräf, *Palmenweihe*, 128–29.

19 Kroos, "Quellen," 89–90, 94n34; Tripps, *Handelnde*, 91–92.

record several payments for repairing an image variously identified as "the painted tabula" and "the tabula with the ass," which "is to be carried on Palm Sunday."[20]

Worshipping Christ through veneration of a cross, a gospel book, or a painting, understood to represent Christ's immediate presence, implicitly authorized a similar veneration of kings, emperors, popes, and archbishops, all of whom claimed to represent Christ in their own persons. We have already seen this principle at work in triumphal royal and papal entries, including some that took place on Palm Sunday itself, others that took place in Rome, and, in the case of Julius II, one that took place both on Palm Sunday and in Rome. It should come as no surprise, therefore, that in Rome the pope himself, rather than an inanimate cross, gospel book, or painting, eventually came to represent the Palm Sunday presence of Christ.

The Mainz pontifical arrived in Rome around 964. Once the capital of the Western Empire, Rome had by the late tenth century fallen into physical, political, and ecclesiastical disrepair. The city was home to little more than classical ruins and a weak papacy in thrall to the German emperors. Since the liturgy, too, was in a state of severe neglect, and popes Leo VIII (964–965) and John XIII (965–972) were both nominated by Otto I, the Mainz pontifical exercised considerable influence on the subsequent shape of the Roman liturgy.[21] Unable to match the German imperial precedent, however, Roman liturgists initially "simplified" the imported pontifical, omitting much of its "unreasonable exuberance."[22]

It was probably a further two centuries before even a brief procession was included in Rome's Palm Sunday liturgy. The first definitive record is found in the *Liber politicus*, compiled sometime between 1140 and 1143 by Benedict, a canon of Saint Peter's Basilica.[23] Palms were blessed after lauds on Palm Sunday in the chapel of Saint Sylvester within the Lateran Palace before being taken to the nearby Triclinium of Leo III, where the pope distributed them. Afterwards, a short and simple procession with palms moved from the Triclinium back to the steps of Saint Sylvester's. There the pope sat on a bench (*subsellium*) while the traditional Palm Sunday antiphons and hymns were sung. Mass followed inside the church.[24]

The later twelfth-century Roman Pontifical, of which multiple copies survive, sets out a Palm Sunday liturgy closer to that of the Romano-German Pontifical, but without the elaborate veneration of the cross.[25] An ordinal compiled between 1213 and 1216, during the last years of the papacy of Innocent III, allows the pope, "if he is there," to

---

20 Dehaisnes, *Documents*, 1:295, 1:387, 2:534, 2:671 (account entries from 1333/4, 1355/6, 1375/6, and 1389/90); Kroos, "Quellen," 90, 94n36.

21 Andrieu, *Ordines*, 1:494–525; Vogel and Elze, *Pontifical*, 1:xvi–xvii.

22 Andrieu, *Pontifical*, 1:11.

23 Benedict, *Liber politicus*, in *Lib. Cens.* 2:139–83 (150); Blaauw, "Contrasts," 386.

24 Benedict, *Liber politicus*, in *Lib. Cens.* 2:139–83 (150); for a plan of the Lateran complex in the twelfth century, see Twyman, *Papal*, xii. The Lateran Cappella di San Silvestro, now restored as part of the Santuario della Scala Santa, should not be confused with the Oratorio di San Silvestro, consecrated in 1246, in the nearby Santi Quattro Coronati complex. For the restored Lateran chapel, see Schroth and Violini, *Cappella*.

25 Andrieu, *Pontifical*, 1:210–14.

receive the homage of the clergy: cardinals and bishops kiss his "right knee," while lower clergy kiss his "foot." The pope then "throws the palm leaves over the people," while others distribute them by hand.[26] The splendour of the papal role greatly impressed Rabban bar Sauma, a Mongol Christian envoy who was in Rome for Easter week in 1288. On Palm Sunday, "from the break of day onwards," he wrote, "tens of thousands of people gathered together before the papal throne, and brought branches of olives," which the pope blessed, and gave to the ranking clergy and nobility, and finally threw "among all the people." Afterwards, to celebrate mass, the pope "put on a red vestment with threads of gold, and ornamented with precious stones, and jacinths, and pearls, down to the soles of his feet, that is to say [his] sandals."[27]

Another thirteenth-century ceremonial, from the reign of Gregory X (1271–1276), proposed that the pope should go "barefoot" (*nudis pedibus*) on Palm Sunday, as well as on Ash Wednesday and the feast of the Purification (Candlemas).[28] In practice, "circumstances such as the state of the streets or the length of the route ... prompted flexible interpretations of this principle. In the long procession of the Purification, the pope would wear slippers (*planelli*) on his bare feet. As a symbolic gesture, only the last few metres of the route ... were traversed literally barefoot." Afterward, "servants would wash the papal feet with hot water and put them in shoes for the mass."[29]

Subsequent papal Palm Sunday ceremonies, whether in Rome or in Avignon during the Great Western Schism (1304–1377), continued the tradition of the blessing and distribution of foliage, ritual homage to the enthroned pope, and a brief procession on foot. The ceremonial compiled by Giacomo Stefaneschi between 1300 and 1340[30] stipulates that "each and every bishop and cardinal" to whom the pope gives a palm frond should kiss the pope's "knee or foot."[31] Stefaneschi had himself been made a cardinal by Boniface VIII in 1295. The Long Ceremonial, composed after 1300 and before 1342 for use in Avignon,[32] is more specific: the senior cardinal bishop removes his mitre, stands before the enthroned pope, presents him with a palm frond, and kisses his hand; other cardinals and prelates also remove their mitres, but then genuflect before the pope, receive from him a palm frond, and kiss his knee; if a king (*rex*) is present, he approaches between the cardinals and the other prelates, but must kiss "the foot of the pope and not the knee"; less prestigious members of the clergy and other privileged laymen are the last to receive a palm, and must also kiss the pope's foot. During this rite of homage, the choir sings "Hosanna filio David, benedictus qui venit in nomine Domini" (Hosanna to the Son of David, blessed is he who comes in the name of the Lord). The entire Palm Sunday ceremony in Avignon took place within the papal palace. Twice, as the papal entourage

26 Van Dijk and Walker, *Ordinal*, 216–17.

27 Budge, *Monks*, 191.

28 Dykmans, *Cérémonial*, 1:24, 201; Blaauw, "Contrasts," 386.

29 Blaauw, "Contrasts," 375–76.

30 Dykmans, *Cérémonial*, 2:131.

31 Dykmans, *Cérémonial*, 2:356, 362.

32 Dykmans, *Cérémonial*, 3:13, 16.

went in procession from the grand banquet hall, where the hierarchical distribution of palms had taken place, to the chapel (now the Chapel of Benedict XII) where mass was celebrated, the pope paused at a window overlooking the grand courtyard or at another "opening," and "threw olive and other tree branches to the people." Palm branches, being less readily available, were reserved for the elite.[33]

Fires devasted the Lateran Basilica in 1308 and 1361. After the return from Avignon to Rome in 1377, the popes resided elsewhere, eventually settling in the renovated Vatican Palace. It is evident from ceremonial books and other sources that the protocol of papal homage and hierarchical dispensation of palms continued to be a major focus of Palm Sunday observation in papal Rome.[34] The humility of Christ's entry into Jerusalem on a donkey was lost in the ceremonial pomp.

On occasion, however, someone (or the remains of someone) other than the pope starred in alternative Palm Sunday celebrations in Rome. On Palm Sunday, April 9, 1430, the presumed relics of Saint Monica, mother of Saint Augustine, were transferred from the cathedral of Ostia, on the coast some fifteen miles away, to a new marble tomb in the Church of Saint Augustine in the centre of Rome. A contemporary sermon, attributed to Pope Martin V but almost certainly written by the Augustinian historian Andrea Biglia (d. 1435),[35] recalls the progress of the relics:

> When the tomb of Blessed Monica had been opened, the [Augustinian] friars ... lifted the body, singing hymns of godly praise at the top of their voices ... With many following, they hastened to the city ... It was Palm Sunday, a day when crowds gather in Rome. Thousands of pilgrims were running to and fro on every side, asking what was happening, and they were told that these were the relics of Blessed Monica, which were to be buried in the city. Those who did not know the name of Blessed Monica were amazed; others, hearing that she was the blessed mother of Augustine, poured out of their houses and lodgings without delay, filling the streets with crowds ... When they entered the city, the streets were not spacious enough for so great a crowd. Everyone longed to look and to touch. Many, unable to gain access, threw hoods or belts or such things, so that they might somehow make contact [with the holy relics] ... Thus, resounding with the hymns and songs of the friars and priests, the body of [Augustine's] mother was translated to the church of her son. There was no lack of clamour from the common people ... nor of the prayers and tears of women.[36]

---

33 Dykmans, *Cérémonial*, 3:201–4.

34 See the instructions for Palm Sunday in the ceremonials of Pierre Ameil, compiled 1375–1401 (Dykmans, *Cérémonial*, 4:117–27), and Patrizi Piccolomini, 1488 (Dykmans, *Oeuvre*, 2:354–65), and the annual Palm Sunday entries in the diary of Johann Burchard, papal master of ceremonies between 1483 and 1506 (Burchard, *Liber*; English translation of volume one only in Burchard, *Diary*).

35 Casamassa, "Autore," 122.

36 *Acta sanctorum*, May 4, 14:495; for the full text of the sermon, see Torelli, *Secoli*, 6:604–15. For the alternative and perhaps more plausible claim that the true relics of Saint Monica had been removed to the Augustinian Abbey of Arrouaise in 1162, see Clark, *Monica*, 164–69.

Several miracles of healing were reported as having taken place either during the procession or in its immediate aftermath. The bones of a saint, no less than the bodies of recently deceased kings, could confer status on their owners or backers by entering a holy city in triumphal public display on Palm Sunday.

A more eccentric piece of Palm Sunday street theatre took place on April 11, 1484, when Giovanni da Correggio, an apocalyptic preacher of noble birth and alchemical pretensions, rode into Rome on Palm Sunday on a white donkey, gathering in his wake a crowd of worshippers who were leaving church after mass carrying blessed palms. The story is told by Correggio's disciple, Lodovico Lazzarelli.[37] Clothed in rich garments and accompanied by four servants on horseback, Correggio first rode "a black snorting horse" through the streets of Rome. Then, leaving the city, "he got off his horse, put sandals on his feet, and dressed and robed himself in bloodstained linen. His hair, parted in the middle after the fashion of the Nazarenes, was crowned with a bloodstained crown of thorns." After adding other biblical, apocryphal, and hermetic symbols, he "offered up a silent prayer. When that was completed, he—who only a little before had spurred on his fiery and warlike horse—humiliated himself and mounted a slow, white, cheap donkey belonging to someone else." From the donkey's shoulder "hung a basket that contained a dry dead man's skull." To Correggio's right, one of his servants sat astride "a large and beautiful horse"; to his left, another "rode a swift and warlike horse." The party reentered the city through the Porta Asinaria, or Asses' Gate.[38] Lazzarelli's insistence that Correggio and his servants ordinarily rode fine horses underlines the theatrical nature of the entry and protects Correggio himself against any personal loss of status: riding a donkey was only an act.

Correggio made several stops along the way to proclaim imminent judgment, striking the dry skull at the end of each "prophetic speech." Resuming his progress, he was "always accompanied by a great crowd of people bearing palm branches which they had just received at High Mass." As Wouter Hanegraaff comments, this "greatly amplif[ied] the intended parallel with Christ's entrance into Jerusalem."[39] Later, Lazzarelli's panagyric begins to strain credibility. He boasts that when Correggio reached the Vatican, the "armed mercenaries" guarding the papal palace "took the arms and staffs with which they usually make way for the Pontiff, and likewise with reverence preceding [Correggio] they shielded him from the crowd, and with great honour kept his way free on all sides." Lazzarelli's Correggio was thus not only honoured by the crowds as an image of Christ but also by the Swiss guards as an alternative to the absent pope.[40] Moreover, after Correggio had repeated his announcement of judgment, his servants dismounted and led his donkey by the hand to the threshold of Saint Peter's, where "this spiritual man jumped from the ass and entered the church surrounded by a dense crowd of people,

---

37 Lazzarelli, "Epistola Enoch," in Hanegraaff and Bouthoorn, *Lodovico*, 107–49.

38 Lazzarelli, "Epistola," 119–32; summary adapted from Hanegraaff, "Pseudo-Lullian," 102–3.

39 Hanegraaff, "Pseudo-Lullian," 103.

40 Sixtus IV (1471–1484) was the first pope to hire Swiss mercenaries as his personal guards, but he "was not present" at Palm Sunday worship on April 11, 1484 (Burchard, *Liber*, 1:9; *Diary*, 5–6). He died on August 12, 1484.

and came to the holy altar of Saint Peter's." Leaving his "mystical apparel" and other trappings, including the skull, as an offering on the altar, Correggio knelt to pray. "And when all these things had been scrupulously done he left the church and went back to his lodgings, riding his horse as before, preceded by the two servants and followed by two others."[41]

Although no references to Correggio's Palm Sunday entry can be found in contemporary historical chronicles of Rome,[42] a somewhat garbled confirmation of the bare facts of Lazzarelli's narrative appears in a chronicle of the town of Cesena by Giuliano Fantaguzzi (1453–1522). Fantaguzzi remembers a "gentleman" who "went to Rome this year upon an ass and dressed in white, and he presented his clothing, on which was a bloody dead man's head, and certain large gilt medallions ... on the altar of Saint Peter's, with certain other prophecies, claiming to be the true Messiah."[43] Hanegraaff is inclined to be more sceptical about the outcome of Correggio's provocative street theatre, thinking it likely that the Swiss guards were not so indulgent, and that Correggio was "arrested on the spot, and never made it to the altar."[44] Whatever the truth of the matter, it is striking that the first man recorded as having ridden a donkey in a Palm Sunday procession of sorts in Rome was not a member of the clergy, but a startlingly eccentric apocalyptic lay preacher.

---

41 Lazzarelli, "Epistola," 132–41.

42 Hanegraaff and Bouthoorn, *Lodovico*, 30.

43 Fantaguzzi, *Cesena Chronicle*, MS Biblioteca Comunale of Cesena, fol. 9r, quoted in McDaniel, "Hermetic," 219; translation from Hanegraaff and Bouthoorn, *Lodovico*, 27.

44 Hanegraaff, "Pseudo-Lullian," 103.

Chapter 7

CRUSADERS, PATRIARCHS, AND EMPERORS

ELITE PALM SUNDAY processions in the Byzantine and, later, Russian empires were also marked by ceremonial splendour. Whereas in the Latin west, supreme power was geographically divided (and often contested) between a pope in Rome and an emperor north of the Alps, eastern patriarchs and emperors or tsars negotiated shared power as neighbours within the same capital city. In Constantinople, shared power required two separate Palm Sunday processions, one presided over by the patriarch, the other by the emperor. Moscow opted for a different approach: the tsar led the patriarch's horse in the city's annual Palm Sunday procession, leaving historians to disagree over which of the two rulers was thereby represented as the more powerful. I consider Moscow in Chapter 8. In the meantime, my discussion of Palm Sunday in Constantinople begins not with the city's annual Greek Orthodox processions, but—by way of a bridge from the Latin west—with a violent exception, when victorious crusaders observed Palm Sunday according to their own rites and a dozen renegade crusaders took advantage of the occasion to loot relics.

Capital of the eastern Roman Empire since the time of Constantine, after whom it was named, Constantinople was captured by the forces of the Fourth Crusade on April 12, 1204. A majority of the crusaders were French; other sizable contingents came from Flanders, the German Empire, and Venice, which, for a substantial fee, had provided the necessary war galleys and transport ships. Diverted from their stated goal of liberating Jerusalem from Muslim rule, and unable to pay the growing debt owed to the Venetians, the crusaders chose to intervene in a dispute over Byzantine imperial succession and attack Constantinople instead. The successful breach of the city's defences took place six days before Palm Sunday.

For three days, crusaders looted the city. Impoverished French and Flemings "rushed in a howling mob down the streets and through the houses, snatching up everything that glittered and destroying whatever they could not carry, pausing only to murder or to rape, or to break open the wine-cellars for their refreshment. Neither monasteries nor churches nor libraries were spared ... Nuns were ravished in their convents. Palaces and hovels alike were entered and wrecked. Wounded women and children lay dying in the streets. For three days the ghastly scenes of pillage and bloodshed continued, till the huge and beautiful city was a shambles."[1] Clerics and Venetians plundered sacred relics and works of art for display back home. Soldiers found lodging in forcefully vacated palaces and houses.

On Palm Sunday (April 18), the victors gathered for worship. Geoffrey of Villehardouin recalled: "The troops of the crusaders and the Venetians ... all rejoiced and gave thanks

---

1 Runciman, *History*, 3:123. See also Queller and Madden, *Fourth*, 192–200; Phillips, *Fourth*, 258–70. Angold, *Fourth*, 100–1, believes that the sack of Constantinople, although "a brutal affair," was "less savage than is often depicted."

to the Lord for the honour and the victory he had granted them, so that those who had been poor now lived in wealth and luxury. Thus they celebrated Palm Sunday and the Easter Day following (*la Pasque Florie et la Grant Pasque après*), with hearts full of joy for the benefits our Lord and Saviour had bestowed on them."[2] The crusaders' Palm Sunday service probably resembled the model set out in the Romano-German Pontifical. No one seems to have sensed the irony of celebrating Christ's peaceful entry into Jerusalem on a donkey so soon after indulging in a military assault on a Christian city.

While this public worship was in full swing, twelve crusaders from the parish of Saint Simeon the Prophet in Venice made their way discreetly to the Church of the Mother of God of the Copper Market, where the relics of Saint Simeon were preserved.[3] The men avoided the public liturgy of thanksgiving not because of a pious desire to worship privately at the tomb of their parish church's patron saint, but because they planned to steal his relics. They had located the church a few days earlier, but postponed the theft until Palm Sunday, when "all the people would be intent on celebrating their festival day, and thus they would be able to complete their desired task more easily and safely."[4] Five men got lost on the way to the church, four stayed outside to guard the doors, and three went inside to carry out the theft. After some hesitation, they broke open successive containers made of stone and lead, the last bound with iron, and retrieved the relics. "A sweet aroma arose as if coming from balsam wood," assuring the men that God approved their action.[5] Hastening back to their ship, the men hid their prize. "On Palm Sunday, the city was in too much chaos for the theft ... to be noticed,"[6] but when the leaders of the Venetian army heard that someone had stolen the body of Saint Simeon, a reward was offered for its "return" to the official collection of sacred booty. The thieves hid the relics in a safer place. Finally, after six months, one of the thieves received permission to return to Venice, quietly took the boxed remains of Saint Simeon with him, and handed them over to the priest of the thieves' parish church in Venice. The relics were installed, with great public rejoicing, in a marble container beneath the church's altar.[7]

Palm Sunday in Constantinople had not always been this fraught. Constantinople was "the city of wonders." Its walls enclosed some eleven and a half square miles and a population numbering in the hundreds of thousands. Its streets and squares displayed a plethora of classical statuary, its churches housed an unrivalled collection of relics, and its successive emperors boasted fabled wealth. The Great Church of the Holy Wisdom

---

2 Villehardouin, *Conquête* 251 (2:54), trans. Shaw, 92–93.

3 For the church, located in the area of Constantinople known as the Copper Market, see Janin, *Églises*, 246–51; *ODB*, 1:407–8. For Saint Simeon, see Luke 2:25–35.

4 *Translatio corporis beati Simeonis prophete de Constantinopoli Venetias* 7 (Chiesa, "Ladri," 455; Perry, "Translatio," 109). Perry, 102, dates the "core" of the *Translatio* to "the years following the installation of the relics in [the Church of] San Simeone Grande [in Venice], sometime after 1205."

5 *Translatio* 12 (Chiesa, "Ladri," 457; Perry, "Translatio," 111).

6 Perry, "Translatio," 104.

7 An alternative story has the relics of Saint Simeon stop at Zadar, on the coast of Croatia (Fondra, *Istoria*, 65–91; Seymour, "Tomb"). The churches of Saint Simeon the Righteous, in Zadar, and San Simeone Profeta (or Grande), in Venice, thus both claim possession of the relics of Saint Simeon.

(*Hagia Sophia*) and the imperial Great Palace were breathtaking in size, splendour, and beauty.[8] Geoffrey of Villehardouin reported that the crusaders, approaching by sea, were amazed at its opulence. They "gazed very intently at the city, having never before imagined there could be so wealthy (*riche*) a place in all the world. They noted the high walls and splendid (*riches*) towers encircling it, its opulent (*riches*) palaces and tall churches, of which there were so many that no one could have believed it to be true if he had not seen it with his own eyes, and viewed the length and breadth of that city, which reigns supreme over all others."[9] The city's public worship was understandably required to match its military, religious, historical, and artistic status.

Palm Sunday was no exception. By at least the tenth century, two independent processions took place on Palm Sunday in Constantinople. One procession was ecclesiastical, the other imperial. Instructions for the former are found in the *Typikon of Hagia Sophia*, a liturgical book from Constantinople's Great Church. The earliest surviving, but incomplete, manuscript of the *Typikon* comes from the end of the ninth or the beginning of the tenth century;[10] the first complete manuscript is thought to be "a late-tenth century copy of a mid-tenth century source."[11]

Both manuscripts include brief instructions for worship on Palm Sunday.[12] A late-night vigil (*pannuchis*) in the Great Church was followed by matins (*orthros*) at the ambo, an elevated platform in the centre of the church.[13] As Palm Sunday dawned, worshippers reassembled about a mile away at the Church of the Forty Martyrs,[14] where the patriarch distributed palms to assisting priests, other clergy, and laity. The Trisagion ("Holy God, holy and mighty, holy and immortal, have mercy on us") was sung. Then the congregation left the church, chanting the feast's designated troparion,[15] "By raising Lazarus from the dead," which ends with the familiar words, "Hosanna in the highest! Blessed is he who comes in the name of the Lord," and is still used in Orthodox churches on Palm Sunday. All then processed on foot through the Forum of Constantine, where they

---

8 Harris, *Constantinople*, 4–17.

9 Villehardouin, *Conquête* 128 (1:130), translation adapted from Villehardouin, *Conquest*, 59.

10 Dmitrievskii, *Opisanie*, 1:1–152. For the date, see Mateos, *Typicon*, xviii. Baldovin, *Urban*, 190, defines a typikon as "a book containing liturgical directions for each feast and fast of the year. It also indicates the proper readings and chants and the place(s) of celebration for the eucharist and other liturgical services."

11 Baldovin, *Urban*, 191. For a scholarly edition of this manuscript, with French translation, see Mateos, *Typicon*.

12 Baldovin, *Urban*, 181–90, gathers abundant evidence of earlier outdoor liturgical processions in Constantinople, but finds among them no record of a Palm Sunday procession.

13 *OBD*, 1:75–76; for the location and design of Hagia Sophia's ambo, see Mathews, *Early*, 92, 98–99.

14 Constantinople's Church of the Forty Martyrs, located near the Philadelphion, was the most important of several churches in the city dedicated to the memory of the Forty Martyrs of Sebasteia, some of whose relics it housed. Built before 609, it was reported to be in ruins in 1420. The Şehzade Mosque, completed in 1548, now stands nearby (Janin, *Églises*, 501; *ODB*, 2:799–800).

15 Jordan, *Synaxarion*, 2:766, defines "troparion" as "a generic term for a poetic stanza used as a refrain for the psalms, the odes and the doxology."

stopped to sing praises to the Triune God, and on to the Great Church for the celebration of the Eucharist.[16]

Yet another manuscript of the *Typikon*, dated to the eleventh century, stipulates an elaborate prologue to the procession, in which the patriarch rode a horse (but not, as I once briefly supposed, a donkey).[17] Unfortunately, the manuscript in question was transferred to the Soviet Union during the Second World War and is now lost.[18] We are therefore dependent on commentary and translated excerpts published earlier in Russian by Alexeii Dmitrievskii.[19] According to Dmitrievskii's translation, the eleventh-century *Typikon* specified:

> At the appointed hour, when the patriarch has donned the archiepiscopal vestments, he holds in one hand the large life-giving cross and in the other hand a palm branch (*pal'moo i baia*) wrapped in whatever kind of sweet-smelling flowers are available at the time. After he covers his head with the cloth veil (τo περίπτάριον),[20] he walks out of the Great Church, gets on a steed (*sadetsya na konya* [= male horse]) and, in the presence of singing ... goes to the Church of the Forty Martyrs.[21]

Dmitrievskii summarizes, in his own words: "From Hagia Sophia, the patriarch processed on a young horse (*na zhrebyati tol'ko*) to the Church of the Forty Martyrs, and thence to the forum of Saint Constantine and back to Hagia Sophia on foot."[22] Elsewhere he cites two Greek passages, one from the lost Soviet manuscript and the other from a Greek manuscript found in Moscow in 1701, that speak of the patriarch riding a "colt" (*pōlos*) on Palm Sunday.[23]

---

16 Mateos, *Typicon*, 2:66–67. Mateos also includes a short paragraph, not found in Dmitrievskii, *Opisanie*, 1:127, which acknowledges an alternative processional route followed by "those who prefer the ancient custom."

17 Flier, "Iconography," 113n7, identifies the rite in Constantinople as "the Procession on the Ass," which I misunderstood on first reading some years ago. Flier uses the same phrase for the Moscow Palm Sunday procession, in which he makes it clear that the "ass" in question was a white horse playing the part of an ass.

18 Mateos, *Typicon*, viii.

19 The manuscript was formerly Codex A 104 of the Royal Library at Dresden, which Dmitrievskii inexplicably numbers both 104 and 140. See Dmitrievski, *Drevneishie*, 260–61, for his own acknowledgment of this confusion.

20 The *periptarion*, more commonly called *epirriptarion* or *epanokalimavkion*, is the cloth veil that covers and hangs down behind an orthodox bishop's cylindrical head covering (*kalimavkion*).

21 Dmitrievskii, "Khozdenie," 70.

22 Dmitrievskii, "Khozdenie," 71. I am grateful to Lisa Woodson not only for her invaluable help in translating this and other Russian passages, but also for helping me to locate and purchase an electronic copy of Dmitrievski, *Drevneishie*, and then scouring it for references to the patriarch's Palm Sunday mount.

23 Dmitrievski, *Drevneishie*, 119–20, 257.

Whether the patriarch's mount was a *pōlos*, a *zhrebya*, or a *konya*, it was certainly not a donkey. Dmitrievskii's purpose in analyzing the Constantinople procession was to compare it to the later Moscow Palm Sunday procession, which he regarded as more "spiritual" precisely because it was a "procession ... on a young donkey (*na oslyati*)." He was well aware, though, that the role of the Russian "donkey" was played by a horse: "The transformation of the colt into a donkey with the aid of a [white linen] blanket was undoubtedly motivated by the desire to make our ritual as sweet and spiritually touching as possible."[24] Dmitrievskii's claim for the spiritual superiority of the Moscow procession depends on the Greek patriarch having ridden an undisguised horse.

Although spatially more circumscribed than its ecclesiastical counterpart, the imperial Palm Sunday procession was in some respects a more elaborate affair, visiting several churches or chapels within the grounds of the Great Palace and taking advantage of all the grandeur of imperial court ceremony.[25] Instructions for the imperial Palm Sunday rituals are found in the *Book of Ceremonies* of Constantine VII Porphyrogenitos (913–959), who "compiled and edited this work from previous and contemporary sources, probably in the latter part of his reign."[26] The liturgy began, on the eve of Palm Sunday, in front of the enamelled icon of the Mother of God in the Church of Saint Demetrios. There, the emperor presented each senator with "a branch with palm leaves, and sweet marjoram, and other sweet-smelling flowers according to the season." To other officials he gave silver crosses, sized according to rank. Then all moved to the adjacent Church of the Mother of God of the Lighthouse for the celebration of first vespers. At the close of the office, the "provosts of the bedchamber" (*praipositoi*) distributed large palm leaves to the "people of the bedchamber" (*kouboukleioi*).[27]

On the morning of Palm Sunday—presumably after the conclusion of the patriarchal procession, which had begun at dawn—the imperial ceremonies resumed in the Chrysotriklinos, the domed ceremonial hall in the heart of the imperial palace. The emperor sat on his throne below a mosaic representing Christ in majesty, "a visual symbol of the theoretical relationship between emperor and Christ," the former ruling on earth with the universal authority of the latter in heaven.[28] Leaders of various ecclesiastical, charitable, and civic groups, bowing deeply, presented gold or silver crosses to

---

24 Dmitrievskii, "Khozdenie," 71. For the Moscow procession, see chap. 8.

25 Baldovin, *Urban*, 168, notes that "the imperial palace ... was not one building, but a conglomeration of buildings that expanded over the centuries." For a plan of the Grand Palace, with all the churches and chapels identified, see the end maps in Constantine, *Livre*, 1.2. For an Arab captive's account of the splendour of Constantinople's imperial processions in the last quarter of the ninth century, see Vasiliev, "Harun-ibn-Yahya."

26 Baldovin, *Urban*, 197. The complete text, with Latin translation, is published in two books in Constantine, *De cerimoniis*; for a facsimile of this edition with an English translation, see Constantine, *Book*; for a scholarly edition of the first book, with French translation and commentary, see Constantine, *Livre*.

27 Constantine, *Livre* 40 (1.1:158–59); Constantine, *Book* 31 (1:170–71). For the churches of Demetrios and the Lighthouse, see Janin, *Églises*, 96, 241–45.

28 Cameron, "Construction," 107, 116.

the emperor to be kissed; others, from the imperial household, bowed and were given crosses by the emperor. As the emperor and his court left the Chrysotriklinos, priests emerged from the Church of the Mother of God of the Lighthouse on the opposite side of a small courtyard, bearing "the church's cross."[29] If Johannes Koder is correct, this was the same relic of the true cross, displayed in an elaborate gilt and enamel reliquary, which is now known, after its present location in the cathedral treasury of Limburg an der Lahn (Hesse, Germany), as the Limburg Staurotheke (Fig. 5). The reliquary, together with its contents, was plundered by crusaders in 1204. While still in Constantinople, the cross was a symbol of imperial military triumph: it is inscribed with a declaration of the emperor's power, when in possession of the true cross, to "crush ... the temerities of the barbarians" just as "Christ with this [cross] formerly smashed the gates of Hades."[30]

With all the participants carrying candles, and the emperor in the privileged position at the rear of the procession, court and clergy continued on foot to two chapels in the Palace of Daphne, the Chapel of the Mother of God and the Chapel of Saint Stephen, in both of which the *ektenē*, a responsory prayer of supplication, was offered.[31] At other stops along the way, groups of palace guards, senators, and other officials prayed for God's blessing on the emperor.[32] Back in the Chrysotriklinos, the emperor stood to the right of the throne room and the patricians stood to the left, leaving the imperial throne itself unoccupied. A deacon placed a gospel book on the throne, signifying the presence of the exalted Christ in their midst,[33] and the company again recited the *ektenē*. A final celebration of the divine liturgy in the Church of the Lighthouse was followed by a meal, for those invited to join the emperor, in the large dining area known as the Hall of Justinian.[34] Oddly, there is no mention on Palm Sunday itself of the palm branches and flowers distributed on Saturday evening. It would appear that only candles and crosses were carried in the imperial Palm Sunday procession.[35]

The *Book of Ceremonies* is not a record of unchanging rituals repeated annually in their entirety from one generation to another. Rather, as Constantine himself makes clear, it gathers together "everything found by our ancestors, passed down by eyewitnesses, or seen by ourselves and introduced in our time," in a conscious attempt to revive lapsed traditions and so to "impress foreigners" and "make the imperial power ... seem more

---

29 Constantine, *Livre* 41 (1.1:160–62); Constantine, *Book* 32 (1:171–74).

30 Koder, "Versinschriften"; Hostetler, "Limburg," 8, provides a translation of the inscription. For the Byzantine practice of carrying relics of the true cross into battle, see Klein, "Sacred," 94–96.

31 For the chapels in the Palace of Daphne, see Janin, *Églises*, 181, 489–90; for the *ektenē*, see Baldovin, *Urban*, 221–22.

32 The verb used (*hupereuchomai*) means not merely to "acclaim" (*acclament*) (Constantine, *Livre* 41.12 [1.1:163]), but to "pray for" (Constantine, *Book* 32 [1:175]).

33 Forsyth, *Throne*, 86–87.

34 Constantine, *Livre* 41 (1.1:162–64, and for editorial comment, 1.2:167–69); Constantine, *Book* 32 (1:174–76); for an alternative partial translation, see Cameron, "Construction," 116–17. For an earlier (September 899) account of the imperial Palm Sunday procession, see Philotheos, "Traité," 196–97.

35 Baumstark, "Solennité," 20.

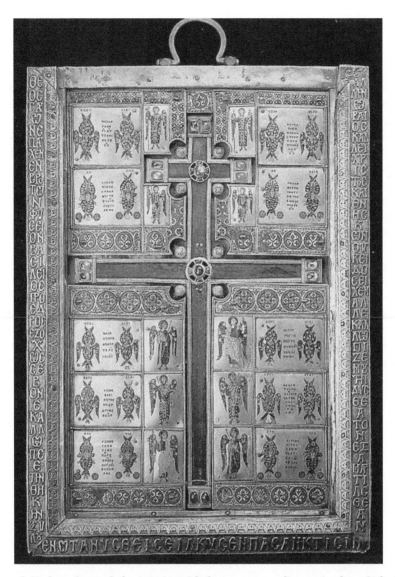

Figure 5 Limburg Staurotheke, interior with the true cross reliquary in place. Cathedral treasury, Limburg an der Lahn. Photographer Michael Benecke, Nentershausen / Ww. Used with permission.

awesome to our subjects." The ceremonies should be like "flowers … that incomparably embellish the imperial splendour."[36] In practice, imperial ceremony may not have been as flawless or as effective as Constantine hoped. Like ceremonies of power everywhere,

---

36 Constantine, *Livre*, 1.1:1–2; Constantine, *Book*, 1:1–4; see also Cameron, "Construction," 118–19.

those set out in the *Book of Ceremonies* "masked the real state of affairs," doggedly cel-ebrating universal and imperial harmony while concealing conflicts between emperor and church, between emperor and the office-holding class, between rival claimants to the throne, and (albeit suppressed) between the powerful and the powerless.[37] Nevertheless, Constantine's idealized vision gives us an idea of the grandeur to which imperial ceremonial aspired and which, in terms of outward show, it may have come close to achieving.

Constantinople never fully recovered from the brutal sack of the city by the forces of the Fourth Crusade in 1204. Churches were vandalized, treasures destroyed, and sacred relics taken home as spoil. Ceremonial suffered. By the middle of the fourteenth century, patriarchal and imperial Palm Sunday processions had been combined into a single short walk from the private apartments of the emperor, along a covered walkway strewn with flowers, its columns twined with branches of myrtle, laurel, and olive, to the Great Church. A gospel book was carried at the head of the procession as a "type of Christ." The emperor followed, carrying a cross. The patriarch of Constantinople, any visiting patriarchs, and five priests carrying "holy icons" brought up the rear.[38] The fall of Constantinople to the Ottoman Turks in 1453 meant a new name for the city (Istanbul), an end to the Byzantine empire, and the transformation of the Great Church into a mosque. The patriarch remained in Constantinople, exercising some measure of spiri-tual influence over an increasingly fragmented network of Orthodox churches. In Greek Orthodox churches today, "the blessed palms are still distributed as of old, but the pro-cession has fallen into disuse."[39]

---

37 Cameron, "Construction," 122–24.

38 Macrides, *Pseudo-Kodinos*, 170–175, and for the date of the compilation of the text ("some time after John VI [Kantakouzenos] came to the throne" in 1347)," 17–18; see also Verpeaux, *Pseudo-Kodinos*, 23, 224–26.

39 Taft, "Holy," 164.

Chapter 8

THE HORSE WITH DONKEY'S EARS

AFTER THE FALL of Constantinople, the most credible claim to preside over a surviving eastern Christian empire came from Moscow, which identified itself both as
heir to the former Byzantine empire and also, to a lesser extent, as the "third Rome,"
heir to the ancient Christian Roman empire established by Constantine.[1] Surpassing
even these glories was the conviction that Moscow ruled over the "New Israel," a nation
chosen by God to defend the true religion against its enemies (including Muslims,
Roman Catholics, Lutherans, and any others not committed to Orthodoxy), to expand
the territorial boundaries in which the true religion was observed, and to do so by the
power of the cross and force of arms.[2] The Moscow Palm Sunday procession witnessed
in 1558 by Anthony Jenkinson, or perhaps by "an anonymous member of his entourage,"[3] reflected these glittering aspirations. The English traveller's description is worth
quoting in full:

> On Palm Sunday, they have a very solemn procession in this manner following:

> First they have a tree of a good bigness, which is made fast upon two sleds,
> as though it were growing there, and it is hanged with apples, raisins, figs,
> and dates, and with many other fruits abundantly. In the midst of the same
> tree stand five boys in white vestures, which sing in the tree before the pro-
> cession. After this there followed certain young men with wax tapers in their
> hands, burning, and a great lantern, that all the light should not go out. After
> them followed two with long banners, and six with round plates set upon long
> staves. The plates were of copper, very full of holes and thin. Then followed
> six carrying painted images upon their shoulders; after the images follow
> certain priests, to the number of one hundred or more, with goodly vestures,
> whereof ten or twelve are of white damask, set and embroidered round about
> with fair and orient pearls, as great as peas, and among them certain sapphires
> and other stones. After them followed the one half of the emperor's noblemen.
> Then cometh the emperor's majesty and the metropolitan, after this manner:

> First, there is a horse, covered with white linen down to the ground, his ears
> being made long with the same cloth, like to an ass's ears. Upon this horse the
> metropolitan sitteth sidelong like a woman. In his lap lieth a fair book with a

---

1 Ostrowski, "Moscow," 175–76, argues that the first record of the rhetorical trope of Third Rome
dates to the late sixteenth century and that "little notice was taken" of it "until 1861"; see also
Ostrowski, *Muscovy*, 219–43.

2 Rowland, "Moscow"; Gruber, *Orthodox*, 23–50, 181–84; for a fuller bibliography, see Kain,
"New," 372n2.

3 Flier, "Iconography," 109.

crucifix of goldsmith's work upon the cover, which he holdeth fast with his left hand, and in his right hand he hath a cross of gold, with which cross he ceaseth not to bless the people as he rideth.

There are to the number of thirty men, which spread abroad their garments before the horse; and as soon as the horse is passed over any of them, they take them up again and run before, and spread them again, so that the horse doth always go on some of them. They which spread the garments are all priests' sons, and for their labours the emperor giveth unto them new garments.

One of the emperor's noblemen leadeth the horse by the head, but the emperor himself, going on foot, leadeth the horse by the end of the rein of his bridle with one of his hands, and in the other of his hands he had a branch of a palm tree. After this followed the rest of the emperor's noblemen and gentlemen, with a great number of other people. In this order they went from one church to another within the castle [Kremlin], about the distance of two flights' [arrows] shot, and so returned again to the emperor's church, where they made an end to their service. Which being done, the emperor's majesty and certain of his noblemen went to the metropolitan's house to dinner, where of delicate fishes and good drinks there was no lack.[4]

The emperor in question was Ivan IV (1547–1584), also known to history as Ivan Grozny (Ivan the Terrible or, in a kinder translation, the Formidable). The metropolitan was Macarius (1542–1563), a close ally and strong supporter of Ivan. Macarius, riding a white horse, played the part of Christ. The horse played the part of Christ's donkey. Ivan went on foot, a gesture that the author of the English account understood as a sign of deference to the metropolitan: "The emperor's majesty ... submitteth himself unto him in many things concerning religious matters, as in leading the metropolitan's horse upon Palm Sunday."[5] Michael Flier disagrees: "The tsar's humility is *not* directed towards the metropolitan as head of the church, but towards the metropolitan as the representation of Christ."[6]

Pursuing this argument further, Flier draws attention to the iconic nature of the procession. Not only did six young men carry processional "painted images," or icons, on their shoulders, but many details of the procession were borrowed from traditional Russian iconography rather than from the biblical narrative. The large, fruit-bearing tree, in which "five boys in white" perched and sang, recalled the tree from which similarly dressed boys gathered fruit or cut branches ahead of Christ's entry in many contemporary icons.[7] The tree's mobility, secured to two sleds at the front of the procession, is

---

4 Morgan and Coote, *Early*, 2:363–64.

5 Morgan and Coote, *Early*, 2:368. Ostrogorsky, "Stratordienst"; Crummey, "Court,"; and Bushkovitch, "Epiphany," 1–4, agree.

6 Flier, "Iconography," 118; Flier, "Breaking," 230.

7 The tree's fruitfulness may also have pointed forward to "the theme of New Jerusalem as a fruitful paradise" (Rowland, "Moscow," 610; see also Rev. 22:2).

logical enough: animate the icon and the tree moves, too.[8] The archbishop's side-saddle posture followed a mode of depicting Christ peculiar to Orthodox icons (Fig. 6).[9] In many icons, Christ's mount is white. The nobles and "other people" who walked behind the archbishop in procession did so in the position occupied by the disciples in Palm Sunday icons. The vested processional clergy recalled the bearded, robed, and cowled Jews of the icons, who greeted Christ at the gate to Jersusalem.[10] Thus, with the single exception of the tsar, all the participants in the procession had counterparts in traditional Russian iconography. Ivan alone played no iconic role, but appeared in his own imperial person: the tsar himself walked with Christ toward Jerusalem. Moreover, "the reins that actually guide[d] the ass [were] not in the hands of the metropolitan." They were held by the tsar: "the moving force of the entire procession [was] given over to him."[11] Dmitry Shvidkovsky accordingly regards the Palm Sunday procession not as an act of submission but as a "sacralization of the power of the tsar," a way of emphasizing "his own special role in the life of the church."[12]

Although the English account of 1558 is the first surviving testimony to the Moscow "donkey walk," an earlier version of the ceremony seems to have been known in Novgorod, where Macarius had served as archbishop for nine years before his promotion to the see of Moscow in 1542. A reference to Gennadius, archbishop of Novgorod from 1484 to 1504, riding "a foal and a donkey" in the city's Palm Sunday procession is found in an addition to the *Tale of the White Cowl*, but like the tale itself the addition is now believed to have been written "after 1589" and to have claimed Gennadius as its author for reasons of contemporary church politics.[13] A more reliable record comes from Palm Sunday 1548, when the two prince-governors of Novgorod are reported to have "led the donkey (*oslya*) which was ridden by the archbishop [Theodosius]" from Saint Sophia Cathedral to the Church of the Entrance into Jerusalem, "both there and back."[14] The same rite is set out in an archiepiscopal ordinary "apparently compiled between 1550 and 1563,"[15] which includes a repeated censing of the archbishop and his donkey (*osyel*).[16] There is no suggestion in the Novgorod records that the animal was anything other than a live donkey; if so, the archbishop of Novgorod may have been the

---

8 The tree's mobility may also be indebted to accounts of an olive tree carried in the Palm Sunday procession in twelfth-century Jerusalem (see chap. 11).

9 Flier, "Iconography," 119; Flier, "Breaking," 232–33; see also Crummey, "Court," 149–50.

10 Examples of such icons can be found at "Entrance of Our Lord into Jerusalem," *Russian Icons*, www.iconrussia.ru/eng/iconography/452/?icon=1.

11 Flier, "Iconography," 120; Flier, "Breaking," 234.

12 Shvidkovsky, *Russian*, 138–39.

13 Rozov, "Povest'," 219, trans. Labunka, *Legend*, 290; for the probable date of composition, see Ostrowski, "Images," 272–74, 283. The phrase "on a foal and a donkey" (*na zhrebyati i osai*) derives from the confusing language of Matt. 21:2–7 rather than processional practice in Novgorod.

14 Kupriyanov, "Otryvki," 48; translation adapted from Labunka, *Legend*, 135.

15 Flier, "Breaking," 221.

16 Golubtsov, "Chinovnik," 256–57; trans. Labunka, *Legend*, 293–95.

Figure 6 *Entrance of Our Lord into Jerusalem*, from the iconostasis of the Cathedral
of the Nativity of Our Lady in Saint Anthony's Monastery, Novgorod.
Tempera on wood, ca. 1560. Novgorod State United Museum.

highest-ranking prelate ever to ride a donkey in a Palm Sunday procession. The white
horse elegantly dressed as a donkey would then have been an innovation introduced in
Moscow by Archbishop Macarius after his arrival from Novgorod.

Two further testimonies to the Moscow Palm Sunday procession survive from the reign
of Ivan IV. The first comes from Heinrich von Staden, a German mercenary who arrived
in Russia in 1564, finding employment in the newly established *oprichnina*, the tsar's
secret police and instrument of terror between 1565 and 1572. In a long letter, written
after his return to western Europe "during the summer of 1576," von Staden twice made
passing reference to Palm Sunday in Moscow. "The bishops of Kazan, Astrakhan, Ryazan,
Vladimir, Vologda, Rostov, Suzdal, Tver, Polotsk, Great Novgorod, Nizhni Novgorod, Pskov,

and Dorpat in Livonia," he wrote, "all … had to appear personally in Moscow every year at the procession of the metropolitan on Palm Sunday."[17] Not only had the number of bishops in attendance grown, but the route of the procession had been extended beyond the walls of the Kremlin to the new Church of the Intercession (Saint Basil's Cathedral), completed in what is now Red Square in 1561. Ivan had ordered the church built to commemorate his decisive victory over the Kazan Tatars in 1552,[18] and its significance was underscored every Palm Sunday, when—as von Staden noted—it was the focal point of "the procession of the metropolitan on Palm Sunday with all the bishops."[19] The largest of the eight surrounding churches (or chapels) within the new building was dedicated to Christ's entry into Jerusalem, and had become the turning point of the Palm Sunday procession before its return to the Kremlin. Ivan thus established an annually enacted "parallel" between his own "triumphant return to Moscow" after the Kazan campaign, when he had entered the city on foot, "and Christ's entry to Jerusalem."[20] Moscow's Palm Sunday procession, like so many others, had become a triumphal entry.

The second foreign eyewitness was Daniel Printz von Buchau, who saw the procession in 1576 while in Moscow as the German imperial ambassador. Printz began his account with the puzzling observation that on Palm Sunday "the metropolitan of Moscow, and the archbishops of the places where they reside, seated on donkeys (*asinae insidentes*), proceed toward the church, which is named after the city of Jerusalem."[21] While the metropolitan archbishop of Moscow is sometimes said to ride a "donkey," after the role played by his mount rather than the animal playing it, I know of no other reference to all the archbishops riding either donkeys or horses dressed as donkeys. I'm inclined to think Printz was mistaken. As for the church named "Jerusalem," the entire Church of the Intercession had by then acquired the popular name of "Jerusalem," at least in part because of its role in the Palm Sunday procession. Printz concludes: "The grand duke (*dux*) himself is accustomed to lead the metropolitan's donkey to the church." Many western European rulers refused to address the leader of "the Grand Duchy of Moscow" as tsar because the title implied a claim to equal status with or even superiority to the Habsburg emperor;[22] hence the lesser title of "duke." For his part, the metropolitan archbishop, elevated to the status of patriarch in 1589, claimed equality with the traditionally preeminent patriarchs of Constantinople, Alexandria, Antioch, and Jerusalem. Giles Fletcher, who in 1588 visited Moscow on behalf of the English crown rather than the Hapsburg empire, used the preferred Russian titles in his subsequent memoir: "On

---

17 Staden, *Aufzeichnungen*, 26–28; translation adapted from Staden, *Land*, 21–22.

18 Shvidkovsky, *Russian*, 126, 138. Red Square (*Krásnaya plóshchad'*) acquired its present name in the seventeenth century: *krásnyy* means either "red" or "beautiful."

19 Staden, *Aufzeichnungen*, 62; translation adapted from Staden, *Land*, 41.

20 Flier, "Church," 43; see also Flier, "Filling," 125.

21 Printz, *Muscoviae*, 711.

22 Madariaga, *Ivan*, 98.

Palm Sunday ... the Patriarch rideth through ... Moscow, the Emperor himself holding his horse's bridle."[23]

Three testimonies to Moscow's Palm Sunday procession also survive from the Russian Time of Troubles or First Civil War (1598–1613), a time of famine and multiple rival claimants to the throne.[24] A brief general observation comes from Peer Peerson, a Swedish agent resident in Moscow between 1602 and 1606, and until at least 1611 an occasional envoy to Russia: "In this part of the city there stands an exceedingly beautiful and artistically rich church, covered with glittering and glistening (*glensenden und gleissenden*) jewels, which is called Jerusalem. To this church, each year on Palm Sunday, the grand duke must lead the patriarch's donkey."[25] Similar language appears in the key to a map of Moscow published by the celebrated Dutch cartographer Hessel Gerritz in 1613: "Church of the Holy Trinity, also called Church of Jerusalem, to which on Palm Sunday the patriarch, sitting on a donkey, is ushered in by the tsar."[26] In both cases, like the unqualified "horse" in Fletcher's account, the "donkey" was no doubt the conventional white horse with long linen ears.

The longest and historically most specific report comes from Conrad Bussow, a German mercenary who lived in Moscow from 1600 to 1611. In July 1610, an invading Polish army under Alexander Gosiewski entered Moscow unopposed and negotiated an invitation to Władysław, son of King Sigismund III of Poland, to become tsar. Władysław never reached Moscow and Gosiewski presided over an "increasingly brutal military dictatorship."[27] By the time Palm Sunday 1611 arrived, tensions between the Polish garrison and the Muscovites had become sporadically violent, and armed revolt was anticipated. "In order to prevent uprising and mutiny," Bussow reports, Gosiewski prohibited the celebration of Palm Sunday.

> For on that day it is the custom for the tsar to come from the Kremlin to the church which they call Jerusalem, while the patriarch rides seated on a donkey, which the tsar leads by a bridle. Before them go the clergy in their priestly vestments, singing Hosanna in their ceremonies. Twenty or more boyar children, clad in red, go before the tsar and spread their garments, over which the tsar walks, as well as the donkey on which the patriarch sits. When the tsar has gone by they pick up the garments, run forward, and once again strew them in his way, and this continues until he reaches Jerusalem church. On sleighs there stands a full-grown tree, which they drag behind the patriarch, and on the sleighs there are also three or four boys, who also sing Hosanna. On the branches of this tree there hang various apple-like fruits. Behind the tree all the

---

23 Fletcher, *Rus*, 141.

24 The standard history of the period is Dunning, *Russia*.

25 Petreius, *Historien*, 5. For Peerson's biographical data, see Orchard, "Petreius."

26 Schilder, *Monumenta* 9:186–89, plate 9. The map itself is believed to have been based on a 1597 Russian original, of which Gerritz acquired a copy; whether the key to the map is also that old is uncertain.

27 Dunning, *Russia*, 413.

princes, boyars, and merchants follow in procession. Many thousands of people converge in order to take part in this festivity. Anyone who can walk will head there, resulting in such a conflux of people that the weak and puny should not be there if they know what is good for them.[28]

Not only was the volatility of such a mass gathering a cause for concern, but Hermogen, the current patriarch, was strongly opposed to the imposition of a Polish Catholic tsar, and the still uncrowned Władysław was not there to lead the patriarch's mount in procession. Learning of the prohibition, the Muscovites became "even more incensed," saying "that it would be better for them all to die than leave this festival uncelebrated." The ban, which had become a provocation rather than a bar to violence, was lifted and the people "were permitted to observe [the Palm Sunday ritual], only instead of the tsar one of the Russian lords" held "the bridle of the donkey on which the patriarch was seated as far as the Jerusalem church." Occupying soldiers were out in force: "The German and foreign regiments and all the Poles were fully armed and on the alert, so that the day passed without tumult."[29] The day's events bore an unintended resemblance to Christ's own entry into Jerusalem, which took place under Roman military occupation and the threat of Jewish revolt.

The uprising, however, had only been delayed. On Tuesday, according to Bussow, "the Muscovites made the first move and slaughtered many Poles who were spending one last night in their previous quarters. They put up barricades and dug trenches in the streets and assembled many thousands strong." Gosiewski sent "several squadrons of lancers" against the revolt, but the cavalry were powerless in the trenched and barricaded streets, and were put to flight by the sustained fire of "Muscovite musketeers." Some four hundred German mercenary musketeers retaliated, firing on the Muscovites from open side streets, and then attacking at close quarters with rapiers. When the Germans returned to barracks, they looked like "butcher's apprentices. Their rapiers, hands, and clothes were covered in blood … They had destroyed many Muscovites but had lost only eight of their own soldiers."[30]

Muscovite resistance resurfaced behind barricades and trenches elsewhere in the city. Unable to use his cavalry against the Russians, Gosiewski ordered his troops "to set fire to the corner houses, and the wind blew to such effect that in twelve and a half minutes" much of Moscow outside the stone-walled Kremlin, where the Poles were based, "was engulfed in flames." Cavalry reinforcements arrived from outside the city; avoiding the remaining barricades, they "roamed about the city, burning, killing, and plundering all that lay in their path." By noon on Wednesday, the uprising was over. "In the course of two days the great metropolis of Moscow" had been "reduced to dung and ashes, and nothing remained except the imperial fortress [i.e., the Kremlin] and its suburb, which were occupied by the [Polish] king's men, and some stone churches." Believing the patriarch Hermogen to have been "the leader and author of all this sedition," the

---

28 Bussow, *Chronicon*, 124; Bussow, *Disturbed*, 160.

29 Bussow, *Chronicon*, 124; translation adapted from Bussow, *Disturbed*, 160–61.

30 Bussow, *Chronicon*, 125–26; Bussow, *Disturbed*, 161–62.

Poles deposed, imprisoned, and starved him to death.[31] In October 1612, a diminished, besieged, and starving Polish garrison finally surrendered to a newly formed national Russian militia. The Polish occupation was over. Michael I (1613–1645), the first of the enduring Romanov dynasty, was crowned tsar the following July. For the next fifty years, Moscow's Palm Sunday procession seems to have enjoyed a measure of peace.

In 1636, Adam Olearius, the secretary and chronicler of an ambitious German trade mission, saw Michael I lead the patriarch in Moscow's Palm Sunday procession. The German visitors "were allotted a wide space opposite the Kremlin gate, and the Russians, more than ten thousand of whom had collected before the Kremlin, were held back," so that the trade delegates "could see clearly" as the procession passed through the open square. In the engraving that accompanies Olearius's published account of the mission (Fig. 7), "a very large, wide, low-slung wagon" is pulled by a single horse, and carries the customary tree, to which are "fastened many apples, figs, and raisins."[32] Walking behind the wagon are "many priests in white choir robes and costly ecclesiastical vestments, carrying banners, crosses, and icons, on long staffs, and singing in unison." Privileged laymen follow, "some of them carrying palm branches." The tsar, or as Olearius calls him,

> the grand duke (*Großfürste*), richly robed and wearing a crown, proceeded arm in arm with two of the most notable state counselors ... He himself led the patriarch's horse by a long rein. The horse was covered with a cloth, and was adorned with long ears, to make it resemble an ass (*Das Pferd war mit Tuche bekleidet, und mit langen Ohren als ein Esel außgemachet*). The patriarch sat sidesaddle on the horse. He wore a round white hat set with very large pearls, and a crown. In his right hand was a golden cross embedded with precious stones, with which he blessed the surrounding people. The people bowed their heads very low and crossed themselves toward him and the cross.

Olearius notably identifies the patriarch's mount by its offstage identity ("horse") rather than its processional role ("donkey"), thus confirming that the "donkeys" mentioned in the intervening records had also been horses with false donkey's ears. "Metropolitans, bishops, and other priests" followed on foot. When the tsar reached the German trade ambassadors, "they bowed to him" and he "sent his senior interpreter ... to ask about their health."[33]

Archdeacon Paul of Aleppo, son and travelling companion of Patriarch Makarios of Antioch, witnessed Moscow's Palm Sunday procession in 1655, the last year before significant changes were made to the rite. In the absence of Alexis I (1645–1676), who was away leading the Russian army in what he regarded as a holy war against Catholic Poland, "the emperor's vice-gerent" led the white horse, which was "all covered with white linen, as white as a shirt, so that nothing of it could be seen but the eyes." On the horse "was a kind of saddle, thickened to the size of a chair, and covered with velvet,

---

31 Bussow, *Chronicon*, 126–28; Bussow, *Disturbed*, 162–65; see also Dunning, *Russia*, 418.

32 The engraving in Olearius, *Offt*, 105, differs somewhat from that in the expanded Olearius, *Vermehrte*, 132, reproduced here.

33 Olearius, *Vermehrte*, 132–33; translation adapted from Olearius, *Travels*, 99–100.

Figure 7 Tsar Michael I leads the patriarch's horse in the Moscow Palm Sunday procession, 1636. Engraving, Adam Olearius, *Vermehrte Newe Beschreibung der Muscowitischen und Perischen Reyse*, 1656.

set on one side ... They brought before the patriarch a chair covered with black cloth, on which, sitting, he was mounted upon the saddle ... with his feet hanging down on one side, and his back leaning against the chair on the other." Patriarch Nikon, newly installed in 1652,[34] wore a vestment "of green velvet; having for its emblems ... the Cherubim and Seraphim, in gold pearls and precious stones; for its border, on both sides, white small clear pearls strung together; and for the red in the middle, valuable red shells." The "archons of the emperor" were also richly dressed "in vests of gold brocade." The procession followed the traditional route from the Cathedral of the Dormition to the Church of the Intercession, where the patriarch was helped off his horse and led inside to "perform the service of the [Palm] Procession," remounting afterward for the return journey.[35] Exceptionally, Paul of Aleppo acknowledged the poor conditions underfoot: "The janissaries, during the previous week, had put the road in order, from the great church to the entrance of the castle-gate, nailing on it planks, and drying the clay with sand; for in this week the ice had begun to thaw, and the rain to fall." His admission gives fresh significance to the "one hundred boys, sons of the janissaries," who had been given from the imperial treasury, "as was customary every year, one hundred cloaks of various colours—green, red, blue, yellow, etc." During the procession, the boys, "fifty on each side, vied with each other in spreading their cloaks ... under the horse's feet across the path; and, when the horse had passed over his cloak, each took it up, and ran forward, to

---

34 Nikon reportedly rode a "donkey" (*oslya*) around the Kremlin after his investiture banquet (Gibbenet, *Istoricheskoe*, 1.1:16; Sevast'yanova, *Materialy*, 46; Shubin, *History*, 2:91). Whether this, too, was a white horse playing the part of a donkey is unclear.

35 Paul of Aleppo, *Travels*, 2:89–92.

spread it again, as before." Despite the protective planks and cloaks, it is hard to imagine that the dignitaries' robes and the horse's white linen remained pristine.[36]

Patriarch Nikon's sweeping reform of Russian Orthodox texts and rituals, imposed in 1656, included substantial changes to Moscow's Palm Sunday procession. Flier has argued that Nikon's aim was "greater historical accuracy,"[37] but mapping events in Jerusalem more accurately onto the local terrain may be a better description. The outward half of the procession was simplified: "the Holy Sovereign Patriarch" went from the Dormition to the Jerusalem Chapel of the Church of the Intercession "on foot, and not on the ass (ne na oslyati)," in a simple "movement with crosses." The return journey began with a dramatization of Christ's appropriation of the donkey. At the Lobnoe Mesto,[38] a stone platform in the square outside the church, an archdeacon read the framing narrative from Mark's gospel, Nikon spoke the words of Christ sending two disciples to fetch the donkey, two priests found the donkey "tied to a nearby post," and a "patriarchal boyar" played the part of the donkey's owner. The "disciples" then led the donkey to the Lobnoe Mesto, where the patriarch was lifted aboard. With Alexis on foot holding the reins, the procession returned through the Kremlin gate to the cathedral.[39] Thus, as Flier understands it, the patriarch more accurately imitated the actions of Christ, walking from "Bethany" (represented by the Church of the Intercession) to "Bethphage" near the "Mount of Olives" (the Lobnoe Mesto), and only then mounting the donkey to ride through the gates of "Jerusalem" (the Kremlin) to the "Holy Sepulchre" (the Cathedral of the Dormition).[40] But the patriarch still wore rich vestments, his "donkey" was still a white horse, and the tsar who held the reins had just waged a holy war against Catholic Christians. For all of the procession's more careful spatial evocation of the biblical narrative, the visual splendour of the rite was still shaped by Nikon's commitment to "Russia's future as a New Israel," to Moscow as a "Russian 'New Jerusalem,'" and to Alexis as the "new Constantine."[41]

Vyacheslav Schwartz's *Palm Sunday in Moscow under Tsar Alexei Mikhailovich: The Procession of the Patriarch on a Donkey*, painted in 1865 (Fig. 1), is also said to have aimed at "historical verisimilitude."[42] The tsar leading the patriarch's horse in the painting is Alexis I and the patriarch atop the horse is Nikon (Fig. 8).[43] The time frame is between

---

36 Paul of Aleppo, *Travels*, 2:89–90.

37 Flier, "Court," 83.

38 Gruber, *Orthodox*, 181, points out that *lobnoe mesto* is "a calque," or loan translation, "of Golgotha," meaning the "place of the skull" or "place of execution" (see Matt. 27:33; Mark 15:22; John 19:17).

39 Dubrovskii, "Patriarshie," 15; partial translation and summary in Flier, "Court," 78–79.

40 Flier, "Court," 81. Although Palm Sunday processions in Jerusalem had ended at the Church of the Holy Sepulchre at least since the time of Egeria (see chap. 5), Christ's own descent from the Mount of Olives ended in "the temple" (Matt. 21:12; Mark 11:11; Luke 19:45).

41 Kain, "Before," 118–20; see also Kain, "New."

42 Vereshchagina, *Viacheslav*, 76.

43 Vereshchagina, *Viacheslav*, 78. Compare the portrait of Nikon in Schwartz's 1867 painting *Patriarch Nikon at the New Jerusalem Monastery* ("Vyacheslav G. Schwartz," *Petroart.ru*, http://petroart.ru/art/sh/shvarc/img/5.jpg).

Figure 8 Vyacheslav Schwartz, *Palm Sunday in Moscow under Tsar Alexei Mikhailovich: The Procession of the Patriarch on a Donkey*, 1865 (detail).

1656 and 1658, the only three years in which both Alexis and Nikon took part. Tsar and patriarch are shown on the return journey, about to enter the Kremlin. Schwartz has compressed the distance between the Jerusalem Church, to the left of the painting, and the walls of the Kremlin, to the right, filling the foreground with the elite heart of the procession. Carefully researched architectural features thus bracket the no less carefully researched vestments, robes, crosses, and other sumptous accoutrements of the privileged members of the procession. The popular crowd is rendered almost invisible, and there is no trace of either ice or mud underfoot. Like Nikon, Schwartz was selective in his choice of historical details.

By the summer of 1658, the relationship between Alexis and Nikon had become strained to breaking point, at least in part because of Nikon's reluctance to acknowledge the tsar "as the senior partner in areas where temporal and spiritual authority overlapped."[44] In July, Nikon withdrew to his favoured New Jerusalem Monastery,[45] but did not resign his office. In his absence, Pitirim, metropolitan of Krutitsy, served as patriarch in his place. Nikon was not pleased, especially when in 1659 Pitirim assumed the part of Christ in the Palm Sunday procession. Nikon wrote to the tsar accusing Pitirim of "daring to pollute by spiritual adultery the chair of the primate of all Russia," an act of

---

44 Longworth, *Alexis*, 126.

45 The New Jerusalem Monastery had been founded by Nikon in 1656 as a patriarchal residence in keeping with the trope of New Israel. It lay within a bend in the River Istra some thirty miles west of Moscow.

presumption by a mere metropolitan "for which nowhere can any precedent or direction be found in holy scriptures."[46] Alexis's reply, delivered orally by messenger, pointed out that Nikon had "abandoned the flock" and so had no business writing of such matters. In any case, Nikon himself had taken part in the ceremony of Palm Sunday when metropolitan of Novgorod, and had subsequently taken no steps to suppress the practice there or elsewhere when he was active as patriarch of Moscow.[47] Undeterred by Nikon's protests, Pitirim rode in the Palm Sunday processions in 1660, 1661, and again, a month after Nikon had formally anathematized him, in 1662.[48]

A contemporary engraving survives of the Palm Sunday procession on March 23, 1662 (Fig. 9). Augustin von Meyerberg was then in Moscow as the leader of a Habsburg imperial embassy, and subsequently supervised a collection of drawings illustrating his time in Russia. One of the engraved drawings shows the return journey of the Palm Sunday procession, stretched between the Lobnoe Mesto and the Kremlin gate. Marginal testimony to Nikon's absence can be found in the key to the drawing, where the rider of the horse is correctly identified as a "metropolitan" rather than the patriarch. Alexis leads Pitirim's horse. Pitirim sits sidesaddle and the horse is draped with a white cloth. On either side of the procession, ranks of musketeers (strel'tsy) prostrate themselves.[49]

By 1665, Pitirim's place had probably been taken by Paul II, who had succeeded him as metropolitan of Krutitsy the previous year.[50] Nikon himself was condemned and deposed by the Great Moscow Synod, convened by Alexis and presided over by the patriarchs of Alexandria and Antioch, in December 1666.[51] Pitirim finally became patriarch in his own right in 1672, but died a year later.

It may seem strange that Schwartz, free to choose any historical pairing of tsar and patriarch, made the disgraced Nikon the dominant figure in his painting. By the second half of the nineteenth century, however, Nikon's reputation had been rehabilitated: he was depicted in scholarly histories and popular biographies alike as a humble representative of the Russian folk, a close friend of the royal family, an advocate of enlightened reform, and a devoted promoter of the cherished idea of Russia as the New Israel.[52] Schwartz's portrayal of Alexis and Nikon in the early glory of their close friendship and

---

46 Palmer, *Patriarch*, 4:164–66, translates Nikon's letter in full. Whereas Palmer parenthetically understands Nikon to find no scriptural warrant for the "ceremony of Palm Sunday," Kevin Kain (personal communication, November 26, 2016) rightly narrows the application to Metropolitan Pitirim's action.

47 Palmer, *Patriarch*, 4:166–69.

48 Palmer, *Patriarch*, 4:313, 324–26, 366.

49 Meyerberg, *Sammlung*, plate 50.

50 Palmer, *Patriarch*, 4:583.

51 For the complex of events leading up to Nikon's deposition, see Kain, "New," 386–93.

52 Kain, "Reading," 169–73; Kain, "Archimandrites," 312–17. The exiled Nikon had received a preliminary pardon from Feodor III in 1681 and a full posthumous pardon from the ecumenical patriarchs in 1682 (Shusherin, *Peasant*, 91–104; Shubin, *History*, 2:131–32).

Figure 9 Metropolitan Pitirim plays the part of Christ in the reformed Moscow Palm Sunday procession, 1662. Engraving, Augustin Freyherr von Meyerberg, *Sammlung von Ansichten, Gebräuchen, Bildnissen, Trachten*, 1827, plate 50.

their shared passion for liturgical reform reflects the prevailing view of his own time. Historical verisimilitude conforms to current expectations.

The generation of Romanovs that followed Alexis presided over the demise of Russian Palm Sunday processions. Feodor III (1676–1682) succeeded his father, Alexis I, as tsar at the age of fifteen. Feodor's participation in public ceremonial was limited by persistent ill health, due to which he was unable to take part in the Palm Sunday procession in either 1676 or 1677.[53] In March 1678, a synodical decree restricted the Palm Sunday procession to Moscow alone, allowing the practice to continue there because it displayed "the humility and submission before Christ our Lord" of the tsar and "our most pious aristocrats."[54] In the same year, Feodor "deigned ... to take the ass's bridle by the end of the reins and to lead the way to the cathedral."[55] By 1681, he was once again too weak to participate.[56]

Feodor was followed by his younger brother, Ivan V, who "had severe visual impairment and perhaps mental handicaps," and his half-brother, Peter I, who displayed a "quick intelligence" and a "liveliness" that verged on "menacing hyperactivity."[57] The two boys were aged fifteen and nine at their joint coronation in June 1682. In 1683, on the

---

53 Bushkovitch, *Peter*, 112.

54 *Akty*, 4:308–9 (no. 223); translation from Flier, "Iconography," 118; see also Crummey, "Court," 134.

55 *Dvortsovye*, 4:31; translation from Hughes, *Sophia*, 45.

56 Bushkovitch, *Peter*, 118n70.

57 Hughes, *Peter*, 19.

first Palm Sunday of their combined reign, Ivan's ill health meant that Peter alone led the patriarch's horse,[58] perhaps setting a precedent for other years. The two ruled jointly until Ivan's death in 1696, after which Peter remained as sole ruler until his own death in 1725. History knows him as Peter the Great.

Peter was notoriously ambivalent toward church ceremonial, and was given at times to drunken parody. In his late teens, he formed a merry company, known as the "Most Comical and Drunken Council," which engaged in gargantuan feasting, excessive drinking, and carnivalesque parodies of court ceremony and religious rites.[59] In 1692, "after lunch on Palm Sunday," the group held their own "procession," starting at Peter's "play court (poteshniy dvor)" in the so-called New German suburb of Moscow where all Protestant and Catholic foreigners were required to live. According to Boris Kurakin, a close associate of the tsar, the drunken council's "mock patriarch was led on a camel through the riverside garden to the French wine cellar. After getting thoroughly drunk there, everyone went home."[60] Such parodies, as James Cracraft points out, "were not mere youthful highjinks," for Peter continued to ridicule ecclesiastical authority and other traditional constraints in this manner until the end of his reign.[61] Some have argued that the relentless mockery was a calculated means of clearing the ground for modernization and further reform.[62]

As for the official Palm Sunday procession, Peter quickly lost interest. In 1694, after the death of his mother in January, Peter declined altogether to take part in the procession.[63] The last recorded observance of Moscow's Palm Sunday procession was in 1696, the year of Ivan's death. Peter's tastes, when he was not indulging in parody of the old religion, ran more to the imported classical grandeur of late-Renaissance absolutism. In September 1696, he staged a magnificent (or overblown) entry for the army on its return from the capture of the Turkish fortress of Azov. The warriors passed through a triumphal arch supported by enormous relief figures of Hercules and Mars. Inscriptions on the vault and pediment further compared Peter to Caesar and Constantine.[64] Palm Sunday, with its false donkey, paled by comparison. Between 1697 and 1700, Peter was away from Moscow during Easter. In 1699 and 1700, the palace records note that "there was no palm ceremony," suggesting that by then even the patriarch had given up on it. The procession appears to have been "simply abandoned, rather than abolished."[65]

---

58 Bushkovitch, *Peter*, 140.

59 Massie, *Peter*, 117–21; Cracraft, *Church*, 11–23; Zitser, *Transfigured*, 63–78. Peter's company may have been modelled in part on French "festive societies" (*sociétés joyeuses*), for which see Beam, *Laughing*.

60 Kurakin, "Gistoriia," 385; see also Cracraft, *Church*, 11. For Peter's "play court" see Zitser, *Transfigured*, 55.

61 Cracraft, *Church*, 12–13.

62 For example, Zitser, *Transfigured*.

63 Bushkovitch, "Epiphany," 15.

64 Wortman, *Scenarios*, 1:42–43.

65 Hughes, *Russia*, 275.

When the ruling patriarch died in October 1700, Peter declined to appoint a successor. No longer constrained by the presence of a patriarch, Peter appropriated Palm Sunday adulation for himself, occasionally being greeted by eminent clergy with the words, "Blessed is he who comes in the name of the Lord."[66] In 1712, Peter moved the Russian capital from Moscow to the newly established city of St. Petersburg. On Palm Sunday, 1718, in front of the tsar and the entire political elite of St. Petersburg, one of Peter's favourite bishops, Feofan Prokopovich, preached a sermon in which he interpreted the biblical narrative of Christ's entry into Jerusalem as a model of Christian loyalty to the tsar as absolute ruler.[67] The opening paragraphs of the sermon are particularly striking. Feofan begins with a flurry of triumphal language, invoking Christ's "triumphal entry" (*torzhestvennii vkhod*), identifying the palm branches as "the emblems of the conqueror" and "Hosanna" as a "triumphant" cry. He then admits that "the Jews welcoming Jesus did not know him to be the King of Heaven," but instead believed him to be an "earthly" ruler, who would soon bring "liberation of the Jewish race from the rule of the Gentiles."[68] Instead of dismissing the Jewish acclamations as a misunderstanding of Jesus's intent, Feofan exalts their actions as a biblically sanctioned model of how any divinely ordained ruler should be honoured, and in particular of how the Russian people should yield unqualified obedience to Tsar Peter. Feofan conveniently ignores the fickleness of the Jewish crowd, which four days later called for Jesus's crucifixion, and goes on to marshall arguments from Scripture and natural law for the duty of subjects to obey government. While this may be consistent with the Russian myth of New Israel, and perhaps even more so with the absolutism of Louis XIV of France and other contemporary western European monarchs, it is hardly impartial biblical exegesis. Peter rewarded Feofan by appointing him bishop of Pskov, third in rank among Russia's dioecesan hierarchy. In 1721, Peter formally abolished the patriarchate, replacing it with the Most Holy Synod. Feofan became first vice-president of the synod, where he served as Peter's chief ideologue. In 1725 he became archbishop of Novgorod.[69]

Feofan's sermon serves as a fitting conclusion to the first part of my book, in which I have shown how triumphal entries and elite Palm Sunday processions appropriated one another's language and iconography in order to exalt human—and frequently military—power, all the while piously claiming humble dependence on divine power. By claiming to model their own triumphal rituals on Christ's entry into Jerusalem, rulers of church and state were able simultaneously to lay claim to Christ's precedent for their own public acts of self-exaltation and to adopt a rhetoric of Christian humility.

Of course, not all Palm Sunday processions were equally prone to such dissonance. For nearly five hundred years after Egeria's report from Jerusalem, Palm Sunday processions had remained free of undue pomp and military pretensions. The same

---

66 Hughes, *Russia*, 275, 452.

67 Prokopovich, *Sochinenia*, 76–93; Prokopovich, "Sermon"; see also Zitser, *Transfigured*, 150–54; Cracraft, *Church*, 57–59.

68 Prokopovich, *Sochinenia*, 76–77; Prokopovich, "Sermon," 14–15.

69 For more on Prokopovich, see Ivanov, *Spiritual*, chaps. 2–4.

was largely true, as we shall see in the second half of Part 3, of processions in which palmesels played a leading role. It was also true, as I have shown elsewhere, of English Palm Sunday processions, where a consecrated host was believed to embody the real, rather than merely vicarious or represented, presence of Christ.[70] But many medieval and early modern Palm Sunday processions, in an area loosely bounded by the imperial capitals of Aachen, Rome, Constantinople, and Moscow, arguably owed as much to classical Roman pomp as to any Christian model. As for royal and papal entries, most were unabashedly triumphal. Perhaps only Celestine V, who rode a donkey towards (but not from) his coronation as pope, managed to enter a city in a manner visually resembling Christ's entry into Jerusalem.

Parody, as the young Tsar Peter recognized, is sometimes the best antidote to pomp. But while parody staged by the tsar entailed no risk to its performers, some parodic acts of sober dissent have been much more hazardous. It is now time to examine two small-scale, unauthorized, and arguably unique civic entries, each of which challenged, at great cost to its primary actor, the kind of pretensions to royal and imperial grandeur, enforced by military power, that we have been studying. In 1656, James Nayler rode into Bristol. More than sixteen hundred years earlier and twice as many miles away, Jesus of Nazareth had ridden into Jerusalem.

---

70 Harris, "Processional," 320–25; Duffy, *Stripping*, 26.

PART TWO:

PARODIES

James Nayler and Jesus of Nazareth

Chapter 9

JAMES NAYLER'S ROYAL PROGRESS

ON FRIDAY, OCTOBER 24, 1656, James Nayler approached Bristol on horseback, accompanied by a small group of men and women reportedly singing "hosanna" and "holy, holy, holy." Nayler was regarded by many, supporters and critics alike, as the leader of the first generation of Quakers in England.[1] It was raining heavily, and the Quakers trudged knee-deep through mud in the part of the road where only horses and carts usually travelled. Some of the women spread their clothes on the ground in front of Nayler. A curious crowd followed the Quakers from the city gates to their inn, where they were able to warm themselves and dry their soaked outer garments before a fire. The city magistrates, believing that the entry embodied a claim that Nayler was Christ, arrested and questioned the members of the group. Nayler was charged with blasphemy, and—along with four of his supporters—was sent to London, where he was tried by the Puritan-dominated parliament. Found guilty, he narrowly escaped the death penalty, and was condemned instead to a series of painful humiliations. In London, he was scourged and pilloried, his tongue was bored through with a red-hot iron (Fig. 10), and his forehead was branded with the letter B for blasphemer. He was then returned to Bristol, where he was made to enter the city seated backwards on a horse, after which he was whipped through the streets and finally imprisoned. In conscious imitation of Christ, Nayler suffered all this without complaint. Released three years later, he died on his way home.[2]

With few exceptions, historians have assumed that Nayler's entry into Bristol was a deliberate "reenactment of Christ's entrance into Jerusalem on Palm Sunday."[3] In a rare qualification of this judgment, Peter Toon distinguished between Nayler's action and its subsequent interpretation by the Bristol magistrates, affirming that Nayler "allowed his

---

1 Damrosch, *Sorrows*, 115. Although George Fox may have founded the Quakers, he would become their undisputed leader only after Nayler's death in 1659.

2 For balanced accounts of Nayler's life, see Brailsford, *Quaker*; Bittle, *James*; Damrosch, *Sorrows*; Neelon, *James*. For contemporary, but hostile, accounts of his entry into Bristol, see the letter of George Bishop to Margaret Fell, dated October 27, 1656, in Nayler, *Works*, 3:549–52; Deacon, *Grand*, 1–3; Farmer, *Sathan*, 2–4 (Nayler, *Works*, 3:558–59); Grigge, *Quaker's*, 3–4. Because the Julian calendar, according to which the year began on March 25, remained in use in England until 1752, Bishop dated his letter "27th 8th month, 1656"; he placed Nayler's entry "on the 6th day of the last week, between the 2d & 3d hour in the afternoon." Farmer, *Sathan*, title page and 2 (Nayler, *Works*, 3:557–58), confirms the date ("the 24 day of October, 1656") and the day of the week ("Friday"). For the speed with which news of Nayler's entry and trial spread to the continent, see Marriott, *Transnational*, 39–47.

3 Loewenstein, *Treacherous*, 227; see also, among many others, Wilson and Merli, "Naylor," 45–46; Bittle, *James*, 104; Damrosch, *Sorrows*, 1, 8, 57, 120, 163; Moore, *Light*, 39; Kuenning, in Nayler, *Works*, 1, iii; 3:iii; Neelon, *James*, xiii, 145; Marriott, *Transnational*, 36.

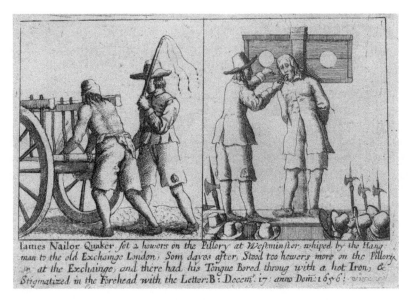

Iames Nailor Quaker *fet a howers on the Pillory at Weftminfter whiped by the Hang-man to the old Exchainge London, Som dayes after, Stood too howers more on the Pillory at the Exchainge, and there had his Tongue Bored throug with a hot Iron, & Stigmatized in the Forehead with the Letter: B: Decem. 17: anno Dom: 1656:*

Figure 10 James Nayler was whipped, pilloried, and had his tongue bored through with a red-hot iron. Etching, 1656. National Portrait Gallery, London.
© National Portrait Gallery, London.

followers to treat him as though he were the Messiah, making the Bristol authorities think he was reenacting Christ's entry into Jerusalem."[4] A few historians, limiting themselves to a careful précis of contemporary testimony, neither refer to Palm Sunday nor dispute the prevailing view.[5] In this chapter, I draw attention to weaknesses in the Palm Sunday interpretation of Nayler's entry. I then propose, as an alternative (and to my mind more persuasive) explanation, that his entry into Bristol was the last in a series of imitation royal entries, together constituting an imitation royal progress, which Nayler and his followers staged between Exeter and Bristol between October 20 and October 24. Finally, with due caution, I suggest that Nayler's progress may have been intended as a parody of triumphal entries, and that in this modified sense his enacted "sign" may after all be said to resemble Christ's anti-triumphal entry into Jerusalem.[6]

---

4 Toon, "Naylor."

5 Fogelklou, *James*, 175–228; Nicholls and Taylor, *Bristol*, 3:93–96

6 During the various stages of his trial, Nayler repeatedly called himself a "sign": Deacon, *Grand*, 18; Rich, *True*, 28 (Nayler, *Works*, 3:711); Burton, *Diary*, 1:47–48, 151 (Nayler, *Works*, 3:677; the excerpts from Burton's diary in Nayler, *Works*, 3:600–91, do not include the first of the two cited passages); Nayler et al., *O England, thy time is come*, in Nayler, *Works*, 3:585–99 (595). Nayler's sustained reluctance to interpret his own "sign" renders any subsequent interpretation, whether by his immediate judges or by later historians, including myself, necessarily tentative.

JAMES NAYLER'S ROYAL PROGRESS

A first weakness in the dominant view of Nayler's entry is that no contemporary witness is reported to have asserted that Nayler's entry into Bristol resembled Christ's entry into Jerusalem. Nor, as far the extensive records of the proceedings go, did those who interrogated Nayler in Bristol or, with one or two possible exceptions, in London. Nor did Nayler himself or any of his followers, despite being given ample opportunity. When the Bristol magistrates asked Nayler, "Wherefore camest thou in such an unusual posture, as two women leading thy horse; others singing Holy, holy, etc., with another before thee bareheaded, knee-deep in the highway mud?" Nayler did not offer the excuse that an attempt to reenact Christ's entry had been spoiled by inclement weather, but answered simply, "It tended to my Father's praise and glory."[7] Martha Simmonds, the leading figure among the women accompanying Nayler, was asked, "What made thee lead his horse into Bristol, and sing, Holy, holy, holy, etc., and spread thy garments before him?" She answered, "I was forced thereto by the power of the Lord."[8]

Four days before he rode into Bristol, Nayler had been released from prison in Exeter, where he had been detained for three months as a vagabond, a charge often brought against travelling Quakers.[9] Dorcas Erbery, who believed herself to have been raised from the dead by Nayler inside Exeter prison, and who remained with him during his ride to Bristol, was asked by the Bristol magistrates, "Why did you sing Holy, holy, etc., before James Nailor [sic] when he rode in?" She replied, "I did not sing then, but they that did were called to it by the Lord."[10] Nayler and his followers may have been avoiding the issue in order not to incriminate themselves, but they did not always exercise the same caution in answer to other questions. Erbery, for example, testified to her own resurrection without equivocation. She was asked, "Jesus Christ hath raised from the dead, hath Nailer [sic] done so?" She responded, "Yes, he raised me from the dead." The magistrate insisted, "How so?" Erbery explained, "I was dead two days, and he laid his hands upon my head, and said, Dorcas arise, and from that day to this, I am alive." Her own mother, she said, witnessed the miracle.[11]

Even in the unlikely event that Nayler and his followers were speaking guardedly on the matter of imitating Christ's entry, the same motives can hardly be attributed to their examiners. The summary of charges drawn up by the Bristol magistrates lists many

---

7 Deacon, *Grand*, 18–19; see also Farmer, *Sathan*, 15 (Nayler, *Works*, 3:568); Rich, *True*, 5 (Nayler, *Works*, 3:697).

8 Deacon, *Grand*, 24; see also Farmer, *Sathan*, 15 (Nayler, *Works*, 3:568).

9 Bittle, *James*, 88.

10 Grigge, *Quaker's*, 10; see also Deacon, *Grand*, 39a. The pagination of Deacon's work is confusing, running from 1 to 24, 33–40, and 33–47, in that order. For those numbers that appear twice, I designate the first sequence 33a–40a and the second sequence 33b–40b.

11 Grigge, *Quaker's*, 11; see also Deacon, *Grand*, 40a. Nayler himself was initially reticent about the nature of Erbery's recovery and his own part in it, telling the Bristol magistrates, "I can do nothing of myself" (Deacon, *Grand*, 18). Three years later, he wrote: "That report as though I had raised Dorcas Erbury [sic] from death, carnally, this I deny also" (Nayler, *Works*, 4:234). Gordon, "Nayler," 40:131, suggests that "in ranter language," talk of raising the dead "merely meant that [Nayler] had revived her spirits"; Nuttall, *James*, 14, agrees.

offences, but the reenactment of Christ's entry is not among them: "James Naylor [*sic*], a most eminent ringleader, and head of that faction [the Quakers] hath lately appeared here amongst us ... in horrid and open blasphemies, expressly avowed and owned by his nearest followers, as that he is the only begotten Son of God, and that there is none other than he; that he is the everlasting Son of righteousness, and that in him the hopes of Israel stand; that he is the King of Israel, and Prince of Peace; and calling him Lord and Master, saying his name shall be no more called James, but Jesus."[12] Historians have recognized that such charges stemmed at least in part from the failure of Nayler's examiners to acknowledge the distinction drawn by early Quakers between the Christ who was crucified in Jerusalem and the Christ understood to dwell in each true believer. So strongly did the Quakers affirm this present manifestation of Christ that they frequently spoke in such exaggerated and flowery language of those in whom Christ dwelt, and especially of those thought to have achieved a kind of sinless perfection, that it sounded as if they regarded individual Quakers as Christ himself.[13] Such rhetoric was prone to misunderstanding by outsiders. It was this apparent claim to be Christ, rather than any specific possibility that Nayler reenacted Christ's entry into Jerusalem, that so disturbed the Bristol authorities.

The same is true of the parliamentary committee that examined Nayler after his arrival in London, and of parliament as a whole when it debated the committee's report. Affirming that "James Nayler did assume the gesture, words, honor, worship, and miracles of our blessed Saviour," as well as his "names and incommunicable attributes and titles,"[14] the report was primarily concerned with establishing that Nayler had allowed himself to be worshipped as if he were Christ. It dwelt at length on the titles, believed by the examiners to be properly exclusive to Christ, that were accorded to Nayler in the writing and speech of his followers. Even when it dealt with the group's entry into Bristol, the report was more interested in establishing that the followers had sung "Holy, holy" to Nayler than it was in any possible mimetic relationship to Christ's entry into Jerusalem.

Only on rare occasions did the committee members or their witnesses come close to using language that could be construed as referring to Palm Sunday. At one point, Nayler distinguished between his "visible" self, to which worship was not due, and the "invisible" Christ within him, to whom worship was due. A committee member responded, "Then you say, that worship was due (to that which you call the invisible in you) to you as was given to Christ at Jerusalem?"[15] Later, an unnamed witness, who had been present at Nayler's examination in Bristol, referred to "the coming of this blasphemer into Bristol,

---

12 Grigge, *Quaker's*, 35.

13 For a helpful discussion of the "maddening exegetical labyrinth" (72) into which Puritans and Quakers wandered when confronting one another on this topic, see Damrosch, *Sorrows*, 69–114. Jacob Adriansz, a Dutch pamphleteer who interviewed Nayler in prison as he awaited trial in London, suffered the same confusion (Hull, *Rise*, 237–38).

14 Rich, *True*, 3–4 (Nayler, *Works*, 3:695).

15 Grigge, *Quaker's*, 9. The speaker appears to acknowledge Nayler's attempted distinction parenthetically, only to reject it with the following clarification: "to you."

in such a manner, personating the Lord Jesus Christ."[16] These two remarks are as close as anyone gets, during legal proceedings that lasted nearly three months, to any reference to Palm Sunday.

The full parliamentary debate made even less of the issue. At one point, Francis Drake, member of parliament for Amersham and a landowner with a history of opposition to religious disturbances,[17] addressed his colleagues: "Did he [Nayler] not suffer himself to be honored as our Saviour, in his riding through all the towns. What would you do if one should ride triumphantly through the country, as a ruler of the nations? Were not he to be proceeded against as a traitor?"[18] Another speaker complained that Nayler "was let out of Exeter gaol, and what was the issue? He rode in triumph, presently after, into Bristol."[19] The ultimate referent may have been Christ's "triumphal" entry into Jerusalem, but the more immediate concern appears to have been with illegitimate claims to political authority. A false claimant to power who rides "triumphantly through the country" in a series of presumptive royal entries, according to Drake, should be tried as a "traitor." The speakers had in mind illegitimate royal entries no less (and, perhaps, more) than blasphemous reenactments of Christ's entry into Jerusalem.

A second weakness in the prevailing interpretation of Nayler's sign is that there is no record of palms or other foliage being used. This, too, is a surprising omission if Nayler intended a straightforward reenactment of Christ's entry. Three of the four gospels report that, as Christ approached Jerusalem, he was met by a crowd bearing "branches of palm trees" or "leafy branches."[20] Although traditional Palm Sunday processions, in which participants carried branches of palm, olive, boxwood, yew, willow, or other foliage, had been banned in England since the Elizabethan Religious Settlement of 1559,[21] the biblical narrative was still familiar. Nayler himself, of course, had never seen a Palm Sunday procession. Nor had any of his followers or accusers, unless they had done so abroad.

Despite the lack of contemporary evidence that Nayler's followers displayed any kind of foliage, the Palm Sunday explanation took such a strong hold on the popular

---

16 Grigge, *Quaker's*, 13.

17 In his capacity as farmer of the manor of Walton-on-Thames, Drake had filed suits of trespass in 1549 against Gerrard Winstanley and other Diggers for occupying nearby St. George's Hill (Gurney, *Brave*, 139, 161–62; for Winstanley's account of the confrontation, see *A Watch-word to the City of London*, in Winstanley, *Complete*, 2:79–101). For a brief biography of Drake, see Winstanley, *Complete*, 2:445–46.

18 Burton, *Diary*, 1:55 (Nayler, *Works*, 3:622).

19 Burton, *Diary*, 1:262.

20 See chap. 10.

21 Palm Sunday processions in England came to a slow and uneven halt during the country's on-again, off-again Reformation. Carrying palms or other foliage in Palm Sunday processions was explictly permitted by Henry VIII in 1539 (Dixon, *History*, 2:164–65), forbidden by Edward VI in 1548 (Dixon, *History*, 2:491), mandated by Mary in 1553 (Dixon, *History*, 4:94, 129), and implictly forbidden along with all other processions "about the church or churchyard, or other place"—with the exception of Rogation Day "perambulations"—by Elizabeth I in 1559 (Dixon, *History*, 5:134; Gee and Hardy, *Documents*, 425–26).

Figure 11 *The Quaker James Naylor's Entry into Bristol.* Engraving, *Alte und neue Schwarm-Geister-Bruth, und Quäcker-Greuel,* 1702.

imagination that some later illustrators added palms and other foliage to their portrayals of Nayler's entry (Fig. 11).[22] A few historians have done likewise. Christopher Hill asserts that "Nayler's symbolic entry into Bristol," included "women ... strewing palms before him."[23] Vera Massey makes the same mistake: "The marchers ... laid branches on the cobbled roadway."[24] Sarah Covington writes of Nayler's "palm-wielding followers."[25] Such additions, flying in the face of the historical record, reinforce the distortions of the prevailing narrative.

"Having no palm fronds," according to David Neelon, "certain members of the entourage cast down their cloaks on the mud before the rider."[26] While there is ample evidence that Nayler's followers threw garments in the road ahead of him, their clothing

---

22 *Alte unde neue Schwarm-Geister-Bruth, und Quäcker-Greuel* (Frankfurt, 1702), between pp. 112 and 113.

23 Hill, *World,* 200; see also Hill, *God's,* 184.

24 Massey, *Clouded,* 58.

25 Covington, "Law's," 272; see also Mack, *Visionary,* 198.

26 Neelon, *James,* 145.

was not a substitute for palms. Members of the Jerusalem crowd had spread both "their cloaks" and unspecified "branches from the trees ... on the road."[27] Nayler's followers could easily have spread both garments and branches of local foliage, but chose only to throw clothing. They did so not only as they entered Bristol but also in other cities along the way from Exeter. Dorcas Erbery was asked by the Bristol magistrates, "Why did you so honor him, as to pull off his stockings, and put your clothes under his feet?" She answered, "Because he is the Lord of Israel, and is worthy of it."[28] Another of the women, Hannah Stranger, admitted that she "spread [her] garments at Wells, etc., to honor him,"[29] and that "she flung her handkerchief before him, because commanded so of the Lord."[30] Her husband, John Stranger, confessed to the parliamentary committee that "he saw others spread garments before [Nayler] in the way from Exon to Bristol."[31] Nayler himself, when asked by the Bristol magistrates, "Did not some spread their clothes on the ground before thee, when thou ridest through Glastonbury and Wells?" answered, "I think they did."[32] Opponents of Nayler repeated these testimonies in their own summaries of events.[33]

Although flinging a handkerchief and gloves and pulling off Nayler's stockings were elaborations on the original story, Nayler's followers were no doubt aware of the biblical precedent of spreading cloaks before Christ. Their actions, however, do not prove that the entries to Glastonbury, Wells, and Bristol were simple reenactments of Christ's entry. After all, the first biblical instance of such a practice was on the occasion of a military coup. When "the commanders of the army" acclaimed Jehu as king of Israel (ca. 842 BCE), "they all took their cloaks and spread them for him on the bare steps."[34] There is also the story of Walter Raleigh laying his cloak over a muddy puddle in the path of Elizabeth I. First published by Thomas Fuller in 1662, the story may well be apocryphal, but it does testify to the belief, only six years after Nayler's entry, that laying a cloak in mud might be a simple act of homage to royalty.[35] While it would be naïve to suppose that the spreading of garments by Nayler's followers contained no reference to Christ's entry, it is worth asking whether homage to royalty may also have been an intended referent.

A third weakness in the prevailing view of Nayler's entry has to do with the words reportedly sung by his followers. George Witherley, who had seen the party struggling

---

27 Matt. 21:8; compare Mark 11:8.

28 Grigge, *Quaker's*, 10.

29 Farmer, *Sathan*, 16 (Nayler, *Works*, 3:569).

30 Deacon, *Grand*, 35a. In the report of the parliamentary committee, the single "handkerchief" has become "two handkerchiefs" (Rich, *True*, 4; Nayler, *Works*, 3:696).

31 Nayler confirmed Stranger's testimony; for both, see Rich, *True*, 4 (Nayler, *Works*, 3:696).

32 Deacon, *Grand*, 19; see also Grigge, *Quaker's*, 6. In a later pamphlet, "Glory to God Almighty" (1659), Nayler repudiated "all their casting off their clothes in the way, their bowings and singings, and all the rest of those wild actions" (Nayler, *Works*, 4:232).

33 Deacon, *Grand*, 3; Farmer, *Sathan*, 3–4 (Nayler, *Works*, 3:559).

34 2 Kings 9:13.

35 Fuller, *History*, 1:419.

knee-deep through the mud outside Bristol and had suggested that they "come in the dry upon the causeway," testified to the city magistrates that he had been unable to make out distinct words: "he saith he knoweth not what they sang, but they made a humming noise."[36] Leo Damrosch comments: "This lack of conventional intelligibility was in fact a deliberate feature of Quaker worship. Just as prayer was to be spontaneous, so also singing ought to be 'making melody in your heart' " to the Lord.[37] Early Quakers, including Nayler himself,[38] scorned the use of prescribed hymns and metrical psalms, but some were open to singing psalms and improvised songs of praise when so moved by the Spirit. Although such spontaneous "singing in the Spirit" could be with intelligible words and phrases, it might also—like the "singing in the Spirit" of the modern charismatic movement—take the form of meaningless syllables or "humming many at once" set to "heavenly" melodies.[39]

But such singing, lacking intelligible content, could not easily have been judged blasphemous. We should not be surprised, therefore, that subsequent accounts added words to Witherley's inchoate "humming." Under questioning, Hannah Stranger admitted to singing "Holy, etc."[40] Dorcas Erbery denied singing "Holy, holy, etc.," but acknowledged that "they that did were called to it by the Lord."[41] Asked if some had sung, "Holy, holy, etc.," as he "rode through Glastonbury and Wells," Nayler replied that "he believed they did."[42] These may have been the only intelligible words they used, intermingled with otherwise unintelligible singing in the Spirit. As for his entry into Bristol, Nayler responded to a question as to whether some had been "singing before thee Holy, holy, holy, Hosannah, etc.," with a careful qualification: "Some there were that … sang praises to the Lord, such songs as the Lord put into their hearts … it might be the song of Holy, holy, holy, etc."[43] He admitted neither that the singing was directed to himself, nor that the women sang, "Hosanna." Nevertheless, in a letter dated October 27, 1656, two days after the examination by the Bristol magistrates, George Bishop wrote to Margaret Fell that Nayler "rode through the town, the women singing as they went, 'Holy, holy, holy, hosannah.'"[44] Bishop and Fell were both Quakers trying to distance themselves from Nayler's actions.

---

36 Farmer, *Sathan*, 3 (Nayler, *Works*, 3:558). Deacon, *Grand*, 2, adds his own hostile gloss to Witherley's testimony: "He saith that they sang, but sometimes with such a buzzing mel-ODIOUS noise that he could not understand what it was."

37 Damrosch, *Sorrows*, 149, citing Eph. 5:19.

38 Nayler, *Works*, 1:320.

39 Carroll, "Singing"; Bloechl, "Illicit," 152–62. For Nayler's defence of "singing in the Spirit," see, e.g., *Works*, 1:96, 228.

40 Deacon, *Grand*, 35a.

41 Grigge, *Quaker's*, 10.

42 Grigge, *Quaker's*, 6.

43 Deacon, *Grand*, 5.

44 Nayler, *Works*, 3:550.

None of Nayler's party admitted to singing "Hosanna." Yet it was this cry, rather than "Holy, holy, holy" that, according to the biblical narrative, the crowd shouted as Christ entered Jerusalem, and the children repeated when he reached the temple area.[45] Nor is there any mention in the records of anyone singing, or being charged with singing, "Blessed is he who comes in the name of the Lord." This acclamation immediately follows "Hosanna" in the gospel accounts,[46] and it had been for more than a millennium the verbal centrepiece of liturgical celebrations of Palm Sunday. If the imitation of Christ's entry had been the main focus of either Nayler's actions or the subsequent interrogations, the omission of this acclamation would have been an odd oversight.

"Holy, holy, holy," on the other hand, has nothing to do with Christ's entry into Jerusalem. It is the cry of the seraphs in Isaiah's vision of God "sitting on a throne, high and lofty." The six-winged angels call to one another, "Holy, holy, holy is the Lord of hosts; the whole earth is full of his glory."[47] The words are heard again in John of Patmos's similar vision of God on his throne. In this instance, the "four living creatures," each with "six wings," sing, "Holy, holy, holy, the Lord God the Almighty, who was and is and is to come."[48] If Nayler's examiners could prove that Nayler had accepted praise from his followers in such terms, they could in good conscience find him guilty of blasphemy. Accordingly, it was this phrase, rather than "Hosanna," on which they focused.

The parliamentary committee probed this matter at length. Under questioning, Dorcas Erbery admitted that those who sang "Holy, Holy" did so to "him that rode upon the horse." Martha Simmonds was asked "whether she did sing the words, 'Holy, Holy,' before the said James Nayler." She answered inconclusively, "It is my life to praise the Lord." Posed the same question, Hannah Stranger "answered, she could not well remember the words." Nayler was reluctant to verify specific words, but clear that whatever words may have been sung were sung to God, not to himself. Asked once, he replied, "There were praises sung to the Lord." Asked a second time, he "answered that he heard those words." A third time, he responded "that there was a psalm sung, such a one as the Lord was pleased to give into the hearts of them that sang. And being asked as to the words of the psalm, whether they were not 'Holy, holy,' said, 'It may be it was; very like it might be so.' "[49] Despite the uncertainty of the witnesses, the committee concluded that "James Nayler riding through a town in Somerset, his company spread their garments and sang, 'Holy, holy,' before him; and also sang the like at his entrance into Bristol."[50]

---

45 Matt. 21:9, 15; Mark 11:9–10; John 12:13.

46 Compare Luke 20:38, which omits "Hosanna," but includes "Blessed is the king who comes in the name of the Lord!"

47 Isa. 6:1–3. The words later became part of the Te Deum.

48 Rev. 4:8.

49 Rich, *True*, 4–5 (Nayler, *Works*, 3:696–67). In 1654, Nayler had protested "that ever I did say that I was as holy, just, and good as God is an untruth, and was never spoken by me, nor ever did it enter into my thoughts" (*Works*, 1:368).

50 Rich, *True*, 4 (Nayler, *Works*, 3:695).

Even so, the words "holy, holy" were not by themselves sufficient proof that Nayler's followers had been worshipping him. To serve that purpose, they had to be amplified to include the more explicit language of Isaiah's and John's visions. The committee therefore appended to their report "some further evidence." One of those responsible for guarding the house to which Nayler and his followers were confined informed the committee "that the usual posture of James Nayler is sitting in a chair," while others kneel or sit on the floor, "singing these and divers other words to the like purpose, viz., 'Holy, holy, holy to the Almighty, to the true God, to the great God; and glory to the Almighty,' etc." Two members of parliament, having been "at the place where Nayler is now a prisoner," reported similar sights and sounds. This information confirmed the members of the committee in their conviction that Nayler was being hailed as the thrice-holy, almighty Lord. But as Richard Rich, one of Nayler's most consistent supporters, objected in his published notes to the committee's report, the singing may have been nothing more than a spontaneous outburst of praise to God. "Are you angry," he asks, "that others should sing praises to the Lord God, and is this your further evidence of James Nayler's blasphemy?"[51]

After the full parliament had found Nayler guilty of "horrid blasphemy,"[52] several opponents of the Quakers quickly published accounts of his acts, his examination, and his punishment. These took it for granted that Nayler's followers had sung to him the songs of angelic worship heard by Isaiah and John of Patmos. John Deacon, who had taken part in the examination in Bristol, told his readers unequivocally that the words sung on the approach to Bristol had been "Holy, holy, holy, Lord God of Sabbath [sic], etc."[53] "Sabbath" is is a misspelling of "Sabaoth," the Hebrew word usually translated "of hosts" or "almighty" in English versions of Isaiah. "The Lord of Hosts" had appeared above Cromwell's profile on the commemorative medal issued after the Battle of Dunbar, but Cromwell had not been charged with blasphemy.[54] Ralph Farmer, a Bristol clergyman, placed on the title page of his account the confident assertion that the women leading Nayler's horse had been "singing 'Hosannah,' and 'Holy, Holy, Holy, Lord God of Israel.' "[55] What may in the first place have been nothing more than spontaneous and often unintelligible singing in the Spirit had become, in the continual hostile retelling, songs of praise to an enthroned divinity. In any case, even if—as seems to me unlikely—Nayler's followers were guilty as charged, their singing would still be no evidence that Nayler intended to reenact Christ's entry into Jerusalem. No one on the first Palm Sunday sang "Holy, holy, holy" to Christ.

A fourth weakness in the prevailing narrative is the fact that Nayler rode a horse, not a donkey. Although the gospels variously report that Jesus rode "a young donkey," "a colt, the foal of a donkey," or simply "a colt,"[56] Christian tradition is united in affirming

---

51 Rich, *True*, 26–27 (Nayler, *Works*, 3:708–9).

52 Burton, *Diary*, 25–143 passim (Nayler, *Works*, 3:602–73); Deacon, *Grand*, 23; Damrosch, *Sorrows*, 196.

53 Deacon, *Grand*, 2. For Deacon's earlier attack on Nayler, see Nayler, *Works*, 3:13–46.

54 See chap. 4.

55 Farmer, *Sathan* (Nayler, *Works*, 3:557).

56 See chap. 10.

that he rode a donkey. All the contemporary accounts of Nayler's entry into Bristol agree that the Quaker leader rode a horse.[57] Most historians have passed over this discrepancy without comment. David Hume noted it, but offered an inadequate explanation. Nayler, he wrote, "entered Bristol, mounted on a horse: I suppose, from the difficulties in that place of finding an ass."[58] Damrosch supposes Hume's attitude to be one of "deadpan mockery ... The entry into Bristol is made ridiculous by the substitution of an English horse for the Biblical ass."[59] Donkeys were not, however, in short supply in rural England at the time; indeed, they may have been more plentiful than horses.[60] It is unlikely that Nayler's decision to ride a horse was prompted by a scarcity of donkeys.

Other scholars have gone further, replacing the horse of the historical records with the donkey required by the Palm Sunday narrative. Christopher Hill writes of "Nayler's symbolic entry into Bristol in 1656, riding on a donkey."[61] Susan Wiseman imagines "the Quaker James Nayler entering Bristol on a donkey in duplication of Christ's entry into Jerusalem."[62] Theodore Wilson and Frank Merli opt for a hybrid: "James Naylor (*sic*) ... rode a mule into Bristol in a pathetic parody of Christ's entry into Jerusalem."[63] The inherited scholarly narrative thus overrides the historical evidence, which states clearly and repeatedly that Nayler rode a horse.

If Nayler had intended a straightforward reenactment of Christ's entry, he would have ridden a donkey. Why then did he ride a horse? The answer may be simple enough: Christ rode a donkey, but kings rode horses. Even royal entries that borrowed the language and iconography of Palm Sunday stopped short of using a donkey; while claiming to imitate Christ, kings rode on horseback or in a horse-drawn carriage. Nayler's horse is further evidence that the primary referent for his enacted sign was not Christ's entry into Jerusalem but more recent royal—or, in the case of Oliver Cromwell, quasi-royal—entries.

A fifth weakness in the standard interpretation of Nayler's entry is that it took place in October, rather than on or near the historical date of the Sunday before Easter. One could make the case that the timing of Nayler's entry was determined by his release from

---

57 Bishop to Fell, in Nayler, *Works*, 3:550; Deacon, *Grand*, 1–3, 5, 18, 24, 39a; Grigge, *Quaker's*, 3, 6; Farmer, *Sathan*, title page, 2–3, 15 (Nayler, *Works*, 3:557–58, 568); see also Hull, *Rise*, 247, who translates two lines of "doggerel verse" from an anonymous Dutch pamphlet published in 1657 as "He [Nayler] rode to Bristol all so quiet, / Upon one wretched, meagre steed."

58 Hume, *History*, 5:431.

59 Damrosch, *Sorrows*, 3.

60 Bough, *Donkey*, 53–54: "By the sixteenth century horses had become scarce because the army had taken them as mounts. Farmers needed a replacement and donkeys were again found to be useful in agriculture. Out in the fields in rural England, donkeys were ploughing, turning water-wheels, transporting the harvest and carrying goods to market." The relative shortage of horses may have been even more acute in the aftermath of the English Civil War.

61 Hill, *World*, 200; see also Hill, *God's*, 184: "on an ass."

62 Wiseman, *Conspiracy*, 53. Others who have made the same mistake include Mack, *Visionary*, 198; Brace, *Idea*, 145; Covington, "Law's," 272.

63 Wilson and Merli, "Naylor's," 45–46.

Exeter prison on October 20, rather than by a liturgical calendar to which Quakers did not adhere. Even so, if Nayler had intended to reenact Christ's entry for a public audience, October was not the best month in which to do so.

A final weakness is the repetition of Nayler's sign. His arrival in Bristol was at least the third in a series of entries staged by Nayler and his followers since leaving Exeter. We have already heard testimony from several members of the party, including Nayler himself, that clothes were strewn in the way and "Holy, holy" was sung in Glastonbury and Wells. Timothy Wedlock, one of four men in Nayler's party, went further, testifying that the sign was not confined to towns. When asked, "Wherefore didst thou honor him in towns, and not elsewhere?" he replied, "We did as well in commons [open countryside] ... in both as the Spirit of the Lord directed us."[64] Such admissions were widely reported elsewhere. John Deacon wrote that "passing through Wells and Glastonbury, this party bestrewed the way with their garments."[65] Ralph Farmer complained that they came to "play their pranks with us" in Bristol, "as well as in other places as they passed through." He, too, named Wells and Glastonbury. Some pages later, he repeated his complaint that they had staged "their pageantry in their way to and in Bristol."[66] Nayler spoke at his trial before parliament of "passing through" and "going into these towns," each time using a plural noun.[67] A parliamentary committee, appointed "to consider ... the great misdemanours and blasphemies of James Nayler, and others, at Bristol and elsewhere,"[68] reported that "his company spread their garments, and sang Holy, Holy, before him" while he rode "through a town in Somerset"—which could designate either Wells or Glastonbury—"and also sang the like at his entrance into Bristol."[69]

Damrosch notes that this repetition of "identical performance[s]" has largely gone "unnoticed by later historians."[70] The simple reason for this oversight may be that the evidence contradicts the prevailing view of historians, including Damrosch, that Nayler was reenacting Christ's entry into Jerusalem. Christ rode into Jerusalem on a donkey only once, but royal entries could be repeated in successive towns, and supplemented between towns by roadside acclamations. Collectively they become a royal progress. Like Nayler's horse, the repetition of his enacted sign suggests that the immediate referent was not Christ's singular entry but the multiple entries of royal and quasi-royal progresses.

None of these weaknesses alone undermines the prevailing view of Nayler's entry into Bristol, but their cumulative effect is enough to call it into serious doubt, leaving historians with perhaps three alternative options. First, we could continue to maintain

---

64 Deacon, *Grand*, 38a.

65 Deacon, *Grand*, 3.

66 Farmer, *Sathan*, 3–4, 20 (Nayler, *Works*, 3:559, 571).

67 Burton, *Diary*, 1:11 (Nayler, *Works*, 3:600), 47.

68 Burton, *Diary*, 1:10.

69 Rich, *True*, 4 (Nayler, *Works*, 3:695).

70 Damrosch, *Sorrows*, 147.

that Nayler and his followers intended to reenact Christ's entry, while admitting that they made a really poor job of it. The weaknesses would then be evidence not of our misreading but of the group's mimetic imprecision or incompetence. Second, we could grant that Nayler and his company did not intend to reenact Christ's entry as such, but still believe that their purpose was to acclaim Nayler as "Christ" or "king" in some way that his accusers were right to regard as the actions of a "blasphemer" or a "traitor." Choosing this option would not, of course, commit us to endorsing parliament's choice of punishment. Third, we could concede that Nayler and his company intended neither to reenact Christ's entry as such nor to acclaim Nayler as "Christ" or "king," but rather to mock those whose royal entries and other shows of power were, from a radical Quaker point of view, blasphemous claims to an authority that properly belongs only to King Jesus. Acknowledging that Nayler's ride from Exeter to Bristol was a pretty shabby imitation of a royal progress, we could point out that mockery is sometimes better served by belittling ridicule than by exaggerated splendour.

I prefer the third option. In October 1656, as we saw at the close of Chapter 4, the time was ripe for a parody of Cromwell's drift towards royal pomp, his perceived aspirations to the throne, and what the radical dissenters understood to be a direct challenge to the exclusive authority of King Jesus. Six months later, such a parody would have been less urgent: in the spring of 1657, Cromwell refused the Second Protectorate Parliament's offer of the crown,[71] a step that Nayler could not have anticipated at the time of his journey from Exeter to Bristol. Nayler shared the concern that Cromwell was setting himself up in opposition to Christ. As a Quaker, too, he would have deplored all hierarchical pomp, even in such comparatively small matters as the demand that he remove his hat and use the polite second person plural ("you" rather than the familiar "thou") in the presence of those who had set themselves up as his social superiors.[72] Moreover, although Quakers did not formally embrace pacifism until 1660,[73] Nayler himself argued strenuously for peaceful non-resistance and a literal interpretation of Christ's command to turn the other cheek.[74]

The Swedish theologian Emilia Fogelklou, in a book first published in 1929 but too little heeded since, recognized that Nayler's entry was much less about Nayler than it was about Cromwell. Nayler's action, she observed, was "a protest against the type of ruler which more and more seemed to become embodied in Cromwell," a "'sign of repentance' that Christ was not to enter with arms or worldly power," and "a contrast to all visible authority and outward show, which had also entered the Protectorate."[75] Douglas Gwyn has since reached a similar conclusion. Although he accepts the conventional narrative that Nayler's followers sang "Holy, Holy, Holy, Hosanna" and cast "their

---

71 Knoppers, *Constructing*, 118–22.

72 Damrosch, *Sorrows*, 52–62. Kuenning, in Nayler, *Works*, 4:iv, notes that "Nayler's own refusal to doff his hat to Judge Steele was what had landed him in Exeter Jail."

73 Fox, *Declaration*; Brailsford, *Quaker*, 11–29; Weddle, *Walking*, 39–54, 234–37.

74 For example, Nayler, *Works*, 4:88.

75 Fogelklou, *James*, 145, 176, 207.

garments in his path, suggesting Jesus' entry into Jerusalem,"[76] Gwyn understands that "Jesus' entry into Jerusalem ... constituted the rejection of hierarchical kingship." He therefore suggests that "Nayler's entry into Bristol offered a similar critique of traditional, hierarchical kingship." He rightly points out, too, that Nayler's "sign was enacted at the very time Parliament was considering whether to make Cromwell's position as Protector hereditary," and that this "monarchical" scheme was "public knowledge and the focus of intense criticism by Friends [Quakers], who bid Cromwell to 'lay the crown at Jesus' feet.'"[77]

Taking only a small step beyond the insights of Fogelklou and Gwyn, a modified third option could suppose that Nayler did, after all, recall Christ's entry, but that he did so in the belief that Christ's entry had itself been a parody, rather than a poor imitation, of imperial triumphal entries. If this were the case, then Nayler's ride from Exeter to Bristol would have resembled Christ's entry not by attempting (and failing) to reenact it with some measure of visible and audible realism, but by sharing its parodic stance towards the conventional triumphal entries of the day. Biblical scholars who now understand Christ's entry as a parody of the imperial and other military entries of his time do so, as we shall see in Chapter 10, in accord with a much older tradition that also understood Christ to be publicly repudiating martial posturing and triumphal pomp. Whether Nayler knew this tradition, reached a similar conclusion from his own meditation on the Christian story, stumbled independently across a kindred form of performance art, or was (as he might have put it) enlightened by the indwelling Christ, is impossible to know. However he may have acquired this belief, it does not seem implausible to suppose that Nayler recalled Christ's entry into Jerusalem conceptually rather than mimetically, imitating Christ's entry by challenging the displays of civic pomp and military power of his own historical context rather than by staging a convincing reenactment of the biblical entry. If this was the case, then Nayler's muddy street theatre was an arguably more faithful and politically subversive commemoration of Christ's entry than anyone has previously dared to imagine.

---

76 Gwyn, *Covenant*, 165–66.

77 Gwyn, *Covenant*, 177.

Chapter 10

JESUS ON A JACKASS

THIS BOOK MIGHT logically (and chronologically) have begun with a close reading of the biblical story of Christ's entry into Jerusalem, paying careful attention to the underlying Greek and Hebrew texts. Recognizing that some readers might find such an opening gambit less than inviting, I have instead postponed consideration of the biblical material until a point in my narrative arc where, I hope, even the most secular reader will be eager to know what the original story actually said. James Nayler's parodic royal progress, indebted in its own way to the same story, provides a hinge on which I can now turn from the triumphal entries and elite Palm Sunday processions of Part 1 to a close reading of the narrative to which they claimed allegiance.

Christian tradition holds that Jesus of Nazareth rode a donkey into Jerusalem five days before his crucifixion, and that the crowd lining the way waved palms. Palms (or branches of other local foliage) were, as we saw in Part 1, a prominent feature of Palm Sunday processions from the earliest mention of such a procession by Egeria. Long a common feature of Roman triumphal entries, they were no less prevalent in the entries of Christian rulers. Live donkeys, by contrast, were absent from Palm Sunday processions until the fifteenth century, and were no less rigorously excluded from triumphal entries that otherwise borrowed freely from the language and iconography of Palm Sunday. Consistent with this bias, the day on which Christ's entry into Jerusalem was commemorated was called Palm (or sometimes Olive or Hosanna) Sunday, but never Donkey Sunday. In this chapter, I suggest that such a bias reversed the biblical evaluation of the crowd's palms and Christ's donkey.

I begin with the donkey, or at least with a fictional question about it. In her novel *Reflections in a Golden Eye* (1941), Carson McCullers wrote: "Leonora Penderton feared neither man, beast, nor the devil; God she had never known. At the very mention of the Lord's name she thought only of her old father who had sometimes read the Bible on a Sunday afternoon. Of that book she remembered two things clearly: one, that Jesus had been crucified at a place called Cavalry [sic] Hill—the other that once He had ridden somewhere on a jackass, and what sort of person would want to ride a jackass?"[1] McCullers's novel is set on an army base somewhere in the southern United States. Leonora Penderton likes horses, which may explain why she confuses Calvary and Cavalry, and why she cannot fathom the kind of person who would want to ride a jackass. Despite her confusion, Penderton anticipates recent scholarship on the nature of Jesus's mount, and poses a question about Jesus's character that goes to the heart of the story of Palm Sunday: "What sort of person would want to ride a jackass?"

Neither Penderton nor her elderly father would have found the term "jackass" in an English translation of the New Testament. Mark's gospel has Jesus send his disciples

---

1 McCullers, *Reflections*, 20–21.

in search of "a colt (*pōlon*) that has never been ridden."[2] Luke uses an almost identical phrase.[3] John specifies that Jesus found "a young donkey" (*onarion* = little donkey), and cites a passage from the Hebrew Bible, where the prophet Zechariah speaks of Israel's king coming "on a donkey's colt" (*epi pōlon onou*).[4] Matthew confuses matters by having Jesus tell his disciples to bring him two animals, "a donkey (*onon*)" and her "colt (*pōlon*)." In support, Matthew provides a longer version of Zechariah's prophecy: "Tell the daughter of Zion, Look, your king is coming to you, humble, and mounted on a donkey (*epi onon*), on a colt, the foal of a donkey (*epi pōlon huion hupozugiou*)."[5] Some scholars have sensibly suggested that Zechariah was using "Hebrew poetic parallelism," whereby one line of poetry paraphrases the previous line, and that the "donkey" and the "colt, the foal of a donkey" were the same animal.[6]

Even more plausibly, Kenneth Way argues for the identity of the donkey and the colt through a careful analysis of the increasingly specific Hebrew terms used by Zechariah: "humble and riding on a donkey (*ḥamōr*), on a colt (*'ayir*), the foal of a donkey (*ben-'athonōth*)." In biblical Hebrew, Way explains, *ḥamōr* "is the general term for donkey, which can be male, female, or an unspecified gender"; *'ayir* "always designates a male equid; it is usually the donkey/jackass, but it may also designate the male hybrid [i.e., mule]"; *'athon* "always designates the female donkey/jenny." The string of donkey terms in Zechariah's prophecy thus moves from the general to the specific: "Zion's king is riding on a donkey [*ḥamōr*], but not just any donkey. He is riding on a jackass ['*ayir*], but not just any jackass. He is riding on a purebred [*ben-'athonōth* = son of a jenny] jackass."[7] The Septuagint's use of *pōlos* to translate *'ayir* is misleading. Zechariah's *'ayir* is not a "young animal," but the adult "offspring of a jenny."[8] Penderton was right: the biblical Jesus rode a jackass.

Whether Jesus himself rode a jackass is another matter. The scholarly quagmire of the "historical Jesus" echoes with the voices of squabbling theologians, and I have no intention of wading into it. Perhaps we can agree simply that Jesus entered Jerusalem— for how else would he be present later in the week at his arrest and crucifixion?—and

---

2 Mark 11:2.

3 Luke 19:30 substitutes *pōpote* for *oupō*: both words mean "not yet" or "never."

4 John 12:14–15; Zech. 9:9.

5 Matt. 21:2–5. Matthew's account perhaps owes too much to the Septuagint, the pre-Christian translation of the Hebrew Bible into Greek, which has Zechariah's messianic king riding rather awkwardly "on an ass and a young foal" (*epi hupozugion kai pōlon neon*).

6 Calvin, *Harmony*, 2:292; more recently, Albright and Mann, *Matthew*, 251–52; Hare, *Matthew*, 238; Blomberg, "Matthew," 63–64. Derrett, "Law," 257, posits the use of an explicative conjunction ("riding on an ass *and* [i.e., namely] on a colt").

7 Way, "Donkey," 113–14. Köhler, *Kleine*, 52–57, had reached the same conclusion, prompting Kümmel, *Promise*, 117, to translate, "riding upon an ass, upon a male ass, the foal of a she-ass."

8 Way, *Donkeys*, 167; see also Köhler, *Kleine*, 56. The gospels' use of the word *pōlos* (colt) famously prompted Bauer, "Colt," to argue on semantic grounds that the biblical Jesus rode a horse. Bauer's argument was quickly refuted by Kuhn, "Reittier," and Michel, "Philologische"; see also Michel's authoritative entry in *TDNT*, s.v. πῶλος (6:959–61).

that, if he rode anything at all—and all the sources agree that he did—it was some kind of donkey.[9] The next step is to address Pendleton's astonished question as to why Jesus would ride such an animal in the first place.

The answer is not what the modern reader might expect. Riding a donkey was not generally regarded in the biblical world as an act of humility. Most people travelled on foot. As an economically "valuable" animal, the donkey "served as a mount for people of high standing." It was "a status symbol," even "so to speak, the 'Mercedes-Benz' of the biblical world."[10] For the messianic king to be described as "humble [Heb: *'onī*; Gk: *praus*] and riding on a donkey" in translations both of Zechariah and of Matthew's citation of Zechariah is misleading; some English versions prefer "gentle."[11] The significance of the donkey for Zechariah is clarified in the next verse: "He [the king] will cut off the chariot from Ephraim and the war-horse from Jerusalem; and the battle bow shall be cut off, and he shall command peace to the nations."[12] The point of the donkey is its unsuitability for war. No one willingly rides a donkey into battle. Zechariah's king comes in peace to establish peace.

Regardless of their disagreements on other matters, biblical scholars generally agree on this point. Leon Morris writes: "The ass ... was the animal of a man of peace, a priest, a merchant or the like ... A conqueror would ride into a city on a war horse ... The ass speaks of peace."[13] Hauerwas concurs: "Victors in battle do not ride into their capital cities ... on asses, but ... on fearsome horses ... This king does not and will not triumph through force of arms."[14] Borg and Crossan harmonize: "This king, riding on a donkey, will banish war from the land—no more chariots, war-horses, or bows. Commanding peace to the nations, he will be a king of peace."[15]

The idea has a long pedigree. Cyril of Jerusalem (313–386) taught his catechumens that Christ came "riding on ass ... not upon a chariot," very different from "a king clad

---

9 Tan, *Zion*, 140: "The best explanation for the existence of such a story is that there was an incident which involved Jesus riding into Jerusalem on an ass."

10 Way, *Donkeys*, 87, 99–100. Roman writers testify to the donkey's worth as a reliable pack, plow, and mill animal, and for its role in breeding mules, the highly valued offspring of a horse and a donkey: see, e.g., Columella, *Agriculture* 7.1 (2:230–33); Varro, *Agriculture* 2.1.14 (320–21), 2.8.3 (392–93), 3.2.4–7 (430–33). Pliny, *Natural* 8.68.167–70 (3:116–19), observed, "The profit made out of she-asses surpasses the richest spoils of war. It is known that in Celtiberia their foals have made 400,000 sesterces per dam, especially when mules are bred." An ordinary pack donkey might sell for something closer to five hundred sesterces, roughly equivalent to about five months' wages for an unskilled laborer. For more on ancient donkey prices, see Duncan-Jones, *Economy*, 249.

11 Zech. 9:9: Bible in Basic English, New Century Version, New International Version (1984). Matt. 21:5: these and other versions; Luz, *Matthew*, 3:7.

12 Zech. 9:10.

13 Morris, *John*, 587; see also Cranfield, *Mark*, 354; McComiskey, "Zechariah," 1166.

14 Hauerwas, *Matthew*, 181; see also Witherington, *Christology*, 107; Luz, *Matthew*, 3:7–8.

15 Borg and Crossan, *Last*, 4; see also Borg, *Jesus*, 174. Writing together, they insist (*Last*, 53) that Jesus's vision of peace entails "an absolute criticism not only of violent domination, but of any religious collaboration with it."

in [imperial] purple ... guarded by spearmen, and sitting on a golden chariot."[16] John Chrysostom (ca. 349–407) told his congregation in Antioch that Christ entered Jerusalem "not with an army in his train, but having an ass alone."[17] Augustine of Hippo (354–430) insisted that "Christ's kingship over Israel was not for the purpose of exacting tribute, of putting swords into his soldier's hands, of subduing his enemies by open warfare; but he was king of Israel in exercising kingly authority over their inward natures."[18] The author of the fifth-century *Incomplete Commentary on Matthew* was moved to soaring rhetoric: "Do you wish to know the gentleness of the one who is coming? Consider the image of his arrival. He does not sit on a golden chariot, shining with priceless purple. Nor is he mounted upon a foaming horse, the lover of discord and quarreling, which has a chest filled with glory's boasting, which sniffs out war from afar and rejoices at the sound of the war trumpet and, when it sees a bloody battle, says in its own heart, 'It is well done.' Rather, he sits upon the ass of tranquility, a friend of peace."[19]

Jesus's arrival in Jerusalem was thus very different from any conventional triumphal entry of his day. When a military victor entered a conquered city, he did so as a warrior at the head of an army, at best promising peace while threatening violence against further resistance, or at worst allowing his troops to rape and pillage. When a Roman general returned home, if his victory had been important enough, he entered the city in triumph, surrounded not only by his own army but also by a lavish processional display of captives and spoils.[20] Even peacetime rulers, entering subject cities to ostentatious displays of welcome, ordinarily did so on horseback with a substantial armed guard. Pontius Pilate, arriving in Jerusalem to preside over an assize at the season of the Jewish Passover, was no exception: "The soldiers who travelled with him would have been an intimidating group ... [of] both infantry and horsemen ... Given the massive increase in Jerusalem's population during the festival, the Jews' prior record of inciting troubles at festivals, the Romans' intention to maintain order, and the analogy of troops required to put down both previous and later disturbances, it is not unlikely that something on the order of one thousand troops would have been with Pilate."[21] Jesus rode a donkey and was accompanied by a small band of unarmed disciples.

----

16 Cyril of Jerusalem, *Catechesis* 12, 10 (*PG* 33:735–38), in W*orks*, 1:232–33.

17 Chrysostom, *Homilies*, 245 (Homily 66, 1).

18 Augustine, *Lectures*, 284 (Tractate 51, 4).

19 *Opus imperfectum*, in *PG* 56:601–946 (col. 637); trans. Simonetti, *Matthew*, 125; see also *Incomplete Commentary*, 2:296. Formerly attributed to John Chrysostom, the *Opus imperfectum* is now thought to have been "written by an Arian bishop or priest, who lived in the second or third quarter of the fifth century" (Van Banning, *Opus*, v). For the argument that parts of it are the work of John Scotus Eriugena (ca. 810–ca. 877), see Piemonte, "Recherches."

20 For the Roman triumph, see Versnel, *Triumphus*; Beard, *Roman*. For a strong argument against the now-discredited notion that Christ's entry was modelled on the imperial *adventus*, see Mathews, *Clash*, 24–39; for genuine New Testament references to Roman triumphs, see 2 Cor. 2:14; Eph. 4:8; Col. 2:15.

21 Kinman, *Jesus*, 170.

Jesus's choice of a donkey affirmed his commitment to peace, but it also allowed him to engage in a parody of military entries. Hans Leander understands Christ's entry into Jerusalem as "a parodic undermining of imperial notions of power."[22] Hauerwas describes it as "an unmistakable political act," one that "parodies the entry of kings and their armies."[23] Borg and Crossan see it as "a deliberate lampoon" of such entries,[24] including that of Pontius Pilate, who probably rode into Jerusalem "seated upon a horse or riding a chariot."[25] Jesus and Pilate may even have ridden into Jerusalem simultaneously from opposite sides of the city, the Jewish teacher on his donkey implicitly critiquing the heavily defended Roman governor on horseback.[26] Jesus's entry was not the "triumphal entry" imagined by a long tradition of subsequent Christian rhetoric and processional performance; it was "nontriumphal,"[27] "atriumphal,"[28] or even "anti-triumphal."[29]

Whether the crowd understood Jesus's parodic and, more importantly, peaceful intent is another matter. The palms offer a clue. John's gospel insists, with double emphasis, that the crowd "went out to meet" Jesus with "palm branches of palm trees" (*ta baia tōn phoinikōn*).[30] Unlike the donkey, palm branches bore connotations of Jewish military victory. In 164 BCE, four years after the Syrian forces of Antiochus IV Epiphanes had sacked Jerusalem and profaned its temple, Judas Maccabeus recaptured most of the city. The rededication of the temple was joyously celebrated for eight days "in the manner of the festival of booths,"[31] which in its full form required temporary shelters to be built with "branches of palm trees, boughs of leafy trees, and willows of the brook."[32] Carrying "ivy-wreathed wands and beautiful branches and also fronds of palm (*phoinikas*)," Judas Maccabeus and his guerrilla warriors "offered thanksgiving" to God, "who had given success" in battle. They also decreed that the feast of dedication (Hanukkah) should be established as an annual Jewish festival.[33] Under Roman rule, the memory of Judas Maccabeus's war of liberation was probably such a strong

---

22 Leander, "With," 323.

23 Hauerwas, *Matthew*, 181–82.

24 Borg and Crossan, *Last*, 32.

25 Kinman, *Jesus*, 160–72.

26 Borg and Crossan, *Last*, 2–5.

27 Duff, "March," 55.

28 Kinman, *Jesus*, 90–122; Blomberg, "Matthew," 65.

29 Crossan, *Jesus*, 128; Borg and Crossan, *Last*, 32.

30 John 12:13, trans. Morris, *John*, 584n38. Mark 11:8 says that members of the crowd spread "leafy branches" (*stibadas*) on the road; Matt. 21:8 calls these "branches from the trees" (*kladous apo tōn dendrōn*); Luke makes no mention of any kind of foliage.

31 2 Macc. 10:6.

32 Lev. 23:40.

33 2 Macc. 10:7–8. For an alternative account of the military exploits of Judas Maccabeus and the recapture of Jerusalem, see 1 Macc. 3–4, and, for the establishment of Hanukkah, Josephus, *Antiquities* 12, 316–26 (*Works* 7:163–69).

component of the feast of dedication that its palm branches became "associated with nationalistic aspirations."[34]

But Judas Maccabeus's victory had been incomplete. The Acra, a citadel fortified by Antiochus Epiphanes within Jerusalem, had held out. Occupied by Syrian forces and Jewish confederates for nearly thirty years, it was finally starved into submission by Simon Maccabeus in 141 BCE. Palm branches featured in Simon's triumphal entry no less than in his brother's: "The Jews entered [the Acra] with praise and palm branches (*baiōn*), and with harps and cymbals and stringed instruments, and with hymns and songs, because a great enemy had been crushed and removed from Israel." Simon declared this day, too, an annual festival.[35] John's gospel draws attention to the Maccabean background, combining terms from both episodes into a single emphatic phrase: "palm branches of palm trees" (*ta baia tōn phoinikōn*).[36]

Against the background of Maccabean resistance, its annual festal commemorations, and John's choice of vocabulary, it is likely that the waving of palm branches during Jesus's entry into Jerusalem signaled the crowd's "nationalistic hopes that in Jesus a messianic liberator had arrived."[37] If so, the crowd failed to understand the peaceful character of the donkey. While the crowd recalled the warfare of the Maccabees, Jesus was "intentionally enacting" Zechariah's prophetic vision, hoping to persuade "a generation headed for war" against the Romans that "the alternative of peace was still open."[38] Or, as R. H. Lightfoot put it, perhaps Jesus rode a donkey "in silent protest against the multitude's misunderstanding of his mission."[39] The order of events in John's gospel implies as much: "Jesus found a young donkey and sat on it" only after the crowd had met him with "branches of palm trees."[40]

The same misunderstanding may explain other elements of the crowd's behaviour. "Spreading their cloaks on the road"[41] may have been "a spontaneous expression of respect,"[42] but it is striking that the only biblical precedent for such a gesture announced a bloody military coup. When "the commanders of the army" acclaimed Jehu as king of Israel (ca. 842 BCE), "they all took their cloaks and spread them for him on the bare steps."

---

34 Farmer, "Palm," 64.

35 1 Macc. 13:49–52. For the building of the Acra, see 1 Macc. 1:33–40. For an alternative account of the recapture and subsequent fate of the Acra, see Josephus, *Antiquities* 13, 208–17 (*Works*, 7:332–37).

36 Farmer, "Palm," 65. 1 Macc. survives in the Septuagint Greek translation of a lost Hebrew original; 2 Macc. was composed in Greek.

37 Köstenberger, "John," 470; see also Lightfoot, *John*, 238; Daly-Denton, "Psalms," 126.

38 Borg, *Jesus*, 174. Cadoux, *Historic*, argues that Jesus's entire ministry was shaped by "his deep interest and concern over the dangerous mutual attitude of Israel and Rome, and his strenuous effort to avert the threatened clash of arms between them" (18); see especially 163–74, 266–79.

39 Lightfoot, in an editorial note to Farmer, "Palm," 66.

40 John 12:12–14.

41 Luke 19:36; see also Matt. 21:8; Mark 11:8.

42 Cranfield, *Mark*, 350.

To secure power and eliminate religious syncretism, Jehu rode to successive slaughters in a chariot, quickly killing every member of the reigning royal family, including "seventy sons" of Ahab, as well as "all his leaders, close friends, and priests."[43] Jehu was the kind of leader that many of Jesus's contemporaries hoped might drive out the Romans. By his "anti-triumphal" entry, Jesus publicly repudiated such a role.

Military aspirations also lurk behind the acclaim shouted by the crowd in all four gospels: "Blessed is he who comes in the name of the Lord!"[44] Psalm 118, from which this cry is taken, is a Jewish "king's hymn of thanksgiving for delivery from death [in battle] and for a military victory."[45] It bristles with such verses as "Yahweh is for me, my Great Warrior, so I shall gloat over my enemies" and the thrice-repeated "in Yahweh's name indeed I cut off their foreskins." The hero is imagined passing through the gates of Jerusalem in triumph: "This is the gate that belongs to Yahweh, let the triumphant enter it."[46] The cry of "Hosanna," which accompanies "Blessed is he who comes in the name of the Lord!" in both Matthew and Mark's gospels,[47] also expresses a longing for liberation from Roman rule. "Hosanna ... is not in any way a cry of praise," but "an ancient liturgical text, a cry to the anointed king for deliverance."[48] It means "save, now" or "save, please," and the phrases in which it appears are best translated as "Save (or help), please, O Son of David!" or "Save (or help), please, O Highest!"[49] In this context, as elsewhere in contemporary Jewish tradition, "it had the meaning, 'Save us from the Romans!' "[50] The actions and words of the crowd surrounding Jesus thus invoke a set of biblical images that are radically different from the one evoked by Jesus's donkey.

Perhaps this is why Luke included the episode in which Jesus paused during his descent from the Mount of Olives to weep over Jerusalem. Jesus addressed the city: "If you, even you, had only recognized on this day the things that make for peace! But ... the days will come upon you, when your enemies will set up ramparts around you and surround you, and hem you in on every side. They will crush you to the ground, you and your children within you, and they will not leave within you one stone upon another."[51] Whether Luke's account was written before or after the First Jewish–Roman War (66–73 CE), which included the Roman destruction of Jerusalem (70 CE),[52] the words ascribed to

---

43 2 Kings 9:13; 10:1, 11.

44 Matt. 21:9; Mark 11:9; Luke 19:38; John 12:12; see also Ps. 118:26.

45 Dahood, *Psalms*, 3:155.

46 Ps. 118:7, 10–12, trans. Dahood, *Psalms*, 3:154.

47 Matt. 21:9; Mark 11:10.

48 Albright and Mann, *Matthew*, 252.

49 Pope, "Hosanna," 291.

50 Leander, "With," 327.

51 Luke 19:41–44.

52 For the early date, see, e.g., Easton, *Luke*, 289; Morris, *Luke*, 360; and, for the late date, Bultmann, *History*, 36, 123; Craddock, *Luke*, 228. Dodd, "Fall," accepts a late date for Luke as a whole, but argues persuasively for an early date of this passage. Evans, *Luke*, 685, qualifies Dodd's conclusions. Kinman, *Jesus*, 137n20, summarizes.

Jesus reinforce the impression that he anticipated the rejection of his message of peace by a generation bent on armed rebellion.

The peace to which Jesus refers in this warning is too often understood by Christians in terms of the relationship of the Jews to God, and the destruction of Jerusalem as the result of the Jews' "failure ... to recognize the salvation that has come in the person of Jesus."[53] But C. F. Evans argues cogently that Jesus's primary concern here "is not the peace (salvation) of God or peace as reconciliation with God, but peace with Rome."[54] Jesus's tears, in other words, have an immediate political context. Whether through supernatural foreknowledge or simple political acumen, he predicts the disastrous consequences for Jerusalem of armed Jewish resistance against Rome. Too many in the crowd around him and in the city below are blinded by a religious nationalism that will only intensify over the next thirty years. Jesus rides a donkey as a sign of peace. The crowd waves palm branches and greets him as a warrior-king. Jesus weeps over their misunderstanding.

I know of no Palm Sunday processions in which Jesus weeps. I know of many Palm Sunday processions and triumphal entries that have celebrated military power. We met several in Part 1. Now, in Part 3, we turn at last to Palm Sunday traditions in which pomp is either muted or altogether absent and in which donkeys, whether wooden or (finally!) alive, play a starring role.

---

53 Chance, *Jerusalem*, 116–17; Bock, *Luke*, 314–15: "Peace with God is not possible for those who reject Jesus."

54 Evans, *Luke*, 684; see also Cadoux, *Historic*, 266–67, 272.

PART THREE:

DONKEYS

I. A Scarcity of Donkeys: From Udine to El Alto

Chapter 11

UNDER MUSLIM RULE

TO THE BEST of my knowledge, the earliest surviving record of anyone riding a live donkey in a Palm Sunday procession comes from Udine, in northeast Italy, in the early fifteenth century. The rider was probably an altar boy. The chapter accounts of Udine cathedral record payment of "twelve soldi [pence]," on Palm Sunday, 1424, "to the boy who went on the ass in place of Christ" (*puero qui fuit super asellum loco Christi*). A similar payment of "fourteen soldi" was made in 1461 "to the young boy who rides the ass with the bell-ringer who leads the colt" (*al puto chel chavalca l'aseno col campanaro che mena l'asenello*). According to Guiseppe Vale, subsequent payments were recorded "almost every year."[1] Since the Aquileian rite used in Udine differed from the standard Roman rite,[2] it may be that the live donkey was also exceptional.

An argument from a thousand years of silence is not conclusive, but a carefully documented silence can still be persuasive. In this chapter, I trace the long absence of donkeys from the records of Palm Sunday processions in Jerusalem. Although such processions began there some two centuries earlier than in Europe, the first reliable record of a live donkey taking part occurs fifty years later than in Udine. The father superior of the Franciscan community in Jerusalem was the rider. The silence from which I argue is thus longer in Jerusalem than it is elsewhere. In Chapter 12, I supplement documentation with explanation, offering a more detailed account of why live donkeys should have been so long excluded from Palm Sunday processions even as the surrounding liturgies freely acknowledged that Christ himself rode a donkey. In Chapter 13, I welcome the more recent proliferation of live donkeys onto the processional stage of Palm Sunday.

I noted earlier the absence of donkeys from Palm Sunday processions in Jerusalem between Egeria's visit to the city around 384 and its capture by Muslim forces in 638.[3] My return to Jerusalem allows me both to document the ongoing absence of donkeys and to expose a few misguided rumours of their presence. It also permits me to celebrate a different kind of ecclesiastical restraint. Under Muslim rule, Palm Sunday processions had little option but to resist the temptations of triumphalism.

Jerusalem fell to the forces of the Rashidun caliph ʿUmar ibn Al-Khattāb in 638, after which it was ruled by various Muslim dynasties until the arrival of the First Crusade in 1099. Muslim rule resumed in 1187. On the whole, Muslim control afforded Christians considerable freedom and continuity of worship. The Palm Sunday ceremonial in the Greek *Typikon of the Holy Sepulchre*, compiled in Jerusalem in 1122 but containing

---

1 Vale, "Liturgia," 29, citing the "libri dei Dapiferi del Capitolo di Aquileia (Udine, Archivio Capitolare)"; see also Bernardi, *Drammaturgica*, 185.

2 For an accessible introduction to the Aquileian rite, see King, *Liturgies*, 1–51.

3 See chap. 5.

materials going back "at least to the first half of the tenth century,"[4] follows much the same pattern as it did in the earlier Armenian and Georgian liturgical books, but it does so in greater detail, suggesting a measure of processional elaboration rather than imposed restrictions during the intervening years.[5] One innovation required an olive tree to be carried the full length of the procession from Bethany and finally placed in front of the rock of Golgotha "in imitation of the crucifixion" (*kata mimēsin tēs staurōseōs*).[6] The Christian historian Yaḥyā ibn Saʿīd al-Anṭākī (d. ca. 1066) confirms the portage of "a large olive tree" through the streets of Jerusalem on Palm Sunday, with stops along the way for "readings and prayers." He adds that the Muslim governor of the city "rode on horseback with all his retinue, accompanying the Christians and parting the crowd."[7] There is no suggestion that anyone rode a donkey in the procession.

There were occasional threats to this freedom. In 938, according to some reports, "Christians were attacked during their Palm Sunday procession and the Muslims set fire to the gates of the Martyrium."[8] More seriously, in 1008, the Fatimid caliph Al-Hakim bi Amr Allah (996–1021) banned Palm Sunday celebrations not only in Jerusalem, but throughout his empire.[9] As part of a broader persecution of Jews and Christians lasting from 1008 until at least 1013, Al-Hakim also ordered the destruction of Jerusalem's Church of the Holy Sepulchre.[10] In 1030, Al-Hakim's son, the new caliph ʿAlī az-Zāhir agreed to allow the rebuilding and redecoration of the church at Byzantine expense, a task that was finally completed in 1048. Palm Sunday ceremonies may have resumed during the rebuilding.

Surviving copies of liturgical books from the crusader kingdom (1099–1187) also offer silent testimony to the absence of donkeys from the city's Palm Sunday procession.[11]

---

4 Uspensky, *Evening*, 167n188.

5 Papadopoulos-Kerameus, "Typikon," 2:1–28. For a summary in French, see Thibaut, *Ordre*, 16–19.

6 Papadopoulos-Kerameus, "Typikon," 2:17, 21; Thibaut, *Ordre*, 18–19, imagines that "several strong men" carried the tree and that the people "stripped" its foliage before placing it "at the foot of Calvary." Perhaps a tree was less offensive to Muslim sensibilities than a processional crucifix.

7 Yaḥyā, *Histoire*, 2:487. Also known as Yahya of Antioch, Yaḥyā was born in Egypt, left the country in 1015 during the caliphate of Al-Hakim bi Amr Allah, resetttled in Antioch, and died ca. 1066 (*ODB*, 3:2213).

8 Armstrong, *Jerusalem*, 256. Grabar, "Al-Ḳuds," 326, is the earliest (1986) reference I can find to this event. Yaḥyā, *Histoire*, 1:799–802, reports that a mob set fire to the gates of the church on the feast of Pentecost, 966.

9 Al-Hakim ruled from Cairo. Yaḥyā, *Histoire*, 2:487–88, notes the effect of the ban in both Egypt and Jerusalem.

10 For a balanced account of Al-Hakim's persecution of Jews and Christians, see Walker, *Caliph*, 205–14; for the political motives behind his destruction of churches, see Pruitt, "Method."

11 Schönfelder, "Prozessionen," 584–86, quotes from a fourteenth-century copy, now owned by the Biblioteka Kapitulna in Wrocław, Poland, of an original manuscript dated to between 1157 and 1187. Kohler, "Rituel," 412–13, quotes from a thirteenth-century ritual book, now owned by the Church of the Holy Sepulchre in Barletta, Italy, which was probably compiled from similar books used in Jerusalem's Church of the Holy Sepulchre before 1187. For English summaries of the Palm

By then, the procession had become even more elaborate, incorporating two distinct groups of worshippers, one representing Christ and his disciples arriving from Bethany, and another representing the crowd that went out from Jerusalem to acclaim him with palm branches. The first, accompanying the Latin patriarch and the relic of the true cross, set out from the tomb of Lazarus, on the southeast slope of the Mount of Olives; the second started at the Temple of the Lord with the blessing of palm and olive branches. Chanting psalms and antiphons along the way, the two groups met outside the city in the Valley of Jehoshaphat. Christ was represented by the conjunction of the true cross and the living patriarch. After the patriarch preached, the two groups entered Jerusalem through the Golden Gate. A boys' choir, on top of the gate, sang "Gloria, laus et honor." The sources agree that the patriarch descended the Mount of Olives carrying the reliquary of the holy cross in his own hands,[12] something he could have done easily enough on foot, but is unlikely to have attempted while riding a donkey. Two twelfth-century pilgrims to Jerusalem, John of Würzburg and Theoderich, also made passing reference to the city's Palm Sunday procession, but neither mentioned a donkey.[13]

The historiated lintel of the church of the Holy Sepulchre, now housed in the Rockefeller Museum in Jerusalem, also dates to the crusader kingdom. Further enlarged and renovated since its initial rebuilding in the previous century, the latest version of the church was consecrated in 1149, but the lintel itself may have been added at any point before the reconquest of the city in 1187 by Ṣalāḥ ad-Dīn Yūsuf ibn Ayyūb, the Ayyubid Sultan of Egypt and Syria, better known in the west as Saladin.[14] Molly Lindner has argued persuasively for an iconographic link between the sculpted images on the lintel and Jerusalem's Palm Sunday procession.[15] The images portray events in the last week of Christ's life from the raising of Lazarus to the Last Supper, including Christ's entry into Jerusalem, but their sequence deviates slightly from the biblical version. Lindner therefore proposes that the lintel reflects the order in which twelfth-century worshippers passed commemorative sites during their processional descent from the Mount of Olives on Palm Sunday. She is careful, however, not to suggest that the sculpted image of Christ on a donkey, now badly damaged,[16] testifies to the twelfth-century processional participation of a live donkey and rider. Visual affirmation that the biblical Christ rode a donkey no more testifies to Palm Sunday processional practice than does the verbal affirmation contained in the day's biblical readings and antiphons.

Sunday processional data contained in these documents, see Lindner, "Topography," 90; Schein, *Gateway*, 101–2.

12 Schönfelder, "Prozessionen," 585; Kohler, "Rituel," 412.

13 John of Würzburg, *Description*, 19; Theoderich, *Description*, 34–35, 40.

14 Borg, "Observations," 40.

15 Lindner, "Topography."

16 The image of "Christ mounted on an ass, with the colt beside the ass," was still intact when Niccolò of Poggibonsi saw it in 1347 (Niccolò da Poggibonsi, *Libro*, 1:51–52; trans. Bellorini and Hoade, 12).

After Ṣalāḥ ad-Dīn's victory restored Muslim rule over Jerusalem, the Franks were expelled, but a small community of Syrian and Armenian Christians was allowed to remain. Four years later, Christian forces recaptured the northern coastal city of Acre (now Akko), which became the capital of a thin coastal crusader kingdom of Jerusalem in exile. In 1192, at the close of the Third Crusade, a treaty negotiated by Ṣalāḥ ad-Dīn and Richard I of England granted unarmed Christian pilgrims and merchants the freedom to visit Jerusalem. The first small Franciscan community in the Holy Land may have been established in Acre as early as 1217.[17]

Two years later, Francis of Assisi himself launched his own mission to the region, travelling via Acre to Egypt, where he arrived during the Fifth Crusade's prolonged siege of Damietta. Taking advantage of a brief truce, Francis reportedly gained an amicable audience with the sultan of Egypt, al-Malik al-Kâmil, before returning home from Acre in 1220.[18] Franciscans established a temporary community in Jerusalem during the thirteenth century,[19] but it was not until 1333 that the order gained a permanent foothold there.[20] After 1342, they regarded themselves as papally appointed custodians of the Holy Land, and the Franciscan father superior in Jerusalem was known as the Guardian of Mount Zion.[21]

It is from this context that the first rumor of a Palm Sunday donkey emerges. According to Miroslav Labunka, "A description of a Palm Sunday procession taking place in thirteenth century Jerusalem ... reveals that the patriarch of that city is riding a foal of an ass in the procession ... [The description] comes from the pen of a Franciscan friar named Caremus."[22] Other scholars had made a similar claim. In 1935, Georg Ostrogorsky had credited "the Franciscan monk Caremus, who visited the Holy Land in the thirteenth century," with the eyewitness testimony that "the archpriest sits on the jenny" during the Palm Sunday procession. In 1898, Aleksei Maltsev, writing in both German and Russian, had pushed the visit of "Careme" or "Karem (*Каремъ*)" back to "the beginning of the thirteenth century," and had quoted at length the friar's account of "the chief shepherd (*Erzhirt/arkhipastyr*), sitting on the donkey (*Esel/oslya*)," riding downhill to Jerusalem and entering the city through the Golden Gate, while the crowd

---

17 Roncaglia, *Francis*, 35; Arce, *Miscelánea*, 3:77–79.

18 Roncaglia, *Francis*, 26–30; for an extended study of the meeting with al-Kâmil, see Tolan, *Saint*. Clareno, *Chronicle*, 28.33, was the first to claim, in 1326, that Francis visited Jerusalem on his way home; see also Tolan, 147–61, and for more on "the legend of Francis's pilgrimage to Jerusalem," 257–93.

19 Roncaglia, *Francis*, 41–45.

20 Tolan, *Saint*, 258.

21 For the relevant papal bulls, "Gratias agimus" and "Nuper charissimae," issued on November 21, 1342 by Clement VI, see *Bullarium*, 6: 95–96; for a translation of the former, see "Juridical Constitution of the Custodian of the Holy Land," *Custodia Terrae Sanctae*, 2011, www.custodia.org/default.asp?id=432. For the duties and privileges of the Father Guardian, see Suriano, *Trattato*, 1.24 (66–67); trans. Bellorini and Hoade, 79.

22 Labunka, *Legend*, 133.

sings hosannas and strews "grass, flowers, and their clothes along the way."[23] Maltsev's unacknowledged source was Konstantin Nikol'skii, who in 1885 had been the first to date Karem's visit to "the beginning of the thirteenth century" and had provided the same long quotation in Russian.[24] Retreating even further to Nikol'skii's source, we uncover the truth behind the persistent rumor. In 1818, a German theologian, Johann Christian Wilhelm Augusti, had quoted the same long description in one of his own volumes, crediting it to "the Franciscan Franciscus Quarêsme, who in the beginning of the seventeenth century (*im Anfange des XVII Jahrhunderts*) was the papal envoy in Palestine." Nikol'skii had not only misread Augusti's date, mistaking XVII for XIII and thus advancing the event by four centuries, but had also obscured the identity of the original eyewitness. Franciscus Quaresmius (1583–1650) served in Jerusalem from 1616 to 1620 and again from 1625 to 1627. During this decade, he wrote a "historical, theological, and moral elucidation of the Holy Land," published in 1639, which includes the description of Palm Sunday faithfully reproduced by Augusti.[25] Although Quaresmius's account is a valuable testimony to Palm Sunday in early seventeenth-century Jerusalem, by which time a live donkey was an established part of the proceedings, it does not bear witness to a thirteenth-century donkey.

Another dubious notice of an early processional donkey comes from Ludolph von Suchem, who travelled widely in the Holy Land and beyond between 1336 and 1341. He wrote: "To [the Golden Gate] on every Palm Sunday, even to this day, a solemn procession of Christians is made before sunrise, and over this gate boys sing *Gloria, laus*, etc. Then the Archbishop of the Armenians enters the gate with an ass (*cum asino*), and is welcomed by the boys and the people even as Christ was there welcomed by the Jews."[26] Ludolph's use of the phrase "cum asino" (with an ass) rather than "super asinam" (on an ass) may mean that he understood the bishop to have walked alongside rather than ridden on the animal. It makes little difference. Ludolph was "a very gullible tourist,"[27] whose secondhand reports are not always to be trusted. His account of the Palm Sunday procession may well be secondhand, for he appears to have spent little time in Jerusalem, devoting to the city only three chapters out of a total of forty-five.

Further doubt is cast on Ludolph's notice by the report of the Franciscan Niccolò da Poggibonsi, who played an active role in Jerusalem's Palm Sunday procession just a few years later in 1347. Niccolò includes a wealth of details, but no donkey:

> Early on Olive Sunday, the bishop of the Armenians was dressed and attired, that is vested, in place of Jesus Christ, and my companion was placed on one side and I on the other of the bishop: we took the place of the apostles, and were so vested; and the crowds of people and Saracens followed us, and so

23 Maltzew, *Begräbniss*, 354–57.

24 Nikol'skii, *Sluzhbakh*, 75–76.

25 Quaresmius, *Historica*, 4.11 (2:254); for an English translation of this passage, see Flier, "Court," 80.

26 Ludolph von Suchem, *De itinere*, 76; translation adapted from Stewart, 100.

27 Kurdian, "Note," 104.

adorned we started on our way toward the Holy Sepulchre, all singing aloud. All the streets and windows of the houses were packed with Saracens, so that none could pass, but the Saracen marshals (*bastonieri*) caused the crowd to make way. Right behind us were carried two big olive trees and on top of them and amid the branches were several men, who pointing to the bishop, cried out words in very shrill voices [which, being in Arabic and Ethiopic, Niccolò could not immediately understand]. And yet the truth is that they spoke very good words and the multitude around them all sang in a loud voice, each one in his own tongue, that which was sung before Christ, as they cast olive branches and their garments on the way."[28]

It is hard to believe that Niccolò, walking alongside the bishop, would not have mentioned a donkey had there been one.

The first definitive reports of a Palm Sunday donkey in Jerusalem date from the late fifteenth century. By then, the Armenian bishop is no longer credited with playing the part of Christ; more plausibly, the donkey has a Franciscan rider. In the 1480s, Felix Fabri wistfully imagined "days of old," when "the Christians possessed the city," and complained that the Palm Sunday procession of his own day was hampered by the presence of Muslims. He did, however, note the presence of a donkey. Christians, he wrote, are forced "to hurry through Palm Sunday." Once they reach Bethphage, "they set one of the brethren in his priestly vestments upon an ass, and accompany him towards the city singing praises. As they descend the Mount of Olives the other Eastern Christians run to meet them with boughs of palm and olive and with strewing of garments in the way, and lead him as far as the brook Cedron, where the procession ends, for they dare not mount up towards the city singing praises in this fashion, lest the Saracens should break up their procession by pelting it with stones."[29] Fabri twice went on pilgrimage to Jerusalem. His first journey lasted from April to October 1480, the second from April 1483 to January 1484. In neither case was he in Jerusalem for Holy Week, so his description of the Palm Sunday procession is necessarily secondhand. His testimony to the use of a donkey, however, is borne out by an unequivocally reliable contemporary witness.

Francesco Suriano, who served as a Franciscan friar in Jerusalem between 1481 and 1484 and again between 1493 and 1515, described the "Olive Sunday" procession of his day. He was more sanguine than Fabri about the procession's effect on the city's Muslims:

All the friars go to Bethphage where they put the Father Guardian on an ass and then proceed in procession with great devotion and tears into Jerusalem to Mount Zion, with palms and olive branches in their hands singing: "Hosanna filio David benedictus qui venit in nomine Domini." And when they draw near to Mount Zion, they are met by all the Armenians,[30] religious and lay, who spread their cloaks and clothes under the ass: the street is decked with flowers and

---

28 Niccolò da Poggibonsi, *Libro*, 1:106–8; translation adapted from Bellorini and Hoade, 24–25.

29 Fabri, *Evagatorium*, 1:369–70; trans. Aubrey Stewart, 1:460.

30 For the cordial relationship between the Franciscans and the Armenian Christian community in Jerusalem, see Suriano, *Trattato*, 1.28 (75–76); trans. Bellorini and Hoade, 88.

carpets and other beautiful things, so that not only the Christians are incited to devotion, but also the Saracens.[31]

Since Suriano was himself, in 1493 and 1512, twice appointed to three-year terms as the Franciscan Guardian of Mount Zion,[32] he wrote as one who had ridden the processional donkey himself. Even so, Bellarmino Bugatti felt compelled to remark, in an editorial note, on the "peculiarity" of "the use of the ass"[33]: he understood Suriano to be testifying to an innovation.

In 1516, the Ottoman Turks gained control of Jerusalem. The rebuilding of the city walls, completed in 1541, included the closure of the Golden Gate, after which the Palm Sunday procession was diverted to Zion Gate in the southern stretch of wall. Further testimony to the Franciscan donkey comes from Boniface of Ragusa, who was in Jerusalem from 1552 to 1564. Like Suriano, he served as Guardian of Zion. Wearing "sacred vestments," and accompanied by "a deacon and a subdeacon, four singers, two candle-bearers, and a thurifer," he wrote, the "Guardian of Mount Zion" greets worshippers at Bethphage after lunch on Palm Sunday. Two friars quickly bring "a female donkey and her colt." The friars place their clothes on both animals, and then help the guardian onto the donkey. A multinational crowd of "Latins, Greeks, Armenians, Copts, Jacobites … Assyrians,[34] Maronites, and Chaldeans" scatters clothes along the way. Those whose clothes are traversed "by the precious animal on which the guardian who represents Christ is seated" are reckoned "blessed." Others scatter flowers and the foliage of trees, while all cry "Hosanna to the son of David."[35]

By the seventeenth century there is evidence not only of growing local resistance to the procession but also of Protestant travellers' scorn. William Lithgow, a Scot, arrived in Jerusalem in 1612 on the morning of Palm Sunday. Despite being, by his own account, "no Popish Catholic," he was met by the Franciscan guardian and twelve friars and provided with lodging in their monastery.[36] Lithgow and six German Protestants refused to take part in the "foolery," watching instead from the top of the cloisters, and taking perverse delight in the procession's interruption by Turkish troops. Lithgow wrote:

> In an apish imitation of Christ, at … Bethphage, there was an ass brought to the Guardian, whereupon he mounted (being as it were, the greater ass, riding upon the lesser) and came riding to Jerusalem. The people cutting down boughs of trees, and also despoiling themselves almost to the skin, bestrewed the way as he rode along, crying, Hosanna, Hosanna, the Son of David, blessed is he that cometh in the name of the Lord, until they came to the south gate of Zion … The Guardian thought to have entered, riding through Jerusalem to his monastery,

---

31 Suriano, *Trattato*, 1.51 (105); trans. Bellorini and Hoade, 118.

32 Bugatti, in Suriano, *Treatise*, 3–11.

33 Suriano, *Treatise*, 118n2.

34 The Assyrian (or Nestorian) Church is now known as the Church of the East.

35 Bonifacius, *Liber*, 30–31.

36 Lithgow, *Totall*, 209–10.

with this shouting convoy of six thousand oriental Christians,[37] because their patriarchs have not that liberty to do so, as this Italian Guardian [does]. Notwithstanding, the clamor of the people incensed so the Turkish garrison lying at this gate that they not only abused the poor Christians in their ignorant devotion, but they pulled the Guardian also from the ass's back, beating him most cruelly, and all the rest of the friars and French pilgrims that were with him. At last entering the convent, most of them came in groaning, and laden with black and bloody blows, whereat I and the other Protestants did laugh in our sleeves to behold their foolish procession so substantially rewarded.[38]

The Ottoman authorities, ruling over Jerusalem from Istanbul, dealt with such disturbances by issuing "an array of conflicting *firmans* [edicts] designed to please, and maintain the balance between" the opposing parties.[39] They repeatedly granted permission to the Franciscans to hold an annual Palm Sunday procession in Jerusalem, while also upholding Muslim complaints that the procession violated Islamic law. In theory, under Ottoman rule, Christians and Jews could worship freely inside pre-existing sacred buildings, but not in public space. The Palm Sunday procession, "with its ritual details and clamourous publicity, must have constituted a major offense to the feelings of all Muslims witnessing it."[40]

In 1641, Sultan Ibrahim I issed a firman stipulating that the Franciscans should be allowed "to hold their ceremony called the donkey of al-'Aziriya [the site of Lazarus's tomb]" on Palm Sunday, "according to their custom and usage," without hindrance or trouble.[41] In 1645, Ibrahim instructed the *qadi* (judge) in Jerusalem to inquire into complaints of the city's Sufi dervishes against the Franciscans and, if neccesary, to prevent the latter from displaying their heresy in public.[42] In defence of their rights, the Franciscans produced the 1641 decree. In 1650, Sultan Mohammed Khan IV ordered somewhat ambiguously that "no one should interfere" with Palm Sunday observances in Jerusalem, "so long as they not harm the religion of my own people."[43] In early 1651, the sultan again directed the *qadi* to investigate the procession. Court records specify the nature of the offence taken: "The Franciscan monks who live in Jerusalem conduct their abbot mounted on a donkey from a nearby village named al-'Aziriya to the city of

---

37 By "oriental Christians," Lithgow means those in Jerusalem whose allegiance is to Greek or other "Eastern" churches rather than to the Roman church represented by the Franciscans.

38 Lithgow, *Totall*, 218–19; for a summary of Lithgow's stay in Jerusalem, see Bosworth, *Intrepid*, 79–90.

39 Peri, *Christianity*, 87.

40 Peri, *Christianity*, 86.

41 Hussein, Sciad, and Gosselin, *Firmans*, 258.

42 Peri, *Christianity*, 87.

43 Hussein, Sciad, and Gosselin, *Firmans*, 294. The edict was issued to satisfy a request from the Austrian ambassador. It identifies Palm Sunday as "the feast that they hold a week before the Feast of the Red Eggs," a reference to the Greek Easter custom of dyeing eggs red to recall the blood of Christ.

Jerusalem. As they march before and behind him spreading their garments in the way, they display their rituals in public, and raise their voices in heresy. Doing this, they climb up the Mount of Olives; then they go down and up again to Jerusalem. Here they get into the city through the Gate of Zion bearing the crucifix in the open, where everybody can see it."[44] The *qadi* ordered the Franciscans "to abstain henceforth from mounting their abbot on a donkey, conducting their ceremonies in public, raising their voices in heresy and from displaying the crucifix in the open, for these things stand in opposition to the Sacred Law."[45] In 1652, Mohammed Khan again ordered that the Franciscans be allowed to hold "their ceremony called the donkey of al-'Aziriya," without "governors, magistrates, natives, dependents, or other people troubling or tormenting them."[46] The contradictory series of directives continued until at least 1711, when Ahmed Khan III was still referring to Palm Sunday as the feast of "the donkey of al-'Aziriya."[47]

Franciscan monopoly of the procession came to an end in 1757. On the eve of Palm Sunday that year, members of the Greek Orthodox community—jealous of the privileges enjoyed by the Latin Christians—stormed the Church of the Holy Sepulchre and the Franciscan monastery: "Incited and armed by their monks, the Greek mob, in the night preceding Palm Sunday, rushed into the basilica with clubs, maces, hooks, poniards and swords; upset the candlesticks, rent the tapestries, broke the lamps and reduced everything to pieces; then turned towards the convent of the Minors[48] to kill the poor friars living there, who had to barricade the doors to escape the violence of those malefactors 'excited by wine and debauch.'"[49] Swayed by the vagaries of European politics, Osman III issed an edict favouring the Greeks, and establishing the Orthodox church's preeminence among Christians in Jerusalem.[50] The Orthodox patriarch did not ride a donkey on Palm Sunday.

Palm Sunday processions in Jerusalem under Muslim rule differed from many of their European counterparts both in their lack of triumphalism and, after the late fifteenth century, in their sustained tradition of high-ranking clergy riding a donkey in imitation of Christ. Perhaps the enforced absence of triumphalism under Muslim rule created an environment in which the Franciscan guardian could ride a donkey without embarrassment. If nothing else, the long history of Palm Sunday in Jerusalem demonstrates that neither triumphalism nor the absence of live donkeys is inherent to the processional celebration of Palm Sunday. Indeed, the constraint of Muslim rule may have prompted a Palm Sunday processional tradition that was more congruent with the biblical narrative than the royal entries and elite processions of Christian Europe.

---

44 Peri, *Christianity*, 86.

45 Peri, *Christianity*, 87–88.

46 Hussein, Sciad, and Gosselin, *Firmans*, 300–1.

47 Hussein, Sciad, and Gosselin, *Firmans*, 485–86. For intermediate references to the feast variously called "Palm Sunday," "the cavalcade," and "the donkey of al-'Aziriya," in the Franciscan collection of edicts in their favour, see Hussein, Sciad, and Gosselin, *Firmans*, 304–5, 327, 355, 358, 450, and 471.

48 The official Latin name of the Franciscan order is Ordo Fratrum Minorum.

49 Baldi, *Question*, 64–65.

50 Wardi, "Question," 391; Peters, *Jerusalem*, 540.

Chapter 12

WHITE HORSES AND IMAGINED DONKEYS

THE QUESTION NATURALLY arises of why, if all Christendom believed that Jesus rode a donkey, there were so few live donkeys and so many white horses in medieval and early modern Palm Sunday processions. Bishops and other high-ranking clergy had not always been reluctant to ride donkeys. Athanasius, bishop of Alexandria from 328 to 373, reportedly reentered the city on a donkey after one of his several periods of exile.[1] Athanasius was no minor ecclesiastical figure: he is now best known as the leading defender of orthodox Christology against Arianism. Athanasius's biographer, Gregory of Nazianzus, compared the bishop's entry to that of Christ: "He rode on a colt (*pōlos*: Fr. *anôn* = little donkey)[2] ... as my Jesus did upon that other colt ... He was welcomed with branches, and multi-colored garments, rich in flowers, were spread before him, and thrown beneath his feet ... Just as at the entry of Christ, those who went ahead of him shouted acclamations and danced."[3]

Martin of Tours (ca. 335–ca. 400) is also said to have ridden a donkey. The source is an "apparently apocryphal legend,"[4] found not in the saint's biography written by Sulpicius Severus, who knew Martin personally, but in a collection of anecdotes about miracles, saints, and their relics compiled by Martin's sixth-century successor Gregory of Tours. According to Gregory, once when Martin was approaching Clermont, the senators of that old Roman city came out to meet him "with horsemen, coaches, chariots, and wagons. Martin was riding a donkey and seated on a very plain saddle." Seeing them approach "in this procession," the saintly bishop said, "What do these people who are approaching us with this magnificence intend for themselves? ... It is not my [intention] to enter their city with this ostentatious parade." Martin immediately "turned the bridle of his donkey around and began to depart on the road by which he had come." The men of Clermont followed him and "humbly" persuaded him to delay his departure long enough to heal the sick who had come out to him from the city.[5] Whether or not the story is true, it reflects Gregory's own disapproval of clergy who embraced the trappings of "an ostentatious parade" when entering a town.

Moreover, both stories attest to the fact that, even as late as the sixth century, it was not considered contrary to the dignity of the church for one of its bishops to ride a donkey. This was soon to change. Although the practical and economic value of the donkey continued until the widespread introduction of the internal combustion engine, the animal's symbolic value suffered greatly under the inclination of Christian authorities to interpret

---

1 Gregory of Naziansus, *Discours* 21.29 (172–73); Gregory, *Select*, 278.

2 Mossay, in Gregory, *Discours*, 173, translates *pōlos* into French as *anôn*, meaning the foal of a donkey, or a little donkey.

3 Gregory, *Discours* 21.29 (172–73); translation adapted from Gregory, *Select*, 278.

4 Van Dam, in Gregory of Tours, *Glory*, 21n9.

5 Gregory of Tours, *Glory* 5 (22–23). I am grateful to Martin Walsh for alerting me to this passage.

the Bible allegorically and tropologically. Biblical narratives featuring a donkey were treated not as records of its practical service to humanity, but as opportunities to draw spiritual and moral lessons for Christian readers. Theologians focused on what they took to be the donkey's slowness, stupidity, and lust.

Ambrose of Milan (340–397) considered the ass "sluggish … vulnerable to captivity, and slower in understanding" than the horse.[6] Isodore of Seville (560–636) agreed, but saw the advantages to humanity of these limitations: "The animal is indeed slow, and offers resistance to no plan; as soon as man wished, he subjected it to his service."[7] Pope Gregory I let his exegetical imagination run riot. In his long and digressive commentary on Job, he took the ass to mean "sometimes the inertness of fools, sometimes the unrestrained indulgence of the wanton, sometimes the simplemindedness of the Gentiles."[8] Variations on these human character traits included unbelief, the inability to understand "deep mysteries," "uncleanness," "wanton inclinations," and lust.[9] Accordingly, Gregory interpreted Christ's entry into Jerusalem on a donkey not as an act of immediate political and religious significance, but as a promise of the future spiritual transformation of the Gentiles. The risen and ascended Christ would "take possession of the simple hearts of the Gentiles to conduct them to the vision of [heavenly] peace, by ruling and ordering them."[10] Such attitudes had practical consequences. In a letter written in 592 to the overseer of the papal estates in Sicily, Gregory acknowledged the receipt of "one miserable horse and five good asses." He added, "I can't ride the horse because it's a wretch, nor the good ones because they're asses."[11] Jörg Traeger, identifying this as the first recorded reference to a papal mount, observes: "It is significant that this pope already rejects the donkey as a riding animal."[12]

The symbolic devaluation of the donkey was sustained and intensified in medieval bestiaries and encyclopedic works of natural history. Hrabanus Maurus, in *De universo* (ca. 845), compressed his predecessors' judgments on the stupidity of the ass into a single dense lump: "The word 'ass' or 'she-ass' sometimes designates the impudence of extravagant or lustful people, sometimes the gentleness of simple people, sometimes the

---

6 Ambrose, *Hexameron* 6.3.11 (*PL* 14:246); Savage's translation, 235 ("The donkey is a slothful and stupid animal, an easy prey to all mischance") may be a little harsh.

7 Isidore, *Étymologies* 12.1.38 (12:65); trans. Throop (unpaged); alternative trans. Barney et al., 249.

8 Gregory the Great, *Moralia* 1.16.23 (36), see also 35.16.40 (1800); trans. Bliss, 1:43; see also 3:689.

9 Gregory the Great, *Moralia* 17.26.38 (872), 2.30.49 (88–89), 27.28.38 (1359), 1.29.41 (47), 7.28.36 (360); trans. Bliss, 2:302–3, 1:100, 3:227, 1:54, 1:391–92. See also Gregory the Great, *Dialogues* 3.34.4 (2:402–3); trans. Zimmerman, 174; Gregory the Great, *Règle* 3.12. (2:328–29); Gregory the Great, *Pastoral*, 36).

10 Gregory the Great, *Moralia* 1.16.23 (37); trans. Bliss, 1:44. Isidore, *De ecclesiasticis* 1.28 (31), trans. Knoebel, 50–51, adopts Gregory's interpretation of Christ's choice of a donkey.

11 Gregory the Great, *Registrum* 2.50 (145); Gregory the Great, *Letters*, 1:105; translation from Franz, *Horseman*, 33–34.

12 Traeger, *Reitende*, 19.

folly of the pagans. Because the ass is a stupid and lustful animal, it mystically symbolizes ... either the Gentile people, on whom the Lord deigned to sit, heading toward Jerusalem, so that he would make them subject to him and would lead them to the heavenly country; or a stupid person, following only the luxury of this world." An ass also signifies "the synagogue of the Jews," or "a stupid person, when it shows him carrying the burdens of his sin, and engaging in the lusts of the flesh until the end of his life."[13] Given this enduring symbolic devaluation of the donkey, it is hardly surprising that high-ranking clerics followed Gregory's sixth-century precedent and refused to ride a donkey, especially on so important a public liturgical occasion as Palm Sunday.

An apparent exception proves this rule. During the Christmas season, some medieval churches welcomed donkeys into the liturgy. At first vespers of the feast of the Circumcision (January 1) in twelfth- and thirteenth-century Beauvais, a donkey was led into the cathedral to the processional chanting of "Orientis partibus," now known as the Song of the Ass.[14] In Autun, an ass was still led in procession on the feast of the Circumcision in the early fifteenth century.[15] Donkeys also took part in seasonal church drama and *tableaux vivants*. In the Benediktbeuern *Christmas Play* and the Laon *Office of the Prophets*, both probably composed in the late twelfth century, the actor playing Balaam rode a donkey. In the latter, a boy "beneath the ass" spoke the animal's lines.[16] By the fourteenth century, the Office of the Prophets in Rouen cathedral was known as the *Office of the Procession of the Ass*.[17] When Francis of Assisi erected a crib for the newborn Christ in Greccio in 1223, he added a live ox and ass to the scene.[18] A live ass also played an important part in the thirteenth-century Padua *Representation of Herod*, recalling the ass that carried the Holy Family to Egypt.[19] Such practices were exceptional. Not only were they limited to the Christmas season, when conventional hierarchies could be reversed in celebration of the good news that God had become

---

13 Hrabanus, *De universo* 7.8 (*PL* 111:212), trans. Throop, 1:226–27; see also Hildegard, *Physica* 7.9 (*PL* 197:1320), trans. Throop, 212. Later bestiaries recycled earlier authorities. Thus, the account of the ass in MS Bodley 764 (Barber, *Bestiary*, 97–99), dated to the 1240s, is an almost verbatim transcription of Hrabanus's ninth-century scorn.

14 Louvet, *Histoire*, 2:300, citing a now-lost manuscript that can be dated between 1160 and 1162; Arlt, *Festoffizium*, 2:3–4. For a full discussion of the Beauvais procession of the ass, and the long history of misleading scholarship on the subject, see Harris, *Sacred*, 74–85, 107–8. The Song of the Ass also opened the feast of the Circumcision in Sens, but there is no evidence that a live ass accompanied the processional chant there (Villetard, *Office*, 86–87, 130–31; Harris, *Sacred*, 101).

15 Harris, *Sacred*, 147–48.

16 Benediktbeuern: Young, *Drama*, 2:175; Bevington, *Medieval*, 183. Laon: Young, *Drama*, 145, 150; Lageux, "Glossing," 692–68. Although most scholars agree that in Laon the boy was concealed beneath the caparisons of a live ass, a few imagine a boy in a donkey costume (Harris, *Sacred*, 124n61).

17 Young, *Drama*, 2:154–71.

18 Bonaventure, *Life*, 110–11.

19 Cattin and Vildera, *Liber*, 2:66; Vecchi, *Uffici*, 176; Young, *Drama*, 1:108; Harris, *Sacred*, 41, 50–53.

human in Christ, but the donkeys were handled exclusively by lower clergy, choirboys, and mendicant Franciscans.

Emperors, popes, and archbishops preferred to ride a white horse or, occasionally, a white mule. The twelfth-century archibishop of Milan, as we have seen, rode a white horse in his city's annual Palm Sunday procession. So did the archbishop of Tours.[20] Popes tended to do so after their coronation and in other triumphal entries, rather than on Palm Sunday. Perhaps the earliest reference to the pope's white horse comes from an ordinal, dating to "around the year 897."[21] Leaving Saint Peter's Basilica after his ordination ceremony, the new pope sat "on a white horse" as he rode in the traditional rite of *possesso* (taking possession) from Saint Peter's Basilica to Saint John Lateran."[22] In 1295, Boniface VIII rode a richly caparisoned "snow-white" horse.[23] It was also customary during the *possesso* for the consecrated host to be carried, near the front of the cavalcade, on a white horse and beneath a baldachin. Thus "the sacramental real presence of the Body of Christ and the person of the Vicar of Christ ... were accorded equal treatment."[24]

The white horse owed its ceremonial status to both imperial and biblical referents. Triumphant Roman generals and emperors were believed to have ridden in chariots pulled by four white horses.[25] Riding a single white horse was more likely the privilege of a young prince of the imperial family.[26] Byzantine emperors and Roman popes, too, preferred a single white horse to a chariot.[27] As for the Bible, the Book of Revelation twice refers to a rider on a "white horse." The first, "bent on conquest,"[28] is generally understood to be a military conqueror. Some commentators have understood him to represent the power of the Roman Empire,[29] a possibility made more likely if the book was written

---

20 Martène, *De antiquis*, 3:75, cites an undated ritual book from Tours, which stipulates that the archbishop, "if present on Palm Sunday," should ride "on a white horse covered with a cloth." For Milan, see chap. 5. Blaauw, "Contrasts," 362, notes that the white horse was "a papal prerogative," which in the tenth century the pope "started to grant ... to other bishops, allowing them to ride a white horse ceremonially 'according to Roman use'."

21 Andrieu, *Ordines*, 4:168, 191.

22 Andrieu, *Ordines*, 4:199.

23 Stefaneschi, *Opus*, 101; Mann, *Lives*, 18:57.

24 Stinger, *Renaissance*, 53.

25 Beard, *Roman*, 234–36; Pliny, *Panegyricus* 22.1 (*Letters*, 2:370–71).

26 Suetonius, *Domitian* 2 (*Lives*, 2:322–25), where the young Domitian rides a "white horse" and Rolfe notes that this was "the usual procedure for a youthful prince." In 29 BCE, according to Suetonius, *Tiberius* 3 (*Lives*, 1:320–21), the young Tiberius and his brother Marcellus each rode one of the trace horses pulling the chariot of their father Octavian in his triumph after the battle of Actium.

27 For the use of a white horse in Byzantine triumphal entries, see McCormick, *Eternal*, 172–73, 182–83, 418; Stephenson, *Legend*, 62–65.

28 Rev. 6:2 (New International Version).

29 For example, Elliott, *Horae*, 1:121–25; Swete, *Apocalypse*, 85–86; Richard, *Apocalypse*, 5, 68–69. Others have understood the first rider to represent "military conquest" in general, or the Parthian threat to Rome in particular (e.g., Roloff, *Revelation*, 86; Smalley, *Revelation*, 150–51).

in the last years of the emperor Domitian (81–96 CE).[30] As a young prince, Domitian had ridden a white horse when his father, Vespasian, and his elder brother, Titus, celebrated their conquest of Jerusalem in 71 CE.[31] Toward the end of his life, he instituted a reign of terror whose victims included Christians.[32] Revelation's second such rider is Christ. Mounted "in righteousness" on a "white horse," he leads "the armies of heaven, wearing fine linen, white and pure … on white horses," to victory over the last enemies of God. Despite the military metaphors, he lacks conventional weapons, bearing only the "sharp sword" of "the word of God," and a shepherd's "rod of iron," with which to protect his people against persecution.[33] The biblical author "does not depict Christ as a great *military* warrior," but as one who "establishes justice and peace "by the power of his word."[34] After his victory, the peaceful city of new Jerusalem is seen "coming down out of heaven."[35] Riding a white horse in triumphal procession allowed popes, emperors, and other Christian rulers not only to trumpet their imperial aspirations but also to represent Christ in his role as eschatological victor.

Thus, when the eighteen-year-old duke (and future emperor) Maximilian I entered Bruges with his new bride in 1477, "there stood above the city gate a very beautiful picture on which the aforesaid noble duke's likeness was depicted in a painting and there was written 'Benedictis qui venit in nomine domini.' "[36] Maximilian rode a white horse draped in cloth of gold. He was in full armour, and he was escorted by a large company of armed men.[37] Although the caption to the duke's portrait acknowledged Jesus's entry into Jerusalem before his passion, the manner of Maximilian's "triumphal" (*triumphelic*) entry anticipated Christ's final advent. Medieval princes preferred a white war-horse to a donkey and the glorification of military victory to the humiliation of self-sacrifice.

Perhaps even more influentially, the ceremonial white horse had become associated with imperial insignia granted to the pope in a forged document commonly known as the *Donation of Constantine*. Claiming to be a solemn legal enactment by the first Christian

---

30 Irenaeus, *Contre* 5.30.3 (384–85); Irenaeus, *Against*, 559–60. See also Brown, *Introduction*, 802–9; Charles, *Critical*, 1:xci–xcvii; Roloff, *Revelation*, 8–12.

31 Suetonius, *Domitian* 2 (*Lives*, 2:322–25).

32 Eusebius, *Ecclesiastical* 3.17–20 (1:234–41); Suetonius, *Domitian* 10–16 (*Lives*, 2:339–57); Brown, *Introduction*, 805–9.

33 Rev. 19:11–16. For the argument that Christ is here portrayed as both warrior and shepherd, see Richard, *Apocalypse*, 146–47.

34 Johnson, *Revelation*, 574.

35 Rev. 21:2.

36 Roovere, *Excellente*, 193a. I am grateful to Elsa Strietman for helping me with this translation. Kipling, *Enter*, 23, mistakenly translates "schildereyn" (painting) as "children," and, 344n, transcribes "voors" (aforesaid) as "voork." For Roovere's authorship of the part of this chronicle covering the years 1440 to 1482, see Oosterman, "De *Excellente*"; Oosterman, "Excellente." For an expanded French paraphrase of Roovere's account of Maximilian's entry into Bruges, see Delepierre, *Chronique*, 113–16.

37 Roovere, *Excellente*, 192b–93a. Although the colour of the horse is not specified in the text, it is white in the accompanying illustration.

emperor, the decree conferred wide-ranging imperial privileges on the pope, including the use of imperial tiara, mantles, sceptres, standards, banners, "and all the pomp of our imperial eminence, and the glory of our power."[38] The original document, now known by its Latin title of *Constitutum Constantini*, is thought to have been written sometime between the accession of Charlemagne's father, Pepin the Short, in 752, and the death of Charlemagne's son, Louis the Pious, in 840.[39] It remained in comparative obscurity until the second half of the eleventh century, when an abbreviated and modified version emerged. The shorter version, now known as the *Donation of Constantine*, added an inaccurate opening summary, which began: "The Emperor Constantine yielded his crown, and all his royal prerogatives in the city of Rome, and in Italy, and in western parts to the Apostolic [See]."[40] Summarized thus, the *Donation* became a potent weapon of the papacy in the ongoing struggle for power between pope and emperor.[41] The *Constitutum*, in both its full and modified version, has been recognized as fraudulent since at least the fifteenth century.

The white horse was not among the imperial privileges specified in the *Constitutum*,[42] but the document did include the apocryphal story of Constantine's ceremonial submission to Pope Sylvester I (314–335), according to which Constantine had crowned Sylvester with the "glittering" papal tiara, and then, "holding the bridle of [the pope's] horse, out of reverence for the Blessed Peter ... performed for him the duty of groom."[43] Recalling this precedent, twelfth-century Roman ritual books stipulated that, after the coronation of an emperor by the pope, the newly crowned monarch should hold the stirrup of the pope's horse steady while its rider mounted, and then lead it a little way by the bridle before mounting his own horse and riding in procession directly behind the pope.[44] This signalled a notable shift in symbolic power. The fictitious Constantine had displayed his own authority by crowning Sylvester before he deigned to lead the pope's horse. The twelfth-century pope claimed the right both to crown and to be served by

---

38 Fuhrmann, *Constitutum* 14 (88); trans. Coleman, in Valla, *Treatise*, 14–15; for an alternative translation, see Valla, *Donation*, trans. Bowerstock, 176–79.

39 Fried, *Donation*, 35, 112.

40 Fried, *Donation*, 148, 151. For the addition of the summary, see Fried, *Donation*, 19; for the distinction between the *Constitutum* and the *Donation of Constantine*, 5; for Latin texts and English translations of both, 129–53.

41 Twyman, *Papal*, 2–3.

42 Traeger, *Reitende*, 12–13, assumes that the privilege of riding a white horse was included among the "diversa ornamenta imperialia" (Fuhrmann, *Constitutum* 14 [88]; Valla, *Treatise*, 14) granted to the pope. Elisabeth Garms-Cornides, reviewing Traeger's book in *The Art Bulletin* 55 (1973): 451–56, dissents, rightly insisting that "the horse is not listed among the symbols of lordship which the emperor assigns or leaves to the pope" (452).

43 Fuhrmann, *Constitutum* 16 (92–93); trans. Coleman, in Valla, *Donation*, 16–17; see also Fried, *Donation*, 136, 144, 149, 152.

44 Elze, *Ordines*, 46 (*Lib. Cens.*, 1:6), 68; Blaauw, "Contrasts," 361–62.

Figure 12 Emperor Constantine leads Pope Sylvester's white horse. Fresco, 1248. Oratorio di San Silvestro, Rome. Wikimedia Commons. Photograph by Matthias Holländer.

the emperor. In subsequent visual representations of Sylvester's coronation, the pope's horse is always white (Fig. 12).[45]

Such precedents effectively made it impossible for a medieval ruler of church or state to ride anything less prestigious than a white horse, but it has not stopped scholars from assuming the presence of a Palm Sunday donkey where none is recorded. We have already noted the mistaken assumption by some that the bishop of Jerusalem rode a donkey in the late fourth century and again at the beginning of the thirteenth century. Others have supposed that the patriarch of Moscow rode a real donkey rather than a white horse dressed as a donkey.[46]

Historians have also imposed a donkey on thirteenth-century Palm Sunday festivities at Quedlinburg Abbey, in northeast Germany. In 1786, Gottfried Voigt published a history of the abbey, in which he affirmed that the bishop of Halberstadt "came to Quedlinburg every year on Palm Sunday, amid the greatest pomp and attended by very many clergy ... In remembrance of Christ's entry into Jerusalem, and to make the people meditate aright on that event, he rode to the town on a donkey or a horse (*auf einem Esel oder*

---

45 The best-known example, reproduced in Fig. 12, is in the Oratorio di San Silvestro in the Santi Quattro Coronati complex in Rome, not far from the Lateran Palace: see Mitchell, "St. Silvester"; Herzman and Stephany, *Dante*, 105–9; Barelli, *Monumental*, 70–75.

46 For example, Ostrogorsky, "Stratordienst," 194; Kantorowicz, "King's," 229.

Pferde)."[47] Later in the same volume, Voigt dropped the alternative "horse" and declared that the bishop "played the part of Jesus, and came to Quedlinburg mounted on a jenny (*auf einer Eselin*)," while "a foal (*Füllen*) went alongside."[48] Subsequent scholars ignored the option of a horse, stating without qualification that the bishop rode, "like the Lord Jesus, humbly on a jenny with its foal,"[49] or conforming the record even more closely to the biblical narrative by having the bishop "ride upon a donkey in procession ... as the people strewed branches before him."[50] One nineteenth-century scholar found the whole thing deeply offensive: "The bishop, representing the Redeemer, riding upon an ass, under the shade of palm branches, surrounded by his clergy, and followed by a numerous train, arrived at and entered the abbey church, amidst the ringing of bells and shouts of Hosannah! After high mass he caused the abbey relics to be exhibited; and with all his attendants and followers, was abundantly feasted throughout the day ... It was only the progress of the public mind that at length put an end to this blasphemous festival."[51]

No one disputes that the abbess was obligated to provide the bishop and his entourage with a lavish banquet after mass in the abbey church. From time to time she tried to end the custom. In 1250, she was able to limit the bishop's company to "no more than sixty horses."[52] The donkey ride, however, is a figment of scholarly imagination. Johann Ludewig, whom Voight acknowledged as his source, had in 1719 merely quoted in passing, without mentioning either Quedlinburg or Halberstadt, an unidentified pontifical's stipulation that "the bishop should ride in with the palm donkey (*Palmesel*) or palm horse (*Palmpferd*)."[53] Voigt assumed that the pontifical was generally binding and that bishop of Halberstadt would also have ridden "a donkey or a horse." Of the two, Voigt much preferred the donkey. But Ludewig's free-floating pontifical had not even specified a live animal. The unidentified bishop, it said, "should ride in *with* the palmesel" (my italics: "*mit* dem Palmesel ... eingeritten komme"). He was to accompany (but not ride!) a conventional wooden palmesel, a life-size processional image of Christ on a donkey. I know of no record of a palmesel in Quedlinburg, and I think it safe to assume that the bishop of Halberstadt and his companions all rode fine horses, unencumbered by either a live donkey or a wheeled wooden palmesel. Their goal was not to represent Christ en route, but to sit down after mass to an excellent banquet.[54]

---

47 Voigt, *Geschichte*, 1:92.

48 Voigt, *Geschichte*, 1:323.

49 Fritsch, *Geschichte*, 1:126. According to Wiepen, *Palmsonntagsprozession*, 15n3, the bishop "rode a jenny," while Malherbe, "Palmezel," 83, has him riding "the foal of a jenny," and assumes that the custom began as early as the time of the abbess Adelaide I (d. 983).

50 Monti, *Sense*, 319, who simplifies Malherbe by dating the practice unequivocally to the tenth century.

51 Cramer, *Denkwürdigkeiten*, 2:174–75.

52 Voigt, *Geschichte*, 1:331.

53 Ludewig, *Erlauterung*, 2:570, cited by Voigt, *Geschichte*, 1:92 n.

54 Hahn, "Relics," 144, assumes that "the riches of the monastery," including some of its impressive collection of relics, were "displayed" during the "elaborate Palm Sunday procession," but this

Figure 13 Charles VIII enters Naples, 1495. Pen drawing tinted with wash. Melchione Ferraiolo, *Una cronaca napoletana figurate del Quattrocento.*

One scholar has even found a donkey in a royal entry. Johannes Tripps claims that when the victorious Charles VIII of France entered Naples in 1495, he did so "in full ceremonial dress on a donkey."[55] Tripps cites as his authority the contemporary Neapolitan chronicler Melchione Ferraiolo (ca. 1443–ca. 1498), whose account of Charles's triumphal entry includes several coloured illustrations of the royal entourage. One depicts a diminutive Charles riding what could be mistaken for a donkey (Fig. 13), but Ferraiolo's modern editor provides a more credible explanation: "The king rides a remarkable little pony proportional to his small stature."[56] Kings did not ride donkeys. Nor did prelates of the medieval church. The first person to follow Christ's example of riding a donkey in public procession on Palm Sunday may have been a nameless altar boy in Udine in 1424.

---

depends on there having been such an annual procession. I know of nothing in the records that precludes the simpler option that the bishop and his companions rode on horseback to the abbey, celebrated mass, and dined.

55 Tripps, *Handelnde*, 98.

56 Filangieri, in Ferraiolo, *Cronaca Napoletana*, 128–29n75. Further confusion arises because of a typographical errror reversing the captions of plates 40 and 41. Plate 40 is identified as "XLI: L'ingresso a Napoli di Carlo VIII," plate 41 as "XL. L'esercitto francese entra a Napoli." Charles and his pony are depicted in plate XL/41. To make matters even more opaque, Filangieri numbers the relevant section of Ferraiolo's text as "75," whereas Coluccia, in Ferraiolo, *Cronaca*, 47, numbers it "77."

Chapter 13

LIVE DONKEYS AT LAST

EVEN AFTER 1424, live donkeys in Palm Sunday processions were few and far between. The Franciscan guardian's use of a donkey under Muslim rule in Jerusalem, between 1480 and 1757, was exceptional. I have found no other record of a high-ranking Roman Catholic cleric riding a donkey on Palm Sunday. The occasional parish priest did so in the nineteenth century, and I'd like to think that some did so before then, but I have yet to find any evidence.

Live donkeys did, however, sometimes appear at other times of the year in civic dramatizations of Christ's entry. In England, for example, a donkey was ridden by the lay actor playing Christ in the York and Chester Corpus Christi dramatizations of the entry into Jerusalem, in the Hereford Corpus Christi procession, and in the Cornish *Ordinalia*. The most enduring of these dramatizations, the York and Chester plays, were suppressed in 1569 and 1575 respectively.[1] Like the occasional use of donkeys in continental church drama and tableaux during the Christmas season,[2] the inclusion of donkeys in English civic drama only sets in starker relief the surprisingly long absence of live donkeys from contemporary Palm Sunday processions throughout Europe.

So does the variety of ways in which the Palm Sunday figure of Christ has more recently been represented on a live donkey. In this chapter, by way of further contrast, I fast-forward to the nineteenth century and beyond, while travelling to places as far from Udine and Jerusalem as Mexico and Bolivia, to consider some of the mimetic options that were ignored by medieval Palm Sunday processions.

I begin in Ecuador. In the capital city of Quito, on the morning of Palm Sunday, 1830, the French traveller M. de Raigecourt attended "the blessing of the branches" in the cathedral. The branches were from palms, rose bushes, and banana trees. Leaving the cathedral afterward, de Raigecourt caught sight of a procession returning to the Franciscan convent. At the heart of the procession, he recalls, was an image of Christ, "which at first I thought was carried by human strength; but the strange movements I saw it make prompted me to examine it closely, at a time when the procession had stopped beneath the arcade of the convent. I then discovered, not without surprise, that the bearer of the

---

1 Harris, "Processional," 324–25. The York Corpus Christi Play, first recorded in 1376, had its "last recorded performance" (before its modern revivals) in 1569 (Beadle, "York," 99). The Chester play, first recorded in 1422, was moved from Corpus Christi to Whitsunday sometime between 1472 and 1521, and last performed in 1575 (Mills, "Chester," 116). Hereford's Corpus Christi procession, according to a surviving list of pageants from 1503, included "The good lord ridyng on an asse with xij appostelles" (Klausner, *Herefordshire*, 115). In the Cornish *Ordinalia*, Jesus rides an ass, accompanied by its foal, while a group of seven boys "bear palms and flowers," which they speak of scattering in Jesus's path along with "olive branches," "bays and ripe box," and their own "best clothes" (Harris, *Cornish*, 87–88).

2 See chap. 12.

figure (*mannequin*) was a donkey, which, troubled by its burden, would certainly have thrown it to the ground, if two men, one on each side, had not been constantly engaged in maintaining its balance, for fear of an accident."[3] Although the donkey was live, the figure of Christ was inanimate.

To the best of my knowledge, the Palm Sunday processional practice of mounting a sculpted life-size image of Christ on a live donkey is exclusive to Latin America. A similar report, albeit with a more amenable donkey, comes from Popayán, Colombia, in 1866. A witness to the city's Palm Sunday procession describes "the statue (*estatua*) which represents Jesus, riding on a well-behaved jenny."[4] A much earlier account may come from seventeenth-century Mexico. In his *Monarquía Indiana* (1615), the Franciscan Juan de Torquemada describes how on Palm Sunday the indigenous Christians of Tlaxcala throw their cloaks on the ground ahead of "the priest and his assistants, who represent Christ and his apostles," while children stationed in trees along the processional route, "sing, 'Benedictus qui venit in nomine Domini, Osana in excelsis,' and throw flowers at the image of Christ our Lord which goes on an ass."[5] Christ was thus represented both by the officiating priest on foot and by an inanimate image mounted on a donkey; the children preferred the latter. Given that a live donkey had been taking part in the annual Franciscan Palm Sunday procession in Jerusalem for well over a century, and that Franciscans were the dominant missionary force in Tlaxcala, Quito, and Popayán, I am inclined to believe that the donkey in Tlaxcala was also live rather than wooden.

Franciscans were also responsible, "sometime in the 1960s," for reviving the tradition in Quito.[6] On Palm Sunday, an articulated image of Christ, his movable limbs clothed in a white tunic and red silk smock, is now annually secured with ropes and belts to a live donkey. Led with a rope halter, the donkey bears his mount through the old city to the Franciscan convent, where an outdoor mass is celebrated on a raised platform. The figure of Christ, dismounted, sits on an episcopal throne near the altar, his sandaled feet unable to reach quite to the floor of the platform.[7]

---

3 Orbigny, *Voyage*, 93, quoting a personal communication from de Raigecourt.

4 Vergara, "Semana," 170.

5 Torquemada, *Monarquía* 17.7 (5:336).

6 Susan Verdi Webster, personal communication, August 22, 2016. Webster adds that the city's Holy Week processions had lapsed "from the late nineteenth to the mid-twentieth century," and that the revived processions were consciously modelled on de Raigecourt's account of Holy Week in 1830 (Orbigny, *Voyage*, 92–96; the 1854 "new edition" of Orbigny's work severely abbreviates de Raigecourt's account of Holy Week and omits a fold-out engraving of the Good Friday procession).

7 Roldán, *Quito*, 2:165–68; "Foto de archivo—Quito, Ecuador—01 de abril 2012—entrada de Jesús a la ciudad en la procesión del Domingo de Ramos," *123RF*, 1 April, 2012, https://es.123rf.com/photo_12993669_quito-ecuador-01-de-abril-2012-entrada-de-jes%C3%BAs-a-la-ciudad-en-la-procesi%C3%B3n-del-domingo-de-ramos.html?fromid=RVhOb2h0bmxMcFRyQmFZQWgwaXlCZz09; "Domingo de Ramos abrió la puertas a la Semana Santa," *La Hora Nacional*, 21 March, 2016, http://lahora.com.ec/index.php/noticias/show/1101927391.

The practice is not exclusively Franciscan. In Panchimalco (El Salvador), children reach out and pet the saddled donkey on which Christ sits somewhat precariously, kept from falling by four "disciples." He wears a voluminous lightweight red cape that billows behind him, supported by four other disciples, and, like everybody else, he carries a bouquet of palms. When the procession reaches the crowded parish church, Christ is lifted from his donkey and carried up the aisle. His articulated right arm is manipulated by one of the disciples so that King Jesus beats time to the music with his bouquet of palms. Seated at the front, to one side, he faces the congregation during mass.[8]

In León (Nicaragua), the Señor del Triunfo wears a jaunty broad-brimmed Nicaraguan sombrero over a long black wig, and a loose-fitting, brightly coloured robe and cape. A brass and percussion band (*chichero*) plays lively march tunes. The Christ figure becomes almost animated, his upright torso, right hand raised in blessing, exaggerating the uneven movements of the donkey beneath him. Crowds line the narrow streets; large numbers join the procession; balloons are released from above. After passing through an imitation city gate, on which is blazoned "Bendito el que viene en el nombre del Señor," Christ and his donkey are met by the city's bishop. The prelate has arrived on foot beneath a processional baldachin, which he now cedes to Christ and his donkey. The band plays "When the Saints Go Marching in." As the procession approaches the cathedral, church bells ring out. Then, to cries of "Viva," the waving of palms by the gathered congregation, and the still-cheerful music of the *chichero*, Christ rides his remarkably docile donkey, still beneath the episcopal baldachin, up the central aisle of the cathedral to the altar, where he finally dismounts.[9]

Allowing a live rider, rather than an articulated image, to ride a donkey in a Palm Sunday procession poses problems of liturgical propriety, verisimilitude, and interpretation. A child, as in fifteenth-century Udine, is an appropriately humble image of Christ and is not demeaned by the low status of his mount, but unlike the donkey, which looks like a donkey, the child doesn't look much like the adult Jesus of Nazareth. On the contrary, the child can look so sweet that the challenge posed by the biblical narrative of a divine king riding a donkey is obscured. This may be the case in twenty-first-century Prague. Since at least 2008, a young boy in a bright red cape and hood has ridden in a

---

8 "Con el Domingo de Ramos inicia la Semana Santa," La Prensa Gráfica Noticias de El Salvador, *YouTube*, April 1, 2012, www.youtube.com/watch?v=0dn11gYg1PI; "Celebración de Domingo de Ramos en Panchimalco," Giovanni Lemus, *La Prensa Gráfica*, April 1, 2012, http://mediacenter. laprensagrafica.com/galerias/g/celebracion-del-domingo-de-ramos-en-panchimalco-y-san-salvador/; "Así se vivió el Domingo de Ramos en Panchimalco," Nelson Dueñas, *Diario1.com*, April 13, 2014, http://diario1.com/nacionales/2014/04/imagenes-asi-vivieron-los-catolicos-el-domingo-de-ramos/.

9 "Domingos de Ramos Jesús del Triunfo 2014 León Nicaragua," *YouTube*, April 13, 2014, www. youtube.com/watch?v=YK6923o_kxU; "Procesión del Domingo de Ramos 2012 Leon Nicaragua," *YouTube*, April 1, 2012, www.youtube.com/watch?v=89OmucF8bR8; "Domingo de Ramos en la Catedral de Leon Nicaragua," Irasema Villacci, *YouTube*, April 13, 2014, www.youtube.com/ watch?v=rPZFVqqdCNY.

Palm Sunday procession through the Malá Strana district from the Church of Our Lady Victorious, home to the celebrated statue of the Infant Jesus of Prague, to the Church of Saint Thomas. There mass is celebrated with the boy and his donkey facing the congregation from the foot of the chancel steps.[10] A second procession has taken place, since at least 2011, within the walls of the castle complex that overlooks Malá Strana, beginning at Saint George's Basilica and ending at the cathedral of Saint Vitus. Although official reports unfailingly refer to a "boy on a donkey" (*chlapec na oslíku*), images of the procession between 2014 and 2016 clearly show a young girl astride the animal.[11]

As a concession to verisimiltude, Palm Sunday activities sometimes feature a live donkey ridden by a young man who has grown his hair long and cultivated a beard for the occasion. This is the case in several communities in the Mexican state of Michoacán, where the Palm Sunday entry is often the first in a series of "dramatizations" (*escenificaciones*) that include the *via crucis* on Friday and the resurrection on Sunday. In Jacona, the Confraternity of Our Lady of Hope stages not only Christ's entry on a donkey, but also the Last Supper, an extremely bloody crucifixion, a hanging of Judas, and finally the resurrection.[12] In Comanja, Holy Week begins with a sombre Palm Sunday procession in which hymns are sung and the young man playing Jesus on a donkey hides his face beneath a mantle. After a lengthy dramatization of Christ's suffering and resurrection, the week ends late on Easter Sunday with a carnivalesque entry of masked Judases dancing with cross-dressed partners, followed late into the night by the lighting of multiple firecracker-filled effigies of Judas that have been strung up above the town's streets.[13]

---

10 "Palm Sunday," *Tischlers in Prague*, March 16, 2008, http://tischlersinprague.blogspot.com/ 2008/03/palm-sunday.html; "Květná neděle 29.3.2015," *Zonerama*, March 29, 2015, https:// taborzs2014.zonerama.com/Album/605673, includes a final image of the boy and donkey inside the church.

11 "Květná neděle v pražské katedrále," *Arcibiskupství pražské intranet*, April 15, 2011, http:// in.apha.cz/-kvetna-nedele-v-prazske-katedrale-2011, confirms the 2011 date, but posts no images. For images from 2014 and 2016, see "13-4-2014 Květná neděle v katedrále," *Arcibiskupství pražské*, April 13, 2014, www.apha.cz/13-4-2014-kvetna-nedele-v-katedrale; "Květná neděle," *Katedrála svatého Víta*, March 20, 2016, www.katedralasvatehovita.cz/cs/fotogalerie/udalosti-zivota-katedraly/velikonoce-2016/kvetna-nedele-2016. "Květná neděle v pražské katedrále," *Arcibiskupství pražské*, March 20, 2016, www.apha.cz/kvetna-nedele-v-prazske-katedrale-2016, should be treated with caution. Not only does it still refer to a "boy (*chlapec*)," rather than a girl (*dívka*) "on a donkey," but it also shows an image of a young man on a donkey, taken not at the Prague cathedral 2016 Palm Sunday procession but at the 2015 Zbraslav Passion Play: compare "18.4.2015 Pašijové hry v areálu Zbraslavského zámku," *Arcibiskupství pražské*, April 18, 2015, www.apha.cz/184-2015-pasijove-hry-ve.

12 "Realizaron Procesión del Domingo de Ramos en Jacona," Leticia E. Becerra Valdez, March 22, 2016, www.viviendomiciudad.com/2016-noticias-jacona/35815; "Viacrucis viviente Jacona 2016," Emmanuel Cota, *YouTube*, April 4, 2016, www.youtube.com/watch?v=benzCVMJ0Kg.

13 "Procesion domingo de ramos 2014 Comanja Michoacan," *YouTube*, April 13, 2014, www. youtube.com/watch?v=PQYp_SrLWAM; "5 Viacrucis Comanja 2016," *YouTube*, March 26, 2016, www.youtube.com/watch?v=dAxXJlWG70Y; "Judas recorriendo las calles Comanja Michoacan

A priest, too, may take the part of Christ on a donkey. Such has been case for well over a hundred years in the small Sicilian town of Prizzi. Guiseppe Pitrè described the tradition in 1876: "In Prizzi, on Palm Sunday," he wrote, "some fifty priests and all the town's confraternities gather" at the Parish Church of Santa Rosalia, overlooking the town. "The confraternity members, each with a palm in his hand, set out first."[14] Those representing the "twelve apostles, also bearing palms, follow"; one, carrying "a lantern in his hand, represents Judas.[15] The clergy come next. Two of the more important guide a recently foaled jenny and, behind her, a foal all adorned with flowers and ribbons." On the jenny is "a priest, dressed like a Jew (*vestito all'ebrea*), who plays Christ." Bringing up the rear is a crowd of laity "with huge branches of olive and other trees."[16]

Nowadays the priest no longer dresses "like a Jew," but is fully vested in alb, stole, and red dalmatic. He raises his right hand throughout the procession in a gesture of blessing, and is followed by a cheerful wind-and-percussion band. Crowds line the streets.[17] Reaching the old town, the procession is greeted outside the Church of Saint Francis by Prizzi's mayor and police commander, who assume responsibility for leading the jenny. A doll-size angel, controlled by rope and pulley, descends with a small palm branch, which the priest accepts "as a sign of peace."[18] From there the procession continues to the cathedral church of Saint George. Holy Week in Prizzi ends on Sunday afternoon with an episode known as "the Encounter" (*L'Incontro*). Two costumed devils, in bright red woollen suits and red metal masks, dance with Death, who wears a yellow suit and a pale leather skull mask. He brandishes a crossbow. Together, Death and the devils try to prevent a meeting and motherly kiss between a statue of the Madonna and another of the risen Christ, but are overcome by two young men representing sword-bearing angels. Their defeat enacts the power of Christ's resurrection over death and the demonic.[19]

Prizzi was not the only town in nineteenth-century Sicily where a priest rode a live donkey on Palm Sunday. In "many Sicilian churches, the most recently ordained of the priests in the community," carrying an olive branch and "preceded by twelve mounted apostles," rode a jenny that had "born only one foal." The procession ended "at the main

2016," *YouTube*, March 28, 2016, www.youtube.com/watch?v=FWaBw-gFeMs; "8 Quema judas Comanja Michoacan 2015," *YouTube*, April 6, 2015, www.youtube.com/watch?v=Py2yW8Fzsa8.

14 There were then five confraternities in Prizzi, all of which had been approved by royal decree in 1831 (*Collezione delle Leggi e de' Decreti Reali del Regno delle Due Sicilie* [1831, sem. 1]: 182, 266, 268–69. Among them was the still-active Confraternity of the Crucified, which is now credited with introducing the Palm Sunday procession to Prizzi (Stanzione, "Settimana," s.v. "Domenica delle Palme").

15 For Judas's lantern, see John 18:3.

16 Pitrè, "Notizie," 110.

17 "Domenica delle Palme 2014," *YouTube*, April 15, 2014, www.youtube.com/watch?v=UGTfLqNjvIQ.

18 Stanzione, "Settimana," s.v. "Domenica delle Palme—Processione delle Palme."

19 Stanzione, "Settimana," s.v. "Domenica di Pasqua—L'Incontro"; "Pasque a Prizzi 2009," *YouTube*, May 6, 2009, www.youtube.com/watch?v=gJQH0zGpr4I.

altar rail of the principle church," where the priest dismounted.[20] In Caccamo, by way of variation on the prevailing theme, a child (*fanciullo*) was dressed "as a priest with a surplice and biretta" and rode "a white ass."[21] This tradition, too, has survived, although the donkey is no longer white. A vested altar boy, imitating the actions of a priest more than those of Christ, makes the sign of the cross over the crowd with his right hand and holds a small crucifix in his left as he rides through the town.[22]

Palm Sunday in the small Sicilian city of Piana degli Albanesi may be unique. The city was founded by Albanian refugees in the late fifteenth century and has maintained its Albanian Italian traditions ever since. Its churches, affiliated with the Italo-Albanian Catholic Church, observe the Byzantine rite in the Greek or Albanian language.[23] The eparch (bishop) of Piana degli Albanesi, wearing the purple mandyas (mantle), black kamilavkion (cylindrical hat), and black epanokalimavkion (veil) of a bishop, rides a donkey in the city's Palm Sunday procession.[24] He may be the highest-ranking priest in western Europe ever to ride a Palm Sunday donkey.

A final example of a priest riding a Palm Sunday donkey comes from Bolivia. A Catholic priest, Sebastián Obermaier, arrived in El Alto in 1978, when it was still a largely indigenous settlemement, experiencing exponential growth in population, on the rim of the altiplano above the capital city of La Paz. He remained there until his death in August 2016. He worked tirelessly on behalf of the poor and disadvantaged, and was described after his death as "a poor man devoted to the poor, a man who in his life placed the highest value on gratitude, the love of God, and the love of his brothers and sisters."[25] For many years, on Palm Sunday, he rode a donkey through his El Alto parish of Villa Adela.[26] In every photograph of the event, Obermaier is vested, smiling, and waving a palm. The donkey is so small that the priest's feet almost touch the ground and his head barely rises above those of his *compadres* who line the street or walk alongside. Obermaier rode the donkey for the last time in March 2016, at eighty-one years of age. He explained

---

20 Pitrè, *Spettacoli*, 137.

21 Pitrè, *Spettacoli*, 78.

22 Buttitta and Minnella, *Pasqua*, 71; Barbara, *Settimana*, s.v. "CACCAMO (Pa) * U Signuruzzu a cavaddu"; "Isignuruzzu a cavaddu domenica delle palme 'CACCAMO'," *YouTube*, March 29, 2015, www.youtube.com/watch?v=7FYB8NECAIM.

23 For more on the Italo-Albanian communities of southern Italy, see Nasse, *Italo-Albanian*.

24 Fonte, *Folklore*, 285–88; Barbara, *Settimana*, s.v. "PIANA DEGLI ALBANESI (Pa) * Pashkët"; "Piana degli Albanesi 'Domenica degli Palme'—Piccolo Grande Italia," *YouTube*, December 28, 2010, www.youtube.com/watch?v=_wps0q776IU; "Pianna degli Albanesi 20 03 2016," Ugo Pirrotta, *YouTube*, March 21, 2016, www.youtube.com/watch?v=TdEIRinzHbw.

25 Eugenio Scarpellini, bishop of El Alto, on the day of Obermaier's death ("Padre Sebastián Obermaier," Micaela Diaz, *Iglesia Viva*, August 2, 2016, www.iglesiaviva.net/2016/08/02/padre-sebastian-obermaier-un-hombre-que-ha-hecho-de-su-vida-un-don-para-todos-los-demas). See also "A missionary priest," Sara Shahriari, *Christian Science Monitor*, June 1, 2010, www.csmonitor.com/World/Making-a-difference/2010/0601/A-missionary-priest-becomes-a-master-builder-in-a-booming-Bolivian-metropolis. For a biography of Obermaier, see Jiménez Mancilla, *Qué linda*.

26 Jiménez Mancilla, *Qué linda*, 142.

afterwards, in words that are especially poignant from someone who survived the last—and arguably most brutal—years of military rule in Bolivia, "The Saviour does not come like a king on a white horse and surrounded by generals, he comes on a donkey."[27]

27 "Paceños asisten masivamente a iglesias en Domingo de Ramos," Jorge Quispe, *La Razón*, March 21, 2016, www.la-razon.com/sociedad/Devocion-pacenos-masivamente-iglesias-Domingo_de_Ramos_0_2457954218.html); see also "The World celebrates Palm Sunday," *Chron*, April 1, 2012, www.chron.com/news/slideshow/The-world-celebrates-Palm-Sunday-41157/photo-2765822.php.

PART THREE:

DONKEYS

**II. Wooden Christs on Wooden Donkeys:
From Augsburg to Chiquitos**

Chapter 14

AN IMAGE OF THE LORD SEATED ON AN ASS

SOME TWO HUNDRED years after Charlemagne rode into Rome in conscious evocation of Christ's entry into Jerusalem and some five hundred years before a live donkey was first ridden in a Palm Sunday procession, a carved wooden "image of the Lord seated on an ass" took part in the annual Palm Sunday procession in Augsburg. The palmesel, as such images came to be known, was a major innovation. Other processional images were carried high above the eye level of those who venerated them, but palmesels were mounted on wheels and pulled at street level, enjoying an unconventional intimacy with those around them. It was possible to make eye contact with the figure of Christ on a palmesel—or even for children to ride behind Christ on the donkey—in a way that was unthinkable with a dignitary mounted on a white horse.

I have argued in earlier chapters that Christ's entry into Jerusalem on a donkey was a repudiation of both Jewish and Roman military triumphs, but that many elite Palm Sunday processions and triumphal entries after the time of Charlemagne, in contrary fashion, evoked Christ's entry to display a militant triumphalism. If Christian Europe produced any enduring Palm Sunday processional tradition that resisted this dissonance, it was that of the palmesel. In Part 3.2, I tell the story of the palmesel from its first appearance in tenth-century Augsburg, through its persecution by sixteenth-century Protestant iconoclasts and its suppression by "enlightened" eighteenth-century Roman Catholic prelates, to its survival and even revival not only in Germany and its immediate neighbours, but as far away as lowland Bolivia.

I thus spend more time on palmesels than on royal entries, triumphal Palm Sunday processions, or even live donkeys. I do so for several reasons. First, others have written at length about royal entries and the processional liturgy of Palm Sunday, but no one has written a performance history of palmesels. Second, palmesels were more popular and, in small towns and rural communities, more widespread than royal entries and elite Palm Sunday processions. Third, palmesels play a much larger part in the history of the processional theatre of Palm Sunday than do live donkeys. Fourth, it is worth showing that the form of processional theatre most compatible with the biblical narrative of Christ's entry into Jerusalem was also the most subject to persecution, not by followers of other religions but by zealous Christians. Fifth, I have personally seen upwards of fifty palmesels on display in churches or museums, and have accompanied three others in procession on Palm Sunday; I have learned to appreciate their unassuming representation of Christ on a donkey. Sixth, the narrative arc of my book moves from dissonance to a greater (though never complete) degree of processional accord with the biblical story. The pomp of royal entries and triumphal Palm Sunday processions began my narrative arc in Part 1. James Nayler's and Jesus of Nazareth's parodic repudiations of military triumphs served as a hinge, in Part 2, on which to turn from dissonance to greater congruence. After a brief consideration of live donkeys in Part 3.1, the comparative modesty, peacefulness, and accessibility of palmesels now completes the arc. I prefer to devote most space to the agreeable end of my story.

Some might ask why I have bothered at all with triumphal pomp and not devoted an entire book to palmesels. My explanation is that palmesels are best appreciated not merely as an endearing (and enduring) folk tradition but as a serious alternative to the dissonant pomp of royal and episcopal triumph. What has gone before provides a necessary context for the full understanding, in Part 3.2, of the processional role of palmesels.

I begin with a moment from Gerhard of Augsburg's *Life of Saint Ulrich*, written within two decades of the death of Ulrich, prince-bishop of Augsburg, in 973.[1] Ulrich had served as prince-bishop of the city for fifty years, and his biography includes an account of Palm Sunday celebrations during his episcopate:

> On that day at dawn, [Ulrich] used to come to the Church of Saint Afra, if he had not already spent the night there. He would sing the mass of the Holy Trinity and bless the palm branches and various other foliage. Then with the gospel book and crosses and banners, and with an image of the Lord seated on an ass (*cum effigie sedentis domini super asinum*), with the clergy and a multitude of people carrying palm branches in their hands, and with chants composed in honour of that same day, he proceeded with great splendour to the hill called Perlach. There, with everything beautifully done, the choir of canons came to meet him, as well as the citizens who had remained in the city, and those from surrounding towns who wanted to join them there in imitating the humility of the children and the rest of the people who [long ago had] strewed the way of the Lord with palm branches and their own clothes. After this, the holy man preached to everyone a most suitable sermon about the Lord's passion, often weeping himself and by his tears causing many others to weep. When his sermon was finished, everyone came to the cathedral church praising God, and there celebrated mass with him. Afterward they all went home.[2]

Augsburg's Palm Sunday celebrations involved two distinct processions. The first began at the Collegiate Church of Saint Afra, then about three-quarters of a mile south of the city,[3] where Ulrich celebrated a votive mass of the Holy Trinity,[4] and blessed "palm branches and various other foliage" for distribution to clergy and to "a multitude of people." Acolytes and other designated bearers lifted richly decorated banners,

---

1 Berschin and Häse, "Einleitung," in Gerhard, *Vita*, 7–8; Berschin, "Realistic," 377–78.

2 Gerhard, *Vita*, 124–27; translation adapted from Mayr-Harting, *Ottonian*, 1:121–22.

3 For a plan of Augsburg in the time of Ulrich, see Groos, "Augsburg," 42. The cathedral occupied the southern quarter of the old Roman city. To its immediate south were the Roman walls, from which the Via Claudia Augusta led to the Church of Saint Afra, which was later (ca. 1006) attached to a Benedectine monastery.

4 A votive mass is not tied to a particular day in the liturgical calendar. According to Beleth, *Summa* 51 (2:88–89), the mass of the Trinity was "at one time"—before the standardization of services for each Sunday and holy day in the liturgical year—the customary rite for use on Sundays.

processional crosses, and a gospel book.[5] Ulrich's surviving vestments, made of the finest silk and gold brocade, and possibly imported from Byzantium, testify to the visible splendour of the occasion.[6] Musically, the procession was embellished with "chants composed in honour of that same day." Whether these were freshly composed in Augsburg or borrowed from the Palm Sunday repertoire of other cities is not clear. "With great splendour," the first procession moved north from Saint Afra's along the old Roman Via Claudia Augusta (now, locally, the elegant Maximilianstrasse) "to the hill called Perlach" (*ad collem qui dicitur perleich*), by which Gerhard meant the open space, then immediately outside the old Roman city walls, that is now called Perlachplatz or Marktplatz.[7] Arriving with the "image of the Lord seated on an ass," this group recalled Christ on his donkey approaching Jerusalem in the company of his disciples.

A second procession recalled the Jewish crowd coming out of Jerusalem to meet Christ. Led by a "choir of canons," and including a large number of citizens from Augsburg and the "surrounding towns," it began "in the city," both in the literal sense that it started at the cathedral, within the city walls, and in the mimetic sense that the walled city of Augsburg now represented the city of Jerusalem, which Christ was about to enter. This group, too, moved in procession "with everything beautifully done."

Those who took part in the two processions spanned the social strata. Ulrich was the son and brother of successive Counts of Dillingen. On his mother's side he was related to the Dukes of Swabia. The canons of the cathedral and of the Collegiate Church of Saint Afra also enjoyed considerable status. As for the lay participants in the procession, Gerhard describes them simply as "citizens" or "a multitude of people" without reference to rank. The processions met at "the hill called Perlach," where Ulrich preached a sermon on Christ's imminent "passion" that brought tears to his own eyes and caused many in the crowd to weep. A single united procession then led the image of Christ on his donkey into "the city," all now joining in "imitating the humility" of those in Jerusalem

---

5 I know of no surviving processional crosses or intact gospel books from Ulrich's episcopate. The Basilica of Saints Ulrich and Afra owns a small gilt-and-enamel reliquary cross, known as the Ulrichskreuz, but the present ornamentation dates to 1494. Munich's Bayerische Staatsbibliothek owns the *Purpur-Evangeliar* (Purple Gospel), generally dated to the episcopate of Hanto of Augsburg (807–816), but its current leather binding dates to the nineteenth century.

6 Müller-Christensen, "Liturgische"; Roeck, *Geschichte*, 41.

7 Roeck, *Geschichte*, 40; Leuppi, *Liber*, 500. Heinrich Vogtherr the Younger's frequently reproduced painting *Perlachtplatz in Winter* (1550), now in Augsburg's Maximillianmuseum, shows open countryside rising to the east beyond Perlachplatz. The "fanciful hill shapes in the background" (Krämer, "Jörg," 118) were added for aesthetic effect rather than representational accuracy. Misled by reproductions of Vogtherr's painting, I previously mistook his fanciful background for Perlach Hill itself, and assumed that the city's Palm Sunday procession had followed "a downhill route from the hill called Perlach" (Harris, "Interpreting," 3). A visit to Augsburg in March 2015 enlightened me. For Vogtherr's painting, see "Augsburg1550.jpg," *Wikimedia Commons*, 27 March, 2006, http://commons.wikimedia.org/wiki/File:Augsburg1550.jpg. For an earlier, almost identical painting, *The Months of October, November, December* (ca. 1531–1550), formerly attributed to Jörg Breu the Elder and now in Berlin's Deutsches Historisches Museum, see Morrall, *Jörg*, 103.

who had "strewed the way of the Lord with palm branches and their own clothes." Mass in the cathedral followed.

Quite when Ulrich introduced the palmesel to Augsburg is unknown.[8] If, while he was a student in the city's monastic school, his exposure to "many processions" gave him "an enduring insight into the festive nature of human beings,"[9] then he may have done so early in his long episcopate. In any case, the sculpted image of Christ on a donkey was a triply innovative addition to the wider church's processional repertoire. First, Christ on the cross was a familiar subject of three-dimensional images; Christ on a donkey was not. Second, unlike other images and processional accoutrements, palmesels were wheeled, not carried. Third, palmesels avoided the urge to "splendour" evident in other processional images of the period. Essen's celebrated Golden Madonna and the jewel-encrusted reliquary statue of Sainte Foy from Conques (France), both of which survive, are two examples of the latter kind.

Palmesels, by contrast, were comparatively simple in execution. The oldest surviving example, originally from Steinen (Switzerland) and now in Zurich's Landesmuseum, has been conservatively dated by its conservators to "around 1055"[10] (Fig. 14). Acquired by the museum in 1893, it had previously been stored "for many decades in the loft of the charnel house" in Steinen,[11] some twenty miles south of Zurich. Remarkably well preserved, it retains its original wheeled platform and much of its original predominantly red and blue polychromy.[12] It gives no sign that it was ever enamelled, gilded, or studded with jewels.[13] Christ's right arm is raised in blessing. His left hand clasps a book to his breast. The lively wooden donkey "strides forward, right foreleg lifted."[14] Pulled at street level, and painted in lifelike colours (or left unpainted) rather than coated in gold or

---

8 For the argument that Ulrich's processional *effigie* was not a statue, but a carved wooden or painted panel, see Adelmann, "Christus," 183–87. For a refutation of Adelmann's hypothesis on linguistic and art historical grounds, see Tripps, *Handelnde*, 89–102. Gerhard of Augsburg's latest editor is satisfied that the *effigie* was "a life-size wooden figure of the Lord sitting on an ass" (Berschin, "Realistic," 378).

9 Bernhart, "Bischof," 23.

10 Flühler-Kreis, Wyer, and Stuppan, *Holzskulpturen*, 1:177, who add (1:179) that radiocarbon dating suggests an even earlier date between 1011 and 1015.

11 Stückelberg, "Palmsonntagsfeier," 30; see also Flühler-Kreis, Wyer, and Stuppan, *Holzskulpturen*, 1:179.

12 Restoration work, including the trimming of Christ's beard, and the loss of Christ's right hand, account for differences between earlier and more recent photographs of the Steinen palmesel: compare Young, *Drama*, 1:94, and Flühler-Kreis, Wyer, and Stuppan, *Holzskulpturen*, 1:176–79.

13 I know of only two late palmesels that may have been decorated with jewels. The palmesel of Nonnberg Abbey, destroyed by order of the archbishop of Salzburg in the late eighteenth century, was reportedly adorned with semi-precious stones (see chap. 17). According to Schatz, "Palmesel," the robe worn by the Christ figure on the fifteenth-century palmesel in Kalbensteinberg's Reiterkirche was once "probably studded with precious [or semi-precious] gems."

14 Horlbeck, "Gloria," 29.

**Figure 14 Palmesel, Steinen, ca. 1055. Schweizerisches Nationalmuseum, Zurich.
Photograph by author.**

enamel, palmesels are inclined by their very design to interpret Christ's entry in terms of humility rather than splendour, and to emphasize his humanity rather than his divinity. Augsburg's palmesel probably resembled its later counterpart in Steinen, and served to moderate the general splendour of Ulrich's Palm Sunday retinue.

The subsequent early history of the palmesel is sketchy at best. Before the thirteenth century, we have only Gerhard of Augsburg's written testimony and two or three surviving palmesels. Of these, the Steinen palmesel is unquestionably the best preserved. A second early palmesel, in Berlin's Bode Museum, lost its donkey in the Second World War. The poplar-wood Christ figure, its carved sky-blue robe secured with a red sash, now sits astride a modern replacement. Dated to "around 1200," the original palmesel and rider

Figure 14 (continued)

are said to have come from a church near Landshut (Bavaria).[15] A third palmesel for which an early date has been claimed is in Erding's Heimatsmuseum (Bavaria). The Christ figure lacks both forearms, while the donkey is missing its ears, lower legs, and feet. The whole stands only just over four feet high. The late-ninetenth-century parish priest considered it "a crude, clumsy, naive work allegedly carved by a man with little artistic skill around 1200."[16] Paul Adelsberger, director of the musem, dates the palmesel to "around the fourteenth century," but admits that that "there are a few experts who believe the figure could be even older and date from the eleventh century."[17] Unfortunately, we know nothing of the performance history of any of these images beyond the fact that the Steinen palmesel, still in possession of its original wheeled platform, was pulled rather than carried in procession. Even so, standing before the Steinen palmesel can evoke a measure of awe: its age, artistic merit, and excellent condition make it a unique witness to the early years of a thousand-year-old performance tradition.

---

15 Beenken, *Romanische*, 134–35, includes a pre-war photograph of the intact sculpture, which he dates to "around 1170–1180." Adelmann, "Christus," 187, and Lipsmeyer, "Jahreslaufbrauchtum," 51, prefer "around 1200," while Vöge, "Romanische," 127, favours "hardly later than 1250." For a colour photograph of the original Christ figure on its modern donkey, see Sailko, "Bassa baviera, palmesel, fine del XII sec.JPG," *Wikimedia Commons*, 18 February 2012, https://commons.wikimedia.org/wiki/File:Bassa_baviera,_palmesel,_fine_del_XII_sec.JPG.

16 Strele, "Palmesel," 138.

17 "Einer der ältesten Palmesel im Erzbistum," *Isargau.de*, March 29, 2004, http://ud04_116.ud04. udmedia.de/cms/media/Sachaussschuesse/Brauchtum/Berichte/Der_aelteste_Palmesel.pdf.

By the thirteenth century, palmesels begin to appear more frequently in the written records. The earliest such account comes from Liège, now in eastern Belgium, but then capital of a largely independent prince-bishopric within the German (or Holy Roman) Empire. Renier of Saint-Jacques, prior of the city's Benedictine abbey of Saint-Jacques, wrote, as part of his 1213 entry in the annals of the abbey: "Nor do we wish to be silent that the people of Huy, when Liège was destroyed, found in a certain church an image of the Saviour sitting on an ass (*immaginem Salvatoris in asino sedentem*), removed it, and setting it in a wagon, took it away in their midst with great joy, and when they had returned to Huy, most piously left it in the Church of the Holy Sepulchre."[18] Wilhelm Vöge understands this as a simple case of looting.[19] But Renier's immediate narrative context was the sack of Liège, including "its churches and its holy places,"[20] by Henry I, duke of Brabant, in May 1212, and the subsequent battle of Steppes, in October 1213, in which the combined forces of the prince-bishop of Liège, the count of Loos, and the citizen militia of Huy defeated Henry's army.[21] It is more likely, therefore, that the citizens of Huy, allies of the Liègeois, happily discovered the palmesel undamaged after the sack of Liège and took it for safekeeping to the Augustinian abbey of Neufmoutier, dedicated to the Holy Sepulchre, near Huy. In any case, Renier's brief notice suggests that the Liège palmesel was a popular object of devotion, known and valued not only by the Liègeois themselves but also by the people of Huy, sixteen miles to the southwest of Liège.

A more detailed, but arguably exceptional, account of the palmesel's role in the Palm Sunday liturgy comes from Essen. Essen abbey, one of the wealthiest in the German empire, was headed by an abbess with remarkable secular and ecclesiastical authority, a "princess of the empire" (*Reichsfürstin*) who exercised all the powers of a prince-bishop but that of ordination. The ladies of the abbey, all of aristocratic birth, were not cloistered nuns but canonesses. By at least 1224, the abbey's collegiate church (*Stiftskirche*) had a separate chapter of priests, serving under a dean who was himself subject to the abbess.[22] A surviving church ordinal, written in the second half of the fourteenth century but reflecting "thirteenth-century liturgical usage,"[23] includes directions for the observance of Palm Sunday.[24]

After compline on the eve of the feast, "the image of Christ sitting on an ass" (*ymaginem Christi sedentem in asino*) was led in an elaborate candlelight procession from the abbey church, around the cemetery, and through the city and central marketplace to

---

18 Renier de Saint-Jacques, "Annales," 670.

19 Vöge, "Romanische," 127.

20 Kurth, *Cité*, 1:120.

21 Kurth, *Cité*, 1:119–25.

22 Kahsnitz, "Gospel," 123–27; Bärsch, "Raum," 165.

23 Lipsmeyer, "Devotion," 22. Arens, *Liber*, viii–ix, makes the case for the ordinal's dependence on thirteenth-century sources. Schilp, "Liber," 192, suggests twelfth-century sources.

24 Arens, *Liber*, 41–47 (Latin), 148–51 (German translation); Lipsmeyer, "Devotion, 22–24 (English summary). The abbey church is now Essen cathedral.

"the Church of Saint Gertrude" (now the Market Church),[25] a distance of some three hundred yards. Carried at the head of the procession were "four gold crosses decorated with precious stones, gems, and enamels,"[26] other images including the celebrated Golden Madonna,[27] reliquaries, and various "banners" (*vexilla*).[28] Then came the scholars of the choir school, the canons, the processional candles, the palmesel, the canonesses (who went only as far as the abbey churchyard), and "finally the people." In keeping with the biblical account of Christ's entry into Jerusalem, the processional order required that "some were preceding and others following Christ on the donkey."[29] As the procession entered Saint Gertude's, it was censed by the church's priest (*plebanus*). The palmesel spent the night "in the middle of the church in front of the choir."[30]

The next morning, after palm branches were blessed and distributed at the abbey church, an almost identical procession made its way to Saint Gertrude's to recover "the image of Christ with the donkey that had been led there yesterday." On arrival, the clergy remained outside while "the people" (*populus*) went inside to retrieve the palmesel. The *plebanus*, carrying an ornate gospel book (*pleonarius*), joined the procession for the return journey.[31] Meanwhile, the canonesses, who had again remained at the abbey church, accompanied this time by the officiant and acolytes, gathered before the huge late-tenth-century seven-branch gilded bronze candlestick that stood in the nave before the altar of the Holy Cross.[32] There they awaited the return of the palmesel.

After entering the abbey church in joyous procession, the palmesel was placed in a prominent position at the west end of the nave, facing east towards the high altar. Three carpets had been laid across the nave between the candelabrum and the image. The canonesses entered the choir stalls to the north of the nave, while the canons and scholars filled those to the south. When all were in place, the *plebanus* and a subdeacon, each with a sacristan, approached the image and stood, one pair on either side, "near the neck of the ass."

---

25 The twelfth-century Marktkirche was dedicated to Saint Gertrude until 1563, when it became the first Protestant church in Essen. Razed by allied bombing during the Second World War, the church was rebuilt in a simplified form. It should not be confused with Essen's nineteenth-century Catholic Church of Saint Gertrude.

26 Kahsnitz, "Gospel," 130; see also Pothmann, "Essener," 142–48.

27 Kahsnitz, "Gospel," 129; Pothmann, "Essener," 137–40; Frings and Gerchow, *Krone*, 66, 270.

28 For the argument that in Essen the processional *vexilla* were not literal "banners" but "the golden crosses and the reliquary containing the Holy Nail," see Kahsnitz, "Gospel," 157. For the eleventh-century reliquary, see Pothmann, "Essener," 150–51; Frings and Gerchow, *Krone*, 272–73. For colour photographs of Essen's surviving processional treasures, see Frings and Gerchow, *Krone*, 66, 166–67, 233–34, 266, 268–77; Falk, *Gold*, 62–101.

29 Arens, *Liber*, 41; compare Matt. 21:9 (Vulgate).

30 Arens, *Liber*, 41.

31 Kahsnitz, "Gospel," 156, defines a *pleonarius* as "a manuscript which contains the complete text of the Gospels, as opposed to a Gospel lectionary or book of pericopes, which contains only the extracts from the Gospels read at mass." Essen Abbey owned two exceptionably fine *pleonarii*.

32 Arens, *Liber*, 42–44, 149. For the candelabrum, which now stands at the west end of the nave, see Pothmann, "Essener," 140–43.

Six canonesses also approached. Standing behind the palmesel, facing east, they led the convent in the Palm Sunday hymn "Gloria, laus et honor." When all had returned to their seats, the clergy sang the antiphon "Pueri Hebraeorum vestimenta prosternebant" (The Hebrew children spread their garments), and eight scholars genuflected on the carpet in front of the image. Then the canonesses sang while the canons, "kneeling, similarly prostrate[d] themselves;" the clergy sang while the canonesses adored (*adorabit*) the image; the canonesses sang once without accompanying action; and the clergy sang again while the officiant and acolytes prostrated themselves in adoration of the image. Finally, while the clergy chanted "Ingrediente Domino in sanctam civitatem," the "image with the ass" was moved to the tomb of Saint Altfrid, the founder of the abbey, located at the foot of the steps leading up to the choir. The image remained there during high mass.[33]

I know of no other case in which a Palm Sunday procession concluded with so elaborate a veneration of the palmesel. Unable to compete for splendour with the abbey's Golden Madonna, processional crosses, gospel books, and multiple reliquaries, the simple palmesel nevertheless outranked these treasures on Palm Sunday. At times, too, the palmesel reversed other established hierarchies, giving greater prominence to "the people" than to the princess-abbess and her clergy. The canonesses remained inside the abbey grounds, while the *populus* followed the palmesel through the streets and alone went into the Church of Saint Gertrude to retrieve the image on Palm Sunday. Even the abbey's male canons stayed outside. Only during the final extended act of adoration did the canonesses reclaim their ceremonial rank.

An ordinal from Zurich's Großmünster (Great Minster), compiled by the cantor Konrad von Mure between 1260 and 1281, bears witness both to lively popular interaction with the palmesel and to an extensive theatrical mapping of Jerusalem onto the local terrain. The ordinal was one of very few liturgical books to survive the systematic plundering of ecclesiastical libraries by the city's Reformed authorities on October 7, 1525.[34] It includes two versions of the city's Palm Sunday rite, both of which were almost certainly "older than Konrad's tenure."[35] One, in the main body of the text, assumes a processional route across the Limmat River to the Lindenhof—then, as now, a public park on a hill overlooking the city—and back again. A second, added in cramped letters across the wide bottom margins, sets out an abbreviated route in the immediate vicinity of the church, to be used in case of bad weather or damage to the bridge across the river.[36] Both map Jerusalem onto the local landscape, but the longer route necessarily does so to better effect, creating a vast and hilly stage set for the day's processional theatre.

---

33 Arens, *Liber*, 44–47, 149–51.

34 Lipsmeyer, "Liber," 139; Germann, "Untergang."

35 Lipsmeyer, "Liber," 141.

36 Leuppi, *Liber*, 238–40; Lipsmeyer, "Liber." An agreement drawn up in 1265 allowed for the procession to be curtailed "on account of intemperate weather or breakage or damage to the bridge or other legitimate impediment" (Leuppi, *Liber*, 241). A later document (ca. 1474) specified that the full procession to and from the Hof took place only "if it is fine and not rainy weather and also if one may cross the bridge" (Wyss, "Geschichte," 450).

The full rite began in the Großmünster after the brief morning office of terce. Palm branches were exorcised and blessed, the day's gospel read, and prayers sung in the chancel. The palms were then aspersed, censed, and distributed to the waiting crowd in the nave, while altars, canons, and people were also sprinkled with sacred water. Sometimes, "to avoid din and tumult," the palms were distributed to what must have been a large—if not somewhat unruly—congregation at the beginning of the ceremony and blessed while already in the hands of the crowd. A procession "with banners" then made its way west across the river and up to the Hof, a distance of about a quarter of a mile. Choir and laity alternated antiphons, versicles, and responses along the way.[37]

Meanwhile, the "image of the Lord on an ass" (*imago domini super asino*)[38] had probably spent the night with the nuns of the Fraumünster abbey, on the same side of the river as the Lindenhof. We know this was the case in the fifteenth century, and there is no reason to believe it was not by then a long-established tradition.[39] After matins, the palmesel was taken in a separate procession from the abbey to the Lindenhof to await the arrival of the procession from the Großmünster. A series of mimetic correspondences was thus set up, in which the Hof represented the Mount of Olives, Zurich stood for Jerusalem, the palmesel and its company took the part of Christ and his disciples approaching the city, and those coming from the Großmünster represented the crowd coming out of Jerusalem to meet him.

When the two groups met at the Hof, the nuns and canons alternated chants, including the standard "Gloria, laus et honor." Then, as the antiphon "Pueri Hebreorum tollentes ramos olivarum" (The Hebrew children lifting olive branches) was sung, "small branches were thrown here and there over the image by the faithful."[40] German speakers used a lively metaphor to describe the action: "the palms were shot (*geschossen*)" at the image.[41] "With several hundred people taking part," it must have been a moment of "spectacular" audience participation.[42]

Further antiphons were sung before a combined procession joyously descended the steep hill into the city. Still singing, choirs, clergy, and crowd crossed the bridge and climbed a shorter hill up to the Großmünster, where "amidst a crowd of laity and clergy" the image of Christ and the donkey was led into the church.[43] Extending the series of

---

37 Leuppi, *Liber*, 238.

38 Leuppi, *Liber*, 239.

39 Lipsmeyer, "Liber," 143; Zeller-Werdmüller, "Nächtliche"; Wyss, *Geschichte*, 450. The nuns were also obliged, according to a 1265 agreement, to provide "a pitcher of wine containing enough for thirty-two cups" (*urna vini que constat ex triginta duobus cifis [=Scyphis]*), apparently for later consumption by the canons of the minster (Leuppi, *Liber*, 241).

40 Leuppi, *Liber*, 239.

41 Wyss, *Geschichte*, 449, citing a document from 1474. In 1524, Gerold Edlibach wrote that "to praise God one shot palms" (*got zů lob den balmenn schoß*) at the image (Jezler, "Beschachend," 51; see also Edlibach, *Chronik*, 269). Bullinger, *Reformationsgeschichte*, 1:160, wrote: "On Palm Sunday, people led the donkey (*Esel*) up to the Hof, and there shot palms (*und da den Balmen schooß*)."

42 Lipsmeyer, "Liber," 143.

43 Leuppi, *Liber*, 240.

mimetic correspondences begun earlier, the Großmünster and its precincts now signi-fied Jerusalem's Temple Mount and perhaps by analogy the heavenly temple entered by Christ at his Ascension.

The shorter version of the day's festivities began with the palmesel stationed near the house occupied by Welcho, stipendiary priest (*plebanus*) of the minster from 1265 to 1282, at what is now Kirchgasse 13.[44] The palmesel faced downhill towards the main (north) door of the Großmünster. A procession made its way through the cloisters and up the street toward the palmesel. The provost, pastor, and most of the other canons, clerics, and scholars waited with the palmesel, while a second group, consisting of the celebrant, acolytes bearing thurible, cross, candles, and banners, and the twelve scholars with the best singing voices, positioned themselves on the far (south) side of the church, overlooking the Wasserkirche (Water Church) and the river.[45] After the choir of scholars sang "Gloria, laus et honor," the provost's group repeated the last verse, and then began to lead the palmesel downhill towards the Großmünster, recalling—albeit on a smaller scale than during the usual descent from the Lindenhof—Christ's ride from the Mount of Olives. This, in turn, was the signal for the celebrant, the choirboys, and others pre-sent to hurry around the outside of the church with palm branches in hand and greet the approaching palmesel, which was then led into the church amid "a crowd of laity and clergy," while the choir sang "Ingrediente Domino in sanctam civitatem."[46] Elizabeth Lipsmeyer believes that, in the shorter version, the palms were shot "in the church" rather than outside.[47]

Von Mure's liturgy for Palm Sunday includes no reference to "great splendour," ornate processional crosses, gospel books, or other prized images accompanying the palmesel in procession. Emil Egli mistakenly believed that the treasured relics of the town's patron saints, Felix and Regula, were carried in procession to the Hof both "on Palm Sunday and after Pentecost,"[48] but only the latter was in fact the case. By at least 1304, on the Wednesday following Pentecost, the venerated relics were carried "to the Hof in a very beautiful and laudable procession" involving the nuns of the Fraumünster, "all the clergy of Zurich, both religious and secular," and numerous laity.[49] By 1524, when Gerold Edlibach recalled it, the Pentecost procession had grown to include not only the relics

---

44 For Welcho's identity and the location of his house, see Leuppi, *Liber*, 239n2, and for plans of the minster and its immediate vicinity, 495–96. For the role of the *plebanus* or *Leutpriester*, variously translated as "people's pastor" or "stipendiary priest," see Dörner, *Kirche*, 127–32.

45 The Wasserkirche, built on a small island in the Limmat, is midway between the Großmünster and the Fraumünster.

46 Leuppi, *Liber*, 239–40; Lipsmeyer, "Liber," 142–43.

47 Lipsmeyer, "Liber," 143. Wyss, *Chronik*, 51, lends support to this view when he reports that in 1524 it was ordered that palms be shot "neither on the Hof nor in the churches."

48 Egli, "Zürich," 158; Farner, *Huldrych*, 3:20, and Garside, *Zwingli*, 85, 88, repeat Egli's error.

49 Ott, "Richtebrief," 233; Barraud Wiener and Jezler, "Liturgie," 135. Bullinger, *Reformationsgeschichte*, 1:160, recalls the "Pentecost Wednesday" procession, in which "the coffins" (*die Särch*) were carried "up to the Hof," before the Reformation.

of Felix and Regula but "all the relics" belonging to "three parishes and three monastic orders" borne in "four large coffins and four small coffins," flanked by members of "the twelve guilds," each guild carrying "four costly candles well gilded with gold" and "other costly things."[50] The absence of comparable markers of conspicuous sanctity or religious grandeur on Palm Sunday, even in Edlibach's day,[51] draws attention again to the natural inclination of the palmesel to insist on a modest interpretation of its role.

Subsequent scattered records add to our knowledge of the performance history (and other adventures) of the Zurich palmesel. In 1425, late at night on the eve of Palm Sunday, Ulrich Grauw, a metalworker, and some companions were together on the Lindenhof. One suspects they had been drinking. Hearing church bells strike two in the morning, one of the men said, "It's time to fetch the donkey." The group walked down to the Fraumünster abbey, where the nuns, praying with the palmesel, begged them not to take it. The men defied the nuns and led the palmesel back up toward the Hof, singing a version of the popular pilgrimage song, "In God's name we go our way, and for his help we longing pray" (*In gottes namen faren wir, siner helff begeren wir*). One man led the impromptu procession by holding aloft a crucifix, which had also been removed from the abbey. At the Hof, the men placed "the donkey and the image of our Lord God" under a shelter, so that it would not be rained on. They later insisted that they had not inflicted any disgrace on the image, but did admit to having broken "a lamp or two" in the course of the raid.[52]

In May 1474, Andreas Hopf, steward of the abbey, and his wife Margaretha established an endowment to pay all eight chaplains of the Fraumünster, as well as the schoolmaster and three scholars in their roles as choirmaster and choirboys, so that "henceforth they might annually and perpetually, early on Palm Sunday after matins, with songs and readings, lead our Lord on the donkey from our aforementioned house of worship to the Zurich Hof, where the palms will then be shot."[53] The abbey's accounts in 1517 confirm payment to the "chaplains for leading the donkey to the Hof," as well as to the sacristan of the parish Church of Saint Peter for ringing the church bells as the procession passed.[54] A curious entry in an eighteenth-century encyclopedic history of Zurich suggests that, while the chaplains and choirboys sang, the hard physical work of hauling the palmesel up the steep incline to the Hof was the responsibility of the city's butchers' guild. The entry, whose primary focus is "little Carnival cakes," claims that the parish priest of Saint Peter's used to give the butchers, every Ash Wednesday, a plate of a hundred and one *Faßnacht-Küchlein* as payment for pulling "the palmesel on Palm Sunday to the chapel on the Hof ... when it was still the time of the papacy." The customary stipend seems to have outlasted the required work, and by the eighteenth century was no longer an

---

50 Edlibach, *Chronik*, 270; see also Dörner, *Kirche*, 173–74.

51 Edlibach, *Chronik*, 269.

52 Zeller-Werdmüller, "Nächtliche."

53 Wyss, "Geschichte," 449–50; Barraud Wiener and Jezler, "Liturgie," 146.

54 Dörner, *Kirche*, 173.

edible gift: "the priest," the entry notes, "now gives them money each year."[55] The Hopfs' bequest and the subsequent payments to chaplains and bell-ringers confirm that the palmesel was not simply delivered to the Hof but was led there in formal liturgical procession. The payment to the butchers uncovers the otherwise hidden contribution of lay muscle. Even Ulrich Grauw and his fellows, in their inebriated effort to emulate the procession, testify both to its existence and to lay familiarity with the palmesel.[56]

---

55 Bluntschli, *Memorabilia*, 129; Barraud Wiener and Jezler, "Liturgie," 146, admit to being unable to find any independent verification of this custom.

56 Barraud Wiener and Jezler, "Liturgie," 139, 146, suggest that the Fraumünster and Saint Peter's each had a palmesel of its own, but I am inclined to think that the evidence they cite refers to a single palmesel, enjoyed on Palm Sunday by all three congregations.

THE LORD GOD BELONGS TO THE BUTCHERS

IN AUGSBURG, ESSEN, and Zurich, the palmesel belonged to a prestigious urban church or abbey. This was not the case everywhere. Steinen, the home of the earliest surviving palmesel, was a much smaller community; it is not known who owned its palmesel in the eleventh century. In late fourteenth-century Zurzach, a small town about twenty-six miles northwest of Zurich on the south (Swiss) bank of the Rhine, the palmesel was pulled in procession by farm labourers, and assigned a much more modest role than its kin in Essen. A surviving ritual book from around 1370 in Zurzach's Collegiate Church of Saint Verena makes it clear that the crucifix, rather than the palmesel, was the cler-ically sanctioned star of the community's Palm Sunday procession. The rubrics grant that "some of our farmworkers go ahead [of the procession] pulling the wagon with the image sitting on a donkey," but it is the veiled Lenten cross that occupies the privileged position at the rear of the procession, surrounded by choirboys, deacons, subdeacons, and finally the dean. Even so, the Palm Sunday cross in Zurzach anticipated Good Friday rather than military victory. At a stop somewhere in the open countryside, the veil was removed from the crucifix, which was then laid flat on the ground, protected beneath by a large cloth. While hymns and antiphons were sung, the dean struck the crucified Christ with a palm branch, a priest's maniple was thrown to recall the crowd casting garments before Christ, and then everyone present threw palm branches at the crucifix.[1] The ritual book makes no further mention of the palmesel, leaving the impression that the clergy only reluctantly allowed the peasants' palmesel even a small part in the procession.

Palmesels in some major urban settings could also be associated with lower caste laity rather than with the clergy. When the German king and future emperor Maximilian I visited the free imperial city of Schwäbisch Hall for Palm Sunday in 1489, he took part in the customary procession of "the Lord Christ sitting on a donkey" (*der Herr Christus auf einem Esel sitzend*) from the Langenfeld Gate to Saint Michael's Church.[2] The palmesel was escorted by the clergy, council members, and common people, and, as the chronicle notes, "the king himself went with them." But when Maximilian "saw Christ led into the church by the ushers (*Häscher*) and bailiffs (*Stadtknechte*)," he voiced his shock: "Oh, my God! Do the people of Hall then have none but beadles and sergeants (*Büttel und Schergen*) who can lead this brave man?" The terms used by the chronicler (*Häscher, Stadtknechte*) and those reportedly used by the king (*Büttel, Schergen*) are more or less "overlapping" terms, ranging from "the euphemistic, to the neutral, to the inten-tionally defaming," that were used to describe minor court officials and "police officers" in early modern Germany. All such positions, because of their necessary proximity to

---

1 Wittwer, *Zurzacher*, 92–93, 197–99; see also Reinle, *Ausstattung*, 212–13.

2 The twelfth-century Langenfelder Tor, now also known as the Crailsheimer Tor, was rebuilt in 1515. The short processional route from the gate to the church is uphill, recalling the ascent to Jerusalem's Temple Mount rather than the descent from the Mount of Olives.

malefactors and executioners, entailed a measure of social dishonour.[3] The king used stronger, more derogatory terms than the chronicler: "beadles" (*Büttel*) ranked lower than "bailiffs" (*Stadtknechte*) because the former "did not participate in the torture and interrogation of 'malefactors' ... and they were not involved in the execution process"; "sergeant" (*Scherge*) was an "explicitly dishonourable" term.[4] Chastened, the council hastily decreed that the palmesel should no longer be led by the bailiffs, but by "two council members (*Rathsherrn*)."[5]

Two palmesels, acquired from Saint Michael's Church by Schwäbisch Hall's Historical Society in 1837, can now be seen in the city's Hällisch-Fränkisches Museum.[6] The older and larger of the two has been dated to "between 1380 and ... 1420,"[7] and is almost certainly the palmesel seen by Maximilian in 1489. With an abnormally long outstretched neck, no eyes, and missing ears, the donkey has an almost abstract appearance. The Christ figure, although it now lacks both feet and forearms, was carved more realistically, especially in its facial features. The second palmesel, only four feet high, has been dated to "around 1505/10."[8] It may have been made after Maximilian's visit, so that the two council members charged with pulling the palmesel would have a lighter load.[9] Both palmesels survived the city's Lutheran Reformation, but were presumably retired soon afterwards along with the church's Palm Sunday procession.

In Biberach an der Riss, another free imperial city, the palmesel was not only pulled in procession but owned and cared for by laymen. We owe our knowledge of Biberach's palmesel to two staunchly Catholic patrician brothers, Joachim I and Heinrich VI von Pflummern, who between them composed first-hand accounts of religious practices in the city as they were immediately before and during the Reformation. Joachim, a city magistrate, ended his account in 1530; Heinrich, chaplain of the city's Hospital Church (*Spitalkirche*) until the Reformation displaced him, began his account where Heinrich left off.[10] Both remembered the city's palmesel with affection.

Ordinarily Biberach's palmesel stood in the Upper Chapel, a beautiful and well-furnished chapel in the grounds of Saint Martin's Church.[11] Once a year, before vespers on the eve of Palm Sunday, the image of "our Lord God on the ass" was placed outside in the churchyard, where "many children and common people" came to greet it. After vespers, the palmesel was taken in "pious procession" to the chapel of Saint Leonard near the

---

3 Stuart, *Defiled*, 136–37. Stuart's book explores in detail the complex and fluid early modern German caste system, in which executioners and skinners ranked the lowest.

4 Stuart, *Defiled*, 98, 136.

5 Crusius, *Schwäbische*, 2:133; see also Zeller, Ausführliche, 678–79; Strele, "Palmesel," 145.

6 Decker, *Bildwerke*, 124–28, 149–52; Strele, "Palmesel," 145.

7 Decker, *Bildwerke*, 127.

8 Decker, *Bildwerke*, 149.

9 Decker, *Bildwerke*, 152.

10 For the full texts of the brothers' chronicles, see Angele, *Altbiberach*, 9–181. For a variant of Joachim's chronicle, see Schilling, "Religiösen," and for a variant of Heinrich's chronicle, Schilling, "Beiträge."

11 Angele, *Altbiberach*, 44; Schilling, "Religiösen," 57.

town's Upper Gate (Fig. 15).[12] Men carrying "guild poles" (*Zunftstangen*)—tall wooden poles topped with ornate carved and painted figures emblematic of the town's guilds—led the way. Priests and choirboys, the latter bearing two small candlesticks (*Stänglin*)[13] and a processional cross, followed. The palmesel, lacking wheels of its own, stood on a small cart, which was pulled by members of the butchers' guild. Other members, bearing guild poles and candles, walked alongside and behind the cart, reflecting the fact that the image of "the Lord God belongs to the butchers" (*Der Herrgott ist der Mezger gesein*).[14] Christ, astride the donkey, was dressed in a blue choir robe (*Chormantel*).[15] Behind the butchers came the town's mayors, burghers, "common men," and finally women of all classes. Church bells rang along the route. After the Marian hymn "Salve Regina" was sung, the palmesel was left overnight in the chapel.[16]

In contemporary Zurich, the butchers pulled the palmesel uphill to the Lindenhof, but the image was still owned by the Großmünster. In Biberach, the butchers owned the palmesel. Although they were neither priests nor patricians, butchers were "honourable artisan[s]" and members of one of "the largest and most honourable guilds" in any early modern German city.[17] As such, they enjoyed a much higher social standing than the bailiffs or beadles who had so shocked Maximilian by pulling the palmesel in Schwäbisch Hall. But their social status was not the primary reason why butchers' guilds were the only lay corporations to take responsibility for a palmesel. There was also a commercial incentive. Palm Sunday and Carnival, when butchers were also disproportionately active,[18] were the liturgical bookends of Lent, the latter heralding its beginning and the former announcing its close. During Lent, the butchers' business suffered from their clients' traditional abstinence from meat. The privilege of taking a leading role during Carnival and Palm Sunday served both as a compensation for the butchers' economic losses and as an effective way for the guild to advertise meat consumption on the traditionally gluttonous Carnival Tuesday and again in anticipation of Easter feasting.[19]

---

12 Angele, *Altbiberach*, 80; Schilling, "Religiösen," 117. Biberach's upper gate, built in 1373 and variously known as the Obertor or Riedlingertor, was demolished in 1870. A small framed mural marks the former location of the gate at the top of what is now Theaterstraße. For the chapel of Saint Leonard, which has also disappeared, see Angele, *Altbiberach*, 50–51; Schilling, "Religiösen," 70–71.

13 For the meaning of *Stänglin* in this context, see Angele, *Altbiberach*, 64, where Joachim notes that "two [choir] school boys with poles and candles on them (*mit Stänglin und Kerzen daruff*)" customarily took part in church processions.

14 Schilling, "Religiösen," 117; see also Angele, *Altbiberach*, 80: "Der Herrgott uff dem Esel hat den Metzgern gehört."

15 *Chormantel* can mean anything from a simple choirboy's robe to a richly embroidered chasuble. In this context, I prefer the more modest garment.

16 Angele, *Altbiberach*, 80–81; Schilling, "Religiösen," 117–18.

17 Stuart, *Defiled*, 18, 35.

18 Nuremberg's Carnival provides the best-known case of a butchers' guild playing a prominent role in the festivities (Sumberg, *Nuremberg*, 26–38). For other examples, see Moser, *Fastnacht*, 140–41, 182, 201–2, 257, 260, 282–85. Since 1904 a butchers' guild has also played a leading role in the Carnival in Oruro, Bolivia (Harris, *Carnival*, 209).

19 Moser, *Fastnacht*, 202. I am grateful to Glenn Ehrstine for first drawing my attention to this explanation.

Figure 15 Obertor (Upper Gate), Biberach, before its demolition in 1870.
Engraving, Konrad Dollonger, *Architektonische Reise-Skizzen* (Stuttgart, 1880–81).
Wikimedia Commons.

In Biberach on Palm Sunday morning, the worshippers divided into two groups. One group met in the church for early mass before going in procession to the Upper Gate, carrying blessed palm or savin juniper branches (*Sevich*).[20] Clergy, choristers, and acolytes each carried "a sea cane or iris" (*Meerrohr oder schwerttelen*).[21] Together, they represented those who went out from Jerusalem to welcome Christ. A second group, led by members of the butchers' guild, retrieved the palmesel from Saint Leonard's chapel and took on the collective role of the disciples approaching Jerusalem from the Mount of Olives with Christ on his donkey. When the first group arrived at the Upper Gate, "our Lord God with the donkey" was waiting for them. The meeting's location was no doubt chosen because its comparative elevation offered a downward slope through the Market Square to the church, allowing Jerusalem to be loosely mapped onto the local terrain. Clergy and people knelt before the image.

Then, in the same processional order as the previous evening, the worshippers led the palmesel down into the town. Arriving in the churchyard, many knelt or prostrated themselves. The choirboys sang with their arms raised to the Christ figure, spread their surplices before the palmesel, and struck one another with "sea canes," recalling the scourging that Christ would face on Good Friday. In like manner, the people "shot" (*haben geschossen*) their palms and juniper branches at the image.[22] Women carried little lights in lanterns; some, their heads modestly covered by rain scarfs, sang. When everyone went into the church for the main mass of the day, the palmesel stayed outside in the churchyard. People took blessed palm and savin branches home; if summer proved stormy, the branches would be put on the fire to improve the weather. After lunch, many children returned to play near the image. Adults, especially women, came to pray in front of it.[23]

Palm Sunday in Biberach was known as "the day of the humble king" (*den tag des demüettigen Königs*).[24] The Christ of the palmesel wore a choir robe, his donkey was pulled in a butcher's cart, and he was acclaimed with local juniper as well as exotic palms. At the close of the procession, rather than continuing into the church, the palmesel stayed in the churchyard; during the afternoon children and women played and prayed in its presence. The image was owned not by the church but by the butchers' guild, whose members walked in the privileged positions next to the image. The secular elite—mayors and burghers—outnumbered the clergy in the procession. As for

---

20 Angele, *Altbiberach*, 82; Schilling, "Religiösen," 119. Grimm, *Deutsches*, 10.1:707, defines *Sevenbaum* as "juniperus sabina"; Angele, *Altbiberach*, 122n31, prefers "Besenstrauch, lat. Genista," i.e., broom.

21 I have been unable to find a translation of *Schwerttelen*, a species of foliage which in Biberach was also strewn in churches and along the processional route during the feast of Corpus Christi (Schilling, "Religiösen," 143). The closest botanical German word I have found is *Schwertlilie* (lit: sword lily), meaning "iris."

22 Schilling, "Religiösen," 119; see also Angele, *Altbiberach*, 82: "waved or ... threw (*gewinkt oder ... zugeworfen*)."

23 Angele, *Altbiberach*, 81–82; Schilling, "Religiösen," 119–20; see also Scribner, *Popular*, 25.

24 Schilling, "Religiösen," 120.

the choirboys striking one another with canes, this must have been a favourite part of the action for energetic young boys.[25] Whereas the theology of Essen's aristocratic canonesses had inclined toward the hierarchical and transcendent, the folk theology of Biberach was immanent and practical. Taking the blessed palms home to protect, if need be, against inclement summer weather was consistent with this folk theology: the Christ who rode a donkey into Biberach cared less about ecclesiastical status than about potential damage to the crops.

Joachim von Pflummern's repeated insistence that everything was done "piously" and "with moderation" was probably intended to counter the threat of iconoclasm. If so, he failed. His brother Heinrich later names the palmesel in a list of Lenten and Holy Week traditions—including the receiving of ashes on Ash Wednesday, Lenten fasting, Maundy Thursday foot washing, the Easter sepulchre, and devotion to various "paintings" (*Tafeln*)—that were abolished by the newly Protestant authorities, briefly sympathetic to the Zwinglian brand of reform, between 1523 and 1530.[26] Then, on the feast day of Saints Peter and Paul (June 29), 1531, an official iconoclastic cleansing of Saint Martin's Church took place, as a result of which the palmesel was handed over to "a bathmaster, who needed it for heating his baths."[27] As firewood, the palmesel could heat the water in which the bathmaster, whose profession overlapped with that of a barber–surgeon,[28] bathed his patients. Michel Rocher (or Neher), the bathmaster in question, did not immediately destroy his prize. First, he displayed the palmesel in his storehouse, "advancing his own schism by shouting that anyone who wanted a good warm bath" could now benefit from the image. Joachim tried to persuade the butchers to donate two florins to save the palmesel, "for it was theirs," but "he got nothing from them." Finally, Rocher carried out his threat and "burned" the palmesel. Heinrich notes, one suspects with some satisfaction, that the bathmaster "died soon afterward."[29] A seventeenth-century retelling of the story, along with other cautionary tales about "the deaths of heretics," has the bathmaster finding his "two fattened pigs" dead in their stall, and two days later dying himself, screaming that he has seen the devil.[30] Happily, Biberach finally settled on a peaceful division of ecclesiastical and civic power. The Parish Church of Saint Martin has been shared by Roman Catholic and Lutheran congregations since 1548.

The palmesel in Schwäbisch Gmünd, yet another free imperial city some sixty miles north of Biberach, survived the religious turmoil of the sixteenth century intact. Despite its isolation in the midst of a predominantly Lutheran region, Schwäbisch Gmünd

---

25 On Palm Sunday in Catalonia, "boys used to stage battles with blows of olive and laurel branches" (Artis-Gener and Moya, *Festes*, 80).

26 Angele, *Altbiberach*, 143; see also Schilling, "Beiträge," 169; Essich, *Geschichte*, 133. For von Pflummern's use of *Tafeln* to designate church paintings, see Angele, *Altbiberach*, 31–32.

27 Essich, *Geschichte*, 130.

28 Stuart, *Defiled*, 106.

29 Angele, *Altbiberach*, 163; see also Schiller, "Beiträge," 203.

30 Ernst, "Tod," 91; Litz, *Reformatorische*, 300.

remained Roman Catholic throughout the Reformation,[31] allowing its palmesel, which had been made "around 1500,"[32] to remain in full use until at least 1800. In Schwäbisch Gmünd, as in Biberach, the butchers' guild owned the palmesel; by the eighteenth century, it had become an even more lively source of entertainment for the town's children than its kin in pre-Reformation Biberach. On the Monday before Palm Sunday, after the sacristan, acolytes, and choirboys had brought the palmesel from the cathedral, children were given donkey rides. For half a farthing, a child rode on the board under the donkey; for a whole farthing, a child could sit next to the Saviour. Around 1800, the chronicler Dominikus Debler reported that between eight and twelve children could ride together around the outside of the cathedral. This lasted as long as the groups could pay.[33]

Such donkey rides were not exclusive to Schwäbisch Gmünd. Perhaps the oldest palmesel still to be found in its church of origin, in Petersthal (Bavaria), bears visible traces of the practice. Possibly made as early as 1310, it was repainted several times over the centuries before being set aside in the wake of the Catholic Enlightenment. "Put away any old where for a long century," it was finally displayed in the Heimatsmuseum in nearby Wertach before being returned to Petersthal's parish church in 1957. Christ's missing forearms, hands and forefeet, the donkey's ears, and the wheeled platform have been replaced with modern substitutes. Christ's crown remains missing. Part of the donkey's back has been worn smooth from children riding behind the Christ figure when the palmesel was still active.[34] Similar wear can be seen on the palmesel in Füssen (Fig. 16).[35] "Boys and girls" (*Buben und Mädel*) were given rides aboard the palmesel in Konstanz.[36] In Vienna, Justus Eberhard Passer, ambassador of Hesse-Darmstadt to the imperial court, noted on March 12 (Palm Sunday), 1682: "Today parents have paid to let their children ride the palmesel at Saint Stephen's [cathedral]."[37] J. G. Jacobi, who taught at the University of Freiburg from 1784 until his death in 1814, remembered from his

---

31 Christ, "Negotiation."

32 Petersohn, "Über," 32.

33 Lipsmeyer, "Jahreslaufbrauchtum," 56; Boosen, "Mittelalterlichen," 17; Kissling, "Palmesel," 113.

34 Herrmann, *Petersthal*, 190–91, 339, 341; see also Reinle, *Ausstattung*, 213; "Eine Rärität: der Palmesel von Petersthal," Verena Scherm and Martin Hock, *YouTube*, 10 April 2014, www.youtube.com/watch?v=u7NvdqIOJJ8.

35 I saw the Füssen palmesel on Friday, March 27, 2015, in the Krippkirche St. Nikolaus, where it was awaiting its role two days later in the town's Palm Sunday procession. Although the palmesel is now pulled by children preparing for their first communion, they are no longer given rides.

36 Birlinger, *Volksthümliches*, 76–77; Federer, "Palmesel," 88; Lipsmeyer, "Jahreslaufbrauchtum," 56; Gugitz, *Jahr*, 1:153.

37 Passer, "Berichte," 335. Schlager, *Wiener-Skizzen*, 12, dates the Vienna palmesel to 1435. In 1784, Josef Richter, an ardent Viennese supporter of the Enlightenment, published a satirical account of the discontinued custom, using one of his several pseudonyms (Obermayr, *Bildergalerie*, 203). Claiming that such rides had been given "in various churches," Richter described crowds of "fathers and mothers," olive branches in hand, running "before or after the donkey," imagining "in their pious simplicity that they were glimpsing a little Christ in their beloved son and heir." The custom, he observed, was financially "very profitable."

**Figure 16 Baroque Palmesel, Füssen, showing wear on the donkey's
back from children riding behind Christ.
Photographs by author.**

childhood that "in various places" children gave a "tip" (*Trinkgeld*) to the sacristan for
rides on the palmesel.[38] The rides were not always sedate affairs. Lipsmeyer observes
that the ride in Freiburg must have been "a hair-raising experience," since it took place
"on top of the lower wall of the churchyard around the cathedral … which was known
until its demolition as the Donkey Wall (*Eselsmauer*)."[39] Gustav Gugitz adds Augsburg,
Fulda, Hirschau, and Rottenburg am Neckar to the list of places where children were
allowed to ride the palmesel.[40]

---

38 Jacobi, *Sämmtliche*, 5:41; see also Wiepen, *Palmsonntagsprozession*, 22–23.

39 Lipsmeyer, "Jahreslaufbrauchtum," 56.

40 Gugitz, *Jahr*, 1:153–54.

Figure 16 (continued)

In eighteenth-century Schwäbisch Gmund, on the afternoon before Palm Sunday, a procession formed outside the cathedral. Stalls selling sweets, pastries, toys, pottery, and other goods had transformed the churchyard into something of an annual market. Children brought (or bought) rattles, whistles, and drums for use in the procession. Every child taking part also had to bring a new piece of clothing, "or else," the chronicler notes, "the palmesel bumps [or bounces] you" (*sonst gumpet dich der Palmesel*). The procession itself was headed by schoolchildren, followed by clergy, who walked ahead of the "festively decorated" palmesel. The image was propelled by six butchers, pushing against the crossbars of a long wooden shaft secured to the front of the palmesel's wheeled platform.[41] It was

---

41 Debler claimed there were "eight" butchers (Kissling, "Palmesel," 113). Contemporary visual images, however, show six butchers at three crossbars (Wenger, *Palmesel*, plates 4–5; Debler and Herrmann, *Chronik*, 16, 112). According to Debler, the butchers claimed this privilege because, in

Figure 17 *Palm Sunday Procession in Schwäbisch Gmünd.* Anonymous oil painting, ca. 1700. © Museum im Prediger, Schwäbisch Gmünd.

accompanied on both sides by other members of the butchers' guild. The butchers' children, both "lads and lasses," were allowed to ride under the donkey, although the privilege was not repeated during the more formal Sunday morning procession. Behind the palmesel came the town council, the officers, the guild members, and finally the women with small children. The procession crossed the Market Place, ending up at its north end inside the Hospital Church.[42] There the palmesel stood overnight, amidst a sea of burning candles, attended by the hospital guards.

On Sunday morning, the procession once again made its way from the cathedral to the Spitalkirche, this time carrying palms but unaccompanied by children's noisemakers (*Krachmaker*). Retrieving the palmesel, the worshippers then made their way back to the cathedral, stopping en route at the baroque Mary Fountain in the centre of the Market Place, where a hymn was sung and a short devotion observed. An anonymous oil painting (ca. 1700), now in the town's Museum im Prediger, depicts both the Saturday and Sunday processions in a single composite image (Fig. 17). The morning's celebrations ended with mass in the cathedral.[43]

After 1801, the procession in Schwäbisch Gmünd was restricted to a sharply curtailed route around the cathedral on Sunday afternoon alone. By the second half of the

---

1546 during the Schmalkaldic War, members of the butchers' guild had recaptured the image from marauding Hessian soldiers (Kissling, "Palmesel," 113).

42 The Spitalkirche was demolished in 1841. A smaller chapel was included in the new hospital building, opened in 1846.

43 Lipsmeyer, "Jahreslaufbrauchtum," 56; Boosen, "Mittelalterlichen," 17–19; Kissling, "Palmesel," 113.

Figure 18 Palmesel, Schwäbisch Gmünd, ca. 1500. Museum im Prediger, Schwäbisch Gmünd. Photograph by author.

nineteenth century, the custom was abandoned altogether, and for more than a century the palmesel stood unused in a chapel in the pilgrimage complex of Saint Salvator outside the town. In 1994, the image was entrusted to the Museum im Prediger. Remarkably, it not only retained its original wheeled platform, but the Christ figure's arms and legs, including all fingers and toes, were also intact.[44] After careful cleaning and restoration, the Schwäbisch Gmünd palmesel is now happily on display in the museum, perhaps the most satisfyingly restored palmesel anywhere (Fig. 18).[45]

---

44 Boosen, "Mittelalterlichen," 13; Petersohn, "Über"; Wenger, *Palmesel*, plates 7–20.

45 I saw the palmesel in March 2015. The museum also owns the torso of a Christ figure (ca. 1400) that was part of an older palmesel belonging to the town's Dominican monastery (Boosen, "Mittelalterlichen," 15–16; Wenger, *Palmesel*, plates 1–2).

Chapter 16

THE PERSECUTION OF THE PALMESEL

THE FATE OF individual palmesels during the Protestant Reformation depended as much on local politics as on general location. The distance from Schwäbisch Hall to Biberach, passing through Schwäbisch Gmünd, is less than a hundred miles. The region has been predominantly Lutheran since the Reformation. Schwäbisch Hall's palmesel survived the city's transition to Lutheranism intact, but no longer took part in a procession. Biberach's palmesel was burned in 1531 during a local spate of Zwinglian iconoclasm. Schwabish Gmund's palmesel not only survived the Reformation under the protection of a doggedly Roman Catholic city council, but also continued active until the mid-nineteenth century. In this chapter, I look more closely at the vagaries of iconoclasm and reform. I begin not in sixteenth-century Germany, but in late fourteenth-century Prague, then the capital of Bohemia, on the eve of the Hussite Revolution.

Prague's best-known palmesel belonged to the cathedral of Saint Vitus, located within the castle complex that still overlooks the city.[1] The cathedral's Palm Sunday procession began outside the castle, probably at Strahov Monastery, where palms and other branches were blessed and distributed. First mentioned in the records in the mid-thirteenth century, the palmesel joined the procession at the high point of the monastery complex. There, choirboys "threw themselves" (rather than merely their garments) in front of the image, and hymns and antiphons were sung. The processional route from Strahov sloped gently downwards, entered the castle through the western gate beside the White Tower, and finally arrived at the cathedral. Choirboys pulled "the donkey with the image of the Saviour" (asell[um] cu[m] ymagine Salvatoris) into the church as far as the entrance to the choir, where it remained during mass.[2]

In 1421, the cathedral's palmesel earned the dubious distinction of being the first processional image of Christ on a donkey known to have been destroyed by iconoclasts.

---

1 Two late fourteenth-century Prague breviaries suggest that the Church of Saint Peter (now the Basilica of Saints Peter and Paul) in the Vyšehrad fortress, and the Church of the Virgin Mary under the Chain in the Malá Strana district, may each also have owned a palmesel (Uličný, "Christ," 30–32; Uličný, "Kristus," 68n15). The latter breviary, owned by the Czech Grand Priory of the Sovereign Military Order of Malta in Prague, where it is labeled R-57, remains unpublished (Petr Uličný, personal communication, August 13–14, 2015).

2 My very brief summary of the cathedral's Palm Sunday procession combines details from several thirteenth- and fourteenth-century sources: see Uličný, "Christ," 25–29; Rataj, "Liturgie," 14–15, 22–27; Machilek, "Liber," 221–22; Horničková, "Heaven," 47. I am grateful to Eliška Poláčková and Petr Uličný, without whose generous help I would have misread these records at several points. In the spirit of appreciative collegial dialogue, however, I believe that Uličny, "Christ," 27, is mistaken when he suggests that the thirteenth-century processional "assello, qui est ducendus in processione" was "a living ass," only later replaced "by a wooden prop that included a statue of Christ." Just as the German word Palmesel refers to a complete wooden image of Christ on a donkey rather than to a mere "palm donkey," live or otherwise, so the Latin word asellus could designate a whole palmesel.

Six years earlier, despite a guarantee of safe passage, the Bohemian reformer Jan Hus had been condemned by the Council of Constance, handed over to the secular authorities, and burned as a heretic. The people of Bohemia responded by intensifying their insistence on independence from Rome in matters of religion and from the German king in matters of linguistic, cultural, and political identity. In 1420, the emperor-elect Sigismund of Luxembourg (who had personally guaranteed and then betrayed Hus's safety) launched the first of five crusades against the Hussite Revolution, only to see his army soundly defeated outside Prague. Internal struggles between conservative and radical forces within Bohemia over the direction of the revolution grew inceasingly violent.[3] Against a background of sporadic massacres and peremptory burnings of "heretics" on both sides, the destruction of the palmesel seems relatively benign.

On June 10, 1421, Jan Želivský, a fiery preacher and leader of the radical forces in Prague, led a group bent on the destruction of idols uphill to the castle. There they removed and burned, in the words of the contemporary Prague chronicler Lawrence of Březová, "excellent images and altarpieces, most of them fine and of great value." Then, "as even clearer evidence of their madness, they displayed the image of Christ seated on a donkey on the battlements (*in cimboriis*, Czech *cimbuří*) of the church, and turning its face toward the city of Meissen, they said blasphemously, 'You, if you are Christ, bless Meissen!' And immediately, throwing the image from the battlements, they broke it into pieces."[4] Petr Uličný believes the "battlements" in question to have been a crenellated outer gallery, facing northwest toward the German city of Meissen, in a part of the cathedral that was pulled down after a disastrous fire in 1541, and that the iconoclasts would have used a crane to haul the palmesel up to the gallery.[5]

A hundred miles away, Meissen was hated by the residents of Prague as both a seat of the Roman Inquisition and an important ally of Sigismund in his campaign against the Hussites. The challenge to bless Meissen was a last derisive chance for the palmesel to prove its devotees' claims that it represented the power and presence of the living Christ. Failing the test, it could be safely destroyed.[6] Personal animosity may also have been at play. Nicholas of Dresden, a radical Hussite greatly admired by Želivský, had been martyred in Meissen sometime between 1417 and 1419.[7] Želivský himself fell out of favour and was beheaded, along with nine associates, by summary order of Prague's magistrates on March 9, 1422.[8]

---

3 For a full account of the causes, factions, and early development of the Hussite Revolution, see Kaminsky, *History*; for the defeat of Sigismund's forces in 1420, see Heymann, *John*, 118–47.

4 Lawrence of Březová, "Kronika," 484.

5 Uličný, "Christ," 25n1, and personal communication, September 2 and October 7, 2015.

6 Bartlová, "Hussite," 66–67. Schnitzler, *Ikonoklasmus*, 91, understands the destruction of the palmesel in Prague not only as an act of religious cleansing but also as a military act of symbolic humiliation and punishment.

7 Kaminsky, *History*, 204, 277n53.

8 Kaminsky, *History*, 460. Despite the iconoclasm of 1421, palmesels continued to appear in the rubrics of Prague cathedral liturgical books for another hundred years. Uličný, "Christ," 25, maintains

A hundred years after Želivský's act of iconoclasm, religious images were widely condemned by reformers elsewhere. The first attacks took place in and around Zurich, which until recently had been experiencing a resurgence of expenditure on church art and paraphernalia, "without precedent" in the city "since the thirteenth century."[9] As part of this resurgence, repairs had been made to the city's palmesel. The Großmünster accounts record payment in 1499 for fitting four wheels to the palmesel.[10] In 1514, the "ropes" (l[e]inen) by which the donkey was pulled were replaced.[11] The following year, the palmesel underwent further renovation: "nails" (naglin) and leather for the donkey's bridle were supplied. A sculptor was paid to repair the donkey's foot, bridle, tail, and cart, as well as Christ's crown. A dyer provided green linen,[12] which in 1516 was made into a robe for "the Saviour on the donkey."[13] In 1517, unspecified repairs to the palmesel were carried out by the minster's "organ bellows-treader" (orgeltretter).[14] Clearly the palmesel was still subject to the wear and tear of an annual passage over steep, cobbled streets.

The repairs, however, were short-lived. In December 1518, Huldrych Zwingli was appointed stipendiary priest (Leutpriester) of the Großmünster. Although Zwingli began to preach against the cult of the saints soon after his arrival in Zurich, it was not until late 1522 that he began explicitly to denounce religious images of saints and other holy figures. His friend, Leo Jud, installed as parish priest of Saint Peter's Church in February

---

that such rubrics testify to the resumption of Palm Sunday processions, including a palmesel, "after the end of the Hussite Wars," while I am inclined to believe that this is a case of liturgical books repeating instructions long after the rites themselves had fallen out of use. For a summary of our discussion, see Harris, "Persecution," 72–73.

9 Garside, Zwingli, 77, and, for an extended discussion, 77–93. Of particular interest is Hans Leu the Elder's panoramic View of Zurich with the Martyrdom of Saints Regula, Felix, and Exuperantius (1497–1502), originally painted for the Großmünster and now in Zurich's Landesmuseum. The scenes of martyrdom in the lower half of the original painting were trimmed and discarded in 1524; the heads of the saints in the top half were overpainted in 1566 and restored in 1937 (Wüthrich and Ruoss, Katalog, 40–43). The remaining painting, in two sections, one showing the left bank of the Limmat and the other the right bank, is now displayed in the same room as the museum's palmesels. A replica of the painting before it was restored can be seen in the Baugeschichtlichen Archiv der Stadt Zürich in the Haus zum Rech. In either case, the city's Palm Sunday processional route, with all the pertinent buildings, bridge, and Hof, can be followed across the five panels of Leu's painting. For colour images of the replica, in which the route is clearer, see "Altartafeln von Hans Leu d.Ä. (Haus zum Rech)," Wikimedia Commons, 29 August, 2011, https://commons. wikimedia.org/wiki/File:Altartafeln_von_Hans_Leu_ d.Ä._(Haus zum Rech)_-_linkes_Limmatufer_ 2011-08-17_15-26-36.JPG.

10 Escher, "Rechnungen," 30:188–89.

11 Escher, "Rechnungen," 31:227.

12 Escher, "Rechnungen," 31:234–38.

13 Escher, "Rechnungen," 31:295.

14 Escher, "Rechnungen," 31:297: "Item den palmesel uff zerichten dem Leinarten vi h." A few lines earlier, "Leinhart" is identified as the "orgeltretter," a man who assisted the organist by working the treadles that inflated the bellows that pumped air through the pipe organ.

1523, was even more vehement. Both men maintained a distinction between their own responsibility to proclaim the biblical case for the removal of images and the sole pre- rogative of the town council to authorize such a removal. Some of those persuaded by Zwingli's and Jud's preaching, however, were unwilling to wait for the council to act.[15]

In September 1523, individual acts of iconoclasm occurred in Zurich and nearby villages, increasing the tension between advocates and opponents of Reformed religion. Indecisive public debates were held. The council sought compromise. A memorandum issued in December permitted the orderly removal of images by individuals who had donated them or congregations that had commissioned them, but otherwise allowed works of art to remain in churches. Paintings with movable panels were to be closed; images and reliquaries were no longer to be carried in procession. The council's caution frustrated the zealous. On December 23, seven men from Zollikon—a village two miles south of Zurich— appeared before the Zurich town council, charged with attacking a palmesel. The men admitted that they had borrowed a key to Zollikon's parish church. They had then removed the parish's "donkey, with the image of our Lord God on it," hacked at it in the churchyard, pulled it to the lake, thrown it in, and sunk it with stones. The council imposed fines of var- ious amounts, depending on the individual's degree of involvement, and released the men.[16]

In June 1524, Zurich's council finally issued an order for the removal of all images from the city's churches. A few days later a committee of lay and clerical leaders was selected to oversee the work,[17] with the help of "blacksmiths, locksmiths, stonemasons, carpenters, and laborers." Over the next "thirteen days," the appointed iconoclasts "went into the churches, locked the doors behind them, and—not without hard work— removed all the images (alle bildner). In time all were broken, burned, and reduced to nothing."[18] It is probably fair to assume that Zurich's palmesel was among the wooden images consigned to the fire. The city's Palm Sunday procession was abolished as "unprofitable" (unnütz) in the same year.[19]

Zollikon and Zurich were not the only communities in the region whose palmesels were destroyed. In 1525, in Amden (St. Gallen), "crosses, banners, altars, images, and the palmesel were piled together in a heap and burned."[20] The same may have happened in May 1529 to the palmesel in Bremgarten (Aargau). After Heinrich Bullinger, a native of the town, had preached there on May 16 (Pentecost Sunday), he noted in his diary: "Not in vain; for the next day they tore down the altars and cast out the images and they

---

15 For the expanding "war against the idols" in Zurich, see Garside, Zwingli, 93–178; Eire, War, 73–86; Wandel, Voracious, 53–101.

16 Egli, Actensammlung, 189–90; Wandel, Voracious, 90–92.

17 The order was issued on June 15 (Bullinger, Reformationsgeschichte, 1:173–74; Egli, Actensammlung, 237). The committee was formed and the work begun on either June 20 (Bullinger, Reformationsgeschichte, 1:175; Wyss, Chronik, 42) or July 2 (Egli, Actensammlung, 240).

18 Bullinger, Reformationsgeschichte, 1:175; see also Wyss, Chronik, 42–43. For modern summa- ries, see Potter, Zwingli, 141–42; Garside, Zwingli, 159–60; Wandel, Voracious, 97–98.

19 Edlibach, Chronik, 269; Wyss, Chronik, 51; Zeller-Werdmüller, "Nächtliche."

20 Arx, Geschichten, 2:488

passed a law against blasphemers, adulterers, and drunkards."[21] Within the week, the people of Bremgarten had called Bullinger to serve as their pastor. He later wrote of the events of May 17 that "idols" (*götzen*) had been "burned" and altars "broken on the ground."[22] The palmesel may well have perished in the fire, but according to another story it was thrown into the river Reuss along with "other images of saints." The river carried it to the neighbouring town of Mellingen, where Catholics wanted to set it in the church, Protestants prevented them, and a butcher severed the donkey's neck and threw it back in the river. The butcher, so the story goes, suffered a goitre by way of punishment.[23] Bremgarten's allegiance to the Reformed faith was short-lived. A Catholic army defeated Zurich's Protestant forces at the battle of Kappel in October 1531. Zwingli was killed in battle, Bremgarten was forcibly returned to Catholicism, and Bullinger fled to Zurich, where he succeeded Zwingli. A new palmesel was delivered to Bremgarten in 1555, but is now lost.[24]

After the battle of Kappel, the Catholic council in Baden (now Baden im Aargau), some ten miles north of Bremgarten, also resolved to commission a new palmesel. The original image "had formerly been pulled in festive procession through the town and to the Matte [Meadow]," since 1424 a public park overlooking the River Limmat.[25] Whether Baden's original palmesel had fallen prey to iconoclasts or old age is unclear. In any case, the council engaged a wood-carver from Zurich, "whose business had been spoiled by the Reformation," to fashion a new palmesel. Discovering his commission, the Zurich authorities raided the artist's workshop and "burned the half-formed donkey."[26] Undeterred, in 1535 the Baden council arranged with another wood-carver, this time in Augsburg, to make "a new Palmesel together with the Lord God on it." Disaster struck in Augsburg, too. "When the donkey was completed and [the carver] was working on the other image [i.e., the Christ figure], it happened, in the providence of God, that [the carver] choked on a wood chip, which flew from nearby into his mouth, so that the Baden councilors were amazed, and horrified, and many people were shocked."[27] In 1540, the councilors complained of the "unseemly behavior" of certain visitors from Zurich, who

---

21 Bullinger, *Diarium*, 17.

22 Bullinger, *Reformationsgeschichte*, 2:62.

23 Busch, "Pritschenschläge," 136; Stückelberg, "Palmesel," 123. Busch, 136, also tells the story of how, some years before the Reformation, the Bremgarten palmesel slipped and fell during the procession, losing its tail in the accident. The mayor, following in his official regalia, kept his composure, righted the donkey, and replaced the tail, allowing the procession to continue. See also Strele, "Palmesel," 153–54. Laugel, *Costumes*, 138, tells a similar story of Ammerschwihr's palmesel in the nineteenth century. Robert Stauder, vice-president of Kaysersberg's Société d'Histoire, told me (April 7, 2017) that when once the tail fell from Kaysersberg's palmesel, the mayor picked it up, licked his fingers, and stuck it back on the donkey's rear end. The story appears to be an urban palmesel legend.

24 Flühler-Kreis, Wyer, and Stuppan, *Holzskulpturen*, 1:185.

25 Fricker, *Geschichte*, 421, 464–65.

26 Fricker, *Geschichte*, 127–28.

27 MS source cited in Fricker, *Geschichte*, 128; see also Strele, "Palmesel," 139.

had interrupted the Palm Sunday procession to the Matte, "causing scandal with much malice, mockery, and laughter."[28] Whether Baden had by then acquired a new palmesel, or was making do with the old one, or even managing without is not clear.

Baden and Bremgarten are less than twenty miles west of Zurich. Amden is about twice as far in the opposite direction. While we may be inclined to dismiss many details of these stories as biased, gullible, or propagandist, together they bear witness to the active destruction of palmesels, old and new, between 1523 and 1540 in Zurich and its surrounding territories. In Baden's case they also testify to the ongoing Catholic affection, despite regional opposition, for the role of the palmesel in the processional theatre of Palm Sunday.

Despite the attacks, a fair number of Swiss palmesels survived.[29] In one of the endearing ironies of the palmesel's history, Zurich's Landesmuseum—a cultural show-piece in the town once responsible for perhaps the most sweeping iconoclasm of the Reformation—owns five full-size palmesels, more than any other single museum. Four were on display when I visited the Landesmuseum in March 2015. The oldest, as we have already seen, is from Steinen (Fig. 14). Another, dated to "around 1510," is from Spiringen (Uri).[30] These two presumably survived the Reformation because they were in parts of the Swiss Federation that remained Catholic. Two more, dated to "the second half of the sixteenth century," from Mellingen (Aargau) and "possibly eastern Switzerland,"[31] were probably commissioned as reassertions of Catholic identity in regions that had sustained or returned to Catholicism. A fifth palmesel, not on display, is "supposedly" from "the canton of Uri" in "the first half of the sixteenth century."[32] Finally, the museum owns a miniature palmesel, only eighteen inches high, that once belonged to the Dominican convent of Saint Katharina in Wil (St. Gallen). Although dated to "the beginning of the sixteenth century,"[33] it was not in the convent on June 18, 1527, when "all the panels and images" were "knocked down and smashed."[34] Instead, the nuns are thought to have brought the palmesel with them when they returned in 1607. Its present curators speculate that the enclosed nuns, "to whom participation in the public Palm Sunday procession was forbidden, pulled the miniature donkey through their cloisters."[35] Palmesels

---

28 Fricker, *Geschichte*, 130.

29 For a complete list of known Swiss palmesels, whether destroyed, lost, or preserved, as of 1894, see Stückelberg, "Palmsonntagsfeier," 29–32; for an updated list, see Broekaert and Knapen, "Inventaris," 253–55.

30 Flühler-Kreis, Wyer, and Stuppan, *Holzskulpturen*, 1:180–81.

31 Flühler-Kreis, Wyer, and Stuppan, *Holzskulpturen*, 1:184–85, 188–89.

32 Flühler-Kreis, Wyer, and Stuppan, *Holzskulpturen*, 1:182–83.

33 Flühler-Kreis, Wyer, and Stuppan, *Holzskulpturen*, 1:186–87.

34 Miles, "Chronik," 310. I understand Miles to date this event to 1527, as do Reeb and Guggenheimer, *Kloster*, 10. Vogler, "Dominkanerinnen," 15–16, opts for 1528.

35 Flühler-Kreis, Wyer, and Stuppan, *Holzskulpturen*, 1:187. For the cloisters, built between 1504 and 1507, see Reeb and Guggenheimer, *Kloster*, 20–23.

can play their part on stages as expansive as the entire city of Zurich or as confined as a convent's arcaded cloisters. Some, even in Zurich, have survived to bear mute testimony.

The gilded treasures of Essen's abbey also survived the Reformation. Essen's palmesel, of less obvious economic value, may not have been so fortunate. Due perhaps to the civic authority of the abbess and the city's late (and moderate Lutheran) adoption of the Reformation, Essen was spared iconoclasm.[36] The city council declared for the Reformation in 1563. Successive abbesses periodically tried to restore Catholicism. The status of religious processions rose and fell. In 1540, the canons of the Stiftskirche had allowed "what remained of the processions" (*die Stuppelheiligenprozession*) to lapse.[37] At the end of the 1550s, processions had been briefly restored. In 1615, Capuchin friars brought to Essen by the abbess again reintroduced Catholic processions to the then Lutheran city.[38] Whether the Palm Sunday procession was still an annual affair even in 1540 is uncertain. In any case, I have found no record of the fate of Essen's palmesel. After its central role in the Palm Sunday processions of the thirteenth and fourteenth century, the image seems to have disappeared from the records.

This is not the case in Ulm, another city in which the Reformation eventually took a Lutheran course. In 1464, the local artist Hans Multscher, one of the more prolific and respected German sculptors of the period, made a palmesel for Ulm Münster. In 1530, the citizens of Ulm voted overwhelmingly in favour of the Reformation, a decision followed, in the summer of 1531, by the officially sanctioned removal of "monstrances and other silver utensils ... panels, altars, paintings, and idols" from the minster.[39] Many were destroyed, but perhaps because of its respected local artistic provenance the palmesel escaped unharmed. The early years of Ulm's Reformation were decidedly Zwinglian, but after the city settled on a more moderate Lutheranism, the palmesel was consigned to the chapels of the Roth and Neithard families inside the minster. It remained on view there, although no longer active in processions, until 1843, when it was given to the city's Verein für Kunst und Altertum (Association for Art and Antiquity), which in turn loaned it to the Ulmer Museum, where it can now be seen. The palmesel retains its large original wagon, as well as two small iron rings, screwed into Christ's left arm, that would once have held a palm or olive branch. Perhaps the most distinctive feature of Multscher's palmesel is its unusual history of having remained on view in a Lutheran church—indeed, perhaps the largest of all Lutheran churches—for three centuries.[40]

---

36 For Luther's opposition to iconoclasm, see Christensen, *Art*, 42–65, and for his sympathy for the palmesel, Burg, "Bildt," 126. For the Reformation and its aftermath in Essen, see Fehse, "Stadt," 219–22; Jahn, *Essener*, 209–31.

37 Fehse, "Stadt," 219; see also Jahn, *Essener*, 213.

38 Fehse, "Stadt," 219–22.

39 Endriss, *Ulmer*, 63.

40 For brief summaries of the Reformation in Ulm, see Coy, *Strangers*, 18; Naujoks, *Obrigkeitsgedanke*, 73–81; for the iconoclasm of 1531, see Endriss, *Ulmer*, 63–66; Litz, *Reformatorische*, 108–22. For the Ulm palmesel, which I saw in March 2015, see Theiss, Wackernagel, and Roth, "Christus," 390–95; "Christus auf dem Palmesel, 1464," *Schule und Archiv Ulm—Ulmer Geschichte im Netz*, www.ulm.de/sixcms/media.php/29/Kirche_03_01_M03.pdf.

Figure 19 Palmesel, Nuremberg, ca. 1378. Germanische Nationalmuseum,
Nuremberg. Photograph by Kater Begemot (Alexander Altenhof).
Used with permission of the museum.

The Germanisches Nationalmuseum in Nuremberg, another city in which
Lutheranism tempered the extremes of Zwinglian iconoclasm, owns four palmesels,
the earliest of which is more or less undamaged and dates to between 1370 and 1380
(Fig. 19). Only Christ's fingers have needed even partial replacement. The colour scheme,
although somewhat faded, is original.[41] The museum identifies the image as coming
"from a Nuremberg church,"[42] but declines to adjudicate between claims advanced on
behalf of two particular churches. In 1910, Walter Josephi suggested that the palmesel
was "perhaps identical" with the image of "our Lord on the donkey, which is used on Palm
Sunday," recorded sometime between 1442 and 1466 in an inventory from Nuremberg's

---

[41] Hess, *Mittelalter*, 434.

[42] "Christus auf dem Palmesel (Figur aus Erlenholz)," *Objektkatalog der Sammlungen des
Germanischen Nationalmuseums*, http://objektkatalog.gnm.de/objekt/Pl.O.153; "Christus auf dem
Palmesel, Nürnberg, um 1370/80, Erlenholz, Germanisches Nationalmuseum, Nürnberg," *Wikimedia
Commons*, April 19, 2015, https://commons.wikimedia.org/wiki/File:Christus_auf_dem_Palmesel_
Nuernberg_um_1370-80_Erlenholz_GNM_Nuernberg-2.jpg.

Frauenkirche.[43] In 1925, Walter Fries called attention to an entry in the 1436 Sacristan's Book of the city's Katherinenkloster.[44] Before vespers on Palm Sunday evening, the nun who served as sacristan was to "lay out a red carpet in front of the high altar" in the convent church, on which she was then to set "the image of our dear Lord on the donkey ... as well as the boards on which the figure stands on Palm Sunday."[45] In Fries' opinion, the Nationalmuseum's fourteenth-century palmesel had "probably" belonged not to the Frauenkirche but to the Katherinenkirche.[46] A simple solution suggests itself: as in Zurich, a single palmesel may have been shared between two churches. The palmesel perhaps belonged to the Frauenkirche, spent the night before Palm Sunday with the nuns of the Katherinenkloster, and on the morning of Palm Sunday was led in procession to meet the main procession coming from the Frauenkirche. The two groups then combined to represent Christ's entry into Jerusalem.

It was probably the same palmesel that prompted the Lutheran reformer Andreas Osiander to complain in a letter written in 1526 of "the trickery (*gauckelspil*) with the Lord God and donkey on Palm Sunday" in Nuremberg. In the same letter he condemned Nuremberg's Good Friday passion play and Corpus Christi procession.[47] Identical language appears in a second document written in Nuremberg in 1528, for which Osiander may also have been responsible.[48] Osiander's objections are consistent with the absence of Palm Sunday, Good Friday, and Corpus Christi from an otherwise generous list, drawn up in 1543, of religious holidays and saints' days that the citizens of Nuremberg were required to observe even after the Reformation.[49] The patrician members of Nuremberg's Council were notably moderate in their attitude to the city's older liturgical and artistic heritage. While they sanctioned the removal of some images from churches, they were consistent in their characteristically Lutheran opposition to radical preachers, public disorder, and icononoclastic violence.[50] If the attribution of the Nationalmuseum's oldest palmesel to "a Nuremberg church" is correct, the city's medieval palmesel was probably retired from active use but otherwise survived the Reformation in good shape.

Osiander was not the only Protestant reformer whose condemnation of the palmesel has survived in print. Sebastian Franck, an independent reformer writing between 1531

---

43 Josephi, *Werke*, 120; Baader, *Beiträge*, 1:89, and for the date of the inventory, 1:74n1.

44 Fries, "Kirche," 108, fig. 25.

45 Jäggi, *Frauenkloster*, 299, 327n310. The image and its supporting platform of wooden "boards" (*tafeln*) would presumably have been placed in a wagon for the procession itself.

46 Fries, "Kirche," 108.

47 Neumann, *Geistliches*, 1:603–4. Osiander had played a leading role in Nuremberg's adoption of the Reformation in 1525. His open letter was addressed to the authorities in Strasbourg, who had somewhat cautiously taken the same course a year earlier.

48 Dünninger and Schopf, *Braüche*, 74.

49 Sehling, *Evangelischen*, 11:537–39.

50 Christensen, "Iconoclasm"; Heal, *Cult*, 102–9. For summaries of the Reformation in Nuremberg, see Strauss, *Nuremberg*, 154–86; Dixon, *Reformation*, 106–8.

and 1533, complained about the "idolatry" of the palmesel, without specifying where (or whether) he had himself seen a palmesel in action. On Palm Sunday, he wrote, "a wooden ass on a trolley is pulled around the town with the image of their God on it; they sing, throw palms before it, and do much idolatry with this wooden God of theirs. The parish priest prostrates himself before this image, and a second priest also creeps up. The children sing and point with their fingers. Two Bacchantes prostrate themselves before it with outlandish ceremony and song, and then everyone throws palms at it: whoever catches the first makes big magic with it."[51]

Augsburg, where the more than one-thousand-year history of palmesels began, is another city whose image of Christ on a donkey—albeit not its earliest one—has survived intact. Augsburg's first palmesel disappears (or has not yet been recovered) from the records after its single mention in Gerhard's *Life of Saint Ulrich*. Eduard Wiepen, unable to find any mention of a palmesel in thirteenth- through sixteenth-century ritual books from Augsburg's cathedral, proposed that the palmesel was a custom "known by everyone" in Augsburg, and therefore in no need of further mention in such a context. The tradition of "leading the palmesel around," he believed, had survived "for centuries" after the time of Ulrich.[52] I'd like to think he was right; he may also have been looking in the wrong place. When a new palmesel was made in the mid-fifteenth century, it was not the cathedral chapter that placed the order, but the head of the Benedictine abbey to which the Church of Saints Ulrich and Afra was by then attached.

The abbey had been founded around 1006; the canons and, later, the monks of the church may have been the keepers of Augsburg's palmesel tradition all along. In 1714, Cornelius Khamm, a respected historian and subprior of the abbey,[53] wrote: "In the same year 1446, Abbot Johannes [IV of Hohenstein] arranged for a sculptor from Ulm, who demanded ten florins for his work, to sculpt an image (*simulacrum*) of Christ sitting on a donkey, which, in memory of our Saviour's triumphal entry into Jerusalem, is nowadays still honoured by boys with palm branches, by the spreading of surplices, and by the shouting of Hosannas, etc., on Palm Sunday."[54] Whether this was a replacement for an older palmesel worn out by centuries of use, or the revival of a long-lapsed tradition, is uncertain. In any case, there is no reason to doubt Khamm's confident testimony that the same palmesel was still in use in 1714.

There is, however, reason to question Khamm's date for the making of the new palmesel. A contemporary notice, in Johannes Frank's *Augsburger Annalen* (1431–1462), places it a decade later. "A master craftsman from Ulm," Frank reports, was paid

---

51 Franck, *Weltbuch*, 131b; translation from Baxandall, *Limewood*, 58. Better known to English-speaking readers is Thomas Kirchmeyer's lengthy mockery, in his *Regnum papisticum*, composed in 1553, of "foolish pageants" of a wheeled "wooden ass ... and image great that on him rides." Kirchmayer's poem was translated into German by Burkard Waldis (1555) and into English by Barnabe Googe (1570). For the relevant lines, see Kirchmayer, *Regnum*, 146–48, trans. Waldis, bk. 3, chap. 15; trans. Googe, 50; Young, *Drama*, 2:526–27, 532–33, lines 1–48.

52 Wiepen, *Palmsonntagsprozession*, 10.

53 Stanonik, "Khamm."

54 Khamm, *Hierarchia*, 3:75; Gerstenberg, "Palmesel," 45–46.

ten florins for carving "the donkey with the Saviour on it," after which a master painter in Augsburg named Jörg was paid a further seven florins for painting it. Jörg also made the wagon that carried the palmesel. The finished image was delivered "on the Friday before Palm Sunday, 1456."[55] Wilhelm Wittwer's *Catalogus Abbatum*, compiled between 1500 and 1512, confirms the precise later date of delivery, as well as the roles of the Ulm sculptor and Augsburg painter, but adds that the latter almost had to "beg" before he was paid, even though he had "donated" the wagon.[56] Marie Schuette explains the discrepancy between the two proposed dates by noting that Khamm frequently mistook a "5" in his source for a "4."[57] The sculptor responsible for the palmesel has been identified as Hans Multscher,[58] who also made the surviving Ulm palmesel. Multscher's modern biographer, Manfred Tripps, affirms the 1456 date for the Augsburg palmesel, citing the early witnesses to this date as well as the palmesel's stylistic similarities with Multscher's other work from the period.[59]

Augsburg's fifteenth-century palmesel survived the Reformation despite periodic outbreaks of iconoclasm. Official policy on religious images in the city vacillated. Throughout the 1520s, Augsburg's city council did its best "to keep the peace and stifle outbursts of violent or public protest, such as vandalism of church property," but made no attempt to privilege either evangelical or Catholic worship.[60] On March 7, 1524, the city council issued a decree "that no one in this city or its realm [should] abuse or insult the images, coats of arms, paintings, and other monuments that hang or stand in the churches, churchyards, or anywhere else by besmirching them, or otherwise damage or break them, without the knowledge and approval of the authorities."[61] The prohibition allowed the orderly removal of images with appropriate approval, but forbade individual acts of iconoclasm. On April 13, in defiance of the ruling, the Lutheran "shoemaker Jorg Nässlin and his servant besmirched, despoiled, and ruined with cow blood all of the plaques in the churchyard and cloister at the [cathedral] Church of Our Lady, which were put there in memory of the dead and were decorated with figures, crucifixes, the Mount of Olives, Our Dear Lady Mary, and images of the saints."[62] Nässlin was banished from the city for a year. In more orderly fashion, in 1533, "two wagonloads of ornaments and precious instruments of the mass" were removed from the formerly Franciscan Barfüßerkirche (Barefoot Church) "to be bought and sold for worldly purposes."[63]

---

55 Frank, "Augsburger," 309–10; Gerstenberg, "Palmesel," 46–47; Tripps, *Hans … Schaffenszeit*, 250.

56 Wittwer, *Catalogus*, 199–200; Gerstenberg, "Palmesel," 47; Tripps, *Hans … Schaffenszeit*, 250.

57 Schuette, *Schwäbische*, 118.

58 Jäger, *Ulms*, 579; Stadler, *Hans*, 171; Gerstenberg, *Hans*, 136–44; Tripps, *Hans … Schaffenszeit*, 270, plates 97–98; Tripps, *Hans … Spätgotik*, 82.

59 Tripps, *Hans … Schaffenszeit*, 251n2, 270.

60 Hanson, *Religious*, 14.

61 Tlusty, *Augsburg*, 7.

62 Sender, *Chroniken*, 155; trans. Tlusty, *Augsburg*, 7.

63 Sender, *Chroniken*, 155; trans. Gray, "Lutheran," 45. "Barfüßer" was the colloquial German name for Franciscan friars.

The palmesel, owned by the abbey of Saints Ulrich and Afra, was not threatened by either incident.

In 1537, however, "a brash young man" by the name of Hans Wesler was elected mayor. On January 17, immediately after Wesler took office, the city council joined him in prohibiting Catholic celebration of the mass. The next day, Wesler "began with the civic workmen to tear down all the altars, paintings, panels, lamps, and more in all the churches in the city, starting with Our Lady and then St. Ulrich, St. Moritz, and other churches."[64] The palmesel escaped this destruction, too, perhaps because it had no immediate association with the mass. Even so, despite the comparatively "mild nature of Protestant iconoclasm in Augsburg,"[65] the palmesel's status remained precarious. The abbey fell into disarray after its church's iconoclastic "cleansing." Some monks renounced their vows, others fled, and for the next decade the church was used for Lutheran services.[66]

In 1547, the Catholic emperor Charles V routed the forces of the Schmalkaldic League of Lutheran princes at the Battle of Mühlberg, and within a year Catholic clergy had returned to Augsburg. The Church of Saint Ulrich was restored to Catholic worship. Although Augsburg retained a Protestant majority, the prosperous Catholic minority "could worship openly again and priests and their processions could be seen on the street."[67] The arrival of the Jesuits in the city in 1580 further encouraged a flourishing of Baroque Catholicism, including "processions that wound their way through Protestant neighborhoods."[68] Perhaps it was under the capable leadership of Jakob Köplin, abbot of Saint Ulrich's from 1548 to 1600,[69] that the Benedictine monks began once again to lead their palmesel in an annual Palm Sunday procession. If so, it may have followed a more circumspect route in the immediate vicinity of the abbey rather than venturing all the way to the cathedral.

Certainly, by 1714, when Khamm wrote, Augsburg's palmesel was again an established tradition, albeit on a much smaller scale. Khamm makes no mention of processional "splendour," noting only "boys with palm branches ... the spreading of surplices, and ... the shouting of Hosannas." According to Anton Birlinger, groups of children were allowed to ride Augsburg's palmesel on Palm Sunday; each child had to pay a "farthing" (*Kreuzer*) for the "great honour."[70] Sixty years later, even that remnant of the once-splendid procession was suppressed. On November 17, 1774, Clemens Wencesalaus, prince-bishop of Augsburg (1768–1812), banned certain "abuse" (*Mißbrauch*) throughout his diocese. Among the casualties was the palmesel: "It is customary, on Palm Sunday or on the

---

64 Tlusty, *Augsburg*, 29.

65 Gray, "Lutheran," 46.

66 Smith, "Sculpting," 208–9.

67 Hanson, *Religious*, 18; Gray, "Lutheran," 46, notes that "most of the prominent patrician and banking families" were Catholic. The Peace of Augsburg (1550) confirmed the city's bi-confessional status.

68 Fisher, *Music*, 3.

69 Friesenegger, *Ulrichs*, 85–86; Smith, "Sculpting," 208–9.

70 Birlinger, *Schwäbisch*, 87.

previous evening, to lead about the image of Christ with the children in the church or around the churchyard, giving rise to unseemly hubbub and diverse other improprieties in the church." Such practices were to "cease for ever."[71] In the wake of similar prohibitions throughout the Catholic Enlightenment, "most palmesels were destroyed ... mutilated,"[72] or "made into firewood,"[73] but Augsburg's resilient palmesel again survived intact. When the abbey of Saint Ulrich was dissolved during the secularization of Bavaria in 1802, ownership of the palmesel passed to the Bavarian state, which eventually auctioned it off for a "knock-down price" (Schleuderpreis). The buyer, bidding through a middleman in Augsburg on behalf of her own institution, was the prioress of Wettenhausen Abbey, some thirty miles west of Augsburg. The nuns acquired the palmesel for the equivalent in today's currency of "ten euros." It was last insured, when on loan for an exhibition elsewhere, for 500,000 euros.[74]

I visited Wettenhasuen abbey in March 2015. It's easy to see why Kurt Gerstenberg called the Wettenhausen sculpture one of "the most noble" of all surviving palmesels.[75] Christ's head is bowed, and his expression is one of quiet suffering, even as his right hand is raised in blessing. He is tall; although the donkey is large for its kind, Christ's feet reach almost to the wheeled platform. The folds of his long robe, descending from his collarbone to his ankles and spreading before and behind over the donkey's back, are finely rendered (Fig. 20). I did, however, notice one puzzling detail: on the lower right inside of Christ's cloak, extending below the belly of the palmesel, is clearly painted in fifteenth-century Gothic numerals the date 1446 (Fig. 21). My initial response was to assume that Cornelius Khamm had been right after all. I now suspect that the date was added by a restorer, keen not only to repair but also to authenticate the palmesel, shortly after the abbey acquired its new treasure, at a time when Kamm's dating was still accepted.[76] Despite this partial repainting, Wettenhausen's palmesel still bears traces of its performance history. Sometime after the image's original construction, a hole was bored in the left rear side of the donkey's neck, in line with Christ's left hand. It was once the practice to thread a palm or olive branch through the circle formed by Christ's fingers and thumb, securing the stem of the branch in the hole beneath. Happily, this record of the palmesel's performance has been allowed to remain.

---

71 Steiner, Acta, 350; Hoeynck, Geschichte, 211.

72 Strele, "Palmesel," 140.

73 Winbeck and Rank, Kloster, 94.

74 Winbeck and Rank, Kloster, 94. Gerstenberg, "Palmesel," 47, dates the acquisition of the palmesel by Wettenhausen Abbey to "the second half of the nineteenth century."

75 Gerstenberg, Hans, 139; see also Tripps, Hans ... Schaffenszeit, 270; Valvekens, "Tentoonstellin gscatalogus," 271.

76 An almost identical "4" can be found on the Prague astronomical clock, whose "numerals were created during the historicist neo-Gothic reconstruction in 1878" ("Pražský orloj—The Prague Astronomical Clock," Stan Marušák, www.orloj.eu/en/orloj_ctyriadvacetnik.htm). I am grateful to Glenn Ehrstine for this information. Khamm's error went unnoticed until 1926, when Gerstenberg, "Palmesel," 46–47, drew attention to Frank's and Wittwer's earlier accounts of the palmesel's delivery in 1456.

Figure 20 Hans Multscher, Palmesel, Augsburg, 1456.
Wettenhausen Abbey. Photograph by author.

Figure 21 Augsburg/Wettenhausen palmesel: 1446, painted in Gothic numerals below
the donkey's belly. Photograph by author.

Chapter 17

BAROQUE SPLENDOUR AND CATHOLIC ENLIGHTENMENT

IN THOSE PARTS of Europe that remained Roman Catholic, the fate of palmesels and other Palm Sunday processional images of Christ on a donkey again varied with location. In the predominantly German Holy Roman Empire, as well as in neighbouring Poland, Catholic opposition to the palmesel and other "superstitions" peaked during the late-eighteenth-century Catholic Enlightenment.[1] Northern Italy, then part of the Empire, suffered a similar suppression of its palmesels. In Spain, where wheeled images of Christ on a donkey were unknown, "a new and specialized genre of sculpture" emerged during the sixteenth century.[2] Penitential confraternities in Seville and elsewhere commissioned the making of life-size images of Christ's passion to be carried in Holy Week processions on the shoulders of teams of bearers. Over the centuries, these portable images, still very much in use throughout Spain and Latin America, have become increasingly elaborate. Images of Christ on a donkey, also carried rather than pulled on wheels, were a late addition to this genre. In this chapter, I focus first on the suppression of palmesels north of the Alps during the Catholic Enlightenment, and secondly on the development of the distinct Spanish tradition of processional images of Christ on a donkey. In Chapter 18, I document the evidence of palmesels in northern Italy, paying particular attention to a surviving example from Verona once believed, according to Protestant slander, to contain the sacred relics of Christ's own donkey.

During what has come to be known as the Catholic Enlightenment, a desire on the part of high-ranking Catholic clergy to "harmonize faith and reason"[3] found expression, at least in part, in a distaste for the excesses of the Baroque and for the perceived improprieties of popular religion. A case in point is the celebrated palmesel of Nonnberg Abbey in Salzburg, now better known as the monastery where Maria von Trapp, of *Sound of Music* fame, was a postulant. Palm Sunday at the abbey had once been a splendid occasion, customarily attended, since at least 1430, by each succeeding prince-archbishop of Salzburg in the first year of his reign. Michael von Küenberg, archbishop from 1554 to 1560, rode to the festivities "on a splendid white horse covered in red velvet, while himself wearing his papal legate's hat and being draped in a purple cloak."[4] The abbey's Palm Sunday celebrations also attracted large crowds of lay worshippers, who came to attend the "annual fair" and to admire "the statue of Christ on the figure of a donkey." The donkey was, by all accounts,

---

[1] For helpful introductions to the Catholic Enlightenment, see Lehner, "Introduction"; Burson, "Introduction."

[2] Webster, *Art*, 57.

[3] Lehner, "Introduction," 2.

[4] Esterl, *Chronik*, 61. Von Küenberg attended the Nonnberg festivities in 1556, having been at the Imperial Diet in Augsburg on Palm Sunday, 1555, the first full year of his rule.

richly adorned with "corals, garnets, and the like." Mistaking these semi-precious stones for precious gems, the common people said that the image was "worth more than a whole kingdom."[5]

Sigismund III von Schrattenbach (1753–1771) was the last prince-archbishop of Salzburg to ride to Nonnberg for the Palm Sunday procession. "Surrounded by his princely household," he rode "on a white palfrey," for which he had provided "a richly embroidered saddle cloth."[6] Schrattenbach's successor, Hieronymus von Colloredo, was a leading figure in the Catholic Enlightenment and decidedly hostile to such popular customs. In a pastoral letter of June 29, 1782, Colloredo ordered the removal from churches of everything "that offends good taste." On November 18, 1785, he issued a decree explicitly forbidding palmesels throughout his diocese.[7] The nuns of Nonnberg Abbey were ordered to destroy their palm donkey. According to one contemporary report, the abbess removed the Christ figure before she "hacked and burned the centuries-old donkey."[8] Another account claims that the donkey was cut into four pieces, one of which was then delivered to the archiepiscopal consistory as proof of the nuns' obedience.[9] The fate of the surviving wooden Christ is unclear. Some say that, by the 1820s, the hollow figure was once again borne in procession on Palm Sunday and then displayed beneath the arched gateway to the abbey; others say that within twenty years of its forced separation from the donkey, "the Christ figure was given away along with various other curiosities."[10]

Nonnberg Abbey was not the only community in the archdiocese to lose its palmesel. The parish priest of Radstadt confirmed in 1786 that the practice of "leading around the palmesel" (*Palmeselherumführen*) had been discontinued four years earlier.[11] In 1897, Richard von Strele, noting that "most palmesels" had been "destroyed or mutilated," named Seekirchen am Wallersee and Zell am Ziller, in addition to Radstadt, as places in the archdiocese where the local community still harboured memories of a palmesel destroyed in the wake of Colloredo's decree.[12] Unusually, Hallein's seventeenth-century palmesel survived and is still active, albeit not in Hallein. Legend has it that the image was thrown into the River Salzach and floated three or four miles downstream to Puch (now Puch bei Hallein), where it was retrieved and hidden in a farmer's barn until it

---

5 Esterl, *Chronik*, 60. For a contemporary (1746) reference to the Nonnberg palmesel, see Martin, "Salzburger," 77:18: "einen hilzernen Ösel ... welcher mit sehr vill kostbaren Sachen angehenckt ist."

6 Adrian, *Salzburger*, 89.

7 Strele, "Palmesel," 140; Reb, *Aufklärung*, 1:480; see also Haslberger, "Salzburger," 69:98, who bitterly chronicles one prohibition after another; Adrian, *Salzburger*, 88. For a 1787 *Pressburger Zeitung* report that the Nonnberg palmesel "is no longer put on display," see Gugitz, *Jahr*, 154. Pressburg, then in Hungary, is now known as Bratislava, Slovakia.

8 Strele, "Palmesel," 142.

9 Adrian, *Salzburger*, 88–89.

10 Adrian, *Salzburger*, 88–89; Strele, "Palmesel," 142.

11 Strele, "Palmesel," 140.

12 Strele, "Palmesel," 141.

could again be safely borne in procession. However it may have reached safety in Puch, it has taken part in the village's Palm Sunday procession almost continuously "since the nineteenth century," only interrupted by a second period of enforced hiding "during National Socialism."[13]

In the first decade of the twentieth century, the Puch palmesel still spent most of the year in its barn, emphatically the property of the common people rather than of the church whose archbishop had ordered its destruction. On the Saturday before Palm Sunday the palmesel was carried to the parish church in lay procession; no priest was present. There the Christ figure, ordinarily dressed only in carved and painted garments, was further clothed in rich processional vestments. Karl Adrian described the effect in 1908: "Christ is wearing a dark blue silk brocade robe, trimmed at the hem with gold braid; a silver heart and silver coins adorn his stomacher (*Brustlatz*). His cape, also bordered with gold, is made of a lightweight, red silk fabric. On his head he has a sort of crown made of green leaves, between which little red flowers serve as decoration, and the three beams of his halo are made of tinsel." From Christ's right hand, raised in blessing, hung the donkey's reins; in his left hand he held "a bouquet of artificial flowers, small, fresh palm branches, and colored breadsticks (*Hobelscheiten*), all held together by a rose-red, silk bow." The juxtaposition of silk brocade vestments and coloured breadsticks is an endearing mix of Baroque excess and folk intimacy. After playing its leading part in the Palm Sunday procession through the village, the vested palmesel remained on display in the church until the Wednesday of Holy Week, when it was returned to its home in the barn.[14]

Nowadays, the palmesel is housed in a gated alcove beneath the church's bell-tower, close by the main entrance to the church, "so that it can be admired throughout the year."[15] On Palm Sunday, Christ still wears a blue robe and a dark pink cape, both made of silk, hemmed with gold trim, and frequently replaced so as always to look new, but he no longer wears a crown of any kind. The reins hang from Christ's left hand, in which he also carries a bouquet of greenery and pussy willow twigs. The donkey wears a fine leather bridle, studded with cowry shells; tucked into the bridle at the animal's forehead is a small bouquet akin to Christ's. Uncharacteristically, the wooden platform on which the palmesel stands has no wheels. Perhaps in Hallein the image was pulled on a wheeled cart, but at least by 1908 in Puch it was carried by four "lads" (*Burschen*).[16] This is still the case: two wooden poles, painted blue to match Christ's robe, are threaded lengthways through elevated metal hoops, one at each corner of the platform. Four young men use these to carry the palmesel, walking with the image supported on their shoulders, such that above their heads Christ's cape billows and the whole image sways, appearing almost animated.[17]

---

13 Gerber, "Osterbräuche"; see also Hutter, "Hochzeits," 607–11.

14 Adrian, *Salzburger*, 89–90; see also Hutter, "Hochzeits," 610; Strele, "Palmesel," 152.

15 Gerber, "Osterbräuche."

16 Adrian, *Salzburger*, 90.

17 For colour images and a brief video of the palmesel in procession in 2016, see Gerber, "Osterbräuche."

Suppression of palmesels by enlightened Catholic prelates was not limited to the archdiocese of Salzburg. Strele provides an incomplete list of other hierarchs who issued edicts or pastoral letters forbidding the use of a palmesel. He includes, from Austria, the archbishop of Vienna[18] and the bishops of Gurk and Wiener-Neustadt; from Germany, the archbishop of Mainz and the bishops of Augsburg,[19] Konstanz,[20] Passau, and Würzburg; from present-day Italy, the bishops of Bressanone (Brixen), Chiusa (Klausen), and Verona; and from the Czech Republic, the archbishop of Prague.[21]

In Poland, the archbishop of Krakow issued a similar decree. Palmesels had been active in Poland since at least the beginning of the fifteenth century. In 1405, the city council of Lviv (Polish, Lwów; now in Ukraine, but then part of Poland) had paid "for the transportation of an image of Jesus on a donkey," perhaps from Krakow, where it may have been made. The image must have been put to immediate, active processional use, for "on the day after Palm Sunday," 1408, a local painter was paid "for repairs to Jesus on the donkey."[22] In 1423, in Wrocław, a bridge collapsed under the weight of the Palm Sunday procession.[23] Many

---

18 Vienna's palmesel "was made in 1435" (Schlager, *Wiener*, 2:10). By 1682, it no longer took part in the city's Palm Sunday procession, but still gave rides to children (Passer, *Berichte*, 335). This custom itself fell into disuse "more than thirty years" before Obermayr, *Bildergalerie*, 202, mocked it in 1784.

19 The parish church of Landsberg am Lech, in the diocese of Augsburg, still houses a well-preserved Baroque palmesel, made in 1671 by the celebrated local sculptor Lorenz Luidl. It was active until about 1802/03, when the Holy Roman Empire, including the diocese of Augsburg, was "secularized" in the wake of the Catholic Enlightenment and the loss of territory to Napoleon's armies (Weißhaar-Keim, *Stadtpfarrkirche*, 15, 19). I saw the Landsberg palmesel in March 2015.

20 The earliest record of a palmesel in Konstanz comes from 1523, when a new palmesel was made to replace the old one. Yet another replacement was made in 1589. For a documentary history of Konstanz's palmesels, their repairs, replacements, and successive prohibitions between 1635 and 1753, see Zinsmaier, "Unbekannte," 70–71n38. Birlinger, *Volksthümliches*, 76–77, dates the final, successful suppression of Konstanz's palmesel to 1784. Rosa Pittà-Settelmeyer, restorer at Konstanz's Rosgartenmuseum, specifies that the palmesel's participation in the Palm Sunday procession was forbidden in 1693, but children's rides aboard the image were allowed to continue until 1784. By then, the palmesel was "in such poor condition" that the priest allowed it be "sawn to pieces. Another of Konstanz's palmesels was burned in the nineteenth century." She adds that the restored palmesel owned by the Rosgartenmuseum is not from Konstanz, but dates to between 1500 and 1510 and "probably comes from Seeschwaben," the part of Swabia on the northern shore of the Bodensee. "It was bought for the museum in 1899 by an antiquarian booskeller in Gottlieben, Switzerland" (personal communication, November 9, 2015). The Rosgartenmuseum palmesel was in storage when I visited in March 2015.

21 Strele, "Palmesel," 140.

22 Walanus, "Imago," 379–84; Kopania, "Animating," 83, 104n24.

23 The bridge in question was Tumski Bridge (German, *Thumbrücke*), crossing the River Odra on the way to the cathedral from the Church of Our Lady on the Sand, where the palms had been blessed. For the route of the procession, see Sobeczko, "Liber," 188–90, 206.

of the people thrown into the river were injured, and several drowned, but "the Palmesel suffered no harm; it only bathed a little."[24]

No Polish palmesels are known to have been lost to iconoclasm during the long Reformation. Protestant disapproval did not spill over into hostile action. The account left by Krzystof Kraiński (1556–1618), a Calvinist preacher, is both mild and informative: "Today ... in Krakow, the city's beadles (oprawcy) will lead a linden-wood donkey, on which Jesus is seated, from the Church of Saint Wojciech ... to the Church of the Virgin Mary. The figure ... used to be led by the Krakow city fathers, but the beadles took over the office, which doesn't make the city fathers angry at them ... Children, dressed in fine and rich garments, throw cloths, reed palms, and pussy willows before the linden-wood Jesus. Throwing flowers in the air ... they point to [the Christ figure], saying: 'This is the one who was to come for the salvation of humankind.' " The singers fall before the cross, while the priest kneels and strikes it with "a rod of marsh reeds." Then the crucifix is raised and all "sing to this mute piece of wood."[25]

It was not Calvinist opposition but Catholic enlightenment that ended the use of palmesels in the diocese of Krakow. A diocesan edict, dated August 10, 1780, banned, among the "multiple appendages" that had battened onto approved forms of worship, the practice of "carrying the Lord Jesus on a donkey in the church" (wożenie Pana Jezusa na osiołku w kościele).[26] By then, it appears, the procession had already been restricted to the interior of the church.

Processional images of Christ on a donkey fared very differently in Spain. The penitential confraternities that dominated Spanish Holy Week processions from the sixteenth century onwards preferred images that recalled the suffering of Christ on Good Friday rather than his supposedly triumphal entry on Palm Sunday. The earliest such images represented Christ carrying the cross, the crucified Christ, and the sorrowing Virgin. Later examples added other moments from the passion narrative, such as Christ's sentencing, whipping, mocking, or crowning with thorns.[27] All were carried at head height and above, rather than pulled on wheels; to "reduce weight" and save expense,

---

24 Pol, Jahrbücher, 1:167; see also Walanus, "Imago," 390n65; Kopania, "Animating," 83, 104n28. Fifteenth-century missals from Kielce and Sandomierz also stipulate the processional use of a palmesel (Lewański, Liturgiczne, 136–37, 143).

25 Kraiński, Postylla, 158v; trans. adapted from Rzegocka, "Performance," 190, and Kopania, "Animating," 81–82, who translate oprawcy as "hangmen" and "torturers or myrmidons." In this context, "beadles" is the more likely meaning. Kolbuszewski, Postyllografja, 201–2, omits "this mute piece of wood" (drewna niemego) from his quotation of the passage; Kopania, "Animating," 102–3n19, and Walanus, "Imago," 386–87, restore it. Confirmation that Krakow's Basilica of the Virgin Mary owned an active palmesel comes from payments recorded in the basilica's account books for repairs "to the statue of the donkey for the Palm Sunday procession" in 1611 and 1619 (Walanus, "Imago," 388n50), and from mention of "the statue of the Lord on a donkey" in an inventory drawn up in 1620 (Grobowski, Skarbniczka, 161).

26 Martynowicz, Annotationes, fols. 86–87, quoted in Lubicz, "Bibljografja," 412.

27 Webster, Art, 89–99.

most were "made of wood (usually hollow) or wood paste."[28] Many, too, were *imágenes de vestir*, made to be clothed in actual garments and requiring only the unclothed parts of the image to be carved and painted in detail. Only the head and hands of the sorrowing Virgin were realistically sculpted, while her clothed "body" was often little more than a conical wooden armature. Some of the images were articulated, having movable or replaceable limbs that allowed the same image of Christ to be represented carrying, nailed to, or being taken down from the cross.[29]

By the late sixteenth century, multifigural tableaux known as *pasos de misterio* were supplementing the earlier single-figure images. One of the oldest such tableaux, making its debut in Seville in 1578, represented Christ's agony in the Garden of Gethsemane. The contract for its original manufacture stipulated that it should include Christ, an angel, and three sleeping apostles, all placed in the appropriate spatial relationship to one another in a realistically represented garden landscape. The tableau, set on a single platform, took a minimum of sixteen men to carry.[30] Over the course of the seventeenth century, Seville's *pasos de misterio* became "ever more elaborate and grandiose,"[31] multiplying the number of figures in each tableau, enlarging and embellishing the supporting platform (*paso*), and making it more difficult to manoeuvre the composite images through the narrow, winding city streets. By the late seventeenth century, the *pasos* had reached their maximum practical dimensions, but the total number of *pasos* has continued to grow. The official program for 2016 listed sixty-one separate portable tableaux each independently making its own slow procession through the crowded streets as part of a schedule stretching from Palm Sunday to Easter Sunday. The greatest number (thirteen) came out on Good Friday, the smallest (one) on Easter Sunday.[32] Suffering, rather than resurrection, is the dominant theme.

Only one of Seville's *pasos* depicts Christ on a donkey. Known officially as "Jesús de la Sagrada Entrada en Jerusalén" (Jesus of the Sacred Entry into Jerusalem) but popularly as "La Borriquita" (the Little Jenny), the *misterio* includes a total of twelve images: Christ on a jenny; a foal alongside its mother; three disciples (James, Peter, and John); six worshipping crowd figures; and a tiny figure of Zacchaeus, who has strayed from earlier in the biblical story and is partly hidden in a tall palm tree (Fig. 22).[33] The oldest of these images (Christ on the donkey, James, Peter, and Zacchaeus) date to the seventeenth

---

28 Webster, *Art*, 57.

29 Webster, *Art*, 57–67.

30 Webster, *Art*, 68–69, 131–34. The original images are believed to have been replaced in 1675 and since restored. The composition of the tableau has also been periodically modified ("Hermandad de Monte-Sion," *Wikipedia*, September 16, 2016, https://es.wikipedia.org/wiki/Hermandad_de_Monte-Sion).

31 Webster, *Art*, 71.

32 "Itinerario oficial Semana Santa de Sevilla," *Semana Santa Sevilla*, March 6, 2016, www.semana-santa.org/itinerario-oficial-semana-santa-de-sevilla.

33 According to Luke 19:1–10, Zacchaeus climbed a sycamore tree to see Jesus as he passed through Jericho on his way to Jerusalem. Luke's account of Christ's entry into Jerusalem follows in 19:28–48.

Figure 22 La Borriquita, Seville, 2006. Wikimedia Commons. Photograph by Ángel Cachón.

century; the newest, a kneeling Hebrew mother and her daughter, were added in 2014. All are dressed in loose clothing, Christ's dark purple-and-gold brocaded robe being the most sumptuous. The images are arranged on a massive, ornately carved gilded wooden *paso*, bordered by six seven-branched gilded candlesticks. Heavy valences hang from the *paso*, concealing the forty-two *costaleros* (bearers) required to carry it slowly through the streets. The borriquita is one of the first *pasos* to come out on Palm Sunday afternoon. Preceded by confraternity members in pointed hoods (*capirotes*), which conceal all but the wearers' eyes,[34] and by altar boys carrying tall silver candlesticks, the *paso* is followed by a brass and percussion band playing solemn marches and by a lengthy cortège of boys in white surplices. Together, they undertake a slow journey to the cathedral and back, lasting about four and a half hours. Although the swaying motion of the *costaleros* partially animates the tableau, Christ on the donkey is still very much an exalted rather than an intimate presence. Christ is closer to those watching from first-floor balconies than he is to those craning their necks upward from the street below. The devotional effect of the Sevillan processional borriquita is very different from that of the palmesel.[35]

Few Spanish borriquitas are both as old and as grandiose as that in Seville. Valladolid's "Borriquilla," plausibly dated to "around the year 1600," is older,[36] but its

---

34 Spanish processional *capirotes* predate the similar hoods worn in the USA by members of the Ku Klux Klan.

35 Search online under "Borriquita" and "Sevilla."

36 Dating the borriquilla is complicated by the loss of its sponsoring confraternity's archives to fire in 1806. Delfín Val and Cantalapiedra, *Semana*, 24, opt for "the last third of the seventeenth

wooden *paso* is smaller, mostly ungilded, and supports half as many images. Christ on his donkey is accompanied by a foal, three disciples, two young men laying blankets in front of the donkey, and another man holding a palm. The figures are made of glued fabric applied to a wooden armature and then polychromed. Only the head, hands, and feet of each image is carved in wood and painted. Christ alone wears additional clothing.[37] There is no shortage, however, of quasi-military pomp and precision surrounding the *paso*'s slow march to the cathedral. All participating members of the confraternity— men, women, and children—wear an identical uniform of green cape over black cassock; white gloves are required. Pointed hoods are saved for later in Holy Week. Twenty-four *costaleros* step and sway in time, visibly supporting the *paso* by means of wooden beams that extend forward and backward from beneath the platform. A police escort marches alongside and behind.[38]

Cartagena's extraordinary Palm Sunday procession, in which a dozen *pasos*—known locally as *tronos* (thrones)—tell the story of Christ from his baptism by John to his entry into Jerusalem, dates only to 1944. A substantial military escort of foot-soldiers from the army, navy, and marines, all armed with rifles and marching in time with the music, begins and ends the procession. The military theme is further emphasized by a disci- plined squadron of young boys dressed as Spanish grenadiers, armed with rifles and bayonets, and by another of men and boys dressed as Roman centurions. The dissonance between the militarized ethos of the procession and the biblical narrative of Christ's entry that it claims to commemorate is at its most extreme when the final *paso* of Christ on the donkey ("La Burrica") is immediately followed by a squadron of fifty or so armed foot-soldiers goose-stepping in unison to a slow drumbeat.[39]

Many other communities in Spain carry a *paso* of Christ on a donkey, of varying size, pomp, and complexity, in processions of varying length and character. None, to the best of my knowledge, is as old as Valladolid's borriquilla; most have been made and set in motion since the close of the Spanish Civil War in 1939. None are wheeled; all are carried.

---

century." Parrado del Olmo, "Entrada," attributes the image to Francisco Giralte (d. 1576) and dates it to "around 1542–1550." Hernández Redondo, "Escultura," 152, prefers a date of "around the year 1600." Pinheiro da Veiga, *Fastigimia*, 19–28, fails to mention the borriquilla in his detailed descrip- tion of Holy Week in Valladolid in 1605, but this may be because he begins his account on Holy Wednesday, three days after Palm Sunday. The first written record of the "paso muy vistoso del triunfo de Cristo en la entrada de Jerusalén" comes from 1750 (Canesi Acevedo, *Historia*, 2:20).

37 Parrado del Olmo, "Entrada"; Hernández Redondo, "Escultura," 151–54; "Cofradía de la Santa Vera Cruz. La entrada triunfal de Jesús en Jerusalén 'La Borriquilla'," Javier Baladrón Alonso, *Arte en Valladolid*, April 12, 2014, http://artevalladolid.blogspot.com/2014/04/cofradia- de-la-santa-vera-cruz-la.html.

38 For a video of the 2103 procession, see "Procesión de la Borriquilla en Valladolid," Alejandro Rebollo, *YouTube*, March 27, 2013, www.youtube.com/watch?v=JaiCsDWuhbM.

39 Search online under "Burrica," "Cartagena," and "España." For a full video of the 2016 proces- sion, in which the *burrica* features between 2:13:15 and 2:18:40, see "Procesión Domingo Ramos— Semana Santa Cartagena," Ayuntamiento de Cartagena CT, March 20, 2016, *YouTube*, www.youtube. com/watch?v=gDqL3TmbxZY.

The Spanish tradition, for all the superficial similarity of its central image to the German palmesel, is a distinct genre. It was introduced some six hundred years after the first palmesel, during the Baroque triumphalism of the Catholic Counter-Reformation, and enjoyed a new burst of popularity during the Catholic triumphalism of the Franco dictatorship. Holy Week festivities, including those of Palm Sunday, are now widely marketed as tourist attractions. Whereas the simple wheeled palmesel may have embodied some form of resistance to the dissonant pomp of royal entries and elite Palm Sunday processions, the Spanish borriquita with its heavyweight *paso* and marching devotees has embraced triumphal pomp and splendour. Moreover, the borriquita looks forward to Christ's passion with greater intensity than is usual in the case of the palmesel. Whereas even the early palmesels tended to celebrate the humility and friendly intimacy of the Christ who chose to ride a donkey, Spanish Holy Week processions developed out of penitential confraternities whose members were committed to imitating in their own flagellated bodies the suffering of Christ. The two traditions employ different processional means because they enact different theological commitments.

Chapter 18

THE DONKEY THAT WALKED ON WATER

TO SPEAK OF an identifiable group of Italian palm donkeys is anachronistic: Italy did not become an independent nation until 1861. The Alpine autonomous region of Trentino-Alto Adige, where references to palmesels are most common, was part of the German and subsequently Austrian empires from the eighth century until its annexation by Italy in 1919. Known alternatively as Sudtirol (South Tyrol), the region is still bilingual. Even Verona, where the best-known Italian palm donkey can still be seen, was long subject to the cultural influence of the predominantly German Holy Roman Empire and, in modern times, belonged to Austria between 1797 and 1866. It might be more accurate, therefore, to speak of palm donkeys south of the Alps, but since all that I mention in this chapter were recorded or are still found in places now inside Italy, it is convenient to describe them with appropriate caution as Italian.

The earliest extant record of an Italian palmesel is found in an inventory taken in 1250 at the former Benedictine abbey of San Gallo in Moggio Udinese. The list of objects used in worship there includes "a wooden ass on which sits an image of Jesus Christ" (*asinus ligneus super quo sedet imago Jesu Christi*).[1] Cornaiano (formerly Girlan) may have owned a palmesel made in the workshop of Hans Schnatterpeck in Merano in 1484.[2] Bolzano (Bozen) cathedral also had a palmesel. In 1488, according to the chapter accounts, payment was made for "four wheels on the donkey and two new axles." Further repairs were made to "the Palm Sunday ass" in 1512 and 1516.[3] A late palmesel is recorded in Chiavenna, on the Swiss border, where a "sacred diary" of church festivities published in 1707 noted that in the city's Palm Sunday procession, members of the Confraternity of Santa Marta "led the statue of Christ the Saviour mounted on the foal of an ass."[4] The fate of these palmesels is unknown.

Three Italian palmesels, one of which has since disappeared, are known to have survived the Catholic Enlightenment. The *Liber processionalis* of the Collegiate Church in San Candido (Innichen), compiled in 1616, describes a Palm Sunday procession from the Romanesque collegiate church to the parish church and back. Unusually, the palmesel remained behind. When the procession returned, Christ and his donkey were waiting in front of the altar of the Holy Cross at the foot of the steps leading up to the choir. There, the image was venerated with antiphonal singing and prostrations reminiscent of those in thirteenth-century Essen. At least by the nineteenth century, matters had become

---

1 Bianchi, *Documenta*, 61; Kretzenbacher, "Palmesel," 86.

2 Broekaert and Knapen, "Inventaris," 255.

3 Neumann, *Geistliches*, 1:139, 185, 213. By contrast, a live donkey may have been used in the Sterzing Palm Sunday Play, performed in Bozen in 1514 (Lipphardt and Roloff, *Geistlichen*, 4:59–60; Tydeman, *Medieval*, 370–72).

4 Macolino, *Diario*, 348, cited in Bernardi, *Drammaturgia*, 305.

**Figure 23 Palmesel, Caldaro/Kaltern, ca. 1498. Museo Civico de Bolzano.
Photograph by author.**

more informal. Choirboys led the palmesel through the town after mass, asking for coins to be donated through a slot in the donkey's back. This tradition lasted "until 1890." The current location of the palmesel, if it still exists, is "unknown."[5]

The palmesel of the parish church of Caldaro (Kaltern) also survived the Catholic Enlightenment. It was found in 1902, unused for a hundred years or so, in the attic of the town's hospital. After some dispute over ownership between church and community, the image was trundled in a cart to the civic musuem in nearby Bolzano, where I saw it in 2013 (Fig. 23).[6] Caldaro's palmesel has been attributed to Hans Klocker (fl. 1478–1500), who is known to have made an altarpiece for the town's parish church around 1498;[7] the palmesel is thought to date to the same period.[8] Sets of holes at each corner of its base suggest that wheels were once fixed to axles in the front and rear. A metal

---

5 Kühebacher, "Prozessionen," 640–41, 651–52.

6 Gallmetzer, "Kalterer"; Pescota, *125 Jahre*, 64.

7 Scheffler, *Klocker*, 12, 17–22, 157–59, plates 2c, 4.

8 Pescota, *125 Jahre*, 64, and Carli, *Scultura*, 37, estimate "around 1498." Scheffler, *Klocker*, prefers "around 1500."

Figure 24 Muletta. Church of Santa Maria in Organo, Verona. Photograph by author.

clasp in the front centre of the base probably secured the shaft by which the palmesel was pulled.[9]

Italy's best-known surviving processional sculpture of Christ on a donkey belongs to the Church of Santa Maria in Organo in Verona, where it is known as the *muletta* (little jenny) (Fig. 24). Its Italian name is by no means the only aspect of its history that makes the muletta exceptional. The Verona image has attracted a dazzling array of myths, origin legends, and misleading scholarship. Moreover, the greatest threat to its survival came neither from the Catholic Enlightenment nor from benign neglect in dusty storage, but from a libellous story spread by a late-seventeenth-century Protestant

---

9 Personal conversation with Stefan Demetz, executive director of the Museo Civico, Bolzano, February 21, 2013.

travel writer and from the ill-considered actions of an early twentieth-century Church of Scotland minister and amateur photographer.

Although a date "around the middle of the thirteenth century"[10] has been claimed for the Verona muletta, the first testimony to its existence comes from 1609. Adriano Banchieri, a monk and composer of sacred music, who visited the Olivetan monastery of Santa Maria in Organo in 1607, described the monastery's Palm Sunday procession as

> an old and devout custom ... Every year on Palm Sunday, after the distribution of the blessed olive branch, there occurs a most notable procession, with a grand assembly of nobility and other people. The ass's foal (*polledretta*), adorned with palms and olive branches, is carried in procession through the city with universal joy of bells and various fireworks. When it is returned to the church, a most solemn Pontifical Mass is sung by the Reverend Father, abbot *pro tem* of that most honoured monastery. This devout custom, observed throughout the city, is called by longstanding use the Feast of the Muletta.[11]

Smaller than most palmesels, for most of its history the muletta was not wheeled but carried by only four monks. The iron loops through which the support poles were inserted survive. For the liturgy that followed, Banchieri composed a Baroque concerted mass with multiple voices and both string and wind instruments.[12] Palm Sunday in seventeenth-century Verona was a lively affair of mixed style, enjoyed by the nobility and the common people alike.

Corroborative testimony comes from Secondo Lancellotti's history of the Olivetan Order (1623). On Palm Sunday, or the feast "of olives" (*olearum*), palms were distributed, the nobility assembled, and "a multitudinous, most illustrious procession" took place. Palms were strewn before "the ass (*asella*) with Christ," which was also honoured with olive branches. The image was "carried most religiously around the whole city, with bells sounding publicly, most brilliant fireworks flashing on all sides ... giving cause for great rejoicing."[13] The image was also included in Verona's annual Corpus Christi procession, where it conferred status on those who marched close to it. On June 20, 1612, the city council issued a judgment against members of the guild of lightermen (*radaroli*) who had refused "to walk solemnly with all the guilds in the aforesaid procession ... but wanted to mingle with the venerable monks of Sta. Maria in Organo, who were in possession of the image of the Saviour seated on the ass, with lighted torches in their hands, which is absurd and not to be endured."[14]

Toward the end of the century, the monks appear to have assigned responsibility for the muletta to the Compagnia della Maestà, a confraternity whose name alluded to

---

10 Francovich, "Contributi," 134.

11 Banchieri, *Conclusioni*, 49–50; trans. Garrett, 45.

12 Banchieri, *Conclusioni*, 50–51; trans. Garrett, 45–46.

13 Lancellotti, *Historiae*, 216.

14 Archivo di Stato di Verona, *Atti del Consiglio*, vol. FFF, fol. 12, quoted in Marchi, "Cristo," 143; Zampieri, *Palio*, 198.

Christ's "parade of extraordinary majesty" into Jerusalem on Palm Sunday.[15] At the same time, four iron wheels were attached to the base of the muletta, so that it could be pulled by means of a rope. But this was considered "too realistic" for enlightened eighteenth-century taste, and a "sgabello grezzo"—described by Gian Paolo Marchi as "a small baldachin of untreated wood"[16]—was made to transport the image in procession. Not long afterward, the muletta lost its place in the procession altogether, the *sgabello* was sold, and the statue was placed in a niche above the altar in a chapel to the north of the high altar. In 1718 the niche was covered with a painting of Christ's entry into Jerusalem, which was itself replaced two years later by a painting of Saint Benedict, whose rule the Olivetans followed.[17]

The cause of this sudden demotion and concealment of the muletta was the story told by Maximilien Misson, an Anglo-French Protestant who travelled through Italy in 1687 and 1688, and subsequently described his journey in *A New Voyage to Italy*. His book, first published in French in 1691 and in English in 1695, "became the standard travel guide to Italy for at least the following fifty years."[18] The story of the Verona muletta first appeared in the second French edition (1694).[19] The source for Misson's story was a French merchant, living in London, who had "often seen" the image carried in procession. "It is believed at Verona," Misson reported,

> that after Christ had made his entrance into Jerusalem, he dismissed the she or he-ass on which he rode, and ordered that he should pass the rest of his days in quiet and liberty. They add that the ass, weary with having wandered so long in Palestine, resolved to visit foreign countries, and to undertake a voyage by sea; nor had he any need of a ship, for the waves became smooth, and the liquid element grew as hard as crystal. After he had visited the islands of Cyprus, Rhodes, Candia [Crete], Malta, and Sicily, he passed over the Gulf of Venice, and stayed some days in the place where that famous city was afterwards built: but the air seeming to be unhealthful, and the pasturage bad among these salt and marshy islands, Martin [the ass] continued his voyage, and mounted the River Adige dry-shod, and coming up to Verona, he made choice of that place for his last residence. After he had lived there some years like an honest ass, he died at last, to the great grief of the confraternity. So lamentable and universal a braying made the echoes to resound through the country, that never was so sad a melody heard at the funeral of such an animal, not even in Arcadia itself. But they quickly found a way to alleviate their grief, for all the honours imaginable being rendered to the blest deceased, the devotees of Verona took care

---

15 Biancolini, *Notizie*, 1:292.

16 Marchi, "Cristo," 145.

17 Marchi, "Cristo," 145–47. Both paintings remain in the church: Andrea Voltolini's *L'Ingresso de Gesù in Gerusalemme* hangs in the left transept, while Simone Brentana's *S. Benedetto* is still above the altar in the chapel of Saint Benedict.

18 Spence, "Misson," 376.

19 Francovich, "Contributi," 146n86; Chambers, *Mediaeval*, 1:333n3.

to preserve his relics, and put them into the belly of an artificial ass, made for that purpose, where they are kept to this day, to the great joy and edification of pious souls. This holy statue is kept in the Church of Notre Dame of the Organs, and four of the lustiest monks in the convent, in pontifical habits, carry it solemnly in procession two or three times every year.[20]

Misson's story was quickly repudiated by learned residents of Verona. Ottavio Alecchi wrote a long letter to a colleague in Zurich on December 16, 1710, in which he asserted: "No one in Verona believes that this ass is really the same as the one that served the Redeemer during his entry into Jerusalem on the Sunday before his passion; or that the wooden mare is covered with the true skin of the aforesaid ass, or that it is enclosed within, as a relic."[21] Misson must have received a similar letter, albeit perhaps from an English Catholic, for in the introduction to the 1714 edition of his book he reported the objection of a correspondent who "cannot fancy, that the good honest priests of Verona, men of great learning, be so simple as to carry in procession the asinine-relic which I mentioned, though there is nothing more certain. His zeal for the church of Rome, of which he is a devout member, has raised in him an indignation at our exposing the ridiculousness of this fine story, and that of the worship which is paid with great ceremonies to the skin and bones of this four-footed saint, who so gravely and miraculously transported himself from Jerusalem to Verona."[22]

Misson's libel has had a long life. It was repeated in the nineteenth century by such influential figures as J. A. Dulaure and F. D. Guerrazzi,[23] and in the twentieth century by E. K. Chambers, Ernst Kantorowicz, and Vera Ostoia.[24] In the twenty-first century, the story has resurfaced in Verona. In a book published there in 2008, Marino Zampieri treats the "scandalous 'festa della muletta'" as a carnivalesque event with its roots in "ancient fertility cults" and "pre-Christian folklore." Paraphrasing Misson at length, Zampieri writes with relish of "the inevitable excesses, the irreverent acts, [and] the carnivalesque celebrations," in which the people of seventeenth-century Verona indulged whenever the muletta was carried in procession.[25] All these writers, from Misson to Zampieri, were careful to label the story of the water-walking donkey and the veneration of its relics in the wooden image as a "legend," but such caution did not extend to the conviction that the people of Verona had believed the tale in the first place.

In fact, the residents of seventeenth-century Verona had attached a very different origin legend to their muletta. Adriano Banchieri, the monk and composer, learned of the local belief during his visit to the monastery of Santa Maria in Organo in 1607. "According to the tradition of ancient writings," he wrote,

---

20 Misson, *New*, 1:198–99.

21 Marchi, *Luoghi*, 129.

22 Misson, *New*, 1:xxviii.

23 Dulaure, *Histoire*, 3:509, quoted with considerable scepticism by Clément, "Drame," 16:33; Guerrazzi, *Asino*, 1:226–27.

24 Chambers, *Mediaeval*, 1:333n3; Kantorowicz, *King's*, 85n105; Ostoia, "Palmesel," 173.

25 Zampieri, *Palio*, 196–99.

the ass's foal ... was industriously carved by a dedicated and venerable hermit who lived at that time in the mountains not far from the town. When it was completed, the hermit placed it in the river Adige where, following the course of the river, it floated into the most illustrious city of Verona, and miraculously stopped at the above monastery. The city came to know of this event, and all the people knew that the carving had been made by the venerable hermit. Therefore, with a solemn ceremony, it was placed in the Church of S. Maria in Organo, of the Olivetan Order, on a glorious altar made of plaster and gold.[26]

A longer version of this story, introduced with the comment "I accept this tradition," was included by Lancellotti in his history of the order. Lancellotti's account identifies the "hermit" as a monk from the monastery of Santa Maria in Organo, who, with his abbot's permission, retired to seek solitude in the forests near Trent, halfway between Verona and Bolzano. When the carved figure of Christ on a donkey was found in the river near the monastic Church of Santa Maria in Organo, it was "reverently carried" by secular clergy to the Basilica of San Lorenzo. At dawn, the image had returned to the river; again it was taken to San Lorenzo. This happened three times before "everyone agreed that God had given [the image] to Santa Maria in Organo ... The hermit had made it with his hands, the Adige had brought it, and it was declared a miracle."[27]

The story was further modified by Edward Wright, another Protestant traveller to Italy between 1720 and 1722, who reported that the ass had been

cut in wood, about four hundred years ago, by a friar of the convent, who left it there ... This ass, as they tell you, was by some means conveyed away from the convent, three several times, and as many times returned of his own accord; how he travelled by land, the story says not, but when he got to the riverside, he took water and swum along a branch of the Adige, which comes just by the convent, and stopped under the bridge that leads to the church. To assure us of the truth of the story, they shewed us the place.[28]

In Wright's version, the wooden donkey was somehow animated, capable of swimming and otherwise moving "of his own accord." Perhaps Wright was influenced by Misson's legend, which he mentioned but had the good grace to admit "was not said to us by the person who showed [the image]." Wright further reported that the image was "preserved with great veneration, as miraculous, in a little vault over the altar in one of the chapels; it is kept covered and not exposed but on great days. Two days in the year it is carried in procession; one of the days is the Feast of Corpus Domini [Corpus Christi]."[29] The other was Palm Sunday.

---

26 Banchieri, *Conclusioni*, 49; translation adapted from Garrett, 45.

27 Lancellotti, *Historiae*, 216. In a personal converstion on February 19, 2013, Umberto Calafà, the custodian of Santa Maria in Organo, told me that a branch of the Adige used to flow directly past the front of the church, following the course of the street now known as the Interrato dell'Acqua Morta. He added, "If the *muletta* had been in the water that long, it would have rotted."

28 Wright, *Observations*, 2:489–90.

29 Wright, *Observations*, 2:490.

Francesco Scipione, Marquis of Maffei, in his four-volume history of Verona (1731–1732), vehemently rejected both Misson's "fable" and Wright's assertion that the ass returned three times "of his own accord," as well as any suggestion that the ass was venerated and thought to be miraculous, all of "which," he wrote, "is most false." "Respect," he insisted, was shown not to the "beast of burden" (giumento) but "to the figure of the Saviour."[30] Giambatista Biancolini, in his equally voluminous history of the churches of Verona (1749–1752), concluded that Lancellotti's origin legend was "rather a fable than a true story." Lancellotti had neither dated the supposed miracle nor offered any proof. Moreover, not a syllable of evidence was to be found in the monastery's archives. Lancellotti was too ready to believe "certain opinions of the common people." The most likely origin of the muletta, in Biancolini's judgment, was that "it was sculpted in Verona by a notable sculptor and lay brother of the monastery, who donated it to the church, where it has since been kept."[31] This view has endured. In 1909, Luigi Simeoni noted that the muletta "is said to be the work of a lay brother of the fifteenth century."[32] In 2002, Luciano Rognini was more specific: the image was "perhaps sculpted by the monk Giovanni, not to be confused with the Olivetan master," Fra Giovanni da Verona (ca. 1457–1525).[33] The latter was responsible for the extraordinary marquetry in the church's choir and sacristy; the former is otherwise unknown.

It might be argued that the legend of the muletta's voyage down the Adige, which rises high in the Italian Alps near the borders of Austria and Switzerland, and flows through Bolzano and Verona before entering the Adriatic south of Venice, was a way of acknowledging the image's northern roots. Géza de Francovich grants that "the Christ seated on the she-mule (mula) of Santa Maria in Organo is certainly of German iconographic provenance," but insists on a local origin and a much earlier date than the written record can verify. Verona's muletta, he argues, is stylistically distinct from German palmesels and consistent with thirteenth-century religious images still to be found in Verona. In particular, he draws attention to the stylistic similarities between the muletta and the mid-thirteenth-century marble statues of Christ and his apostles in Verona's Basilica San Zeno Maggiore.[34] Fernanda de' Maffei has suggested further evidence for the early date. In an exhibition catalogue prepared jointly with Francovich, Maffei draws attention to the stone relief of Jesus's entry into Jerusalem on the outer façade of the Sepolcro di Cansignorio at the Arche Scaligere in Verona (1376). On this panel, she wrote, "the artist reproduces, albeit with a few distinct accents, the 'Muleta' of S. Maria in Organo."[35] If this were true, it would place the muletta in Verona at least by the late fourteenth century. To my eye, the affinity between the stone relief and marble

30 Maffei, Verona, 3:288–92.
31 Biancolini, Notizie, 1:290–93.
32 Simeoni, Verona, 313.
33 Rognini, Chiesa, 51
34 Francovich, "Contributi," 134–36.
35 Maffei and Francovich, Mostra, 43.

statues, on the one hand, and the wooden muletta, on the other hand, remains at best suggestive rather than definitive.[36]

Whatever its origin may have been, the muletta's concealment behind the painting of Saint Benedict was subject to reprieve at least once a year. The painting was hung on hinges,[37] allowing it to be swung open on Palm Sunday to reveal the muletta.[38] Otherwise the palm donkey remained out of sight. When Adolphe Didron visited Verona in 1854, he mistakenly asked in the cathedral to see "the remains of the donkey of 'the flight into Egypt.'" Informed about the wooden image in Santa Maria in Organo, he made his way there, but was unable to find the hidden muletta.[39] Alexander Robertson, who served as the Church of Scotland minister in Venice, was more fortunate. Visiting Verona in December 1902, he was shown the muletta, and wrote respectfully of his experience shortly afterwards.[40]

But in March 1910, Carmeolo Tranchese, then a Jesuit student of theology at Saint Beuno's college in Wales, wrote an impassioned letter to Silvinio Tomba, secretary to the bishop of Verona. Tranchese complained that articles about a "church of the ass" in Livorno (Italy) had been published in Canadian Protestant newspapers. Although a Catholic newspaper had refuted the calumny, a conference on the subject had been organized by a Mrs. Miller. Hearing of the furore, Robertson had written a letter to a friend, Hugh Acland-Troyte, then in Lugano, Switzerland, confirming the existence of the image of Christ on a donkey in Verona, and paraphrasing his earlier published comments. Since the question had arisen, he added, he had made a second visit to Verona, where the sacristan of Santa Maria in Organo had kindly allowed him to take a photograph of the muletta. Robertson had set up magnesium lights, climbed ("*sic,*" wrote the horrified Tranchese!) on the altar in the chapel of Saint Benedict, and succeeded in taking a photograph of the statue in its niche. Moreover, Robertson repeated the slanderous story first advanced by Misson, and sent a copy of his photograph to Acland-Troyte, who duly forwarded it to Mrs. Miller. Tranchese was furious. Receiving Tranchese's letter, the bishop of Verona ordered that the statue no longer be shown indiscriminately to members of the public.[41]

As late as 1965, however, the painting was still swung open on Palm Sunday. The muletta was spectacularly raised into view in its niche by means of a set of cogs and

---

36 On my visit to Verona in February 2013, I was able to examine the marble statues in the Basilica San Zeno, but not the relief at the Scaligeri Tombs, which were closed to the public. For the latter, I have relied on Napione, *Arche,* plates XII and 176.

37 Robertson, *Roman,* 195.

38 Biancolini, *Notizie,* 1:316.

39 Didron, editorial note to Clément, "Drame," 16:33.

40 Robertson, *Roman,* 195.

41 Marchi, "Cristo," 151–55; Marchi, *Luoghi,* 133–37. After his ordination in Wales in September 1910, Tranchese was assigned to a parish in New Mexico. As the priest of Our Lady of Guadalupe in San Antonio, Texas, from 1932–1953, he gained a national reputation as a defender of Mexican Americans and advocate of social justice ("Tranchese, Carmelo Antonio," Donald L. Zelman, *Handbook of Texas Online,* www.tshaonline.org/handbook/online/articles/ftr20).

pulleys in a tiny storage room behind the altar. Since then—happily for visitors at other times of the year—the muletta has been displayed all year round on a pedestal beside the altar in the chapel of Saint Benedict. Christ is dressed in blue and red robes and seated on a golden saddle blanket, all carved and painted. His right hand blesses visitors; his left hand holds a gospel book. The jenny's diminutive size, large brown eyes, and laid-back ears give her an air of docile approachability; the visitor is inclined to pet her. In February 2013, the church's long-serving custodian, Umberto Calafà, told me that he still remembered seeing the annual appearance of the muletta when he was a boy. He kindly showed me the storage room from which the muletta used to be raised into its niche. The mechanism by which it was raised no longer exists,[42] but the muletta itself, despite all the slanders directed against it, has proved remarkably durable.

---

42 Umberto Calafà, personal conversation, February 19, 2013.

Chapter 19

SURVIVALS AND REVIVALS

GIVEN THE LEVEL of religious hostility, wartime damage, benign neglect, and malicious libel that palmesels have suffered over the centuries, it is perhaps surprising that so many have survived. An inventory published in 2006 lists 105 surviving full-size palmesels in Germany, sixteen in Switzerland, twelve in Austria, seven in France, and one or two each in Belgium, England, the Netherlands, Italy, Poland, and the Czech Republic. It also notes a few miniature palmesels, several Christ figures or donkeys that have survived without their other half, and three complete palmesels owned by museums in the United States.[1] Many of the full-size palmesels were rescued from rarely used chapels, charnel houses, attics, barns, and other out-of-sight storage to which they had been confined by changing tastes and ecclesiastical suppression. Others were acquired at state auctions or bought from private owners, antique dealers, or historical societies. Several museums have lovingly restored their acquisitions. Those still owned by churches have been given greater visibility or, in some cases, placed back in service. A few newly made palmesels have been added, such that there are now more than a dozen active palmesels scattered across Europe. We have already noted an Austrian example in Puch bei Hallein. In this chapter, I introduce others from Austria, Germany, Poland, Alsace, Belgium, and even outside Europe, in Bolivia and possibly Paraguay.

I begin with a personal account. In March 2015, I took part in two very different Palm Sunday processions, each involving a palmesel, in the adjacent Austrian communities of Hall in Tirol and Thaur, a few miles east of Innsbruck. Hall's palmesel, housed in the Parish Church of Saint Nicholas, dates to 1430, when it was endowed by the Confraternity of Our Lady.[2] It starred in the town's annual Palm Sunday procession until 1826, when it succumbed to the aftermath of the Catholic Enlightenment and was retired from use. The tradition was reinstated by the parish priest in 1968.[3] Thaur's palmesel belongs to the Parish Church of the Assumption of Mary; it was made in 1772,[4] and has remained in use ever since.

On the afternoon before Palm Sunday, I visited both palmesels in their home churches. Hall's parish church is Gothic in structure, Baroque in decoration, and imposing in scale. The vast and pillared retable behind the Baroque high altar rises as high as the columns of the Gothic arches lining the nave, the vaulted ceilings are lavishly painted with scenes of hagiographic triumph, and most of the gilded figures of saints on the walls and pillars are larger than life. The palmesel stood on its wheeled platform at the foot of the steps in front of the new post-Vatican II altar, facing down the nave towards the church's west

---

1 Broekaert and Knapen, "Inventaris."

2 Friedrich and Schmitz-Esser, *Pfarrkirche*, 23.

3 Streng and Bakay, *Wilde*, 99; Schenk, *Christliche*, 46.

4 A note, still affixed to the breast of the Christ figure in 1904, read "Benefactor Fecit Franciscus Antonius Egger, Procurator hic loco anno post Christum natum 1772" ("Palmsonntagbrauch," 5–6).

doors. With his right hand Christ blessed anyone who entered. His left hand held loose leather reins.[5] Small as the palmesel was by comparison with so much else in the church, this life-size image at the centre of the building somehow acted as a visual magnet, reducing the psychological scale of its surroundings.

Thaur's parish church is smaller and less ornate than its counterpart in Hall; its palmesel, too, is smaller. About three-quarters life size and mounted on a sturdy wheeled wooden platform, it stood sideways on, facing across the nave from what, in a larger church, might have been the south transept. Christ was dressed in a maroon robe under a gold-hemmed cardinal-red cape secured around the waist with a large bow. His right hand was raised in blessing; his left hand held a tall olive branch and loose red reins.[6] The palmesel had been strategically positioned so that Christ's gaze was fixed on a painted wooden crucifix hanging on the opposite wall. Two very different placement decisions had thus been made on behalf of the Hall and Thaur palmesels: the Christ of the former welcomed visitors, the Christ of the latter contemplated his passion.

Palm Sunday dawned cold but clear. A crowd gathered in Hall's old market square, some wearing traditional regional dress, but most clothed informally for warmth. Olive branches were trundled into the square on an old wooden cart and freely distributed. Young men leaned *Palmstangen* (palm poles)—enormous stripped branches decorated with olive, boxwood, pussy willow, pretzels, and coloured ribbons—against the façades of buildings. Some poles were more than thirty feet tall. Children clutched smaller, more manageable *Palmlatten* (palm laths). The town band arrived and warmed up by playing what I think was a polka.

At nine-thirty, a dozen older men in suits, each carrying a late Baroque *Zunftstange* (guild pole), walked in formation down the sloping cobbled street from the church into the square. The poles, about fifteen feet tall and firmer than the *Palmstangen*, were topped with small carved figures emblematic of the town's guilds. Behind the pole-bearers came a dozen girls and boys in cardinal-red cassocks and white surplices, pushing together against a series of wooden bars spliced through a long rope tied to the metal shaft in front of the palmesel's wheeled platform. The palmesel's downward progress alluded to Christ's much steeper descent from the Mount of Olives. Clutching our olive branches, we recalled the crowd that greeted him.

The procession halted at the Mary Fountain, just beyond the entrance to the square. The parish priest presided over a short outdoor liturgy, during which olive branches were blessed, the crowd was sprinkled liberally with holy water, a gospel account of Christ's entry was read, and a Palm Sunday antiphon was sung. An expanded procession then set out on a brief counterclockwise circuit of the old town (Fig. 25). The band led the way, followed by palm poles, young women in traditional dirndl dresses, guild poles,

---

5 For a photograph, see Harris, "Inanimate," 181.

6 Pfaundler, *Sankt*, 37, notes that the Thaur Christ's limbs are movable, in the manner of articulated processional images elsewhere. Although I was unable to verify this in any detail, I did note that Christ's feet moved as the image travelled over rough ground; see also Victoria and Albert Museum, "Religious," especially the footage between 3:04 and 3:18.

Figure 25 Palm Sunday procession, Hall in Tirol, 2015. Photograph by author.

palmesel, priest, and warmly dressed crowd. Others lined the route to watch the procession pass. We were back at the parish church in time for mass at ten.

The church was packed. All seats were filled, leaving standing room only. Even the chancel in front of the Baroque high altar was dense with worshippers. Children sat on the floor or on a parent's shoulders. The palmesel again stood at the foot of the chancel steps, facing the length of the nave. Even the palm poles, the longer ones carefully lowered so that they could be carried horizontally on the shoulders of two men, had been taken inside. The service itself was both orthodox and informal. As well as traditional Catholic chants, we sang Paul Gerhardt's great Lutheran hymn "O Haupt voll Blut und Wunden" (O Sacred Head, Now Wounded) to Bach's arrangement of the melody, and another hymn, whose words I didn't catch, to the tune of "Michael, Row the Boat Ashore." Communicants formed three lines, the central file receiving the host from the priest immediately in front of the palmesel. After the service was over, several worshippers, both children and adults, had their photographs taken next to Christ and his donkey. The presence of the palmesel had once again reduced the psychological scale of the building to more intimate human proportions.

Hall's Palm Sunday liturgy was informal, joyous, and inclusive. One might suppose that the palmesel had been freed for such an interpretation of its role by its fresh beginning in 1968, shortly after the liberalizing pronouncements of the Second Vatican Council. But there is reason to believe that Hall's palmesel had long been inclined to a light-hearted and even mischievous interpretation of its role. An old report claims that the donkey's hollow belly was "filled" beforehand with "consecrated wafers." When "the palmesel was dragged rumbling through the cobbled streets, the wafers would fall one after another through an opened flap; the young people tussled with one another for the blessed gift."[7]

Thaur has only a short procession, followed by mass, on the morning of Palm Sunday; its main procession takes place in the afternoon.[8] The palmesel takes part in both, but I was there only for the latter. As the parish church clock struck one, three acolytes left the building by its west door. One boy carried the same painted wooden crucifix at which the palmesel's Christ had gazed the previous day. Christ and his donkey followed, pulled by eight boy acolytes using a rope-and-wooden-bar mechanism similar to that in Hall. The crucifix was held facing backward so that, throughout the two-hour procession, the Christ on the donkey remained focused on his approaching passion. A surplus of nine priests followed, wearing white lace surplices and either black or white cassocks. Villagers waited at a bend in the narrow lane leading from the church. Some of the palm laths carried by older boys concealed—amid the foliage, pretzels, and ribbons—a tiny model palmesel. As the procession approached, men and boys took their designated place between the crucifix and the palmesel. Women and girls waited until the palmesel had passed before taking their place behind the priests. Following the example of a small minority of couples, my wife and I walked among the women, many of whom prayed the rosary in unison throughout the procession. So, I gather, did the men at the front of the procession.[9]

For half an hour or so, a sinuous column of some three hundred people climbed a steep, winding, and increasingly narrow path out of Thaur (Fig. 26), passing at first through Alpine meadows and eventually through dense woods, until we reached the chapel of Saint Romedius, about half a mile in distance and some five hundred feet in altitude above the parish church. Snow-capped peaks rose behind the chapel. The more zealous (or curious) members of the crowd pressed inside. Most men sat to the right, all the women to the left. The priests knelt facing the single Baroque altar, at the back of which was displayed a skull in a large gilt reliquary, believed by some to be the skull of Romedius himself.[10] Thaur's parish priest invoked a very long list of saints, imploring them, one by one, to intercede for us. The palmesel stood to the right, facing across the aisle (Fig. 27).

After the prayers, the men left the chapel first, followed in processional order by the acolytes, the palmesel, the priests, and the women. Again facing the crucifix, the procession headed back downhill. A nun led the trailing women in loud repetitions of

---

7 Streng and Bakay, *Wilde*, 99. Perhaps, like the English "singing cakes" thrown on choirboys during some English Palm Sunday processions (Harris, "Processional," 323–24), the Hall wafers were in fact unconsecrated.

8 For a short film of both processions, see Victoria and Albert Museum, "Religious." Earlier accounts of Palm Sunday in Thaur ("Palmsonntagbrauch"; Renk, "Palmesel"; Pfaundler, *Sankt*, 32–39) make no mention of the morning procession, which is probably a more recent innovation.

9 See the video footage of the 2010 procession at "Thaur (Tirol) 'Palmeselprozession zum Romedikirchl'," *YouTube*, March 29, 2010, www.youtube.com/watch?v=KzGCvh49s8g.

10 Pfaundler, *Sankt*, 114–17.

Figure 26 Palm Sunday procession, Thaur, 2015. Photograph by author.

the rosary. At a fork in the path, we turned toward the neighbouring village of Rum. A small deputation of two priests, four acolytes (two girls and two boys), and a huddle of lay men and women met us at the edge of the village; as we approached Rum's small parish church, the mood grew more cheerful and inclusive. Girls as well as boys carried *Palmlatten* hiding miniature palmesels among the foliage and pretzels. I found standing room just inside the west door of the church. Pliable *Palmstangen* had been arranged in an arc across the east end of the nave. Rum's parish priest led a short service facing the congregation, and a choir in the loft over my head sang a hymn to a dulcet Austrian folk tune. After the service, fresh pretzels were distributed outside to the crowd. The procession re-formed and made its way, through vineyards just beginning to turn green, back to Thaur, still praying the rosary. We arrived at the church, as scheduled, precisely as the clock struck three.

Unlike the morning procession in Hall—and with the possible exception of the intermezzo in Rum—Thaur's afternoon procession had been a Lenten penitential rite rather than a celebration of Christ's entry into Jerusalem. The palmesel may have been physically at the heart of the procession, but only the priests and acolytes were close to it. The rest of us, lacking surplices and cassocks, had none of the sense of intimacy with Christ on his donkey that the worshippers in Hall had enjoyed. The palmesel's role was to model for us proper Lenten contemplation of the suffering endured by Christ on Good Friday. Some of this may be due to the uninterrupted nature of the tradition in Thaur. Between 1650 and 1750, Baroque Catholicism in southern Germany and Austria saw an "expansion, even explosion, of pilgrimage piety," in which growing numbers of

**Figure 27 Palmesel, Thaur, 1772. Chapel of Saint Romedius, Palm Sunday, 2015.
Photograph by author.**

communal pilgrimage processions made their way to both distant and local shrines.[11]
Thaur's Palm Sunday procession to the chapel of Saint Romedius was a late example of
the local variety: the palmesel was made in 1772, while the chapel was newly rebuilt "at
the end of the eighteenth century."[12] The surviving rite has preserved much of the character of a late-eighteenth-century rural pilgrimage procession, including its penitential

---

11 Forster, *Catholic Germany*, 166–67; see also Forster, *Catholic Revival*, 61–105.
12 Pfaundler, *Sankt*, 46.

nature, separation of the sexes, and recital of the rosary. Even in Thaur, however, the church's palmesel comes nowhere close to embracing the triumphal interpretation of the Palm Sunday narrative that once shaped royal entries and elite Palm Sunday processions. Palmesels may differ in their interpretation of the story, even in communities as close to one another as Hall and Thaur,[13] but they do not easily yield to pomp or to the celebration of military triumph.

The nontriumphal character of the image is also evident in other German towns with active palmesels. Kößlarn has two. The older one remained in almost continuous service, albeit not always as part of a liturgical procession, for over five hundred years until its retirement in 2001. Church accounts record payment in 1481 of "25 Pfund und 15 Pfennig" to the local artist Hans Nagl for making a "holy sepulchre" and a palmesel for use during Holy Week.[14] Repairs to the palmesel were first recorded in 1605. Further repairs were needed a century later, in part because it was by then an established custom for the palmesel to make house-to-house visits after mass, occasioning additional wear and tear. In 1704, a florin paid for "two new wheels and a new shaft" for the "trolley on which our dear Lord rides about the market town on Palm Sunday." In 1711, renovations were made to the palmesel itself. The palmesel's participation in Kößlarn's Palm Sunday procession ended in 1783, in the wake of the Catholic Enlightenment. For safekeeping, Christ and his donkey were hidden abeove the church vaults.[15]

House-to-house visits resumed after the secularization of the prince-bishopric of Passau in 1803, and with only occasional lapses have continued ever since.[16] Further repairs were needed in 1912: among other defects, Christ's right hand had come loose. By 1950, four acolytes (Meßbuben) were pulling the palmesel from house to house, surrounded by a cheerful group of children. Mothers brought babies in arms to the door to "give the Lord Jesus a little kiss (Busserl)" and to catch hold of the donkey's ears. The acolytes then went indoors to sing "more or less skillfully" the Palm Sunday antiphon "Pueri Hebraeorum," for which they were rewarded with coins. After afternoon prayers, the palmesel and its entourage continued to country houses owned by "those faithful to the church and tradition," where the boys were paid in doughnuts.[17] The afternoon tour ended badly in 1969. Approaching a steep descent into town, most of the boys jumped onto the handcart beneath the palmesel; the smallest child climbed astride the donkey itself. The cart and its load hurtled down the hill, but "by the worst luck" everyone ended up in a roadside ditch. The boys were unhurt, but the palmesel broke two of its legs.[18]

---

13 For more on the interpretive versatility of the palmesel, see Harris, "Inanimate."

14 Zue, "Bayerns," 6; Butz, "Dein," 52. Peinkofer, "Niederbayerischen," 82, reports payment of "25 Pfund und 1 Pfennig."

15 Zue, "Bayerns," 6; Butz, "Palmsonntag," 144; Binder, "Palmesel," 83.

16 Butz, "Dein," 53.

17 Peinkofer, "Niederbayerischen," 81–82; see also Zue, "Bayerns," who includes a photo of a child kissing the Saviour and adds the detail of the donkey's ears.

18 Zue, "Bayerns," 7.

In 1977 the repaired palmesel was returned to service, this time as part of an expanded Palm Sunday procession in which many parishioners carried *Palmbuschen*, bound bundles of boxwood and catkin, some several feet high. House-to-house visits within the town were resumed, but the outlying tour was not. The Latin antiphon—by then frequently garbled by the acolytes—was replaced with a simple German song inviting the Christ who "formerly rode through Jerusalem on a donkey … to be today a guest in this house."[19] In 2001, after another broken leg, the elderly palmesel was safely retired to the Kirchenmuseum, where it is now on display, fully restored. A second, smaller palmesel was made, and has since starred in the church's Palm Sunday procession. For the rest of the year, the younger palmesel can be seen in a specially designed box window from which Christ and his donkey, the former's right hand raised in blessing, look out over the street that runs downhill beside the museum. Steps lead up to the window, permitting pedestrians the intimacy of eye contact.[20]

Other active German palmesels date from the late fifteenth to the early twenty-first century. The palmesel at the Church of Saint Jodokus in Bad Oberdorf was made around 1470, perhaps in the workshop of Hans Multscher in Ulm, and restored in 1936.[21] Since 1963, it has taken part in an annual Palm Sunday procession to the neighbouring village of Bad Hindelang. Choirgirls pull the image, followed by the priest, a lively wind band, and parishioners carrying *Palmbuschen*.[22] Built "around 1690," the palmesel in Kühbach bei Aichach's Church of Saint Magnus participated in the Palm Sunday procession until 1850. Rescued from dusty storage by a schoolteacher in 1930, the image was restored and returned to processional service two years later. The acolytes take the palmesel on house-to-house visits in the afternoon.[23] Oberstdorf's palmesel was made in 1729. On the eve of Palm Sunday, it used to be taken in procession from the Parish Church to the Chapel of Saint Nicholas (Klausenkapelle), returning in a second procession the next morning. Surviving the secularization of Bavaria, retirement to inactivity, and a fire that swept through Oberstdorf in 1865, the palmesel was moved to the baroque Josefskapelle outside town in 1903. It now returns each Palm Sunday to take part in a procession from the primary school to the parish church.[24] Füssen's palmesel, of uncertain date but probably "baroque,"[25] has since 2010 played the leading role in an ecumenical Palm Sunday procession, shared by two Roman Catholic churches, a Lutheran church, and a largely immigrant Syrian Orthodox church. The gospel account of Christ's entry into Jerusalem is

---

19 Butz, "Dein," 53–54; for the garbled Latin, see Zue, "Bayerns," 7.

20 Butz, "Prächtige;" search online under "Kößlarn" and "Palmsonntag" or "Palmesel."

21 Broekaert and Knapen, "Inventaris," 241; Miller, *Allgäuer*, 39, 81.

22 Search online under "Palmsonntag" and "Bad Oberdorf" or "Bad Hindelang.

23 Christl, *300 Jahre*, 83–84; Lipsmeyer, "Jahreslaufbrauchtum," 55; "Palmesel Prozession in Kühbach," *Bistum Augsburg*, www.bistum-augsburg.de/Pfarreiengemeinschaften/Kuehbach/Brauchtum/Palmesel-Prozession.

24 "Der Rokokobildhauer Franz Xaver Schmädl," Alex Rößle, *Oberstdorf Lexicon*, March 22, 2015, www.oberstdorf-lexikon.de/schmaedl-franz-xaver.html.

25 Broekaert and Knapen, "Inventaris," 243.

read in both Aramaic and German.[26] A brand new unpainted wooden palmesel, of impressive contemporary design, made its first processional appearance in Odenthal in 2008.[27]

Further east, the best-known surviving Polish palmesel is now on show in the National Museum in Krakow (Fig. 28). Dated to "the third decade of the sixteenth century,"[28] it was found in the attic of the parish church in Szydłowiec by a prominent Warsaw ecclesiastical architect, Konstanty Wojciechowski, around 1886. After Wojciechowski pointed out the palmesel's value, the parish priest offered it as payment for architectural services. Wojciechowski subsequently donated the palmesel to Prince Michał Piotr Radziwiłł for display in his recently restored ancestral home, Nieberów Palace. In 1904, the prince's widow gave the palmesel to the National Museum.[29] The Szydłowiec palmesel retains its original wheeled platform, complete with the metal rings to which ropes were attached for pulling, but it lacks two fingers of Christ's right hand, as well as reins and bridle. The donkey's missing ears were replaced in the 1970s.[30] Another surviving palmesel, from "the first quarter of the sixteenth century," belongs to the convent of the Poor Clares in Stary Sącz.[31] Barely four feet high, it is still lovingly clothed and decorated by the nuns before the start of Holy Week.[32]

Poznań's Jesuit church also once owned a palmesel. Tomasz Młodzianowski (1622–1686), who served as rector of the Jesuit church and college between 1680 and 1683, was troubled by the amused response to the image of visiting "Poles, Swedes ... Brandenburgers ... or these turbaned Turks." He ordered the palmesel placed out of public view in the vestry, where it was construed by some sensitive priests as a form of criticism, tantamount to "You are an ass." When Młodzianowski discovered that the palmesel had again been removed, this time to a stable built especially for it by a well-known citizen, he wished the image well: "Let the Lord God also build a house for him in heaven."[33] Poznań now owns a different palmesel. The city's National Museum acquired a German palmesel at the end of the Second World War. Of uncertain provenance, but possibly made in Ulm in "the last decade of the fifteenth century," it arrived in the museum in 1945, "having been removed from storage in a depot left by retreating German troops in Gębice."[34]

---

26 Search online under "Füssen" and "Palmsonntag" or "Palmesel."

27 "Palmsonntag 2008," *Pfarrgemeined St. Pankratius*, www.pankratius-odenthal.de/content/ ?page=kirchenjahr&Menu=170.

28 Walanus, "Chrystus," 137.

29 Marcinkowski, "Chrystus," 27.

30 Walanus, "Chrystus," 136; "Jesus Christ Sitting on the Palm Sunday Donkey," *Wirtualne Muzea Małopolski*, http://muzea.malopolska.pl/en/obiekty/-/a/26885/1493728.

31 Kopania, "Animating," 80; Trajdos, "Wit," 348–49.

32 Sułkowska, "Obrzędy"; "Klaryski, Stary Sącz (Trójca Święta), Rzeźba / Chrystus na osiołku, 1. połowa XVI w.," Patrycja Ziomek, *Hereditas Monasteriorum*, February 18, 2015, http://pw.kasaty. pl/index.php/en/mobilium/Mobilium/3830.html?search=Stare+Troki.

33 Młodzianowski, *Kazanie*, 81–82, and, for a partial translation, Kopania, "Animating," 84.

34 Kopania, "Animating," 104n30; Woziński, "Rzeźba," 75–77, 87–91. Two Polish palmesels, formerly housed in museums in Wrocław (Breslau), are known to have been lost during the war (Kopania, "Animating," 83; Bela, "Palm," 27).

**Figure 28 Palmesel, Szydłowiec, ca, 1530. National Museum, Krakow.
Photograph by Martin Walsh.**

None of the three surviving palmesels now in Poland is processionally active. Happily, two new palmesels have revived the tradition. In 1968, in Tokarnia, a small village near Myślenice, the parish priest of the Church of Our Lady of the Snows invited a local sculptor, Józef Wrona, to make a new palmesel. Older residents of the community could still remember seeing inactive palmesels inside churches in Tokarnia, Myślenice, and Łętownia at the end of the nineteenth century,[35] but none had survived. Wrona is said

---

35 Janicka-Krzywda, "Elementy," 485.

to have modelled his replacement image on the sixteenth-century Szydłowiec palmesel, prompting one scholar to call the Tokarnia image "an extraordinary reanimation of the old Palmesel."[36] From an artistic point of view, the Tokarnia palmesel falls short of its older model, but it has a folk charm of its own, and is evidently much loved by the people of the village. On Palm Sunday it is pulled in procession in the vicinity of the church, accompanied by hand-held "palm trees" made of bound willow branches and decorated with coloured ribbons, crepe paper, flowers, boxwood, and pussy willow. Some are as tall as thirty feet.[37] Another "reanimation" of an older palmesel can be found in Nowy Sącz. In 2003, the old wooden Church of Saints Peter and Paul in the nearby village of Łososina Dolnej, which had been replaced some years previously by a new brick building, was dismantled, moved, reconstructed, and reconsecrated in Sądecki Ethnographic Park, on the edge of Nowy Sącz. The park commissioned a replica of the diminutive palmesel owned by the convent of the Poor Clares in Stary Sącz. On Palm Sunday, after the new palmesel is led in outdoor procession, mass is celebrated inside the old church.[38]

Just as palmesels travelled east from Germany into Poland, so they travelled west into parts of the predominantly German Holy Roman Empire that are now in Alsace, Belgium, and the Netherlands. Although several survive in Alsace, only one is active. Ammerschwihr's fifteenth-century palmesel was initially retired sometime in the nineteenth century, when its condition was judged too dilapidated for it to be safely led in procession. For many years the image did little more on Palm Sunday than move from the choir in the parish church, where it was ordinarily displayed, to the small square outside.[39] "Miraculously saved" during the fierce Allied aerial bombardment of the village in January 1945,[40] it was fully restored and returned to full processional use in 1957. I took part in Ammerschwihr's Palm Sunday procession in April 2017. Accompanied by a single priest, laity from six parishes, and a lively brass band, Christ and his donkey made their way from the Porte Haute, at the upper end of the village (Fig. 29), through sloping cobbled streets down to the church, thus mapping Jerusalem onto the Alsatian landscape.

36 Bela, "Palm," 30.

37 Search online under "Tokarnia" and "Niedziela Palmowa." For a video of the 2015 procession, see "Niedziela Palmowa—Tokarnia 2015," Józef Zięba, *YouTube*, April 1, 2015, see www.youtube.com/watch?v=_qj8neV9MQ4.

38 "Procesja z Jezuskiem palmowym w Skansenie," *Sądeczanin*, March 29, 2015, http://archiwum.sadeczanin.info/wiadomosci,5/14-00-niedziela-palmowa-w-skansenie,70764#.WA_Ft8kbiCM.

39 Kraus, *Kunst*, 2:18; Laugel, *Costumes*, 138; "La procession de l'âne des Rameaux," Thierry Gachon, *L'Alsace*, March 28, 2015, www.lalsace.fr/actualite/2015/03/28/la-procession-de-l-ane-des-rameaux.

40 "Le Palmesel d'Ammerschwihr," Thierry Gachon, *L'Alsace*, photo 3/10, March 14, 2016, www.lalsace.fr/actualite/2014/04/13/la-palmesel-d-ammerschwihr. Kladstrup, *Wine*, 192, reports that Ammerschwihr's "statues of saints," presumably including the palmesel, found shelter in the deepest wine cellar in the village, known locally as the Cellar of Hell (Cave de l'Enfer). "People still refer to it as the time the saints went to hell."

Figure 29 Palm Sunday procession, Ammerschwihr, 2017. Photograph by author.

Less than two miles away, Kaysersberg's Musée Historique houses the parish church's fifteenth-century palmesel (Fig. 30). Both the Christ figure and his donkey are remarkably well preserved: the original polychrome of Christ's robes is still bright and all his limbs are intact. Touched, Christ's feet move back and forth. Loosely attached at the ankles, behind the hem of his carved robe, they would have visibly jiggled whenever the palmesel was pulled over cobbles, partially animating the figure.[41] Three more inactive but variously restored Alsatian palmesels can be seen within fifty miles of Ammerschwihr.[42] Three other full-size palmesels, originally from Germany, are owned by museums in Strasbourg and Paris.[43]

---

41 I saw Kaysersberg's palmesel in April 2017. I am grateful to Robert Stauder, who showed me the mobility of Christ's feet. For more on Kaysersberg's palmesel, see Stückelberg, "Palmesel," 121, 124; Broekaert and Valvekens, "Palmezel," 144.

42 Broekaert and Knapen, "Inventaris," 256. A diminutive late-fifteenth-century palmesel from Sundgau is in the Musée d'Interlinden in Colmar. Further south, an eighteenth-century palmesel from Murbach can be seen in Guebwiller's Musée Théodore Deck et des Pays du Florival. Finally, an unpainted wooden palmesel is fixed, out of reach, to the wall of the bell-tower chapel in the Parish Church of Saint Martin in Spechbach-le-Haut; the viewer below can clearly see the date of 1733 carved in the donkey's underbelly. I saw all three palmesels during visits to the region in 2015 and 2017.

43 Strasbourg's Musée de l'Oeuvre Notre-Dame owns both a full-size palmesel from Nesselwang, the Christ figure of which dates to "the 1480s" while the donkey and wagon are nineteenth-century

Figure 30 Palmesel, fifteenth century. Musée Historique, Kaysersberg. Photograph by Ji-Elle. Used with permission of the museum.

Belgium boasts two active palmesels. The older of the two, belonging to the Church of Saint Gorgonius in Hoegaarden and believed to have been made in the first half of the sixteenth century, was restored between 1980 and 1981. Its platform lacks wheels, but supports a wooden frame that allows the image to be carried on the shoulders of four "disciples." Twelve "apostles" follow, each identified by an iconographic symbol and a sash bearing his apostolic name.[44] After the blessing of the palms inside the church,

---

replacements (Guillot de Suduirat, *Dévotion*, 125–30; Joubert, "Étude"; Miller, *Allgäuer*, 48), and a miniature, just eight inches high and made of tin in "the second half of the thirteenth century," from the Dominican convent of Unterlinden, in Colmar (Haedecke, *Zinn*, 47–50). In Paris, the Musée de Cluny acquired a late-fifteenth-century palmesel from Baden-Württemberg in 2005 ("Christ des Rameaux," *Musée de Cluny*, www.musee-moyenage.fr/collection/oeuvre/christ-des-rameaux.html). In 2008, the Louvre acquired a palmesel, dated to "ca. 1515–1525," previously owned by the château de La Rochelambert and originally from Memmingen (Guillot de Suduirat, *Dévotion*, 299–303; Broekaert and Valvekens, "Palmezel," 142). I saw all of these in April, 2017. The Château d'Esplas, near Rebourgil, also owns a palmesel, "datable to the end of the 15th or the beginning of the 16th century" ("Le Christ des Rameaux," *Château d'Esplas*, www.chateau-esplas.fr/visite/christ-des-rameaux.asp).

44 Broekaert and Valvekens, "Palmezel," 116–18; Valvekens, "Tentoonstellingscatalogus," 263–65; Smeyers, "Palmezel"; Crab and Van Buyten, "Palmezels," 126–27.

the procession circles the building, returning for high mass. At the appropriate moment during the reading of the gospel, the twelve "apostles" temporarily retreat in confusion to the sacristy, representing the biblical flight of the apostles after Jesus's arrest.[45] During communion, the celebrant partakes with the "apostles" and "disciples," recalling the Last Supper.[46] Local tradition claims that the palmesel has been carried in procession since the foundation of the Confraternity of the Twelve Apostles in 1631,[47] but there is no definitive evidence to this effect.

The neighbouring town of Tienen (Tirlemont) celebrated Palm Sunday "with an image of the Saviour sitting on a donkey and with apostles" as late as 1693.[48] An "enlightened" nineteenth-century antiquarian looked back on the practice with contempt:

> The Palm Sunday procession in Tirlemont was the height of the ridiculous. It began with the twelve apostles dressed like clowns (*en scaramouches*), their heads decked out with enormous black wigs, their faces stained with soot, and goatees on their chins. The traitor Judas alone wore a red wig. A statue of Christ followed, mounted on a donkey and holding in his hand a palm branch laden with figs, raisins, and oublies [traditional round biscuits], which children tried to pull off during the march. The clergy went ahead of the Holy Sacrament, and made their way to a garden which was supposed to be the Garden of Olives, where medieval (*gothiques*) hymns were sung, and where each character represented, in a comic—not to say ridiculous—fashion, something of what happened before Jesus's passion.[49]

Happily, a new palmesel, made for Tienen's Parish Church of Saint Germanus in 1997, has since been carried in a dignified fashion each Palm Sunday by four "disciples," while accompanied by "apostles," clergy, and laity dressed against the cold.[50]

---

45 Matt. 26:56.

46 Wuyts, *Hoegaarden*, 11–15; "Hoegaarden viert Palmzondag," *VTM Nieuws*, April 13, 2014, http://nieuws.vtm.be/binnenland/87727-hoegaarden-viert-palmzondag.

47 "Palmprocessie (Hoegaarden)," *LECA*, March 20, 2016, www.lecavzw.be/tradities/feesten/palmprocessie-hoegaarden. Niederer, "Palmzondag," 158–60, argues for a continuous tradition on the basis of the age of the confraternity, the presumed date of the Hoegaarden palmesel, and the existence of other palmesels in the region since at least 1213 in Liège (see chap. 14). Wuyts, *Hoegaarden*, 10–11, admits that the Palm Sunday procession was suspended "for twelve years" during the French annexation of the Low Countries after the French Revolution. Ruelens, "Procession," cites a 1928 report. The earliest photographs I have found of the Hoegaarden palmesel date to 1944 ("Christus op de palmezel," *Belgian Art Links and Tools*, http://balat.kikirpa.be/object/6496); another, published in 1946, can be seen in Peeters, *Eigen*, 347.

48 Niederer, "Palmzondag," 159, dates this to 1698; Paul Kempeneers, "Een palmezel in Tienen in 1693," February 21, 1997, www.kempeneers.org/sprokkels/sprokkel-7-044.html, describes the entry more precisely as a note added in 1698 to a 1693 accounts book.

49 Schayes, *Essai*, 158–59; see also Reinsberg-Düringsfeld, *Calendrier*, 1:212–13.

50 "Processie eindigt met apostelbroodjes," Raymond Billen, *Nieuwsblad*, March 14, 2016, www.nieuwsblad.be/cnt/blrbi_02181720; "Palmezels in Tienen en Hoegaarden," *Kerknet*, April 12, 2011,

In Antwerp (Anvers), a "statue of the Saviour sitting on a donkey used to be taken in procession on a low cart." In 1487, it was decreed that only those who had visited Jerusalem would be allowed to pull the palmesel.[51] In 1566, the image was "broken" by iconoclasts, but four years later, restored to "renewed splendour," it again took part in a revived procession. By the late eighteenth century, although qualified pilgrims still enjoyed their privileged place in the procession, the palmesel itself had been relegated to stationary display inside the cathedral.[52]

Elsewhere in northern Europe, in the late fifteenth century, Amsterdam's "big wooden donkey (*grooten houten Ezel*), on which a wooden man sat," was accompanied by twelve "apostles." Unlike its counterpart in Hoegaarden, it was pulled on wheels rather than carried. The distinguished members of the sponsoring "Illustrious Brotherhood of the Holy Land" were known colloquially as *Jerusalems-Vaarders* (Jerusalem Pilgrims). Like those who pulled Antwerp's palmesel, they had all been on pilgrimage to the Holy City.[53] Erasmus may have had either the Amsterdam or the Antwerp palmesel in mind when he wrote, in 1526, "Those who have been to Jerusalem are dubbed knights and address one another as 'brother.' On Palm Sunday they behave ridiculously, dragging an ass by a rope—themselves not very different from the wooden ass they pull."[54] Three more surviving palmesels, all originally from Germany, can be seen in museums in the Netherlands and, across the Channel, in England.[55]

Palmesels can also be found in American museums. Three are in the United States, at the New York's Cloisters Museum, the Detroit Institute of Arts, and the University of Wisconsin-Madison's Chazen Museum of Art. Those in New York and Detroit are

---

http://archief.kerknet.be/aartsbisdom/nieuws_detail.php?ID=377&nieuwsID=99040; "20ste Palmommegang in Tienen," Christian Hennuy, *HLN.BE*, March 15, 2016, www.hln.be/regio/tienen-vroeger-en-nu/20ste-palmommegang-in-tienen-c45172.

51 Diercxsens, *Antverpia*, 3:134; see also Reinsberg-Düringsfeld, *Calendrier*, 209. Schayes, *Essai*, 158, misunderstood Diercxsens to mean that a live "pilgrim who had made the voyage to Jerusalem," rather than a wooden image of Christ, rode the wooden donkey.

52 Diercxsens, *Antverpia*, 3:134; Mertens and Torfs, *Geschiedenis*, 3:418–19. There may also have been active palmesels, now lost or destroyed, in Leuven and Zoutleeuw (Smeyers, "Palmezel," 229; Broekaert and Knapen, "Inventaris," 240; also, for Leuven, Schayes, *Essai*, 158; Van Even, *Monographie*, 9). Another surviving palmesel, dated to "around 1530–1550," perhaps from Picardy in northern France, and thought to have been active "until the beginning of the twentieth century," is owned by the Musée de Louvain-la-Neuve (Trizna, "Christ"; Lefftz, "Christ").

53 Le Long, *Historische*, 489–90; see also Adelmann, "Christus," 192; "Jerusalem aan de Zeedijk," Suzette van 't Hof, *AmsterdamMuseum.nl*, March 20, 2016, http://hart.amsterdammuseum.nl/nl/page/54491/020.

54 Erasmus, *Opera*, 1.3:747; Erasmus, *Collected*, 40:1104.

55 Broekaert and Knapen, "Inventaris," 240. Enschede's Rijksmuseum Twenthe owns a fourteenth-century palmesel from southern Germany; Utrecht's Rijksmuseum Het Catherijnconvent owns a sixteenth-century palmesel from the lower Rhine; London's Victoria and Albert Museum's palmesel has been dated to "around 1470–1490" and may have been made in Ulm.

thought to be German in origin and have been dated to the fifteenth century.[56] The exact provenance of the Madison palmesel is unknown, but it is believed to have been made around 1450 somewhere in the Austrian Tyrol.[57] None of these, of course, is native to the Americas. For that we must turn to a small but important museum in Paraguay.

Unnoticed by most histories of the palmesel, the Museo Diocesano de Artes Jesuíticas, in the small Paraguayan town of Santa María de Fe, a former Jesuit community some hundred miles southeast of the capital city of Asunción, houses a remarkable collection of fifty-four wooden statues of Christ, the Virgin Mary, various saints, and (as part of the nativity scene) animals. Carved in solid cedar by indigenous Guaraní artists or by their European Jesuit teachers in the late seventeenth or early eighteenth century, these works of Baroque art belonged to the Jesuit mission church, which was built sometime around 1670 but destroyed by fire in 1889.[58] Also in the museum, but possibly from the late eighteenth century, is a processional sculpture of "Jesús en el burro" (Jesus on the donkey) (Fig. 31).[59] The head, hands, and feet of the Christ figure are carved and painted in detail, but the rest of his body, most of which is hidden beneath his robe, is more rudimentary. His legs are visibly "articulated, that is hinged" at the hip and knee joints (Fig. 32).[60] The image is still active on Palm Sunday. Set on a modern wooden litter with two long bars on either side, it is carried in procession from a small hill ("El Cerrito"), at the east end of town, to the new church, built in traditional style in 1954, at the west end (Fig. 33).[61]

The Spanish custom of carrying processional images on raised *pasos* is now the norm throughout most of Spanish America. The largest are those in Antigua Guatemala, which require as many as a hundred men (or women) at a time to carry them.[62] In Paraguay, smaller but still ornate images of Christ on a donkey, in which the Christ figure wears elaborate robes and a long black wig, are carried in procession in Asunción and in the nearby cities of Limpio and Capiata.[63] A more appealing image, at least to my taste, can be seen in the parish church of Guazacuá, a small rural community some seventy-five miles west of Santa María de Fe. There the wooden donkey's genuine saddle and stirrups are typical of the region, and the articulated Christ is able to dismount. Photographs in

---

56 For New York, see Wixom, "Medieval," 42–43; "Palmesel," *The Met*, www.metmuseum.org/collection/the-collection-online/search/471557. For Detroit, see Richardson, "Three"; Corgan, "Late."

57 Horlbeck, "Gloria."

58 McNaspy and Blanch, *Lost*, 48–59; Trento, *Reducciones*, 128–37; Hebblethwaite, *Paraguay*, 206–8, Hebblethwaite, *From*, 57–59, 63–66. Frings and Übelmesser, *Paracuaria*, 100, count "fifty-six statues."

59 For additional photographs of the Santa María image, see McNaspy and Blanch, *Lost*, 54; Frings and Übelmesser, *Paracuaria*, plate 38.

60 Margaret Hebblethwaite, personal communication, July 4, 2016; Corinna Gramatke, personal communication, February 24, 2017.

61 Hebblethwaite, *Paraguay*, 207, 210; Hebblethwaite, *From*, 36, 64.

62 Search online under "Semana Santa" and "Antigua Guatemala."

63 Search online under "Domingo de Ramos" and "Asunción," "Limpio," or "Capiata."

Figure 31 Jesús en el burro. Museo Diocesano de Artes Jesuíticas, Santa María de Fe. Photograph by Christian Ender.

my possession include one of the Guazacuá Christ seated casually on a bench, wearing what looks like a loose white cotton outfit, his feet not quite reaching the ground. The saddled donkey stands nearby. Iron hoops in its base indicate that this image, too, was once carried in procession.[64] Even so, I'd like to think that the simple images of Christ on a donkey in Santa María de Fe, Guazacuá, and elsewhere in the aptly named Misiones department of southern Paraguay were originally wheeled and only later conformed to the more onerous Spanish style.

Wheeled processional palm donkeys remain popular among the descendants of the Chiquitos Indians who settled in the Jesuit reductions of lowland Bolivia: "In all the mission villages [in the province of Chiquitos] is found a little donkey (*borriquito*) on a wheeled platform, on which is seated a processional [image of] Christ, which can be dressed for the purpose of staging the Palm Sunday procession."[65] San José de Chiquitos

---

64 Photographs by Margaret Hebblethwaite, personal communication, June 13, 2016.

65 Querejazu, "Equipamiento," 654.

Figure 32 Jesús en el burro (articulated). Museo Diocesano de Artes Jesuíticas, Santa María de Fe. Photograph by Fernando Franceschelli on behalf of TU-München-Lehrstuhl für Restaurierung, Kunsttechnologie und Konservierungswissenschaft.

is perhaps the best-known example. There, palms are blessed during both the six and nine o'clock masses, "with the goal of driving the devil from the town." At midday, pulled on a wheeled trolley, "the image of Jesus of Nazareth mounted on a donkey" is "stolen" from the church, and taken to a temporary chapel, designated "Bethany," on the far edge of the community. "In the late afternoon, carrying the blessed palms, the clergy and all the Catholic community accompany" two processional statues, "the Child of the Palms and the Mounted Nazarene on his donkey, from Bethany to the church," recalling Christ's

**Figure 33 Palm Sunday procession, Santa María de Fe.
Photograph by Margaret Hebblethwaite.**

entry into Jerusalem. On their arrival at the church, both images are received with a shower of yellow flowers (Fig. 34), the fluttering of palms, the chiming of bells, songs of acclamation as the son of David, king of Israel, and the sound of bass drums and violins." A complete processional circuit of the town follows (Fig. 2). Returning to the church, the worshippers find the doors closed, signifying "the denial of Jesus of Nazareth by the Jewish people." The head of the indigenous town council strikes the doors three times with his staff of office (*báculo*), and the procession is admitted to the playing of violins within.[66]

The tradition of wheeled wooden images of Christ on a donkey probably travelled to the Americas with German-speaking Jesuit missionaries in the late seventeenth and early eighteenth centuries. The first Jesuits had arrived in South America in 1550. By 1609, their successors had begun to establish a network of "reductions," communities of Christianized but not necessarily Europeanized Indians, which eventually spread across territory in what is now Paraguay, northeastern Argentina, southern Brazil, and lowland Bolivia. Surviving church buildings, religious sculptures, and musical scores bear testimony to the remarkable artistic development of the Jesuit reductions.[67] Between 1690 and the suppression of the Jesuits in 1767, most of the new missionaries arriving

---

66 Cambará Flores, "Semana"; Eckhart Kühne, "Semana Santa y fiesta patronal en San José de Chiquitos," in Querejazu, *Misiones*, 557–63 (558).

67 Caraman, *Lost*; McNaspy and Blanch, *Lost*; Querejazu, *Misiones*; Buelow, *History*, 405–6.

Figure 34 Palm Sunday, San José de Chiquitos, 2011.
Photograph by Limber Leonel Cambara Flores.

in the reductions were from the Austrian Empire, southern Germany, and Switzerland,[68] an influx that demonstrably shaped the Baroque musical tastes of the Jesuit reductions.[69] Surviving woodcarvings (such as those in Santa María de Fe) and other architectural features of the Jesuit churches also reflect this regional influence. So, I suspect, does the lasting popularity of processional wheeled wooden palm donkeys in the former Jesuit settlements of lowland Bolivia. In the early eighteenth century, the palmesel was still widely used in German-speaking Catholic Europe. The tradition escaped to the Americas before the reforms of the Catholic Englightenment.

---

68 Caraman, *Lost*, 98. Anton Sepp, one of the best-known Jesuit missionaries to work in the reductions, was born in Kaltern (now Caldaro) in 1655. As a boy, he would have known (and perhaps ridden) the town's palmesel, which is now in the Museo Civico in Bolzano (see chap. 18). Sepp served in Santa María de Fe between 1694 and 1696.

69 Buelow, *History*, 406; Gerardo Huseby, Irma Ruiz, and Leonardo J. Waisman, "Un Panorama de la Música en Chiquitos," in Querejazu, *Misiones*, 659–70.

Conclusion

CHRIST DISMEMBERED AND THE BOMBING OF LÜBECK

IN THE EARLY hours of Palm Sunday, March 29, 1942, the British Royal Air Force launched the most destructive bombing raid of the Second World War so far. Lübeck, a major German port on the Baltic coast and once the largest and most prosperous city in the Hanseatic League, was chosen as a target not for industrial reasons, but "because it contained many timbered buildings dating from medieval times" and was thus a suitable site "to experiment with a bombing technique using a high proportion of incendiaries."[1] The resulting firestorm destroyed the cathedral and two of the city's main churches, along with much of the medieval city centre (Fig. 35). Nearly two thousand buildings were destroyed, a thousand people killed, and more than fifteen thousand people left homeless. The timing of the raid, on the morning of Palm Sunday, was chosen to take advantage of the visibility provided by a full moon.[2]

Displayed in the fourteenth-century monastery church (Klosterkirche) of Preetz, some forty miles north of Lübeck, is the lovingly restored remnant of a radically damaged palmesel. The headless, armless, and legless torso of Christ sits astride the equally muti-lated torso of the donkey (Fig. 36). Dated to around 1300, the remnant not only shows persuasive signs of the artistry of its sculptor but is also of remarkable historical value as the northernmost surviving evidence of the palmesel tradition. The damage to the image was almost certainly the work of Protestant iconoclasts. Markus Freitag, leader of the 2009 restoration project, reported: "The violent removal (Beraubung) of the figure's most important parts, as well as the marks of hacking on the robe covering [Christ's] right thigh, suggest malicious destruction."[3] There is, of course, no historical connection between the Palm Sunday bombing of Lübeck and Preetz's butchered palmesel, but the coincidental juxtaposition of the two offers a suggestive pair of mental images with which to close this book.

Consciously or otherwise, the bombing of Lübeck was a stark rejection of Jesus's choice of a donkey over the military option of a chariot or a war-horse. Whatever stra-tegic (and even moral) justifications may (or may not) be offered in defence of the bombing of Lübeck, the scale of its violence reminds us that violations of Palm Sunday by nominally Christian leaders were not restricted to the long Middle Ages. Forty miles north, Preetz's truncated image of Christ on a donkey serves as a poignant reminder of the neglect or outright hostility suffered by so many palmesels between the Hussite Revolution and the twentieth century. The mistreatment of palmesels—whether incited

---

1 Grayling, Among, 51; see also Harris, Bomber, 105.

2 Meyer, "Ersten," 723–28; Diefendorf, Wake, 100.

3 Freitag, "Klosterkirch"; "Abgeschlossene Restaurierungsarbeiten," Gesellschaft der Freunde des Klosters Preetz, August 26, 2015, http://klosterfreunde-kloster-preetz.de/restaurierungen.html; Haastrup, "Medieval," 137–38.

Figure 35 Bombing of Lübeck, Palm Sunday, 1942. German Federal Archives.

by Zwingli's sermons, the decrees of "enlightened" archbishops, or mere changes in taste—is consistent with a widespread rejection, especially among the elite and powerful, of the implications of Christ's choice to ride a donkey. Zwingli, it will be remembered, died in battle, and archbishops still rode white horses in the eighteenth century. Together, Lübeck and Preetz serve as emblems of the violence with which Christ's Palm Sunday refusal of violence has too often been met, not only by the Romans and disappointed Jews who collaborated in his crucifixion, but also—and for much longer and with greater loss of life—by those who, for nearly two millennia, have invoked the name of Christ as a justification for triumphal pomp, sectarian violence, and full-scale war.

My book is a work of historical scholarship, but it is also a quiet protest against any repudiation, in the name of Christianity, of the model of Christ on a donkey. I have affirmed the verdict of biblical scholars that the gospel narratives present Christ's entry into Jerusalem as a parody of triumphal Roman pomp and a public refusal of armed Jewish rebellion. Early Palm Sunday processions were fairly simple commemorative local pilgrimages. Ostentatious embrace of triumphalism entered Palm Sunday observance only after Charlemagne had appropriated the language and iconography of the feast for his victorious entry into Rome in 774. Elite Palm Sunday processions followed suit by appropriating the language and iconography of triumphal entries. James Nayler's parodic royal progress from Exeter to Bristol in 1656 may have been closer in spirit to Christ's entry into Jerusalem than any more dignified triumphal parade had ever been.

The conspicuous absence of live donkeys from Palm Sunday processions before the fifteenth century is another measure of the discomfort among those who wielded even small and local power in church or state with the practical implications of Christ's choice

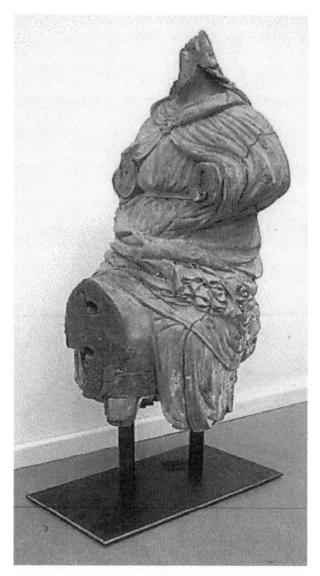

Figure 36 Palmesel torso, Monastery Church, Preetz. Photograph © Dipl.-Restauratoren VDR Dorothée Simmert & Markus Freitag, Rieseby/Kiel.

of mount. Even so, some found a way to celebrate Christ's preference without riding a donkey themselves. Sometime in the second half of the tenth century in Augsburg, the first recorded palmesel made its appearance in a Palm Sunday procession. Pulled on a wheeled platform at ground level rather than carried at shoulder height, palmesels embodied the intimacy and gentleness of the biblical Christ on a donkey. Palm Sunday in Biberach shortly before the Reformation was known as "the day of the humble king." Children could ride with Jesus on the wooden donkey.

Despite attacks on palmesels by Protestant iconoclasts and Catholic archbishops, and despite a tendency in Baroque Spain and Spanish America to elevate images of Christ on a donkey to complex and gilded splendour, the palmesel has survived. It is now enjoying something of a revival, prized by museums and displayed in churches and often lovingly restored. In a growing number of locations, as far apart as Poland and Bolivia, palmesels are active in Palm Sunday processions. Live donkeys are also belatedly taking part in Palm Sunday processions as far apart as the Czech Republic and Nicaragua. Christ on a donkey is again raising a quiet protest against those those who invoke false gods to justify the trappings of power or the glories of war.

BIBLIOGRAPHY

Abū Yūsuf Ya'qub. *Le livre de l'impôt foncier (Kitâb el-kharâdj)*. Translated by E. Fagnan. Paris: Paul Geuthner, 1921.

Acta sanctorum. 68 vols. Paris: 1863–1870.

Adamson, J. S. A. "Oliver Cromwell and the Long Parliament." In *Oliver Cromwell and the English Revolution*, edited by John Morrill, 49–92. London: Longman, 1990.

Adelmann, Josef Anselm von. "Christus auf dem Palmesel." *Zeitschrift für Volkskunde* 63 (1967): 182–200.

Adrian, Karl. *Salzburger Volksspiele, Aufzüge und Tänze*. Salzburg: Huber, 1908.

Akty, sobrannye v bibliotekakh i arkhivakh Rossiiskoi Imperii Arkheograficheskoiu ekspediitsieiu. 4 vols. St. Petersburg: 1836.

Albert of Aachen. *Historia Ierosolimitana: History of the Journey to Jerusalem*. Edited and translated by Susan B. Edington. Oxford: Clarendon, 2007.

Albright, W. F., and C. S. Mann. *Matthew*. AB 26. Garden City: Doubleday, 1971.

Alcuin of York. *Carmina*. Edited by Ernst Dümmler. MGH,PLMA 1:160–351. Berlin: 1881.

——. *Epistolae*. Edited by Ernst Dümmler. MGH,E 4:1–493. Munich: Monumenta Germaniae Historica, 1994.

Aldhelm. *Prosa de Virginitate cum glose latina atque anglosaxonica*. 2 vols. CCSL 124–124A. Edited by Scott Gwara. Turnhout: Brepols, 2001.

——. *The Prose Works*. Translated by Michael Lapidge and Michael Herren. Ipswich: Brewer, 1979.

Althoff, Gerd. *Otto III*. Translated by Phyllis G. Jestice. University Park: Pennsylvania State University Press, 2003.

Amalarius of Metz. *Liber Officialis*. Vol. 2 of *Amalarii episcopi opera liturgica omnia*. Edited by J. M. Hanssens. Vatican City: Biblioteca Apostolica Vaticana, 1948.

Ambrose of Milan. *Hexameron, Paradise, and Cain and Abel*. Translated by John J. Savage. FC 42. New York: Fathers of the Church, 1961.

Andrieu, Michel. *Les Ordines romani du haut moyen âge*. 5 vols. Louvain: Spicilegium Sacrum Lovaniense, 1931–1961.

——. *Le Pontifical romain au moyen-âge*. 4 vols. Vatican City: Biblioteca Apostolica Vaticana, 1938–1941.

Angele, Albert. *Altbiberach um die Jahre der Reformation*. Biberach: Biberacher Verlagsdruckerei, 1962.

Angilbert. *Institutio sancti Angilberti abbatis de diversitate officiorum (800–811)*. Edited by D. K. Hallinger, D. M. Wegener, and D. H. Frank. CCM 1:283–303. Siegburg: Schmitt, 1963.

Anglo, Sydney. *Spectacle, Pageantry, and Early Tudor Policy*. Oxford: Clarendon, 1969.

Angold, Michael. *The Fourth Crusade: Event and Context*. Harlow: Pearson, 2003.

"Annales sancti Amandi, Tiliani, Laubacenses et Petaviani." Edited by Georg Heinrich Pertz. MGH,SS 1:3–18. Hannover: 1826.

Another Victory in Lancashire Obtained against the Scots ... together, with the manner of my Lord General Cromwels comming up, and noble Reception by the City of London. London: 1651.

Arce, Agustín. *Miscelánea de Tierra Santa.* 4 vols. Jerusalem: Franciscan Printing Press, 1974.

Arens, Franz. *Der Liber ordinarius der Essener Stiftskirche.* Paderborn: Pape, 1908.

Arlt, Wulf. *Ein Festoffizium des Mittelalters aus Beauvais in seiner liturgischen und musikalischen Bedeutung.* 2 vols. [1] Darstellungsband und [2] Editionsband. Cologne: Arno Volk Verlag, 1970.

Armstrong, Karen. *Jerusalem.* New York: Knopf, 1996.

Artís-Gener, Avel·lí, and Bienve Moya. *Festes populars a Catalunya.* Barcelona: HMB, 1980.

Astronomus. *Vita Hludowici imparatoris.* Edited by Ernst Tremp. MGH,FIGA,USSE 64. Hannover: Hahn, 1995.

Arx, Ildefons von. *Geschichten des Kantons St. Gallen.* 3 vols. 1810–1813. Reprint, Rorschach: Löpfe-Benz, 1987.

Augusti, Johann Christian Wilhelm. *Denkwürdigkeiten aus der christlichen Archäologie.* 12 vols. Leipzig: 1817–1831.

Augustine of Hippo. *Lectures or Tractates on the Gospel according to St. John.* Translated by John Gibb and James Innes. NPNF,FS 7:4–780. 1888. Reprint, Grand Rapids: Eerdmans, 1986.

Baader, J. *Beiträge zur Kunstgeschichte Nürnbergs.* 2 vols. Nördlingen: 1860–1862.

Baldi, Pasquale. *The Question of the Holy Places.* Rome: Instituto Pio IX, 1919.

Baldovin, John F. *The Urban Character of Christian Worship: The Origins, Development, and Meaning of Stational Liturgy.* OAE 228. Rome: Pontificium Institutum Orientalium Studiorum, 1987.

Banchieri, Adriano. *Conclusioni nel suono dell'organo.* 1609. Reprint, New York: Broude, 1975.

———. *Conclusions for Playing the Organ.* Translated by Lee R. Garrett. Colorado Springs: Colorado College Music Press, 1982.

Banting, H. M. J. *Two Anglo-Saxon Pontificals (the Egbert and Sidney Sussex Pontificals).* HBS 104. London: Boydell, 1989.

Barbara, Mariano. *La Settimana Santa in Sicilia.* https://pasqualions.wordpress.com.

Barber, Richard. *Bestiary, Being an English Version of the Bodleian Library, Oxford M.S. Bodley 764.* Woodbridge: Boydell, 1993.

Barelli, Lia. *The Monumental Complex of Santi Quattro Coronati in Rome.* Translated by Christopher McDowell. Rome: Viella, 2009.

Barraud Wiener, Christine, and Peter Jezler. "Liturgie, Stadttopographie und Herrschaft nach den Prozessionen des Zürcher Liber Ordinarius." In *Der Liber Ordinarius des Konrad von Mure*, edited by Heidi Leuppi, 127–56. Freiburg: Universitätsverlag Freiburg Schweiz, 1995.

Bärsch, Jürgen. "Raum und Bewegung im mittelalticher Gottesdienst: Anmerkungen zur Prozessionsliturgie in der Essener Stiftskirche nach dem Zeugnis des Liber Ordinarius vom Ende des 14. Jahrhunderts." In *Heiliger Raum: Architektur, Kunst und Liturgie in mittelalterlichen Kathedralen und Stiftskirchen*, edited by Franz Kohlschein und Peter Wünsche, 163–86. Münster: Aschendorff, 1998.

Bartlová, Milena. "Hussite Iconcoclasm." In *From Hus to Luther: Visual Culture in the Bohemian Reformation (1380–1620)*, edited by Kateřina Horničková and Michal Šroněk, 57–70. Turnhout: Brepols, 2016.

Bauer, Walter. "The 'Colt' of Palm Sunday (Der Palmesel)." Translated by F. W. Gingrich. *JBL* 72 (1953): 220–29.

Baum, Julius. *Gotische Bildwerke Schwabens*. Augsburg: Filser, 1921.

Baumstark, Anton. *Comparative Liturgy*. Revised Bernard Botte. Translated by F. L. Cross. Westminster, MD: Newman Press, 1958.

——. "La solennité des palmes dans l'ancienne et la nouvelle Rome." *Irénikon* 13 (1936): 3–24.

Baxandall, Michael. *The Limewood Sculptors of Renaissance Germany, 1475–1525*. New Haven: Yale University Press, 1980.

Beadle, Richard. "The York Cycle." *CCMET*, 85–108.

Beam, Sara. *Laughing Matters: Farce and the Making of Absolutism in France*. Ithaca: Cornell University Press, 2007.

Beard, Mary. *The Roman Triumph*. Cambridge, MA: Belknap, 2007.

Becher, Matthias. "Neue Überlegungen zum Geburtsdatum Karls des Grossen." *Francia* 19 (1992): 37–60.

Beenken, Hermann. *Romanische Skulptur in Deutschland (11. und 12. Jahrhundert)*. Leipzig: Klinkhardt & Biermann, 1924.

Bela, Teresa. "Palm Sunday Processions in Poland." *The Early Drama, Art, and Music Review* 12 (1990): 25–31.

Beleth, Iohannes. *Summa de ecclesiasticis officis*. Edited by Herbert Douteil. 2 vols. CCCM 41–41A. Turnhout: Brepols, 1976.

Bergeron, David M. "Charles I's Edinburgh Pageant." *Renaissance Studies* 6 (1992): 173–84.

——. *English Civic Pageantry 1558–1642*. Rev. ed. Tempe: Arizona Center for Medieval and Renaissance Studies, 2003.

Bernard of Clairvaux. *Five Books on Consideration: Advice to a Pope*. Translated by John D. Anderson and Elizabeth T. Kennan. Kalamazoo: Cistercian Publications, 1976.

——. *Opera*. Edited by J. Leclercq, H. Rochais, and C. H. Talbot. 8 vols. Rome: Editiones Cistercienses, 1957–1977.

——. *St. Bernard's Sermons for the Seasons and Principal Festivals of the Year*. Translated by Ailbe J. Liddy. 3 vols. Westminster, MD: Carroll Press, 1950.

Bernardi, Claudio. *La drammaturgia della Settimana Santa in Italia*. Milan: Vita e Pensiero, 1991.

Bernhardt, John W. *Itinerant Kingship and Royal Monasteries in Early Medieval Germany, c. 936–1075*. Cambridge: Cambridge University Press, 1993.

Bernhart, Joseph. "Bischof Udalrich von Augsburg." In *Augusta, 955–1955*, edited by Hermann Rinn, 19–52. Munich: Rinn, 1955.

Berschin, Walter. "Realistic Writing in the Tenth Century: Gerhard of Augsburg's 'Vita S. Uodalrici.'" In *Aspects of the Language of Latin Prose*, edited by Tobias Reinhardt, Michael Lapidge, and J. N. Adams, 377–82. Oxford: Oxford University Press, 2005.

Bevington, David, ed. *Medieval Drama*. 1975. Reprint, Indianapolis: Hackett, 2012.

Bianchi, Giuseppe. *Documenta historiae forojuliensis saeculi XIII*. Vienna: 1861.

Biancolini, Giambatista. *Notizie storiche delle chiese di Verona*. 4 vols. Verona, 1749–1752.

Binder, Egon M. "Der Palmesel von Kößlarn." In *Das Rottal: Ein starkes Stück Bayern*, edited by Dieter Vogel, 82–83. Vilsbiburg: Kiebitz, 2011.

Birlinger, Anton. *Schwäbisch-Augsburgisches Wörterbuch*. Munich: 1864.

———. ed. *Volksthümliches aus Schwaben*. 2 vols. Freiburg, 1862.

Bittle, William G. *James Nayler, 1618–1660: The Quaker Indicted by Parliament*. York: William Sessions, 1986.

Blaauw, Sible de. "Contrasts in Processional Liturgy: A Typology of Outdoor Processions in Twelfth-Century Rome." In *Art, Cérémonial et Liturgie au Moyen Âge*, edited by Nicolas Bock, Peter Kurmann, Serena Romano, and Jean-Michel Spieser, 357–96. Rome: Viella, 2002.

Blázquez, Ricardo. *La Semana Santa Bilbaina*. Bilbao: La Gran Enciclopedia Vasca, 2002.

Bloechl, Olivia. "The Illicit Voice of Prophecy." In *Structures of Feeling in Seventeenth-Century Cultural Expression*, edited by Susan McClary, 147–72. Toronto: University of Toronto Press, 2013.

Blomberg, Craig L. "Matthew." In *Commentary on the New Testament Use of the Old Testament*, edited by G. K. Beale and D. A. Carson, 1–110. Grand Rapids: Baker, 2007.

Bludau, August. *Die Pilgerreise der Aetheria*. Paderborn: Schöningh, 1927.

Bluntschli, Hans Heinrich. *Memorabilia Tigurina, oder Merkwürdigkeiten der Stadt und Landschaft Zürich*. Zurich: 1742.

Blythe, James M. *The Life and Works of Tolomeo Fiadoni (Ptolemy of Lucca)*. Turnhout: Brepols, 2009.

Bobbio Missal, The: A Gallican Mass-Book (Ms. Paris. Lat 13246). Edited by E. A. Lowe, André Wilmart, and H. A. Wilson. 3 vols. HBS 53, 58, 61. London: Henry Bradshaw Society, 1917–1924.

Bock, Darrell L. *Luke*. Downers Grove: InterVarsity, 1994.

Böhmer, J. F., ed. *Regesta Imperii*. 14 vols. Hildesheim: Olms, 1966–1972.

Bonaventure. *The Life of St. Francis*. Translated by Ewert Cousins. New York: HarperOne, 2005.

Bonifacius Stephanis [Boniface of Ragusa]. *Liber de perenni cultu Terrae Sanctae et de fructuosa eius peregrinatione*. Venice: 1875.

Boosen, Monika. "Die mittelalterlichen Palmeselgruppen aus Schwäbisch Gmünd." In Wenger, 13–26.

Bordeaux Pilgrim. *Itinerarium Burdigalense*. Edited by P. Geyer and O. Cuntz. In *Itineraria et Alia Geographica*, edited by E. Franceschini, R. Weber, and P. Geyer, 1:1–26. 2 vols. CCSL 175–76. Turnhout: Brepols, 1965.

———. *Itinerary from Bordeaux to Jerusalem*. Translated by Aubrey Stewart. LPPTS 1. 1887. Reprint, New York: AMS, 1971.

Borders, James, and Lance W. Brunner, eds. *Early medieval chants from Nonantola*. 4 vols. Madison: A-R Editions, 1996–1999.

Boretius, Alfred, and Victor Krause, eds. *Capitularia Regum Francorum*. 2 vols. MGH,L 2. Hanover: 1883–1897.

Borg, Alan. "Observations on the Historiated Lintel of the Holy Sepulchre, Jerusalem." *Journal of the Warburg and Courtauld Institutes* 32 (1969): 25–40.

Borg, Marcus J. *Jesus: A New Vision*. San Francisco: Harper & Row, 1987.

Borg, Marcus J., and John Dominic Crossan. *The Last Week: The Day-by-Day Account of Jesus's Final Week in Jerusalem.* San Francisco: HarperSanFrancisco, 2006.

Bornscheuer, Lothar. *Miseriae Regum.* Berlin: de Gruyter, 1968.

Bosworth, Clifford Edmund. *An Intrepid Scot: William Lithgow of Lanark's Travels in the Ottoman Lands, North Africa and Central Europe, 1609–21.* Aldershot: Ashgate, 2006.

Bough, Jill. *Donkey.* London: Reaktion, 2011.

Brace, Laura. *The Idea of Property in Seventeenth-Century England.* Manchester: Manchester University Press, 1998.

Brailsford, Mabel Richmond. *A Quaker from Cromwell's Army.* New York: Macmillan, 1927.

Broekaert, Marijke, and Luc Knapen. "Inventaris van bewaarde en verdwenen palmezels in Europa." In Knapen, 239–59.

Broekaert, Marijke, and Patrick Valvekens. "De palmezel: oorsprong, iconografie en geografische verspreidung." In Knapen, 113–58.

Brown, Peter. *The Cult of the Saints.* Chicago: University of Chicago Press, 1981.

Brown, Raymond E. *An Introduction to the New Testament.* New York: Doubleday, 1997.

Brown, T. S. *Gentlemen and Officers: Imperial Administration and Aristocratic Power in Byzantine Italy A.D. 554–800.* London: British School at Rome, 1984.

Budge, E. A. Wallis. *The Monks of Ḳûblâi Khân, Emperor of China.* London: Religious Tract Society, 1928.

Buelow, George J. *A History of Baroque Music.* Bloomington: Indiana University Press, 2004.

Bullarium Franciscanum Romanorum Pontificum. 7 vols. Edited by Giovanni Giacinto Sbaraglia and Konrad Eubel. Rome: 1759–1904.

Bullinger, Heinrich. *Diarium (Annales vitae) der Jahre 1505–1574.* Edited by Emil Egli. Basel: Basler Buch- und Antiquariats-Handlung, 1904.

——. *Reformationsgeschichte.* Edited by J. J. Hottinger and H. H. Vögeli. 3 vols. 1838–1840. Reprint, Zurich: Theologische Buchhandlung, 1985.

Bultmann, Rudolf. *The History of the Synoptic Tradition.* 1921. Translated by John Marsh. Oxford: Blackwell, 1963.

Burchard, Johann. *The Diary of John Burchard.* Vol. 1. Translated by Arnold Harris Mathew. London: Griffiths, 1910.

——. *Liber Notarum.* Edited by Enrico Celani. RIS, 2nd series 32.1. Città di Castello: S. Lapi, 1906–1942.

Burg, Christian von. "'Das bildt vnsers Herren ab dem esel geschlagen': Der Palmesel in den Riten der Zerstörung." In *Macht und Ohnmacht der Bilder: Reformatorischer Bildersturm im Kontext der europäischen Geschichte*, edited by Peter Blickle, 117–41. Munich: Oldenbourg, 2002.

Burson, Jeffrey D. "Introduction: Catholicism and Enlightenment, Past, Present, and Future." In *Enlightenment and Catholicism in Europe*, edited by Jeffrey D. Burson and Ulrich L. Lehner, 1–37. Notre Dame: University of Notre Dame Press, 2014.

Burton, Thomas. *Diary of Thomas Burton, Esq., Member in the Parliaments of Oliver and Richard Cromwell, from 1656 to 1659.* Edited by John Towill Rutt. 4 vols. London: 1828.

Busch, Moritz. "Pritschenschläge deutschen Volkshumors." *Die Gartenlaube*. 1876. 84–86, 136–39.

Bushkovitch, Paul A. "The Epiphany Ceremony of the Russian Court in the Sixteenth and Seventeenth Centuries." *Russian Review* 49 (1990): 1–17.

——. *Peter the Great: The Struggle for Power, 1671–1725*. Cambridge: Cambridge University Press, 2001.

Bussow, Conrad. *Chronicon Moscovitum*. In *Rereum Rossicarum scriptores exteri*, 1:1–136. 2 vols. St. Petersburg: 1851–1868.

——. *The Disturbed State of the Russian Realm*. Edited and translated by G. Edward Orchard. Montreal: McGill-Queen's University Press, 1994.

Buttitta, Antonino, and Melo Minnella. *Pasqua in Sicilia*. Palermo: Promolibri, 2003.

Butz, Hanns. "Dein König kommt: Ein uralter Palmsonntagsbrauch in Kößlarn wurde neu belebt." *Die lebendige Zelle* 39 (1996): 52–54.

——. "Palmsonntag." In *Kunstreich—Wehrhaft—Gnadenvoll: Wallfahrtsgeshichte und Sakralkunst in der Kirchenburg Kösslarn*, edited by Ludger Drost, 144–46. Salzweg: Landkreis Passau Kulturreferat, 2009.

——. "Prächtige Prozession trotz kühlem Wetter." *Kösslarner Marktblatt* 2 (July 2015): 31.

Bynum, Caroline Walker. *Christian Materiality*. New York: Zone, 2011.

Cabaniss, Allen, trans. *Son of Charlemagne: A Contemporary Life of Louis the Pious*. Syracuse: Syracuse University Press, 1961.

Cabrol, Fernand. *Les églises de Jérusalem: La discipline et la liturgie au IVe siècle*. Paris: 1895.

Cadoux, Cecil John. *The Historic Mission of Jesus*. New York: Harper, 1943.

Calendar of State Papers and Manuscripts, Relating to English Affairs, Existing in the Archives and Collections of Venice, and in Other Libraries of Northern Italy. 38 vols. in 40. 1890–1947. Reprint, Nendeln: Kraus, 1970.

Calvin, John. *A Harmony of the Gospels*. Translated by A. W. Morrison and T. H. L. Parker. 3 vols. Grand Rapids: Eerdmans, 1972.

Cambara Flores, Limber Leonel. "Semana Santa en San José de Chiquitos." *Crónicas Chiquitanas*, April 20, 2011. http://totito64.blogspot.com/2011/04/semana-santa-en-san-jose-de-chiquitos.html. (Blog removed 2018.)

The Cambridge Companion to Medieval English Theatre. Edited by Richard Beadle. Cambridge: Cambridge University Press, 1994.

Cameron, Averil. "The Construction of Court Ritual: The Byzantine 'Book of Ceremonies.'" In *Rituals of Royalty: Power and Ceremonial in Traditional Societies*, edited by David Cannadine and Simon Price, 106–36. Cambridge: Cambridge University Press, 1987.

Canesí Acevedo, Manuel. *Historia de Valladolid: 1750*. Edited by Celso Almuiña. 3 vols. Valladolid: Pinciano, 1996.

Capp, B. S. *The Fifth Monarchy Men*. London: Faber and Faber, 1972.

Caraman, Philip. *The Lost Paradise: The Jesuit Republic in South America*. New York: Seabury, 1976.

Carli, Enzo. *La scultura lignea italiana del XII al XVI secolo*. Milan: Electa, 1960.

Carrington, Samuel. *The History of the Life and Death of His Most Serene Highness, Oliver, Late Lord-Protector.* London: 1659.

Carroll, Kenneth L. "Singing in the Spirit in Early Quakerism." *Quaker History* 73.1 (1984): 1–13.

Casamassa, Antonio. "L'autore di un prettoso discorso di Martino V." *Miscellanea Pio Paschini*, 2:109–25. 2 vols. Rome: Facultas Theologica Pontificii Athenaei Lateranensis, 1948–1949.

Caspar, Eric, ed. *Fragmenta registri Stephani V. papae.* MGH,E 7:334–53. Berlin: Weidmann, 1928.

———. ed. *Registrum Iohannis VIII. papae.* MGH,E 7:1–312. Berlin: Weidmann, 1928.

Cattin, Giulio, and Anna Vildera. *Il "Liber Ordinarius" della chiesa padovana.* 2 vols. Padua: Instituto per la Storia Ecclesiastica Padovana, 2002.

Chabot, J.-B., ed. and trans. *Chronique de Michel le Syrien, Patriarch Jacobite d'Antioche (1166–1199).* 4 vols. Brussels: Culture et Civilisation, 1963.

Chambers, E. K. *The Mediaeval Stage.* 2 vols. London: Oxford University Press, 1903.

Champagne, Marie Thérèse, and Ra'anan S. Boustan. "Walking in the Shadows of the Past: The Jewish Experience in Rome in the Twelfth Century." *Medieval Encounters* 17 (2011): 464–94.

Chance, J. Bradley. *Jerusalem, the Temple, and the New Age in Luke-Acts.* Macon: Mercer University Press, 1988.

Charles, R. H. *A Critical and Exegetical Commentary on The Revelation of St. John.* 2 vols. Edinburgh: T & T Clark, 1920.

Chiesa, Paolo. "Ladri di relique a Costantinopolo durante la quarta crociata: La traslazione a Venezia del corpo di Simeone profeta." *Studi Medievali* 36 (1995): 431–59.

Christ, Martin. "Negotiation and Power: The Failure of the Reformation in Schwäbish Gmünd c.1500–80." *Reinvention: A Journal of Undergraduate Research* 5.1 (2012). www.warwick.ac.uk/reinventionjournal/issues/volume5issue1/christ.

Christensen, Carl C. *Art and the Reformation in Germany.* Athens, OH: Ohio University Press, 1979.

———. "Iconoclasm and the Preservation of Ecclesiastical Art in Reformation Nürnberg." *Archiv für Reformationsgeschichte* 61 (1970): 205–21.

Christl, Karl. *300 Jahre barocke Pfarrkirche in Kühbach.* Kühbach: Pfarrgemeinde, 1989.

Chrysostom, John. *Homilies on the Gospel of St. John.* Translated by Philip Schaff. NPNF,FS 14:1–334. 1889. Reprint, Grand Rapids: Eerdmans, 1989.

Clareno, Angelo. *A Chronicle or History of the Seven Tribulations of the Order of Brothers Minor.* Translated by David Burr and E. Randolph Daniel. St. Bonaventure: Franciscan Institute Publications, 2005.

Clark, Gillian. *Monica: An Ordinary Saint.* New York: Oxford University Press, 2015.

Clarke, William. *The Clarke Papers: Selections from the Papers of William Clarke.* Edited by C. H. Firth. 4 vols. Camden Second Series 49, 54, 61–62. 1891–1901. Reprint, London: Johnson Reprint, 1965.

Clément, Félix. "Drame liturgique: l'âne au moyen age." *Annales Archéologiques* 15 (1855): 373–86; 16 (1856): 26–38.

Coit, Charles Wheeler. *The Life of Charles the First*. Boston: Houghton Mifflin, 1926.

Columella, Lucius Junius Moderatus. *On Agriculture*. 3 vols. Translated by Harrison Boyd Ash, E. S. Forster, and Edward H. Heffner. LCL. Cambridge, MA: Harvard University Press, 1941–1955.

Constantine VII Porphyrogennetos. *The Book of Ceremonies*. Translated by Ann Moffatt and Maxeme Tall. 2 vols. Canberra: Australian Association for Byzantine Studies, 2012.

——. *De ceremoniis aulae Byzantinae. Libri duo*. Edited by Johann Jacob Reiske. 2 vols. CSCO 16–17. Bonn: 1829–1830.

——. *Le livre des cérémonies*. Edited by Albert Vogt. 2 vols., each in 2 parts. 1935–1940. Reprint, Paris: Belles Lettres, 1967.

Conybeare, F. C. "Antiochus Strategos' Account of the Sack of Jerusalem in A. D. 614." *English Historical Review* 25 (1910): 502–17.

——. ed. *Rituale Armenorum*. Oxford: Clarendon, 1905.

Cooper, James. *Four Scottish Coronations*. Aberdeen: Aberdeen and Glasgow Ecclesiological Societies, 1902.

Copeland, William John. *Hymns for the Week, and Hymns for the Seasons*. London: 1848.

Corgan, Catherine. "A Late Gothic Palmesel." *Bulletin of the Detroit Institute of Arts* 37 (1957–1958): 66–67.

Coulet, Noël. "De l'intégration à l'exclusion: La place des juifs dans les cérémonies d'entrée solonnelle au Moyen Age." *Annales. Histoire, Sciences Sociales* 34 (1979): 672–83.

Covington, Susan. "'Law's Bloody Inflictions': Judicial Wounding and Resistance in Seventeenth-Century England." In *Structures of Feeling in Seventeenth-Century Cultural Expression*, edited by Susan McClary, 272–95. Toronto: University of Toronto Press, 2013.

Coy, Jason P. *Strangers and Misfits: Banishment, Social Control, and Authority in Early Modern Germany*. Leiden: Brill, 2008.

Crab, J., and Leo Van Buyten. "De Palmezels." In *350 Jaar Palmzondagtraditie te Hoegaarden*, edited by Leo Van Buyten, 126–31. Hoegaarden: 1981.

Cracraft, James. *The Church Reform of Peter the Great*. Stanford: Stanford University Press, 1971.

Craddock, Fred B. *Luke*. Louisville: John Knox Press, 1990.

Cramer, Friedrich. *Denkwürdigkeiten der Gräfin Maria Aurora Königsmark und der Königsmarkschen Familie*. 2 vols. Leipzig, 1836.

Cranfield, C. E. B. *The Gospel According to St Mark*. Cambridge: Cambridge University Press, 1959.

Cromwell, Oliver. *The Writings and Speeches of Oliver Cromwell*. Edited by Wilbur Cortez Abbott. 4 vols. Cambridge, MA: Harvard University Press, 1937–1947.

Crossan, John Dominic. *Jesus: A Revolutionary Biography*. San Francisco: HarperSanFrancisco, 1994.

Cruciano, Fabrizio. *Teatro nel Rinascimento, Roma 1450–1550*. Rome: Bulzoni, 1983.

Crummey, Robert O. "Court Spectacles in Seventeenth-Century Russia: Illusion and Reality." In *Essays in Honor of A. A. Zimin*, edited by Daniel Clarke Waugh, 130–58. Columbus: Slavica, 1983.

Crusius, Martin. *Schwäbische Chronick*. 2 vols. Frankfurt: 1733.

Cyril of Jerusalem. *The Works of Saint Cyril of Jerusalem*. Translated by Leo P. McCauley and Anthony A. Stephenson. 2 vols. FC 61, 64. Washington, DC: Catholic University of America Press, 1969–1970.

Dahood, Mitchell. *Psalms*. AB 16–17A. 3 vols. Garden City: Doubleday, 1965–1970.

Daly-Denton, Margaret. "The Psalms in John's Gospel." In *The Psalms in the New Testament*, edited by Steve Moyise and Maarten J. J. Menken, 119–37. London: T & T Clark, 2004.

Damrosch, Leo. *The Sorrows of the Quaker Jesus*. Cambridge, MA: Harvard University Press, 1996.

Davis, Raymond, trans. *The Book of Pontiffs (Liber Pontificalis)*. TTH 6. Rev. ed. Liverpool: Liverpool University Press, 2000.

———. *The Lives of the Eighth-Century Popes (Liber Pontificalis)*. TTH 13. Liverpool: Liverpool University Press, 1992.

Deacon, John. *The Grand Imposter Examined*. London: 1657.

Debler, Werner H. A., and Klaus Jürgen Herrmann, eds. *Die Chronik des Dominikus Debler 1756–1836*. Schwäbisch Gmünd: Einhorn, 2006.

Decker, Bernhard. *Die Bildwerke des Mittelalters und der Frührenaissance 1200–1565*. Sigmaringen: Thorbecke, 1994.

Dehaisnes, [Chrétien]. *Documents et extraits divers concernant l'histoire de l'art dans la Flandre, l'Artois et le Hainaut avant le XVe siècle*. 2 vols. Lille: 1886.

Delepierre, Octave. *Chronique de L'Abbaye de Saint André*. Bruges: 1839.

Delfín Val, José, and Francisco Cantalapiedra. *Semana Santa en Valladolid*. Valladolid: Lex Nova, 1974.

Derrett, J. Duncan M. "Law in the New Testament: The Palm Sunday Colt." *Novum Testamentum* 13 (1971): 241–58.

[De Santi, Angelo]. "La domenica delle palme nella storia liturgica." *La Civiltà Cattolica* 57 (1906): 3–18, 159–77.

Devos, Paul. "La date du Voyage d'Égérie." *Analecta Bollandiana* 85 (1967): 165–94.

Diefendorf, Jeffry M. *In the Wake of War: The Reconstruction of German Cities after World War II*. New York: Oxford University Press, 1993.

Diercxsens, Jean Charles. *Antverpia Christo nascens et crescens*. 7 vols. Antwerp: 1773.

Dixon, C. Scott. *The Reformation in Germany*. Oxford: Blackwell, 2002.

Dixon, Richard Watson. *History of the Church of England from the Abolition of the Roman Jurisdiction*. 6 vols. London: 1878–1892.

Dmitrievskii, Aleksei. *Drevneishie patriarchie tipikony sviatogrobskii Ierusalamskij i Velikoi Konstantinopol'skoi Tserkvi*. Kiev: Gorbunov, 1907.

———. "Khozdenie patriarka Konstantinopol'skogo na zhrebiati v nedeliu vaii v IX I X vekakh." In *Sbornik statei v chest' akademika Alekselia Ivanovicha Sobolevskogo*, edited by V. N. Perettsa, 69–76. Leningrad: Ixdatel'stvo Akademii nauk SSSR, 1928.

———. ed. *Opisanie liturgitseskich rukopisej*. 3 vols. 1895–1917. Reprint, Hildesheim: Olms, 1965.

Dodd, C. H. "The Fall of Jerusalem and the 'Abomination of Desolation.'" *Journal of Roman Studies* 37 (1947): 47–54.

Dörner, Gerald. *Kirche, Klerus und kirchliches Leben in Zürich von der Brunschen Revolution (1336) bis zur Reformation (1523)*. Würzburg: Königshausen und Neumann, 1996.

Drijvers, Jan Willem. "Heraclius and the *Restitutio Crucis*." In *The Reign of Heraclius (610–641)*, edited by Gerrit J. Reinink and Bernard H. Stolte, 175–90. Leuven: Peeters, 2002.

[?Drummond, William]. *The Entertainment of the High and Mighty Monarch Charles King of Great Britaine, France, and Ireland*. Edinburgh: 1633.

Dubrovskii, Nikolai. "Patriarshie vykhody." *Chteniya v Imperatorskom' Obshchestvye istoriy i drevnostey rossiyskikh* 69 (1869), fasc. 2.5.

Duff, Paul Brooks. "The March of the Divine Warrior and the Advent of the Greco-Roman King: Mark's Account of Jesus' Entry into Jerusalem." *JBL* 111 (1992): 55–71.

Duffy, Eamon. *The Stripping of the Altars*. New Haven: Yale University Press, 1992.

Dulaure, J. A. *Histoire physique, civile et morale des environs de Paris*. 8 vols. Paris: Guillaume, 1821–1825.

Duncan-Jones, Richard. *The Economy of the Roman Empire*. 2nd ed. Cambridge: Cambridge University Press, 1982.

Dunning, Chester S. L. *Russia's First Civil War*. University Park: Pennsylvania State University Press, 2001.

Dünninger, Josef, and Horst Schopf, eds. *Bräuche und Feste in fränkischen Jahreslauf*. Kulmbach: Freunde der Plassenburg, 1971.

Durand, Guillaume. *Rationale divinorum officiorum*. Edited by A. Davril and T. M. Thibodeau. 3 vols. CCCM 140–140B. Turnholt: Brepols, 1995–2000.

Dutton, Paul Edward. "Eriugena, the Royal Poet." In *Jean Scot Écrivain*, edited by G.-H. Allard, 51–80. Montreal: Bellarmin, 1986.

Dvortsovye razriady. 4 vols. St. Petersburg: 1850–1855.

Dykmans, Marc. *Le Cérémonial papal de la fin du moyen âge à la Renaissance*. 4 vols. Brussels: Institut Historique Belge de Rome, 1977–1985.

———. *L'Oeuvre de Patrizi Piccolomini ou Le Cérémonial papal de la première Renaissance*. 2 vols. Vatican City: Biblioteca Apostolica Vaticana, 1980–1982.

Easton, Burton Scott. *The Gospel According to St. Luke*. New York: Scribner, 1926.

Edlibach, Gerold. *Gerold Edlibach's Chronik*. Edited by Johann Martin Usteri. Zurich: 1847.

Egeria. *Diary of a Pilgrimage*. Translated by George E. Gingras. ACW 38. New York: Newman Press, 1970.

———. *Egeria's Travels*. Translated by John Wilkinson. London: S.P.C.K., 1971.

———. *Égérie: Journal de voyage (Itinéraire)*. Translated by Pierre Maraval. SC 296. Paris: Éditions du Cerf, 1982.

———. *Éthérie: Journal de voyage*. Translated by Héléne Pétré. SC 21. Paris: Éditions du Cerf, 1948.

———. *Itinerarium Egeriae*. Edited by E. Franceschini and R. Weber. In *Itineraria et alia geographica*, edited by E. Franceschini, R. Weber, and P. Geyer, 1:27–103. 2 vols. CCSL 175–76. Turnhout: Brepols, 1965.

Egli, Emil. *Actensammlung zur Geschichte der Zürcher Reformation in den Jahren 1519–1533*. Zurich: 1879.

———. "Zürich am Vorabend der Reformation." *Zürcher Taschenbuch* NF19 (1896): 151–75.

Eire, Carlos M. N. *War Against the Idols*. Cambridge: Cambridge University Press, 1986.

Eisenstein, Sergei. *Ivan the Terrible*. Translated by A. E. Ellis. London: Faber and Faber, 1985.

Ekonomou, Andrew J. *Byzantine Rome and the Greek Popes: Eastern Influences on Rome and the Papacy from Gregory the Great to Zacharias, A.D. 590-752*. Lanham: Lexington, 2007.

Elliott, E. B. *Horae Apocalypticae*. 4 vols. 3rd ed. London: 1847.

Elze, Reinhard, ed. *Die Ordines für die Weihe und Krönung des Kaisers und der Kaiserin*. MGH,FIGA,USSE 9. Hannover: Hahn, 1960.

Endriss, Julius. *Das Ulmer Reformationsjahr 1531*. Ulm: Höhn, 1931.

Erasmus. *Collected Works*, edited by R. J. Schoek and B. M. Corrigan. 86 vols. Toronto: University of Toronto Press, 1974–.

———. "Iulius Exclusus." Edited by S. Seidel Menchi. In *Opera Omnia* 1.8: 1–297.

———. "Julius Excluded from Heaven." Translated by Michael J. Heath. In *Collected Works*, 27:155–97.

———. *Opera Omnia*. Edited by J. H. Waszink. 9 vols. Amsterdam: North-Holland Publishing, 1969–.

———. *Opus Epistolarum Des. Erasmi Roterodami*. Edited by P. S. Allen, H. M. Allen, and H. W. Garrod. 12 vols. Oxford: Clarendon, 1906–1958.

Ermold le Noir [Ermoldus Nigellus]. *Poème sur Louis le Pieux et Épitres au roi Pépin*. Edited by Edmond Farel. Paris: Champion, 1932.

Ernst, Viktor. "Der Tod der Ketzer." *Blätter für württembergische Kirchengeschichte* 1 (1897): 90–91.

Escher, Konrad. "Rechnungen und Akten zur Baugeschichte und Ausstattung des Grossmünsters in Zürich. I, Bis 1525." *Anzeiger für schweizerisches Altertumskunde* NF 29 (1927): 176–91, 243–57; 30 (1928): 56–64, 114–23, 181–91, 248–54; 31 (1929): 69–76, 140–44, 227–38, 292–306; 32 (1927–1930): 57–63, 133–42.

Essich, Christian Friedrich. *Geschichte der Reformation zu Biberach, vom Jahr 1517 bis zum Jahr 1650*. Ulm: 1817.

Esterl, Franz. *Chronik des adeligen Benediktiner-Frauen-Stiftes Nonnberg in Salzburg*. Salzburg: 1841.

Étaix, Raymond. "Le recueil de sermons composé par Raban Maur pour Haistulfe de Mayence." *Revue des Études Augustiniennes* 32 (1986): 124–37.

Eusebius. *The Ecclesiastical History*. Translated by Kirsopp Lake, J. E. L. Oulton, and H. J. Lawlor. 2 vols. LCL. Cambridge, MA: Harvard University Press, 1926–1932.

———. *Life of Constantine*. Translated by Averil Cameron and Stuart G. Hall. Oxford: Clarendon, 1999.

Evans, C. F. *Saint Luke*. TPI New Testament Commentaries. Philadelphia: Trinity, 1990.

Evelyn, John. *The Diary of John Evelyn*. Edited by E. S. de Beer. 6 vols. Oxford: Clarendon, 1955.

Fabri, Felix. *Evagatorium in Terrae Sanctae, Arabiae et Egypti peregrinationem*. Edited by C. D. Hassler. 3 vols. Stuttgart: 1843–1849.

———. *The Wanderings of Felix Fabri*. Translated by Aubrey Stewart. 2 vols. LPPTS 7–10. 1893. Reprint, New York: AMS, 1971.

The Faithfull Narrative of the late Testimony and Demand made to Oliver Cromwel, and his Powers, on the Behalf of the Lords Prisoners. London: 1654 [=1655].

Falk, Birgitta, ed. *Gold vor Schwarz: der Essener Domschatz auf Zollverein.* Essen: Klartext, 2008.

Farmer, Ralph. *Sathan Inthron'd in his Chair of Pestilence.* London: 1657.

Farmer, W. R. "The Palm Branches in John 12, 13." *Journal of Theological Studies* n.s. 3 (1952): 62–66.

Farner, Oskar. *Huldrych Zwingli.* 4 vols. Zurich: Zwingli-Verlag, 1943–1960.

Federer, Fritz. "Der Palmesel und die Palmprozession in Baden." *Badische Heimat* 21 (1934): 75–91.

Fehse, Monika. "Die Stadt Essen von den Anfängen bis 1803." In *Essen: Geschichte einer Stadt*, edited by Ulrich Borsdorf, 169–233. Bottrop: Pomp, 2002.

Férotin, Marius, ed. *Le liber ordinum en usage dans l'église wisigothique et mozarabe d'Espagne du cinquième au onzième siècle.* 1904. Rome: Edizioni Liturgiche, 1996.

——. "Le véritable auteur de la "Peregriniato Silviae: La vierge espagnole Éthéria." *Revue des questions historiques* 74 (1903): 369–97.

Ferraiolo, Melchione. *Una cronaca napoletana figurata del Quattrocento.* Edited by Riccardo Filangieri. Naples: L'Arte Tipografica, 1956.

Fiey, J. M. *Mossoul chrétienne.* Beirut: Imprimerie Catholique, 1959.

Fisher, Alexander J. *Music and Religious Identity in Counter-Reformation Augsburg, 1580–1630.* Aldershot: Ashgate, 2004.

Fletcher, Giles. *Of the Rus Commonwealth.* 1591. Edited by Albert J. Schmidt. Ithaca: Cornell University Press, 1966.

Flier, Michael S. "Breaking the Code: The Image of the Tsar in the Muscovite Palm Sunday Ritual." In *Medieval Russian Culture*, vol. 2, edited by Michael S. Flier and Daniel Rowland, 213–42. Berkeley: University of California Press, 1994.

——. "The Church of the Savior on the Blood." In *Christianity and the Eastern Slavs*, vol. 2, *Russian Culture in Modern Times*, edited by Robert P. Hughes and Irina Paperno, 25–48. Berkeley: University of California Press, 1994.

——. "Court Ceremony in an Age of Reform: Patriarch Nikon and the Palm Sunday Ritual." In *Religion and Culture in Early Modern Russia and Ukraine*, edited by Samuel H. Baron and Nancy Shields Kollman, 73–95. Dekalb: Northern Illionois University, 1997.

——. "Filling in the Blanks: The Church of the Intercession and the Architectonics of Medieval Muscovite Ritual." *Harvard Ukrainian Studies* 19 (1995): 120–37.

——. "The Iconography of Royal Procession: Ivan the Terrible and the Muscovite Palm Sunday Ritual." In *European Monarchy: Its Evolution and Practice from Roman Antiquity to Modern Times*, edited by Heinz Duchhardt, Richard A. Jackson, and David Sturdy, 109–25. Stuttgart: Steiner, 1992.

Flühler-Kreis, Dione, Peter Wyer, and Donat Stuppan. *Die Holzskulpturen des Mittelalters: Katalog der Sammlung des Schweizerischen Landesmuseums Zürich.* 2 vols. Zurich: Schweizerisches Landesmuseum, 2007.

Fogelklou, Emilia. *James Nayler: The Rebel Saint, 1618-1660.* Translated by Lajla Yapp. London: Benn, 1931.

Fondra, Lorenzo. *Istoria della insigne reliquia di San Simoeone profeta chi si venera in Zara.* Zara [Zadar]: 1855.

Fonte, Mario. *Il folklore religiosa in Sicilia.* Catania: Greco, 2001.

Forster, Marc R. *Catholic Germany from the Reformation to the Enlightenment.* Basingstoke: Palgrave Macmillan, 2007.

——. *Catholic Revival in the Age of the Baroque: Religious Identity in Southwest Germany, 1550–1750.* Cambridge: Cambridge University Press, 2001.

Forsyth, Ilene H. *The Throne of Wisdom: Wood Sculptures of the Madonna in Romanesque France.* Princeton: Princeton University Press, 1972.

Fox, George. *A Declaration from the Harmless and Innocent People of God Called Quakers.* London: n.d.

Franck, Sebastian. *Weltbüch.* 1534. Reprint, Ulm: 1542.

Francovich, Géza de. "Contributi alla scultura romanica veronese." *Rivista del R. Istituto d'archeologia e storia dell'arte* 9 (1942): 103–47.

Frank, Johannes. "Augsburger Annalen." In *Die Chroniken der deutschen Städte*, 25:283–340. 36 vols. Lepizig: Hirzel, 1862–1931.

Franz, Patricia M. "The Horseman as a Work of Art: The Construction of Elite Identities in Early Modern Europe." PhD diss., City University of New York: 2006.

Frati, Luigi, ed. *Le due spedizioni militari di Giulio II tratte dal diario di Paride Grassi Bolognese maestro delle cerimonie della cappella papale.* Bologna: 1886.

Freitag, Markus. "Klosterkirche Preetz: Restaurierung einer gotischen Figur des Palmesel-Christus." Restoration report, 2009.

Fricker, Bartholomaeus. *Geschichte der Stadt und Bäder zu Baden.* Aarau: 1880.

Fried, Johannes. *Donation of Constantine and Constitutum Constantini.* Translated by David Wigg-Wolf. Berlin: de Gruyter, 2007.

Friedrich, Verena, and Romedio Schmitz-Esser. *Pfarrkirche St. Nikolaus und Kapellen.* Passau: Peda, 2007.

Fries, Walter. "Kirche und Kloster zu St. Katharina in Nürnberg." *Mitteilungen des Vereins für Geschichte der Stadt Nürnberg* 25 (1924): 1–144.

Friesenegger, J. M. *Die St. Ulrichs-Kirche in Augsburg.* Augsburg: Seitz, 1900.

Frings, Jutta, and Jan Gerchow, eds. *Krone und Schleier: Kunst aus mittelalterlichen Frauenklöstern.* Munich: Hirmer, 2005.

Frings, Paul, and Josef Übelmesser, eds. *Paracuaria: Die Kunstschätze des Jesuitenstaats in Paraguay.* Mainz: Matthias-Grünewald-Verlag, 1982.

Fritsch, Johann Heinrich. *Geschichte des vormaligen Reichstifts und der Stadt Quedlinburg.* 2 vols. Quedlinburg: 1828.

Frolow, Anatole. "La Vraie Croix et les expéditions d'Héraclius en Perse." *Revue des études byzantines* 11 (1953): 88–105.

Frye, Susan. *Elizabeth I: The Competition for Representation.* New York: Oxford University Press, 1993.

Fuhrmann, Horst. *Das Constitutum Constantini (Konstantinische Schenkung): Text.* MGH,FIGA,USSE 10. Hannover: Hansche Buchhandlung, 1964.

Fulcher of Chartres. *Historia Hierosolymitana (1095–1127).* Edited by Heinrich Hagenmeyer. Heidelberg: Winter, 1913.

——. *A History of the Expedition to Jerusalem (1095-1127)*. Translated by Frances Rita Ryan. Knoxville: University of Tennessee Press, 1969.

Fuller, Thomas. *The History of the Worthies of England*. 1662. Edited by P. Austin Nuttall. 3 vols. London: 1840.

Gallmetzer, Valentin. "Wie der Kalterer Palmesel in das Bozner Museum kam." *Der Schlern* 11 (1930): 207–8.

Gamurrini, G. F., ed. *S. Hilarii: Tractatus de mysteriis et hymni, et S. Silviae Aquitanae: Peregrinatio ad Loca Sancta*. Rome: 1887.

Ganshof, F. L. "Over de geboortedatum van Karel de Grote." In *Dancwerc: opstellen aangeboden aan Prof. Dr. D.Th. Enklaar ter gelegenheid van zijn vijfenzestigste verjaardag*, edited by W. Jappe Alberts, 43–55. Groningen: Wolters, 1959.

Garitte, Gérard, ed. *La prise de Jérusalem par les Perses en 614*. 2 vols. in 1. CSCO 202–3. Louvain: Secrétariat du CSCO, 1960.

Garside, Charles, Jr. *Zwingli and the Arts*. New Haven: Yale University Press, 1966.

Gee, Henry, and William John Hardy. *Documents Illustrative of English Church History*. London: 1896.

George of Pisidia. *Giorgio di Pisidia: Poemi. 1. Panegirici epici*. Edited by Agostino Pertusi. Ettal: Buch-Kunstverlag, 1959.

Gerber, Barbara. "Osterbräuche: der Pucher Palmesel hat Geschichte!" *Tennengau Magazin*, April 6, 2017. http://magazin.tennengau.com/pucher-palmesel#.Vi5l2 SvGp1A.

Gerhard of Augsburg. *Vita Sancti Uodalrici*. Edited and translated by Walter Berschin and Angelika Häse. Heidelberg: Winter, 1993.

Germann, Martin. "Der Untergang der mittelalterlichen Bibliotheken Zürichs: der Büchersturm von 1525." In *Bilderstreit: Kulturwandel in Zwinglis Reformation*, edited by Hans-Dietrich Altendorf and Peter Jezler, 103–7. Zurich: Theologischer Verlag, 1984.

Gerstenberg, Kurt. "Der Palmesel in Wettenhausen." *Repertorium für Kunstwissenschaft* 47 (1926): 45–53.

——. *Hans Multscher*. Leipzig: Insel, 1928.

Gibbenet, N. *Istoricheskoe issledovanie dela Patriarkha Nikona*. 2 vols. in 4. St. Petersburg: 1882–1884.

Glaber, Rodulfus. *Historiarum libri quinque*. Edited and translated by John France. Oxford: Clarendon, 1989.

Godfrey of Viterbo. *Pantheon*. Edited by Lodovico Antonio Muratori. Rerum italicarum scriptores 7:347–520. Milan, 1723–1751.

Golinelli, Paolo. *Il papa contadino: Celestino V e il suo tempo*. Firenze: Camunia, 1996.

Golubtsov, Alexander. "Chinovnik Novgorodskago Sofiyskago sobora." *Chteniya v Imperatorskom' Obshchestvye istoriy i drevnostey rossiyskikh* 189 (1899), fasc. 2.

Gordon, Alexander. "Nayler, James." In *Dictionary of National Biography, 1885–1900*, edited by Leslie Stephen and Sidney Lee, 40:130–33. 63 vols. London, 1885–1901.

Gottron, Adam B. "Die Stationsfeiern in Mainzer Stiften." *Mainzer Zeitschrift* 48 (1953): 19–26.

Grabar, Oleg. "Al-Ḳuds." In *The Encyclopedia of Islam*. New ed. 13 vols. Edited by H. A. R. Gibbs, 5:322–44. Leiden: Brill, 1960–2006.

Gräf, Herman J. *Palmenweihe und Palmenprozession in der lateinischen Liturgie*. Kaldenkirchen: Steyler, 1959.

Grafton, Richard. *Grafton's Abridgement of the Chronicles of England*. London: 1572.

Gray, Emily Fisher. "Lutheran Churches and Confessional Competition in Augsburg." In *Lutheran Churches in Early Modern Europe*, edited by Andrew Spicer, 39–62. Farnham: Ashgate, 2012.

Grayling, A. C. *Among the Dead Cities*. London: Bloomsbury, 2006.

Gregory the Great. *Dialogues*. Edited by Albert de Vogüé, translated by Paul Antin. 3 vols. SC 251, 260, 265. Paris: Éditions du Cerf, 1979–1980.

——. *Dialogues*. Translated by Odo John Zimmerman. FC 39. New York: Fathers of the Church, 1959.

——. *The Letters of Gregory the Great*. Translated by John R. C. Martyn. 3 vols. Toronto: Pontifical Institute of Mediaeval Studies, 2004.

——. *Moralia in Job*. Edited by Marci Adriaen. 1 vol. in 3. CCSL 143, 143A, 143B. Turnholt: Brepols, 1979–1985.

——. *Morals on the Book of Job*. Translated by James Bliss. 3 vols. in 4. Oxford, 1844–1850.

——. *Pastoral Practice*. Translated by John Leinenweber. Harrisburg: Trinity, 1998.

——. *Registrum Epistolarum*. Edited by Dag Norberg. 1 vol. in 2. CCSL 140, 140A. Turnhout: Brepols, 1982.

——. *Règle Pastorale*. Edited by Bruno Judic and Floribert Rommel, translated by Charles Morel. 2 vols. SC 381–82. Paris: Éditions du Cerf, 1992.

Gregory of Nazianzus. *Discours 20–23*. Translated by Justin Mossay and Guy Lafontaine. SC 270. Paris: Éditions du Cerf, 1980.

——. *Select Orations*. Translated by Charles Gordon Browne and James Edward Swallow. NPNF,SS 7:185–434. 1894. Reprint, Grand Rapids: Eerdmans, 1986.

Gregory of Tours. *Glory of the Confessors*. Translated by Raymond Van Dam. TTH,LS 4. Liverpool: Liverpool University Press, 1988.

Grigge, William. *The Quaker's Jesus*. London: 1658.

Grimm, Jacob, and Wilhelm Grimm. *Deutsches Wörterbuch*. 16 vols in 32. Leipzig: Hirzel, 1854–1954.

Grobowski, Ambroży. *Skarbniczka nasjez archeologii*. Lipsk: 1854.

Groos, Walter. "Augsburg zur Zeit Bischof Ulrichs." *Zeitschrift des Historischen Vereins für Schwaben* 67 (1973): 39–46.

Gruber, Isaiah. *Orthodox Russia in Crisis*. De Kalb: Northern Illinois University Press, 2012.

Grumel, V. "La reposition de la Vraie Croix à Jérusalem par Héraclius." *Byzantinische Forschungen* 1 (1966): 139–49.

Guerrazzi, F. D. *L'asino*. 3rd ed. 3 vols. Turin: 1858.

Gugitz, Gustav. *Das Jahr und seine Feste im Volksbrauch Österreichs*. 2 vols. Vienna: Hollinek, 1949–1950.

Guillot de Suduirat, Sophie. *Dévotion et séduction*. Paris: Somogy, 2015.

Gurney, John. *Brave Community: The Digger Movement in the English Revolution*. Manchester: Manchester University Press, 2007.

Gwyn, Douglas. *The Covenant Crucified: Quakers and the Rise of Capitalism*. Wallingford: Pendle Hill Publications, 1995.

Haastrup, Ulla. "Medieval Props in the Liturgical Drama." *Hafnia: Copenhagen Papers in the History of Art* 11 (1987): 133–70.

Haedeke, Hanns-Ulrich. *Zinn: Ein Handbuch für Sammler und Liebhaber*. Braunschweig: Klinkhardt & Biermann, 1973.

Hahn, Cynthia. "Relics and Reliquaries: The Construction of Imperial Memory and Meaning, with Particular Attention to Treasuries at Conques, Aachen, and Quedlinburg." In *Representing History, 900–1300: Art, Music, History*, edited by Robert A Maxwell, 133–47. University Park: Pennsylvania State University Press, 2010.

Halkin, Léon-E. *Erasmus*. Translated by John Tonkin. Oxford: Blackwell, 1993.

Hallinger, Kassius, ed. *Consuetudines cluniacensium antiquiores cum redactionibus derivatis*. CCM 7,2. Siegburg: Schmitt, 1983.

——. *Consuetudinum saeculi X/XI/XII, monumenta, introductiones*. CCM 7,1. Siegburg: Schmitt, 1984.

Hanegraaff, Wouter. "Pseudo-Lullian Alchemy and the Mercurial Phoenix: Giovanni da Correggio's *De Quercu Iulii pontificis sive De lapide philosophico*." In *Chymists and Chymistry*, edited by Lawrence Principe, 101–12. Sagamore Beach: Science History Publications/USA, 2007.

Hanegraaff, Wouter, and Ruud M. Bouthoorn. *Lodovico Lazzarelli (1447–1500)*. Tempe: Arizona Center for Medieval and Renaissance Studies, 2005.

Hanson, Michele Zelinsky. *Religious Identity in an Early Reformation Community: Augsburg, 1517 to 1555*. Leiden: Brill, 2009.

Hardison Jr., O. B. *Christian Rite and Christian Drama in the Middle Ages*. Baltimore: John Hopkins Press, 1965.

Hare, Douglas R. A. *Matthew*. Louisville: John Knox Press, 1993.

Harris, Arthur. *Bomber Offensive*. New York: Macmillan, 1947.

Harris, Jonathan. *Constantinople: Capital of Byzantium*. London: Continuum, 2007.

Harris, Markham, trans. *The Cornish Ordinalia: A Medieval Dramatic Trilogy*. Washington, DC: Catholic University of America Press, 1969.

Harris, Max. *Carnival and Other Christian Festivals*. Austin: University of Texas Press, 2003.

——. "Charlemagne, Triumphal Entries, and Palm Sunday Processions: How Wrong Was Kantorowicz?" *EMD* 20 (2016): 83–103.

——. "Inanimate Performers: The Animation and Interpretive Versatility of the Palmesel." In *Medieval Theatre Performance: Actors, Dancers, Automata, and their Audiences*, edited by Philip Butterworth and Katie Normington, 179–96. Martlesham: Boydell and Brewer, 2017.

——. "Interpreting the Role of Christ and His Donkey: The Palmesel as Actor in the Processional Theatre of Palm Sunday." *EMD* 16 (2012): 1–16.

——. "The Persecution of the Palmesel: Iconoclasm and Survival in Prague, Zurich, and Augsburg." *EMD* 17 (2013): 69–94.

———. "The Processional Theatre of Palm Sunday." In *The Routledge Companion to Early Drama and Performance*, edited by Pamela King, 316–31. London: Routledge, 2017.

———. *Sacred Folly: A New History of the Feast of Fools*. Ithaca: Cornell University Press, 2011.

Haslberger, Felix Audactus. "Die Salzburger Chronik des Felix Audactus Haslberger." Edited by Franz Martin. *Mitteilungen der Gesellschaft für Salzburger Landeskunde* 67 (1927): 33–64; 68 (1928): 51–68; 69 (1929): 97–119; 74 (1934): 159–68.

Hauerwas, Stanley. *Matthew*. Grand Rapids: Brazos, 2006.

Heal, Bridget. *The Cult of the Virgin Mary in Early Modern Germany*. Cambridge: Cambridge University Press, 2007.

Hebblethwaite, Margaret. *From Santa María with Love*. London: Darton, Longman and Todd, 2011.

———. *Paraguay*. 2nd ed. Chalfont St. Peter: Bradt Travel Guides, 2014.

Hen, Yitzhak, and Rob Meens, eds. *The Bobbio Missal*. Cambridge: Cambridge University Press, 2004.

Hernández Redondo, José Ignacio. "La escultura procesional de la Cofradía de la Vera Cruz de Valladolid." In *Actas: IV Congreso Internacional de Hermandades y Cofradías de la Santa Vera Cruz*, edited by José-Andrés Casquero Fernández, 149–72. Zamora: Cofradía de la Santa Vera Cruz de Zamora, 2009.

Herrmann, Norbert. *Petersthal*. Kempten: Verlag für Heimatpflege, 1976.

Herzman, Ronald B., and William A. Stephany. "Dante and the Frescoes at Santi Quattro Coronati." *Speculum* 87 (2012): 95–146.

Hesbert, René Jean, ed. *Corpus antiphonalium officii*. 6 vols. Rome: Herder, 1963–1979.

Hess, Daniel, and Jutter Zander-Seidel. *Mittelalter: Kunst und Kultur von der Spätantike bis zum 15. Jahrhundert*. Nuremberg: Verlag des Germanischen Nationalmuseums, 2007.

Heymann, Frederick G. *John Žižka and the Hussite Revolution*. Princeton: Princeton University Press, 1955.

Hildegard of Bingen. *Physica*. Translated by Priscilla Throop. Rochester: Healing Arts, 1998.

Hill, Christopher. *The Experience of Defeat*. New York: Viking, 1984.

———. *God's Englishman*. London: Weidenfield and Nicolson, 1970.

———. *The World Turned Upside Down*. New York: Viking, 1972.

Hoeynck, F. A. *Geschichte der kirchlichen Liturgie des Bistums Augsburg*. Augsburg: 1889.

Holland, Clive. *Tyrol and Its People*. London: Methuen, 1909.

Horlbeck, Frank R. "Gloria, Laud and Honor: The Palmesel and Palm Sunday." *Elvehjem Museum of Art Bulletin* (1977–1978): 26–37.

Horničková, Kateřina. "In Heaven and on Earth: Church Treasures in Late Medieval Bohemia." PhD diss., Central European University, Budapest: 2009. www.etd.ceu.hu/2009/mphhok01.pdf.

Hostetler, Brad. "The Limburg Staurotheke." *Athanor* 30 (2012): 7–13.

Howes, John. *John Howes' MS., 1582*. Edited by William Lempriere. London: 1904.

Hrabanus Maurus. *De Universo: The Peculiar Properties of Words and Their Mystical Significance*. Translated by Priscilla Throop. 2 vols. Charlotte: MedievalMS, 2009.

Hughes, Lindsey. *Peter the Great.* New Haven: Yale University Press, 2002.

——. *Russia in the Age of Peter the Great.* New Haven: Yale University Press, 1998.

——. *Sophia, Regent of Russia, 1657–1704.* New Haven: Yale University Press, 1990.

Huglo, Michel. "Observations codicologiques sur l'antiphonaire de Compiègne (Paris, B.N. lat. 17436)." In *De Musica et Cantu*, edited by Peter Cahn and Ann-Katrin Heimer, 117–30. Hildesheim: Olms, 1993.

Huizinga, Johan. *Erasmus.* Translated by F. Hopman. New York: Scribner's, 1924.

Hull, William I. *The Rise of Quakerism in Amsterdam, 1655–1665.* Swarthmore: Swarthmore College, 1938.

Hume, David. *The History of England from the Invasion of Julius Caesar to the Revolution in 1688.* 6 vols. 1754–1762. London: 1848.

Hussein, Joseph, Félix Sciad, and Noel Gosselin, eds. and trans. *Firmans Ottomans.* 1934. Reprint, Jerusalem: Franciscan Printing Press, 1986.

Hutter, Ernestine. "Hochzeits-, Faschings- und andere Bräuche." In *Puch bei Hallein: Geschichte und Gegenwart einer Salzburger Gemeinde*, edited by Gerhard Ammerer. Puch bei Hallein: Gemeindamt Puch, 1998.

Incomplete Commentary on Matthew (Opus Imperfectum). Translated by James A. Kellerman. 2 vols. Ancient Christian Texts. Downers Grove: IVP Academic, 2010.

Irenaeus. *Against Heresies.* Translated by Alexander Roberts and James Donaldson. ANF 1:307–567. 1903. Reprint, Grand Rapids: Eerdmanns, 1989.

——. *Contre les hérésies.* Book 5, vol. 2. Edited and translated by Adelin Rousseau, Louis Doutreleau, and Charles Mercier. SC 153. Paris: Éditions du Cerf, 1969.

Isidore of Seville. *De ecclesiasticis officiis.* Edited by Christopher M. Lawson. CCSL 113. Turnhout: Brepols, 1989.

——. *De ecclesiasticis officiis.* Translated by Thomas L. Knoebel. ACW 61. New York: Newman Press, 2008.

——. *Étymologies.* Edited and translated by Jacques André. 19 vols. Paris: Belles Lettres, 1981–.

——. *Etymologies.* Translated by Stephen A. Barney, W. J. Lewis, and J. A. Beach. Cambridge: Cambridge University Press, 2006.

——. *Etymologies.* Translated by Priscilla Throop. 2 vols. Charlotte: MedievalMS, 2005.

Ivanov, Andrey V. *A Spiritual Revolution: The Impact of the Reformation and Enlightenment in Orthodox Russia.* Madison: University of Wisconsin Press, forthcoming.

Jacob of Voragine. *The Golden Legend.* Translated by William Granger Ryan. 2 vols. Princeton: Princeton University Press, 1993.

Jacobi, J. G. *Sämmtliche Werke.* 8 vols. Zurich: 1819–1822.

Jacobsson, Ritva. "The Antiphoner of Compiègne: Paris BNF lat. 17436." In *The Divine Office in the Latin Middle Ages*, edited by Margot E. Fassler and Rebecca A. Baltzer, 147–78. New York: Oxford University Press, 2000.

Jacquot, Jean, and Elie Konigson. *Les fêtes de la Renaissance.* 3 vols. Paris: Centre National de la Recherche Scientifique, 1956–1975.

Jaffé, Philip, Paul Ewald, Ferdinand Kaltenbrunner, S. Loewenfeld, and Wilhelm Wattenbach, eds. *Regesta pontificum romanorum ab condita ecclesia ad annum post Christum natum MCXCVII.* 2 vols. 2nd ed. Leipzig: 1885–1888.

Jäger, Carl. *Ulms Verfassungs, bürgerliches und commercielles Leben im Mittelalter.* Stuttgart: 1831.

Jäggi, Carola. *Frauenklöster im Spätmittelalter.* Petersberg: Imhof, 2006.

Jahn, Robert. *Essener Geschichte.* Essen: Baedecker, 1957.

Janicka-Krzywda, Urszula. "Elementy widowisk i misteriów religijnich w obrezedowosci ludowej okresu Wielkiego Tygodnia na obszarze Polski poludniowej." *Nasza Przeszosc* 98 (2002): 465–502.

Janin, R. *Les églises et les monastères.* Pt. 1, vol. 3 of *La géographie ecclésiastique de l'empire byzantin,* edited by V. Laurent. Paris: Institut français d'études byzantines, 1953.

Jezler, Peter. " 'Da beschachend vil grosser endrungen': Gerold Edlibachs Aufzeichnungen über die Zürcher Reformation 1520–1526." In Hans-Dietrich Altendorf and Peter Jezler, *Bilderstreit: Kulturwandel in Zwinglis Reformation,* 41–74. Zurich: Theologischer Verlag, 1984.

Jiménez Mancilla. *¡Qué linda es la vida! Vida y obra de Sebastián Obermaier.* La Paz: ASES Comunicación y el Gato Lector, 2008.

John of Würzburg. *Description of the Holy Land.* Translated by Aubrey Stewart. LPPTS 5, fasc. 2. 1896. Reprint, New York: AMS, 1971.

Johnson, Alan. *Revelation.* Grand Rapids: Zondervan, 1996.

Jordan, Robert H., ed. and trans. *The Synaxarion of the Monastery of the Theotokos Evergetis.* 3 vols. Belfast: Belfast Byzantine Enterprises, 2000–2007.

Josephi, Walter. *Die Werke plastischer Kunst.* Nuremberg: Verlag des Germanisches Nationalmuseum, 1910.

Josephus, Flavius. *Works.* Translated by H. St. J. Thackeray, Ralph Marcus, Allen Wikgren, and Louis Feldman. 10 vols. LCL. Cambridge, MA: Harvard University Press, 1926–1981.

Joubert, Marion. "Étude et restauration du *Christ des Rameaux* du musée de l'Oeuvre Notre-Dame de Strasbourg." *CeROArt* 4 (2014). http://ceroart.revues.org/4010.

Kaegi, Walter Emil. *Heraclius.* New York: Cambridge University Press, 2003.

Kahsnitz, Rainer. "The Gospel Book of Abbess Svanhild of Essen in the John Rylands Library." Translated by F. Taylor. *Bulletin of the John Rylands University Library of Manchester* 53 (1970): 122–66.

Kain, Kevin M. "Archimandrites and Antiquities: The Creation of Orthodox-Based Russian National Identity at Resurrection 'New Jerusalem' Monastery in the Nineteenth Century." In *Monasticism in Eastern Europe and the Former Soviet Republics,* edited by Ines Angeli Murzaku, 308–29. London: Routledge, 2016.

——. "Before New Jerusalem: Patriarch Nikon's Iverskii and Krestnyi Monasteries." *Russian History* 39 (2012): 112–70.

——. " 'New Jerusalem' in Seventeenth-Century Russia: The Image of a New Orthodox Holy Land." *Cahiers du Monde Russe* 58.3 (2017): 371–94.

——. "Reading Between the (Confessional) Lines: The Intersection of Old Believer Manuscript Books and Images with Print Cultures of Late Imperial Russia." In *The Space of the Book: Print Culture in the Russian Social Imagination,* edited by Miranda Remnek, 165–200. Toronto: University of Toronto Press, 2011.

Kaminsky, Howard. *A History of the Hussite Revolution*. Berkeley: University of California Press, 1967.

Kantorowicz, Ernst H. "The 'King's Advent' and the Enigmatic Panels in the Doors of Santa Sabina." *Art Bulletin* 26 (1944): 207–31.

——. *The King's Two Bodies*. Princeton: Princeton University Press, 1957.

——. *Laudes Regiae*. Berkeley: University of California Press, 1946.

Kettemann, Walter. " 'Chronicon Moissiacense' und 'Chronicon Anianense'. Synoptische Edition der Handschriften Paris BN lat. 4886, f. 43v–f. 54v, und Paris BN lat. 5941, f. 2r–f. 49v." In Walter Ketteman, "Subsidia Anianensia." PhD diss., Gerhard-Mercator-Universität-Gesamthochschule Duisburg: 2000, Beilage 2. https://duepublico.uni-duisburg-essen.de/servlets/DerivateServlet/Derivate-19910/Kettemann_Diss.pdf.

Khamm, Corbinian. *Hierarchia Augustana chronologica tripartita in partem cathedralem, collegialem, et regularem*. 5 vols. Augsburg: 1709–1719.

King, Archdale A. *Liturgies of the Past*. London: Longman, Green, 1959.

Kinman, Brent. *Jesus' Entry into Jerusalem*. Leiden: Brill, 1995.

Kinney, Arthur F., ed. *Elizabethan Backgrounds*. Hamden: Archon, 1975.

Kinser, Samuel L. "The Entry of Triumphant Sovereignty, Rome 1507, Paris 1549." Paper delivered at the Annual Meeting of the American Historical Association, San Francisco, January 1994.

Kipling, Gordon. *Enter the King: Theatre, Liturgy, and Ritual in the Medieval Civic Triumph*. Oxford: Clarendon, 1998.

Kirchmayer, Thomas [Naogeorg(us), Thomas]. *Das Päpstisch Reÿsch*. Translated by Burkard Waldis. Strasbourg: 1555.

——. *Regnum papisticum*. 1555. Reprint, Basel: 1559.

——. *Reprint of The Popish Kingdome..., written in Latin verse by Thomas Naogeorgus, and Englyshed by Barnabe Googe, 1570*. Edited by Robert Charles Hope. London: 1880.

Kissling, Hermann. "Der Palmesel." In *Die Chronik des Dominikus Debler 1756–1836*, edited by Werner H. A. Debler and Klaus Jürgen Herrmann, 113. Schwäbisch Gmünd: Einhorn, 2006.

Kladstrup, Don, and Petie Kladstrup. *Wine and War*. New York: Broadway, 2001.

Klausner, David N. *Herefordshire, Worcestershire*. Records of Early English Drama. Toronto: University of Toronto Press, 1990.

Klein, Holger A. "Sacred Relics and Imperial Ceremonies at the Great Palace of Constantinople." In *Visualisierungen von Herrschaft*. Edited by Franz Alto Bauer, 79–99. Istanbul: Ege Yayınları, 2006.

Knapen, Luc, and Patrick Valvekens, eds. *De palmezelprocessie: Een (on)bekend West-Europees fenomeen?* Leeuven: Peeters, 2006.

Knoppers, Laura Lunger. *Constructing Cromwell*. Cambridge: Cambridge University Press, 2000.

Koder, Johannes. "Zu den Versinschriften der Limburger Staurothek." *Archiv für mittelrheinische Kirchengeschichte* 37 (1985): 11–31.

Kohler, C. "Un rituel et un bréviaire du Saint-Sépulcre de Jérusalem (XIIe –XIIIe siècle)." *Revue de l'Orient Latin* 8 (1900–1901): 383–500.

Köhler, Ludwig. *Kleine Lichter: Fünfzig Bibelstellen erklärt*. Zurich: Zwingli-Verlag, 1945.

Kohlschein, Franz, and Peter Wünsche, eds. *Heiliger Raum: Architektur, Kunst und Liturgie in mittelalterlichen Kathedralen und Stiftskirchen*. Münster: Aschendorff, 1998.

Kolbuszewski, Kazimierz. *Postyllografja polska XVI I XVII wieku*. Krakow: Polska Akademia Umiejętności, 1921.

Kopania, Kamil. "Animating Christ in Late Medieval and Early Modern Poland." *Preternature* 4 (2015): 78–109.

Köstenberger, Andreas J. "John." In *Commentary on the New Testament Use of the Old Testament*, edited by G. K. Beale and D. A. Carson, 415–512. Grand Rapids: Baker, 2007.

Kraiński, Krzysztof. *Postylla Kościoła Powszechnego apostolskiego*. Łaszczów: 1611.

Krämer, Gode. "Jörg Breu d. Ä. (Werkstatt)." In *Welt im Umbruch: Augsburg zwischen Renaissance und Barock*, 1:117–20. 3 vols. Augsburg: Augsburger Druck- und Verlagshaus, 1980–1981.

Kraus, Franz Zaver. *Kunst und Alterthum in Elsass-Lothringen*. 4 vols. Strasbourg: 1876–1884.

Kretzenbacher, Leopold. "Palmesel-Umfahrten in Steiermark." *Blätter für Heimatkunde* 27 (1953): 83–90.

Kroos, Renate. "Quellen zur liturgischen Benutzung des Domes und zu seiner Austattung." In *Der Magdeburger Dom*, edited by Ernst Ullman, 88–97. Lepizig: Seemann, 1989.

Kühebacher, Egon. "Prozessionen des Stiftes Innichen im frühen 17. Jahrhundert." *Der Schlern* 60 (1986): 637–72.

Kuhn, Heinz-Wolfgang. "Das Reittier Jesu in der Einzugsgeschichte des Markusevangeliums." *Zeitschrift für die neutestamentliche Wissenschaft und die Kunde der älteren Kirche* 50 (1959): 82–91.

Kümmel, Werner Georg. *Promise and Fulfilment: The Eschatological Message of Jesus*. Translated by Dorothea M. Barton. Naperville: Allenson, 1957.

Kupriyanov, I. K. "Otryvki iz' Raskhodnykh knig Sofiyskago doma za 1548-y god." *Izvyestiya Imperatorskago Russkago Arkheologicheskago Obshchestva* 3 (1861): 32–54.

Kurakin, Boris Ivanovich. "Gistoriia o tsare Petre Aleksieeviche." 1723–1727. In *Rossiiu podnial na dyby*, edited by N. I. Pavlenko, 1:351–90. 2 vols. Moscow: Molodaya gvardiia, 1987.

Kurdian, H. "A Note on the 'Description of the Holy Land and of the Way Thither' by Ludolph Von Suchem (1350)." *Journal of the American Oriental Society* 55 (1935): 102–4.

Kurth, Godefroid. *La Cité de Liège au Moyen-Âge*. 3 vols. Brussels: Dewit, 1909–1910.

Labunka, Miroslav. *The Legend of the Novogorodian White Cowl*. Munich: Ukrainische Freie Universität, 1998.

Lactantius. "On the Deaths of the Persecutors." In Lactantius, *The Minor Works*, translated by Mary Francis McDonald, 119–203. FC 54. Washington, DC: Catholic University of America Press, 1965.

Lagueux, Robert C. "Glossing Christmas: Liturgy, Music, Exegesis, and Drama in High Medieval Laon." PhD diss., Yale University: 2004.

Lancellotti, Secondo. *Historiae Olivetanae*. Venice: 1623.

Lapidge, Michael. "Ecgbehrt." In *The Blackwell Encyclopedia of Anglo-Saxon England*, edited by Michael Lapidge, John Blair, Simon Keynes, and Donald Scragg, 157. Oxford: Blackwell, 1999.

Laugel, A. *Costumes et Coutumes d'Alsace*. Strasbourg: Fischbach, 1902.

Lawrence of Březová. "Kronika Husitská," edited by Jaroslav Goll. In *Fontes rerum Bohemicarum* 5:327–534. 7 vols. 1873–1932. Reprint, Hildesheim: Olms, 2004.

Leander, Hans. "With Homi Bhabha at the Jerusalem City Gates: A Postcolonial Reading of the 'Triumphant' Entry (Mark 11.1–11)." *Journal for the Study of the New Testament* 32 (2010): 309–35.

Lebrun, François. *Histoire d'Angers*. Toulouse: Privat, 1975.

Leclercq, H. "Semaine Sainte." In *Dictionnaire d'archéologie chrétienne et de liturgie*, edited by Fernand Cabrol and Henri Leclerq, 15:1151–85. 15 vols. Paris: Letouzet et Ané, 1907–1953.

Lefftz, M. "Le Christ des Rameaux." In *La Musée de Louvain-la-Neuve: Florilège*, edited by Joël Roucloux and François Degouys, 94–95. Louvain-la-Neuve: Musée de Louvain-la-Neuve, 2010.

Lehner, Ulrich L. "Introduction: The Many Faces of the Catholic Enlightenment." In *A Companion to the Catholic Enlightenment in Europe*, edited by Ulrich L. Lerner and Michael Printy, 1–61. Leiden: Brill, 2010.

Le Long, Isaak. *Historische beschryvinge van de Reformatie der stadt Amsterdam*. Amsterdam: 1729.

Lerner, Robert E. *Ernst Kantorowicz: A Life*. Princeton: Princeton University Press, 2017.

Leuppi, Heidi, ed. *Der Liber Ordinarius des Konrad von Mure*. Freiburg: Universitätsverlag Freiburg Schweiz, 1995.

Lewański, Julian, ed. *Liturgiczne łacińskie dramatyzacje Wielkiego Tygodnia XI–XVI w.* Lublin: Towarzystwo Naukowe Katolickiego Uniwersytetu Lubelskiego, 1999.

Liber Censuum de l'église romaine, Le. Edited by Paul Fabre and L. Duchesne. 3 vols. Paris: Fontemoing, 1910–1952.

Liber pontificalis, Le. Edited by L. Duchesne. 3 vols. Paris: de Boccard, 1955–1957.

Lightfoot, R. H. *St. John's Gospel*. Oxford: Clarendon, 1956.

Lindner, Molly. "Topography and Iconography in Twelfth-Century Jerusalem." In *The Horns of Hattin*, edited by B. Z. Kedar, 81–98. London: Variorum, 1992.

Lipphardt, Walther, and Hans-Gert Roloff. *Die geistlichen Spiele des Sterzinger Spielarchivs*. 6 vols. Bern: Peter Lang, 1980–1996.

Lipsmeyer, Elizabeth. "Devotion and Decorum: Intention and Quality in Medieval German Sculpture." *Gesta* 34 (1995): 20–27.

——. "Jahreslaufbrauchtum: Palmsonntag-Christus und Palmesel." *Volkskunst: Zeitschrift für volkstümliche Sachkultur* 12 (1989): 50–58.

——. "The 'Liber Ordinarius' by Konrad von Mure and Palm Sunday Observance in Thirteenth-Century Zürich." *Manuscripta* 32 (1988): 139–45.

Lithgow, William. *The Totall Discourse of the Rare Adventures and Painfull Peregrinations of long Nineteene Years Travayles from Scotland to the most famous Kingdomes in Europe, Asia and Affrica*. 1632. Reprint, Glasgow: MacLehose, 1906.

Litz, Gudrun. *Die reformatorische Bilderfrage in den schwäbischen Reichstädten*. Tübingen: Mohr Siebeck, 2007.

Liudprand of Cremona. "Concerning King Otto." In *The Complete Works of Liudprand of Cremona*, translated by Paolo Squatriti, 219–37. Washington, DC: Catholic University of America Press, 2007.

———. "Historia Ottonis." In *Opera Omnia*, edited by P. Chiesa, 167–83. CCCM 156. Turnholt: Brepols, 1998.

Loewenstein, David. *Treacherous Faith*. Oxford: Oxford University Press, 2013.

Longin, Émile. *Les paroisses d'Angers avant la Révolution d'après Thorode*. Angers: 1889.

Longworth, Philip. *Alexis, Tsar of All the Russias*. London: Secker & Warburg, 1984.

Louvet, Pierre. *Histoire et antiquitez du pais de Beauvais*. 2 vols. Beauvais: 1631–1635.

Loyn, H. R., and John Percival. *The Reign of Charlemagne*. London: Edward Arnold, 1975.

Lubicz, Rafał. "Bibljografja, krytyka i wiadomośći bieżące: Przeglad katolicki, tygodnik, Warszawa." *Wisła: miesięcznik geograficzno-etnograficzny* 7 (1893): 410–13.

Ludewig, Johann Peter. *Vollständige Erläuterung der Güldenen Bulle*. 2 vols. Frankfurt: 1716–1719.

Ludolph von Suchem. *De itinere terrae sanctae liber*. Edited by Ferdinand Deycks. Stuttgart: 1851.

———. *Description of the Holy Land and of the Way Thither*. Translated by Aubrey Stewart. LPPTS 12, fasc. 3. 1895. Reprint, New York: AMS, 1971.

Luz, Ulrich. *Matthew*. Translated by James E. Crouch. 3 vols. Minneapolis: Fortress, 2000–2007.

MacCormack, Sabine G. *Art and Ceremony in Late Antiquity*. Berkeley: University of California Press, 1981.

———. "Change and Continuity in Late Antiquity: The Ceremony of 'Adventus'." *Historia: Zeitschrift für Alte Geschichte* 21 (1972): 721–52.

MacCulloch, Diarmaid. *Christianity: The First Three Thousand Years*. New York: Viking, 2010.

Machilek, Franz. "Der Liber brevarius der Kathedralkirche St. Veit zu Prag von ca. 1384 und seine topographischen Angaben." In *Heiliger Raum: Architektur, Kunst und Liturgie in mittelalterlichen Kathedralen und Stiftskirchen*, edited by Franz Kohlschein and Peter Wünsche, 207–24. Münster: Aschendorff, 1998.

Machyn, Henry. *The Diary of Henry Machyn*. Edited by John Gough Nichols. London: 1848.

Mack, Phyllis. *Visionary Women: Ecstatic Prophecy in Seventeenth-Century England*. Berkeley: University of California Press, 1992.

Macolino, Gian Giacomo. *Diario sacro perpetuo che contiene le feste mobili del Signore e le feste de santi ... nelle chiese del borgo e contado di Chiavenna*. Milan: 1707.

Macrides, Ruth, J. A. Munitz, and Dmiter Angelov. *Psuedo-Kodinos and the Constantinopolitan Court*. Farnham: Ashgate, 2013.

Madariaga, Isabel de. *Ivan the Terrible*. New Haven: Yale University Press, 2005.

Maffei, Fernanda de', and Géza de Francovich. *Mostra di sculture lignee medioevali: Museo Poldo Pezzoli*. Milan: Edizioni dell'Ente manifestazioni milanesi, 1957.

Maffei, Scipione. *Verona illustrata*. 4 vols. in 2. Verona: 1731–1732.

Magistretti, Marco, ed. *Beroldus, sive Ecclesiae Ambrosianae Mediolanensis Kalendarium et Ordines, saec. XII*. Milan: 1894.

———. *Manuale Ambrosianum ex codice saec. XI*. 3 vols. in 2. 1897–1905. Reprint, Nendeln: Kraus, 1971.

Malherbe, Georges. "Le 'Palmezel'." *Bulletin paroissial liturgique* 14.5 (1932), 81–90.

Maltzew, Alexios von [Alexei Maltzev]. *Begräbniss-Ritus und einige specielle und alterthümliche Gottesdienste der Orthodox-Katholischen Kirche des Morgenlandes.* Berlin: 1898.

Mann, Horace K. *The Lives of the Popes in the Middle Ages.* 18 vols in 19. 2nd ed. London: Kegan Paul, Trench, Trubner, 1925–1932.

Marchi, Gian Paolo. "Il Cristo delle Palme di S. Maria in Organo a Verona." *Nove historia* 14 (1962): 140–57.

——. *Luoghi letterari.* Verona: Fiorini, 2001.

Marcinkowski, Wojciech. "Chrystus na osiołku z Szydłowca." *Spotkania z Zabyttkami* 2012 (3–4): 26–31.

Marriott, Brandon. *Transnational Networks and Cross-Religious Exchange in the Seventeenth-Century Mediterranean and Atlantic Worlds.* Farnham: Ashgate, 2015.

Martène, Edmond. *De antiquis ecclesiae ritibus editio novissima.* New ed. 4 vols. Antwerp: 1763–1764.

Martin, Franz. "Vom Salzburger Fürstenhof um die Mitte des 18. Jahrhunderts." *Mitteilungen der Gesellschaft für Salzburger Landeskunde* 77 (1937): 1–48; 78 (1938): 89–136.

Martynowicz, Sebastian. *Annotationes summopere necessariae Clero tam saeculari quam Regular.* Lublin: 1782.

Massey, Vera. *The Clouded Quaker Star: James Nayler, 1618–1660.* York: Sessions, 1999.

Massie, Robert K. *Peter the Great.* New York: Knopf, 1981.

Mateos, Juan, ed. *Le Typicon de la Grande Église: Ms. Saint-Croix no. 40, Xᵉ siècle.* 2 vols. OAE 166–67. Rome: Pontificium Institutum Orientalium Studiorum, 1962–1963.

Mathews, Thomas F. *The Clash of Gods: A Reinterpretation of Early Christian Art.* 1993. Rev. ed. Princeton: Princeton University Press, 1999.

——. *The Early Churches of Constantinople.* University Park: Pennsylvania State University Press, 1971.

Mayr-Harting, Henry. *Ottonian Book Illumination.* 2 vols. London: Harvey Miller, 1991.

McComiskey, Thomas E. "Zechariah." In *The Minor Prophets*, edited by Thomas E. McComiskey, 3:1003–244. 3 vols. Grand Rapids: Baker, 1992–1998.

McCormick, Michael. *Eternal Victory: Triumphal Rulership in Late Antiquity, Byzantium, and the Early Medieval West.* Cambridge: Cambridge University Press, 1986.

McCullers, Carson. *Reflections in a Golden Eye.* 1941. Reprint, New York: New Directions, 1950.

McDaniel, W. B. "An Hermetic Plague-Tract by Johannes Mercurius Corrigiensis." *Transactions and Studies of the College of Physicians of Philadelphia*, ser. 4, 9 (1941–1942): 96–111, 217–25.

McNaspy, C. J., and J. M. Blanch. *Lost Cities of Paraguay.* Chicago: Loyola University Press, 1982.

Mellinkoff, Ruth. "Riding Backwards: Theme of Humiliation and Evil." *Viator* 4 (1973): 153–76.

Mertens, F. H., and K. L. Torfs. *Geschiedenis van Antwerpen.* 7 vols. Antwerp: 1845–1853.

Meyer, Gerhard. "Vom Ersten Weltkrieg bis 1985: Lübeck im Kräftefeld rasch wechselnder Verhältnisse." In *Lübeckische Geschichte*, edited by Antjekathrin Grassman, 677–756. 2nd ed. Lübeck: Schmidt-Römhild, 1989.

Meyerberg, Augustin Freyherr von. *Sammlung von Ansichten, Gebräuchen, Bildnissen, Trachten*. Edited by Friedrich Adelung. St. Petersburg: 1827.

Michel, Otto. "Eine philologische Frage zur Einzugsgeschichte." *New Testament Studies* 6 (1959): 81–82.

Miles, Hermann. "Die Chronik des Hermann Miles." Edited by Ernst Götzinger. *Mitteilungen zur vaterländischen Geschichte* 28 (1902): 275–385.

Miller, Albrecht. *Allgäuer Bildschnitzer der Spätgotik*. Kempten: Verlag für Heimatpflege, 1969.

Mills, David. "The Chester Cycle." *CCMET*, 109–33.

Miłosz, Czesław. *The History of Polish Literature*. 2nd ed. Berkeley: University of California Press, 1983.

Misson, Maximilien. *A New Voyage to Italy*. 1695. 4th ed. 4 vols. London: 1714.

Mitchell, John. "St. Silvester and Constantine at the SS. Quattro Coronati." In *Federico II e l'arte del duecento italiano*, edited by Angiola Maria Romanini, 2:15–32. 2 vols. Galatina: Congedo, 1980.

Młodzianowski, Tomasz. *Kazania i homilyie na niedźiele doroczne*. Poznań: 1681. www.dbc.wroc.pl/dlibra/docmetadata?id=12840&from=publication.

Monti, James. *A Sense of the Sacred*. San Francisco: Ignatius Press, 2012.

——. *The Week of Salvation*. Huntington: Our Sunday Visitor, 1993.

Moore, Rosemary. *The Light in Their Consciences: Early Quakers in Britain 1646–1666*. University Park: Pennsylvania State University Press, 2000.

Morgan, E. Delmar, and C. H. Coote, eds. *Early Voyages and Travels to Russia and Persia by Anthony Jenkinson and Other Englishmen*. 2 vols. London: 1886.

Morrall, Andrew. *Jörg Breu the Elder: Art, Culture, and Belief in Reformation Augsburg*. Aldershot: Ashgate, 2001.

Morris, Colin. *The Sepulchre of Christ and the Medieval West*. Oxford: Oxford University Press, 2005.

Morris, Leon. *The Gospel According to John*. Grand Rapids: Eerdmans, 1971.

——. *Luke: An Introduction and Commentary*. Rev. ed. Grand Rapids: Eerdmans, 1988.

Moser, Dietz-Rüdiger. *Fastnacht-Fasching-Karneval*. Graz: Kaleidoskop, 1986.

Muir, Edward. *Civic Ritual in Renaissance Venice*. Princeton: Princeton University Press, 1981.

Müller-Christensen, Sigrid. "Liturgische Gewänder mit den Namen des Heiligen Ulrich." In *Augusta, 955–1955*, edited by Hermann Rinn, 53–60. Munich: Rinn, 1955.

Mulryne, J. R., Helen Watanabe-Kelly, and Margaret Shewring, eds. *Europa Triumphans: Court and Civic Festivals in Early Modern Europe*. 2 vols. Aldershot: Ashgate, 2004.

Napione, Ettore. *Le Arche Scaligere de Verona*. Venice: Allemandi, 2009.

Nasse, George Nicholas. *The Italo-Albanian Villages of Southern Italy*. Washington, DC: National Academy of Sciences, 1964.

Naujoks, Eberhard. *Obrigkeitsgedanke, Zunftverfassung und Reformation.* Stuttgart: Kohlhammer, 1958.

Nayler, James. *The Works of James Nayler.* Edited by Licia Kuenning. 4 vols. Farmington: Quaker Heritage, 2003–2009.

Neelon, David. *James Nayler.* Becket: Leadings, 2009.

Nelson, Janet L. *Charles the Bald.* London: Longman, 1992.

Neumann, Bernd. *Geistliches Schauspiel im Zeugnis der Zeit.* 2 vols. Munich: Artemis, 1987.

Niccolò da Poggibonsi. *Libro d'Oltramare*, edited by Alberto Bacchi della Lega. 2 vols. 1881. Reprint, Bologna: Commissione per i testi di lingua, 1968.

——. *A Voyage Beyond the Seas.* Translated by T. Bellorini and E. Hoade. Jerusalem: Franciscan Press, 1945.

Nichols, John. *The Progresses, Processions, and Magnificent Festivities of King James the First.* 4 vols. London: 1828.

Nicholls, J. F., and John Taylor. *Bristol Past and Present.* 3 vols. Bristol: 1881–1882.

Niederer, J. "Palmzondag te Hougaerde." *Volkskunde* 20 (1909): 157–62.

Nikol'skii, Konstantin. *O Sluzhbakh Russkoi Tserkvi byvshikh v prezhnikh pechatnykh bogosluzhebnykh knigakh.* St. Petersburg: Tovarishchestva Obshchestvennaia Pol'za, 1885.

Noble, Thomas F. X., trans. *Charlemagne and Louis the Pious: The Lives by Einhard, Notker, Ermoldus, Thegan, and the Astronomer.* University Park: Pennsylvania State University Press, 2009.

Nuttall, Geoffrey F. *James Nayler.* London: Friends' Historical Society, 1954.

Obermayr, von [Josef Richter]. *Bildergalerie katholischer Mißbräuche.* Frankfurt: 1784.

Olearius, Adam. *Offt begehrte Beschreibung der Newen Orientalischen Reise.* Schleswig: 1647.

——. *The Travels of Olearius in Seventeenth-Century Russia.* Edited and translated by Samuel H. Baron. Stanford: Stanford University Press, 1967.

——. *Vermehrte Newe Beschreibung der Muscowitischen und Persischen Reyse.* 1656. Edited by Dieter Lohmeier. Tübingen: Niemwyer, 1971.

Oosterman, Johan. "De 'Excellente cronike van Vlaenderen' en Anthonis de Roovere." *Tijdschrift voor Nederlandse taal- en letterkunde* 118 (2002): 22–37.

——. "Excellente Cronike van Vlaenderen." *The Encyclopedia of the Medieval Chronicle,* edited by Graeme Dunphy, 1:600–1. 2 vols. Leiden: Brill, 2010.

Orbigny, Alcide d'. *Voyage pittoresque dans les deux Ameriques.* Paris: 1836.

Orchard, G. Edward. "Petreius." In *The Modern Encyclopedia of Russian and Soviet History,* edited by Joseph L. Wieczynski, 28:18–19. 60 vols. Gulf Breeze: Academic International Press, 1976–1995.

Ortroy, François van. "S. Pierre Célestin et ses premiers biographes." *Analecta Bollandiana* 16 (1897): 365–487.

Ostoia, Vera K. "A Palmesel at the Cloisters." *Metropolitan Museum of Art Bulletin* n.s. 14, no. 7 (1956): 170–73.

Ostrogorsky, Georg. "Zum Stratordienst des Herrschers in der Byzantinisch-Slavischen Welt." *Seminarium Kondakovianum* 7 (1935): 187–204.

Ostrowski, Donald. "Images of the White Cowl." In *The New Muscovite Cultural History: A Collection in Honor of Daniel B. Rowland*, edited by Valerie Kivelson, Karen Petrone, Nancy Shields Kollmann, and Michael S. Flier, 271–84. Bloomington: Slavica, 2009.

———. "'Moscow the Third Rome' as Historical Ghost." In *Byzantium: Faith and Power (1261–1557): Perspectives on Late Byzantine Art and Culture*, edited by Sarah T. Brooks, 170–79. New York: Metropolitan Museum of Art, 2006.

———. *Muscovy and the Mongols*. Cambridge: Cambridge University Press, 1998.

Ott, Friedrich. "Der Richtebrief der Burger von Zurich." *Archiv für Schweizerische Geschichte* 5 (1847): 149–291.

"Otto I: Diplome." MGH,DRIG 1:80–638. Hannover: 1879–1884.

Oxford Dictionary of Byzantium. Edited by Alexander P. Kazhdan. New York: Oxford University Press, 1991.

Oxford Latin Dictionary. Edited by P. G. W. Glare. Oxford: Clarendon, 1982.

Palmer, William. *The Patriarch and the Tsar*. 6 vols. London: 1871–1876.

"Palmsonntagbrauch in Tirol." *Innsbrucker Nachrichten*, March 26, 1904, 5–6.

Papadopoulos-Kerameus, A., ed. "Typikon de l'Église de Jérusalem pour la Semaine Sainte." In *Analekta hierosolymitike stachyologias*, edited by A. Papadopoulos-Kerameus, 2:1–254. 5 vols. 1894. Brussels: Culture et Civilisation, 1963.

Paravacini-Bagliani, Agostino. *The Pope's Body*. Translated by David S. Peterson. Chicago: University of Chicago Press, 2000.

Parkes, Henry. *The Making of Liturgy in the Ottonian Church*. Cambridge: Cambridge University Press, 2015.

Parrado del Olmo, Jesús María. "La entrada triunfal de Jesús en Jerusalén (La Borriquilla)." In *El árbol de la vida*, 55–57. Segovia: Edades de Hombre, 2003.

Passer, Justus Eberhard. "Berichte des hessen-darmstädtischen Gesandten Justus Eberh. Passer an die Landgräfin Elisabeth Dorothea über die Vorgänge am kaiserlichen Hofe und in Wien von 1680 bis 1683." Edited by Ludwig Baur. *Archiv für österreichische Geschichte* 37 (1867): 271–409.

Patrologiae cursus completus [...] series Graeca. Edited by J. P. Migne. 161 vols. Paris: 1857–1864.

Patrologiae cursus completus [...] series Latina. Edited by J. P. Migne. 221 vols. Paris: 1844–1864.

Paul of Aleppo. *The Travels of Macarius, Patriarch of Antioch*. Translated by F. C. Balfour. 2 vols. London: 1829–1836.

Paul the Deacon. *Historia Langobardorum*. Hannover: 1878.

———. *History of the Lombards*. Translated by William Dudley Foulke. Edited by Edward Peters. 1904. Reprint, Philadelphia: University of Pennsylvania Press, 1974.

Peeters, K. C. *Eigen aard: grepen uit de Vlaamse folkore*. Antwerp: De Vlijt, 1946.

Peinkofer, Max. "Von niederbayerischen Palmeseln." *Bayerisches Jahrbuch für Volkskunde* 1 (1950): 79–85.

Peri, Oded. *Christianity under Islam in Jerusalem*. Leiden: Brill, 2001.

Perry, David M. "The *Translatio Symonensis* and the Seven Thieves." In *The Fourth Crusade: Event, Aftermath, and Perceptions*, edited by Thomas Madden, 89–112. Aldershot: Ashgate, 2008.

Pertz, G. H., and Friedrich Kurze. *Annales Fuldenses, sive Annales regni Francorum orientalis*. SRG 52. Hannover: 1891.

——. *Annales Regni Francorum*. MGH,SS,USSE 6. Hannover: 1895.

Pescota, Toni. *125 Jahre Museumsverein Bozen 1882–2007*. Bolzano: Raetia, 2007.

Peters, F. E. *Jerusalem: The Holy City in the Eyes of Chroniclers, Visitors, Pilgrims, and Prophets from the Days of Abraham to the Beginnings of Modern Times*. Princeton: Princeton University Press, 1985.

Petersohn, Hermann Rudolf. "Über die Alterung und Erhaltung von Kunstwerken, oder: 'Bitte nicht berühren'." In Wenger, 27–41.

Petreius, Petrus [Peer Peerson]. *Historien und Bericht von dem Grossfürstenthrumb Muschkow*. Vol. 9 of *Early Exploration of Russia*. Edited by Marshall Poe. 12 vols. London: Routledge Curzon, 2003.

Pfaundler, Wolfgang von. *Sankt Romedius*. Vienna: Herold, 1961.

Phillips, Jonathan. *The Fourth Crusade and the Sack of Constantinople*. London: Cape, 2004.

Phillips, Margaret Mann. *The 'Adages' of Erasmus*. Cambridge: Cambridge University Press, 1964.

Philotheos. "Le traité de Philothée." In *Les listes de préséance byzantines des IXe et Xe siècles*, edited by Nicolas Oikonomidès, 65–235. Paris: Centre National de la Recherche Scientifique, 1972.

Piemonte, Gustavo A. "Recherches sur les '*Tractatus in Matheum*' attribués à Jean Scot." In *Johannes Scottus Eriugena: The Bible and Hermeneutics*, edited by Gerd Van Riel, Carlos Steel, and James McEvoy, 321–50. Leuven: University Press, 1996.

Pinheiro da Veiga, Thomé. *Fastigimia*. Edited by José Pereira de Sampaio. Porto: Domingo Augusto da Silva, 1911.

Pitrè, Guiseppe. "Notizie delle sacre rappresentazioni in Sicilia." *Archivio storico siciliano* n.s. 1 (1876): 65–111, 143–87.

——. *Spettacoli e feste popolari siciliane*. Palermo: 1881.

Pliny. *Letters and Panegyricus*. Translated by Betty Radice. 2 vols. LCL. Cambridge, MA: Harvard University Press, 1969.

——. *Natural History*. Translated by H. Rackham, W. H. S. Jones, and D. E. Eichholz. 10 vols. LCL. Cambridge, MA: Harvard University Press, 1949–1962.

Pol, Nikolaus. *Jahrbücher der Stadt Breslau*. Edited by Johann Gustav Büsching. 5 vols. Breslau: 1813–1824.

Pope, Marvin H. "Hosanna." In *The Anchor Bible Dictionary*, edited by David Noel Freedman, 3:290–91. 6 vols. New York: Doubleday, 1992.

Pothmann, Alfred. "Der Essener Kirchenschatz aus der Frühzeit der Stiftsgeschichte." In *Herrschaft, Bildung und Gebet: Gründung und Anfänge des Frauenstifts Essen*, edited by Günter Berghaus, Thomas Schilp, and Michael Schlagheck, 135–53. Essen: Klartext, 2000.

Potter, G. R. *Zwingli*. Cambridge: Cambridge University Press, 1976.

Poupardin, René. "The Carolingian Kingdoms (840–877)." *Cambridge Medieval History* 3:23–54. Cambridge: Cambridge University Press, 1957.

Printz von Buchau, Daniel. *Muscoviae ortus, et progressus*. SRL 2:687–728. Riga: 1848.

Prokopovich, Feofan. "Sermon on Royal Authority and Honor." Translated by Horace G. Lunt. In *Russian Intellectual History*, edited by Marc Raeff, 14–30. New York: Harcourt, Brace, 1966.

——. *Sochinenia*. Edited by I. P. Eremin. Moscow: Academii Nauk, 1961.

Pruitt, Jennifer. "Method in Madness: Recontextualizing the Destruction of Churches in the Fatimid Era." *Muqarnas* 30 (2013): 119–39.

Putman, Hans. *L'église et l'Islam sous Timothée I (780–823)*. Beirut: Dar el-Machreq, 1975.

Quaresmius, Franciscus. *Historica theologica et moralis terrae sanctae elucidatio*. Edited by Cypriano da Tarvisio. 2 vols. 1639. Venice: 1880–1881.

Queller, Donald E., and Thomas F. Madden. *The Fourth Crusade: The Conquest of Constantinople*. 2nd ed. Philadelphia: University of Pennsylvania Press, 1997.

Querejazu, Pedro. "El equipamiento artístico en las misiones de Chiquitos." In Querejazu, *Las Misiones Jesuíticas de Chiquitos*, 651–58. La Paz: Fundación BHN, 1995.

——, ed. *Las Misiones Jesuíticas de Chiquitos*. La Paz: Fundación BHN, 1995.

Rabe, Susan A. *Faith, Art, and Politics at Saint-Riquier*. Philadelphia: University of Pennsylvania Press, 1995.

Rataj, Michal. "Liturgie květné neděle v českých chorálních pramenech." Master's thesis, Charles University, Prague: 1999. www.michalrataj.com/files/dominica_palmarum. pdf.

Reb, Sylvaine. *L'Aufklärung catholique à Salzbourg*. 2 vols. Berne: Lang, 1995.

Reeb, Claudia, and Dorothee Guggenheimer. *Kloster St. Katharinen, St. Gallen*. Bern: Gesellschaft für Schweizerische Kunstgeschichte, 2013.

Reinle, Adolf. *Die Ausstattung deutsche Kirchen im Mittelalter*. Darmstadt: Wissenschaftliche Buchgesellschaft, 1988.

Reinsberg-Düringsfeld, Otto von. *Calendrier Belge*. 2 vols. Brussels: 1861.

Renier de Saint-Jacques. "Reineri annales." In MGH,SS 16:651–80. 1859. Reprint, Stuttgart: Hiersmann, 1963.

Renk, Anton. "Vom Palmesel in Thaur." In Renk, *Werke*, 4:23–34. 4 vols. Munich: Müller, 1907–1908.

Renoux, Athanase, ed. *Le Codex Arménien Jérusalem 121*. PO 35,1 (1970); 36,2 (1971).

Rich, Robert. *A True Narrative of the Examination, Tryall, and Sufferings of James Nayler*. London: 1657.

Richard, Pablo. *Apocalypse: A People's Commentary on the Book of Revelation*. Maryknoll: Orbis, 1995.

Richardson, E. P. "Three Late Gothic Wood Sculptures." *The Art Quarterly* 3 (1940): 340–47.

Roberts, Michael, ed. and trans. *Swedish Diplomats at Cromwell's Court 1655–1656*. Camden Fourth Series 36. London: Royal Historical Society, 1988.

Robertson, Alexander. *The Roman Catholic Church in Italy*. London: Morgan and Scott, 1905.

Roeck, Bernd. *Geschichte Augsburgs*. Munich: Beck, 2005.

Rogers, P. G. *The Fifth Monarchy Men*. London: Oxford University Press, 1966.

Rognini, Luciano. *La chiesa di S. Maria in Organo: guida storico-artistica*. Verona: 2002.

Roldán, Alfredo Fuentes. *Quito: Tradiciones*. 2 vols. Quito: Abya-Yala, 1995–1999.

Roloff, Jürgen. *The Revelation of John*. Translated by John E. Alsup. Minneapolis: Fortress, 1993.

Roncaglia, Martiniano. *St. Francis of Assisi and the Middle East*. Translated by Stephen A. Janto. Cairo: Franciscan Center of Oriental Studies, 1957.

Rondeau, Louis. *Histoire de la paroisse Saint-Michel du Tertre d'Angers*. Angers: 1891.

Roovere, Anthonis de. *Die excellente cronike van Vlaenderen*. Antwerp: 1531.

Rowland, Daniel B. "Moscow—The Third Rome or the New Israel?" *The Russian Review* 55 (1996): 591–614.

Rozov, N. N. "Povest' o novgorodskom belom klobuke kak pamiatnik obshcherusskoy publitsistiki XV veka." *Trudy Otdela drevnerusskoĭ literatury* 9 (1953): 178–219.

Ruelens, Charles. "La procession du dimanche des rameaux à Hougaerde." *Folklore Brabançon* 8 (1928–1929): 332.

Runciman, Steven. *A History of the Crusades*. 3 vols. Cambridge: Cambridge University Press, 1951.

Ryan, J. Joseph. "Pseudo-Alcuin's *Liber de divinis officiis* and the *Liber 'Dominus vobiscum'* of St. Peter Damiani." *Mediaeval Studies* 14 (1952): 159–63.

Rzegocka, Jolanta. "Performance and Sculpture: Forms of Religious Display in Early Modern Krakow." *EMD* 9 (2005): 177–94.

Sanudo, Marino. *I diarii di Marino Sanuto*. Edited by F. Stefani, R. Fulin, N. Barozzi, and G. Berchet. 58 vols. 1879–1903. Reprint, Bologna: Forni, 1969–1970.

Schatz, Helmut. "Der Palmesel von Kalbensteinberg." http://frankenland.franconica.uni-wuerzburg.de/login/data/2004_24.pdf.

Schayes, A. G. B. *Essai historique sur les usages, les croyances, les traditions, les cérémonies, et pratiques religieuses et civiles des Belges anciens et modernes*. Louvain: 1834.

Scheffler, Gisela. *Hans Klocker: Beobachtungen zum Schnitzaltar der Pacherzeit in Südtirol*. Innsbruck: Wagner, 1967.

Schein, Sylvia. *Gateway to the Heavenly City: Crusader Jerusalem and the Catholic West (1099–1187)*. Aldershot: Ashgate, 2005.

Schenk, Günter. *Christliche Volksfeste in Europa*. Innsbruck: Tyrolia, 2006.

Schick, Robert. *The Christian Communities of Palestine from Byzantine to Islamic Rule*. Princeton: Darwin, 1995.

Schilder, Günter. *Monumenta cartographica Neerlandica*. Vol. 9. *Hessel Gerritsz (1580/81–1632)*. Houten: Hes & De Graaf, 2013.

Schilling, A., ed. "Beiträge zur Geschichte der Einführung der Reformation in Biberach." *Freiburger Diöcesan Archiv* 9 (1875): 141–238.

———. "Die religiösen und kirchlichen Zustände der ehemaligen Reichstadt Biberach unmittelbar vor Einführung der Reformation." *Freiburger Diöcesan Archiv* 19 (1887): 1–191.

Schilp, Thomas. "Liber ordinarius." In *Gold vor Schwarz: der Essener Domschatz auf Zollverein*, edited by Birgitta Falk, 192–93. Essen: Klartext, 2008.

Schlager, J. E. *Wiener-Skizzen aus dem Mittelalter*. 5 vols (1–2 + NF 1–3). Vienna: 1835–1846.

Schnitzler, Norbert. *Ikonoklasmus—Bildersturm: Theologisches Bilderstreit und ikonoklastisches Handeln während des 15. Und 16. Jahrhunderts*. Munich: Fink, 1996.

Schnorr von Carolsfeld, H. "Das Chronicon Laurissense breve." *Neues Archiv* 36.1 (1910): 13–39.

Scholz, Bernard Walter, and Barbara Rogers, trans. *Carolingian Chronicles*. Ann Arbor: University of Michigan Press, 1970.

Schönfelder, Albert. "Die Prozessionen der Lateiner in Jerusalem zur Zeit der Kreuzzüge." *Historisches Jahrbuch* 32 (1911): 578–97.

Schroth, Mary Angela, and Paolo Violini. *La Cappella di San Silvestro*. Rome: Campisano, 2009.

Schuette, Marie. *Der Schwäbische Schnitzaltar*. Strasbourg: Heitz, 1907.

Scribner, R. W. *Popular Culture and Popular Movements in Reformation Germany*. London: Hambledon, 1987.

Sehling, Emil, and Anneliese Sprengler-Ruppenthal. *Die evangelischen Kirchenordnung des XVI. Jahrhunderts*. 24 vols. Leipzig: Reisland, and Tubingen: Mohr, 1902–.

Sender, Clemens. *Die Chronik von Clemens Sender von den ältesten Zeiten der Stadt bis zum Jahre 1536*. Vol. 23 of *Die Chroniken der deutschen Städte*, 36 vols. Lepizig: Hirzel, 1862–1931.

Sevast'yanova, S. K. *Materialy k "Letopisi zhinzni i leteraturnoy deyatel'nosti patriarkha Nikona."* St. Petersburg: Bulanin, 2003.

Severus of Antioch. *Les homiliae cathedrales de Sévère d'Antioch. Introduction générale à toutes les homélies. Homélies CXX à CXXV*. Edited and translated by Maurice Brière. PO 29,1 (1961).

Seymour Jr., Charles. "The Tomb of Saint Simeon the Prophet, in San Simeone Grande, Venice." *Gesta* 15 (YEAR): 193–200.

Sharpe, Kevin. *The Personal Rule of Charles I*. New Haven: Yale University Press, 1992.

Shaw, Christine. *Julius II: The Warrior Pope*. Oxford: Blackwell, 1993.

Sherwood, Roy. *Oliver Cromwell: King in All But Name 1653–1658*. New York: St. Martin's, 1997.

Shubin, Daniel H. *A History of Russian Christianity*. 4 vols. New York: Algora, 2004–2006.

Shusherin, Ioann. *From Peasant to Patriarch*. 1681–1686. Translated by Kevin M. Kain and Katia Levintova. Lanham: Lexington Books, 2007.

Shvidkovsky, Dmitry. *Russian Architecture and the West*. Translated by Antony Wood. New Haven: Yale University Press, 2007.

Signorelli, G. "La domenica delle Palme a Siracusa." *L'illustrazione populare* 27 (March 30, 1890): 195–98.

Simeoni, Luigi. *Verona: guida storico-artistica della città e provincia*. Verona: Baroni, 1909.

Simonetti, Manlio, ed. *Matthew 14–28*. Downers Grove: InterVarsity, 2002.

Ślusarek, Robert, ed. *Dziedzictwo kulturowe świętej Kingi. Katalog wystawy zrealizowanej ze zbiorów klasztoru sióstr klarysek w Starym Sączu*. Nowy Sącz: Muzeum Okręgowe, 2013.

Smalley, Stephen S. *The Revelation to John*. Downers Grove: InterVarsity, 2005.

Smeyers, Maurits. "Palmezel." In *Erasmus en Leuven*, edited by Jan Roegiers, 229–30. Louvain: Stedelijk Museum, 1969.

Smith, Jeffrey Chipps. "Sculpting Sacred Theatre: Hans Degler and the Basilica of St Ulrich and Afra in Augsburg." In *Die Erschließung des Raumes*, edited by Karin Friedrich, 1:207–28. 2 vols. Wiesbaden: Harrassowitz, 2014.

Smuts, R. Malcolm. "Public Ceremony and Royal Charisma: The English Royal Entry in London, 1485–1642." In *The First Modern Society: Essays in English History in Honor of Lawrence Stone*, edited by A. L. Bier, David Cannadine, and James M. Rosenheim, 65–93. Cambridge: Cambridge University Press, 1989.

Sobeczko, Helmut. "Der Liber Ordinarius der Breslauer Kathedrale von 1563 und seine Ortsangaben für die Feier der Liturgie." In *Heiliger Raum: Architektur, Kunst und Liturgie in mittelalterlichen Kathedralen und Stiftskirchen*, edited by Franz Kohlschein and Peter Wünsche, 187–206. Münster: Aschendorff, 1998.

Spätling, Luchesius G., and Peter Dinter, eds. *Consuetudines Fructuarienses-Sanblasianae.* 2 vols. CCM 12. Siegburg: Schmitt, 1985–1987.

A Speech of Delaration of the Dread King of Scots upon the Death of Montrosse. London: 1650.

Spence, Craig. "Misson, Francis Maximilian (c.1650–1722)." *Oxford Dictionary of National Biography*, edited by H. C. G. Matthew and Brian Harrison, 38:376–77. 60 vols. Oxford: Oxford University Press, 2004.

Staab, Franz. *Das Erzstift Mainz im 10. Und 11. Jahrhundert.* Bingen am Rhein: Vereinigung der Heimatfreunde am Mittelrhein, 2008.

Staden, Heinrich von. *Aufzeichnungen über den Moskauer Staat.* Edited by Fritz T. Epstein. 2nd ed. Hamburg: Cram, De Gruyter, 1964.

———. *The Land and Government of Muscovy.* Translated by Thomas Esper. Stanford: Stanford University Press, 1967.

Stadler, Franz J. *Hans Multscher und seine Werkstatt.* Strasbourg: Heitz, 1907.

Stanonik, Franz. "Khamm, Cornelius." In *Allgemeine deutsche Biographie*, edited by R. von Liliencron, F. X. von Wegele, and Anton Bettelheim, 15:703. 56 vols. Leipzig: 1875–1912.

Stanzione, Francesco. "La Settimana Santa a Prizzi (PA)." *La Settimana Santa in Sicilia* (blog), January 1, 2010. http://lamiasettimanasanta4g7.blogspot.com/2011/04/domenica-delle-palme-processione-delle.html.

Stefaneschi, Giacomo. *Opus metricum.* In *Monumenta Coelestiana*, edited by Franz Xavier Seppelt, 1–146. Paderborn: Schöningh, 1921.

Steiner, Joseph Anton. *Acta selecta Ecclesiae Augustanae.* Augsburg: 1785.

Stephenson, Paul. *The Legend of Basil the Bulgar-Slayer.* Cambridge: Cambridge University Press, 2003.

Stewart, Alan. *The Cradle King: A Life of James VI and I.* London: Chatto & Windus, 2003.

Stinger, Charles L. *The Renaissance in Rome.* Bloomington: Indiana University Press, 1985.

Stone, Lawrence. *The Crisis of the Aristocracy, 1558–1641.* Oxford: Clarendon, 1965.

Story, Joanna. "The Carolingians and the Oratory of Saint Peter the Shepherd." In *Old Saint Peter's, Rome*, edited by Rosamond McKitterick, John Osborne, Carol M. Richardson, and Joanna Story, 257–73. Cambridge: Cambridge University Press, 2013.

Stow, Kenneth. *The Jews in Rome.* 2 vols. Leiden: Brill, 1995–1996.

Strauss, Gerald. *Nuremberg in the Sixteenth Century.* Rev. ed. Bloomington: Indiana University Press, 1976.

Strele, Richard von. "Der Palmesel: Eine culturhistorische Skizze." *Zeitschrift des Deutschen und Österreichischen Alpenvereins* 28 (1897): 135–54.

Streng, Petra, and Gunter Bakay. *Wilde, Hexen, Heilige: Lebendige Tiroler Bräuche im Jahreslauf.* Innsbruck: Loewenzahn, 2005.

Stroll, Mary. "Calixtus II: A Reinterpretation of his Election and the End of the Investiture Contest." *Studies in Medieval and Renaissance History* n.s. 3 (1980): 1–53.

Strong, Roy. *The Tudor and Stuart Monarchy: Pageantry, Painting, Iconography.* 3 vols. Woodbridge: Boydell, 1995–1998.

Stuart, Kathy. *Defiled Trades and Social Outcasts.* Cambridge: Cambridge University Press, 1999.

Stückelberg, E. A. "Der Palmesel." *Revue Alsacienne Illustrée* 10 (1908): 118–28.

———. "Palmsonntagsfeier im Mittelater." In *Festbuch zur Eröffnung des Historischen Museums,* 17–36. Basel: 1894.

Suetonius. *Lives of the Caesars and Lives of Illustrious Men.* Translated by J. C. Rolfe. 2 vols. LCL. Rev. ed. Cambridge, MA: Harvard University Press, 1997–1998.

Sułkowska, D. "Obrzędy Wielkiego Tygodnia w klasztorze." *Kurier Starosądecki* 16, nr. 163–64 (April 2006), 24. www.kurier.stary.sacz.pl/ks163-4.pdf.

Sumberg, Samuel Leslie. *The Nuremberg Schembart Carnival.* New York: Columbia University Press, 1941.

Suriano, Francesco. *Il trattato di Terra Santa e dell'oriente.* Edited by Girolamo Golubovich. Milan: Artiquianelli, 1900.

———. *Treatise on the Holy Land.* Translated by Thephilus Bellorini and Eugene Hoade, with a preface and notes by Bellarmino Bagatti. Jerusalem: Franciscan Press, 1949.

Sweeney, Jon M. *The Pope Who Quit.* New York: Image, 2012.

Swete, Henry Barclay. *The Apocalypse of St John.* 3rd ed. 1909. Reprint, Grand Rapids: Eerdmans, 1951.

Taft, Robert F. "Holy Week in the Byzantine Tradition." In *Between Memory and Hope,* edited by Maxwell E. Johnson, 155–81. Collegeville: Liturgical Press, 2000.

Tan, Kim Huat. *The Zion Traditions and the Aims of Jesus.* Cambridge: Cambridge University Press, 1997.

Tarchnischvili, Michel, ed. *Le grand lectionnaire de l'Église de Jérusalem (V^e–VIIe siècle).* 4 vols. CSCO 188–89, 204–5. Louvain: Secrétariat du CSCO, 1959.

Tedallini, Sebastiano de Branca. "Diario Romano." Edited by Paolo Piccolomini. RIS, second series, 23.3, part 3, 231–445. Città di Castello: Lapi, 1904.

Theiss, Harald, Rudolph Wackernagel, and Michael Roth. "Christus auf dem Palmesel." In *Hans Multscher, Bildhauer der Spätgotik in Ulm,* edited by Brigitte Reinhardt and Michael Roth, 390–95. Ulm: Süddeutsche Verlagsgesellschaft, 1997.

Theoderich. *Description of the Holy Places.* Translated by Aubrey Stewart. LPPTS 5, fasc. 4. 1896. Reprint, New York: AMS, 1971.

Theodulf of Orléans. *Carmina.* Edited by Ernst Dummler. MGH,PLMA 1:437–581. Berlin: 1881.

——. *Theodulf of Orléans: The Verse*. Translated by Theodore M. Andersson, Åslaug Ommundsen, and Leslie S. B. MacCoull. Tempe: Arizona Center for Medieval and Renaissance Studies, 2014.

Theological Dictionary of the New Testament. Edited by Gerhard Kittel and Gerhard Freidrich. Translated by Geoffrey W. Bromiley. 10 vols. Grand Rapids: Eerdmans, 1964–1976.

Theophanes Confessor. *The Chronicle of Theophanes Confessor*. Translated by Cyril Mango and Roger Scott. Oxford: Clarendon, 1997.

——. *Chronographia*. Edited by Charles de Boor. 2 vols. Leipzig: 1883–1885.

Thibaut, J.-B. *Ordre des offices de la Semaine Sainte à Jérusalem du IVe au Xe siècle*. Paris: Maison de la Bonne Presse, 1926.

Thietmar of Merseburg. *Die Chronik des Bischofs Thietmar von Merseburg*. Edited by Robert Holzmann. MGH,SRG,NS 9. Munich: Monumenta Germaniae Historica, 1996.

——. *Ottonian Germany: The Chronicon of Thietmar of Merseburg*. Translated by David A. Warner. Manchester: Manchester University Press, 2001.

Thomson, R. W., and James Howard-Johnston, eds. and trans. *The Armenian History Attributed to Sebeos*. 1 vol. in 2. TTH 31. Liverpool: Liverpool University Press, 1999.

Thurloe, John. *A collection of the state papers of John Thurloe*. 7 vols. London: 1742.

Tlusty, B. Ann, ed. *Augsburg During the Reformation Era*. Indianapolis: Hackett, 2012.

Tolan, John. *Saint Francis and the Sultan*. Oxford: Oxford University Press, 2009.

Tolomeo da Lucca [Bartolomeo Fiadoni]. *Historia ecclesiastica nova*. Edited by Ottavio Clavuot and Ludwig Schmugge. MGH,SS 39. Hannover: Hahn, 2009.

Toon, Peter. "Naylor, James." In *The New International Dictionary of the Christian Church*, edited by J. D. Douglas. Grand Rapids: Zondervan, 1978.

Torelli, Luigi. *Secoli Agostiniani*. 8 vols. Bologna: 1659–1685.

Torquemada, Juan de. *Monarquía Indiana*. 7 vols. Mexico City: Universidad Nacional Autónoma de México, 1975–1983.

Traeger, Jörg. *Der reitende Papst*. Munich: Schnell & Steiner, 1970.

Trajdos, Ewa. "Wit Stosz inscenizatorem? Grupa rzeźb ruchomych I ich związki z teatrem średniowiecznym." *Pamiętnik teatralny* 13 (1964): 333–52.

Trento, Aldo. *Reducciones jesuíticas: el paraíso en el Paraguay*. Asunción: Parroquia San Rafael, 2003.

Tripps, Johannes. *Das handelnde Bildwerk in der Gotik*. Berlin: Mann, 1998.

Tripps, Manfred. *Hans Multscher: Meister de Spätgotik*. Leutkirch: Heimatpflege Leutkirch, 1993.

——. *Hans Multscher: Seine Ulmer Schaffenszeit 1427–1467*. Weißenhorn: Konrad, 1969.

Tritton, A. S. *The Caliphs and Their Non-Muslim Sujects*. 2nd ed. London: Cass, 1970.

Trizna, Jāzeps. "Le *Christ des Rameaux* de la collection Frans Van Hamme." In *Mélanges d'archéologie et d'histoire de l'art offerts au professeur Jacques Lavalleye*, 291–96. Louvain: Université de Louvain, 1970.

Trombley, Frank R., and John W. Watt, trans. *The Chronicle of Pseudo-Joshua the Stylite*. TTH 32. Liverpool: Liverpool University Press, 2000.

Twyman, Susan. *Papal Ceremonial at Rome in the Twelfth Century*. HBS, Subsidia 4. London: Boydell, 2002.

Tydeman, William, ed. *The Medieval European Stage, 500–1550*. Cambridge: Cambridge University Press, 2001.

Tyrer, John Walton. *Historical Survey of Holy Week*. London: Oxford University Press, 1932.

Uličný, Petr. "Christ in Motion: Portable Objects and Scenographic Environments in the Liturgy of Medieval Bohemia." *Theatralia* 44 (2011): 24–64.

———. "Kristus z Litovle a topografie Svatého týdne (Jeruzalémskékaple)." In *Gotické klenoty v kapli sv. Jiří v Litovli*, edited by Vladimir Maňas, 61–69. Litovel: Řimskokatolická farnost Litovel, 2012.

The Unparalleld Monarch. Or, The Portraiture of a Matchless Prince, exprest in some shadows of His Highness my Lord Protector. London: 1656.

Uspensky, N. D. *Evening Worship in the Orthodox Church*. Translated by Paul Lazor. Crestwood: St Vladimir's Seminary Press, 1985.

Vale, Guiseppe. "La liturgia nella chiesa patriarcale di Aquileia." In *Mostra di codici liturgici aquileiesi*, 13–32. Udine: Arte Grafiche Friulane, 1968.

Valla, Lorenzo. *On the Donation of Constantine*. Translated by G. W. Bowerstock. Cambridge, MA: Harvard University Press, 2007.

———. *Treatise on the Donation of Constantine*. Translated by Christopher B. Coleman. New Haven: Yale University Press, 1922.

Valvekens, Patrick. "Tentoonstellingscatalogus." In Knapen, 261–362.

Van Banning, J. *Opus Imperfectum in Matthaeum: Praefatio*. CCSL 87B. Turnhout: Brepols, 1988.

Van Dijk, Stephen J. P., and John Hazelden Walker. *The Ordinal of the Papal Court from Innocent III to Boniface VIII and Related Documents*. Fribourg: The University Press, 1975.

Van Even, Edward. *Monographie de l'église de Saint-Pierre à Louvain*. Brussels: 1858.

Varro, Marcus Terentius. *On Agriculture*. In Cato and Varro, *On Agriculture*, translated by William Davis Hooper and Harrison Boyd Ash. LCL. Cambridge, MA: Harvard University Press, 1979.

Vasiliev, A. "Harun-ibn-Yahya and His Description of Constantinople." *Seminarium Kondakovianum* 5 (1932): 149–63.

Vecchi, Giuseppe, ed. *Uffici drammatici padovani*. Florence: Olschki, 1954.

Vereshchagina, A. *Viacheslav Grigor'evich Shvarts, 1838–1869*. Leningrad: Iskusstvo, 1960.

Vergara Vergara, José María. "La Semana Santa en Popayan." In *Museo de Cuadros de Costumbres*, 1:167–75. 2 vols. Bogotá: 1866.

Verpeaux, Jean, ed. and trans. *Pseudo-Kodinos: Traité des offices*. Paris: Centre National de la Recherche Scientifique, 1966.

Versnel, H. S. *Triumphus: An Inquiry into the Origin, Development and Meaning of the Roman Triumph*. Leiden: Brill, 1970.

Victoria and Albert Museum. "Religious Processions 1300–1500." *YouTube*, November 23, 2009. www.youtube.com/watch?v=oIGfXwleeQA.http.

Villehardouin, Geoffroi de. *The Conquest of Constantinople*. In *Joinvile and Villehardouin: Chronicles of the Crusades*, translated by M. R. B. Shaw. London: Penguin, 1963.

——. *La conquête de Constantinople*. Edited and translated by Edmond Faral. 2 vols. Paris: Société d'édition "Les Belles lettres," 1938–1939.

Villetard, Henri, ed. *Office de Pierre de Corbeil (Office de la Circoncision) improprement appelé "Office des Fous"*. Paris: Picard, 1907.

Vöge, Wilhelm. "Romanische und frühgotische Holzstatuen." 1908. Reprint, in Wilhelm Vöge, *Bildhauer des Mittelalters*, 127–29. Berlin: Mann, 1958.

Vogel, Cyrille, and Reinhard Elze. *Le Pontifical romano-germanique du dixième siècle*. 3 vols. Vatican City: Biblioteca Apostolica Vaticana, 1963–1972.

Vogler, Katharina. "Das Dominkanerinnen-Kloster St. Katharina in St. Gallen zur Zeit der Reformation." *Zeitschrift für schweizerische Kirchengeschichte* 28 (1934): 1–19, 105–16, 161–83, 256–71.

Voigt, Gottfried Christian. *Geschichte des Stifts Quedlinburg*. 3 vols. Leipzig: 1786–1793.

Walanus, Wojciech. "Chrystus na osiołku z Szydłowca." In *Wokół Wita Stwosza*, edited by Dobrosława Horzela and Adam Organisty, 134–37. Krakow: Muzeum Narodowe w Krakowie, 2005.

——. "*Imago Ihesu in Asino*: O niezachowanym dziele sztuki gotyckiej we Lwowie." In *Fides Ars Scientia: Studia dedykowane pamięci Księdza Kanonika Augustyna Mednisa*, edited by Andrzej Betlej and Józef Skrabski, 379–90. Tarnów: Muzeum Okręgowe w Tarnowie, 2008.

Walker, Paul E. *Caliph of Cairo: Al-Hakim bi-Amr Allah, 996–1021*. Cairo: American University in Cairo Press, 2009.

Wandel, Lee Palmer. *Voracious Idols and Violent Hands: Iconoclasm in Reformation Zurich, Strasbourg, and Basel*. Cambridge: Cambridge University Press, 1994.

Wardi, Chaim. "The Question of the Holy Places in Ottoman Times." In *Studies on Palestine during the Ottoman Period*, edited by Moshe Ma'oz, 385–93. Jerusalem: Magnes, 1975.

Warkentin, Germaine, ed. *The Queen's Majesty's Passage and Related Documents*. Toronto: Centre for Renaissance and Reformation Studies, 2004.

Warner, David A. "Thietmar of Merseburg on Rituals of Kingship." *Viator* 26 (1995): 53–76.

Way, Kenneth C. "Donkey Domain: Zechariah 9:9 and Lexical Semantics." *JBL* 129 (2010): 105–14.

——. *Donkeys in the Biblical World*. Winona Lake: Eisenbrauns, 2011.

Webster, Susan Verdi. *Art and Ritual in Golden-Age Spain*. Princeton: Princeton University Press, 1998.

Weddle, Meredith Baldwin. *Walking in the Way of Peace: Quaker Pacifism in the Seventeenth Century*. New York: Oxford University Press, 2001.

Wedel, Lupold von. "Journey through England and Scotland Made by Lupold von Wedel in the Years 1584 and 1585." Translated by Gottfried von Bülow. *Transactions of the Royal Historical Society*, n.s. 9 (1895): 223–70.

Weißhaar-Keim, Heide. *Stadtpfarrkirche Mariae Himmelfahrt, Landsberg am Lech*. Regensburg: Schnell & Steiner, 2010.

Wemple, Suzanne Fonay. *Women in Frankish Society*. Philadelphia: University of Pennsylvania Press, 1981.

Wenger, Alfons, Monika Boosen, Gabriele Holthuis, and Hermann Rudolf Petersohn. *Der Palmesel: Geschichte, Kult und Kunst*. Schwäbisch Gmünd: Museum für Natur & Stadtkultur, 2000.

Whitelock, Bulstrode. *Memorials of the English Affairs from the Beginning of the Reign of Charles the First to the Happy Restoration of King Charles the Second*. 4 vols. Oxford: 1853.

Wiepen, Eduard. *Palmsonntagsprozession und Palmesel*. Bonn: Hanstein, 1903.

Williams, Watkin. *Monastic Studies*. Manchester: Manchester University Press, 1938.

Wilson, Arthur. *The History of Great Britain, Being the Life and Reign of King James the First*. London: 1653.

Wilson, Theodore A., and Frank J. Merli. "Naylor's Case and the Dilemma of the Protectorate." *Historical Journal* (University of Birmingham) 10 (1965): 44–59.

Winbeck, Katharina, and Gertrud Rank. *Kloster Wettenhausen: Geschichte und kulturelle Bedeutung*. Lindenberg im Allgäu: Fink, 2011.

Winstanley, Gerrard. *The Complete Works of Gerrard Winstanley*. Edited by Thomas N. Corns, Ann Hughes, and David Loewenstein. 2 vols. Oxford: Oxford University Press, 2009.

Wiseman, Susan. *Conspiracy and Virtue: Women, Writing, and Politics in Seventeenth-Century England*. Oxford: Oxford University Press, 2006.

Witherington, Ben. *The Christology of Jesus*. Minneapolis: Fortress, 1990.

Wittwer, Peter. *Der Zurzacher Liber Ordinarius und seine Beziehungen zur Marbacher Liturgie*. Fribourg: Academic Press, 2004.

Wittwer, Wilhelm. *Catalogus Abbatum monasterii SS. Udalrici et Afrae Augustenis*. In *Archiv für die Geschichte des Bisthums Augsburg*, edited by Anton Steichele, 3:10–437. 3 vols. Augsburg: 1856–1860.

Wixom, William D. *Medieval Sculpture at The Cloisters*. The Metropolitan Museum of Art Bulletin, n.s. 46, 1988–1989.

[Wolfhelm of Brauweiler]. *Brunwilarensis monasterii fundatorum actus*. Edited by Georg Waitz. MGH,SS 14:121–41. Hannover: 1883.

Wortman, Richard S. *Scenarios of Power: Myth and Ceremony in Russian Monarchy*. 2 vols. Princeton: Princeton University Press, 1995–2000.

Woziński, Andrzej. "Rzeźba Chrystusa na osiołku z Muzeum Narodowego w Poznaniu." *Studia muzealne* 16 (1992): 75–96.

Wright, Edward. *Some Observations Made in Travelling through France, Italy, &c. in the Years 1720, 1721, and 1722*. 2 vols. London: 1730.

Würdtwein, Stephan Alexander. *Commentatio historico-liturgica de stationibus ecclesiae Moguntinae*. Mainz: 1782.

Wüthrich, Lucas, and Mylène Ruoss. *Katalog der Gemälde: Schweizerisches Landesmuseum Zürich*. Zurich: Schweizerisches Landesmuseum, 1996.

Wuyts, Leontine. *Hoegaarden en zijn palmprocessie*. Antwerp: Vlaamse Toeristische Bibliotheek, 1975.

Wyss, Bernhard. *Die Chronik des Bernhard Wyss, 1519–1530*. Edited by Georg Finsler. Basel: Basler Buch- und Antiquariats-Handlung, 1901.

Wyss, Georg von. *Geschichte der Abtei Zürich*. Zurich: 1853.

Yaḥyā ibn Saʿīd al-Anṭākī. *Histoire de Yahya-ibn-Saʿid d'Antioche, continuateur de Saʿid-ibn-Bitriq*. 3 vols. Vols. 1–2. Edited and translated by I. Kratchkovsky and A. Vasilev. PO 18 (1924): 699–833, 23 (1932): 347–550. Vol. 3. Edited and translated by I. Kratchkovsky, Françoise Micheau, and Gérard Troupeau. PO 47 (1997): 371–559.

Yarnold, Edward. *Cyril of Jerusalem*. London: Routledge, 2000.

Young, Karl. *The Drama of the Medieval Church*. 2 vols. Oxford: Clarendon, 1933.

Zampieri, Marino. *Il palio, il porco e il gallo*. Verona: Cierre, 2008.

Zeller, Andreas Christoph. *Ausführliche Merkwürdigkeiten der hochfurstlichen würtembergischen Universitæt und Stadt Tübingen*. Tübingen: 1743.

Zeller-Werdmüller, H. "Nächtliche Spazierfahrt eines Palmesel." *Anzeiger für schweizerische Altertumskunde*, n.s. 2 (1900): 67.

Zinsmaier, P. "Eine unbekannte Quelle zur Geschichte der mittelalterlichen Liturgie im Konstanzer Münster." *Zeitschrift für die Geschichte des Oberrheins* N.F. 65 (1956): 52–104.

Zitser, Ernest A. *The Transfigured Kingdom: Sacred Parody and Charismatic Authority at the Court of Peter the Great*. Ithaca: Cornell University Press, 2004.

Zue, Gerold. "Bayerns 'dienstältester' Palmesel." *Altbayerische Heimatpost* 30.12 (1978): 6–7.

INDEX